Comparative Syntax

Comparative Syntax

Ian Roberts

Professor of Linguistics at the Universtiy of Wales, Bangor

A member of the Hodder Headline Group
LONDON • NEW YORK • SYDNEY • AUCKLAND

This book is dedicated to
Lucia Cavalli-Roberts

First published in Great Britain in 1997 by
Arnold, a member of the Hodder Headline Group
338 Euston Road, London NW1 3BH
175 Fifth Avenue, New York, NY10010

Distributed exclusively in the USA by
St Martin's Press Inc.
175 Fifth Avenue, New York, NY 10010

British Library Cataloguing in Publication Data
A catalogue record for this book is available from the British Library

Library of Congress Cataloging-in-Publication Data
Roberts, Ian G.
Comparative syntax/Ian Roberts.
p.   cm.
Includes bibliographical references and index.
ISBN 0-340-67659-0.—ISBN 0-340-59286-9 (pbk.)
1. Grammar, Comparative and general—Syntax.   2. Principles and
parameters (Linguistics)   I. Title.
P291.R58 1996
415—dc20   96-11678

ISBN 0 340 59286 9 (Pb)
ISBN 0 340 67659 0 (Hb)

Composition in 10^{1}/2/12^{1}/2 Times by Anneset, Weston-super-Mare, Somerset
Printed and bound in Great Britain by J W Arrowsmith Ltd, Bristol

Contents

List of Tables

Acknowledgements

This book is based on teaching carried out in many places over a period of years. I'd like in particular to thank the students who attended my classes during various visits to Brazil in the period 1989–94, and also my Brazilian colleagues – especially Mary Kato and Ilza Ribeiro – for making the visits possible (and so enjoyable). I'd also like to thank my colleagues and students at the University of Wales, Bangor, especially Anna Roussou, Siobhán Cottell, Najib Jarad and Pamela MacDonald. I'd like to acknowledge Luigi Rizzi's influence on this book, as on all my work. Thanks also to Andrew Radford for his helpful comments.

Ian Roberts
Bangor
October, 1995

List of Abbreviations

Those abbreviations are listed that are not explained the first time they are introduced in the text.

ACC	Accusative case (or Case)
ABS	Absolutive case
Agr	Agreement
AP	Adjective Phrase
ASP	Aspect marker
Aux	Auxiliary
CAUSE	Causative affix
DAT	Dative case (or Case)
D	Determiner
Det	Determiner
ERG	Ergative case
F	Feminine
GEN	Genitive
LOG	Logophor
M	Masculine
N	Neuter
NOM	Nominative case (or Case)
Neg	Negation
NP	Noun Phrase
O	Object
Pl	Plural (preceded by an Arabic numeral, denotes the relevant person, e.g. 3Pl = third person plural)
Poss	Possessor
PRE	Prefix
PRES	Present
PST	Past
Q	Question particle
S	Sentence
SCL	Subject clitic
Sg	Singular (preceded by an Arabic numeral, denotes the relevant person, e.g. 3Sg = third person singular)
SUF	Suffix
T	Tense
TOP	Topic Marker
VP	Verb Phrase

Introduction

What This Book is About

Take a step outside your mind and imagine someone talking. If possible, try to imagine someone speaking a language you don't know. Nothing could be more human and at the same time more foreign. What has someone who speaks a foreign language got that you haven't? What have you got that people who don't speak English haven't (I'm assuming that, since you're reading this book, you know English)? This book is about part of the answer to these questions.

In a real sense, this is a book about the human mind. Think again of the person talking. There must be something in their mind that makes language possible. What is it? Since all humans know at least one language (except for some truly rare exceptions), what is in the human mind that makes language possible? And – here's the core of the matter for us – what is different about the minds of speakers of different languages?

Scientific ethics prevent us from trying to answer these questions by opening up people's heads and having a look inside. In any case, we wouldn't really know what to look for. Nowadays most people believe that cognitive capacities like language are physically located in the brain (this idea is supported by the observation that if someone gets a hard enough knock on the head, their cognitive and linguistic abilities are affected). But we really know very little about how the details of neurology are related to cognitive abilities. One of the great mysteries of our time is how the physical substance of the brain can produce perception, consciousness, memory, and – of most concern to us – language.

So, in our ignorance, we can try to understand language by looking at what people really know. In a sense, it's a metaphorical way of looking inside people's heads. To do this, we construct theories of language, or of specific parts of language, like syntax. This book is an introduction to the most influential theory of syntax of the last decade or so.

Think again of the person speaking. One obvious answer to the question: 'what's in their head that makes this possible?' is 'Words'. No one would seriously doubt that anyone who can speak a language has some kind of mental list of words of that language somewhere in their head. This list is known as the **lexicon**. But without syntax, some way of putting these words together, languages are at best shopping lists. The **syntax** is what makes the lexicon go; it turns the shopping list into news, interesting stuff about who's doing what to whom, when, and why. In short, syntax makes sentences that make sense (of some kind). Shopping lists (and dictionaries) aren't much good at that, which is perhaps why a lot of people find them pretty boring.

Here's a sentence that makes some kind of sense (it is attributed to the 1960s pop artist Andy Warhol):

(1) In the future, everyone will be famous for 15 minutes

Anyone who speaks English can recognize this sentence as English and tell you what it means. In fact, they are rather unlikely to react to any aspect of the sentence's form, although they might have something to say about the meaning (and perhaps about Andy Warhol more generally). This is an immediate, intuitive, and almost involuntary reaction. You can't *help* understanding your own language.

Our next sentence makes rather less sense:

(2) Minutes 15 for famous be will everyone, future the in

Here I've just pulled the rather banal trick of reversing the order of the words. Once you figure that out, the sentence can be recognized as the same as (1). However, if someone came up to you on the street and uttered (2), you would most likely consider them to be mad, foreign, or playing some bizarre kind of language game (or some combination of these). Unlike (1), (2) is a syntactically ill-formed sentence, as any native speaker of English is immediately able to recognize.

The sentence in (2) is obviously an extreme case. What about the next little trio?

(3a) In the future will everyone for 15 minutes famous be

(3b) In the future will be everyone famous for 15 minutes

(3c) Future, everyone minutes 15 for famous be will

I think most English speakers would agree that (3a) is, to say the least, awkward, although not incomprehensible (and less obviously a trick than (2)); (3b) could almost be a perfectly fine English question, but that order of words cannot be understood as a statement in English; (3c) is definitely bordering on the grossly bizarre again. However, and here's the rub of the whole intellectual endeavour that this book attempts to lure you into, *the orders of the words in (3) are all perfectly natural ways of saying (1) in other languages.* Example (3a) is the German order, (3b) the Welsh order, and (3c) the Japanese. If we plug the relevant lexica into the orders, we get grammatical sentences in the respective languages (there are a few differences of detail as compared to (3), but we can safely ignore those for now):

(4a) In der Zukunft wird jeder   für 15 Minuten berühmt sein
      In the future   will everyone for 15 minutes famous   be

(4b) Yn y dyfodol, bydd   pawb   yn enwog am 15 munud
      In the future will be everyone in famous for 15 minutes

(4c) Shorai wa,   daremo   ga   15 hun   kan yumei ni   naru desho
      Future TOP, everyone NOM 15 minutes for famous DAT be   will

Why should this state of affairs exist? Why should different languages require us to order the words and phrases of our utterances in differing ways? This book tries to present a theory which can give us an explanation of this state of affairs. As you might imagine, this theory, although rather complex, has implications for other areas of linguistics and many intellectual rewards. I hope by the time you get to the end of this book you will understand something that, reading this for the first time, you don't yet know about.

As we said above, in connection with (1), our reactions to sentences of our native language are immediate and intuitive. You just *know* that the word order of sentences in your own language is OK (native speakers of English may care to look back at example (1) at this point). In fact, the vast majority of people would never pay the slightest heed to the order of the words. Normally, syntax passes completely unremarked. However, it is a remarkable thing, as I hope to convince you. The unconscious ability to make lists into meanings is known as native-speaker **competence**. The differences among the sentences in (3) show us that native-speaker competences differ, in the sense that the same word order can have a different grammatical status in different languages (a comparison of your reaction as a native speaker of English to (1) with your reaction to (3) reveals this). Recent syntactic theory has been devoted to explaining these kinds of differences among languages, and in the chapters to follow I'll introduce the central ideas of this theory.

But here comes a very important point. Your reactions to (1) attest that native-speaker competence is an intuitive, unconscious mental capacity. I take it that there is no reason to believe that people from different parts of the world have a different mental make-up. So it's the same mental ability that causes Germans to accept (3a), Welsh-speakers (3b), and Japanese people (3c). In short, it must be that the same basic ability underlies the competence of all humans in their native language, whatever that language might be. For this reason, our theory must be universal in scope: we need to propose a **Universal Grammar**.

Wait a minute. We've just been talking about differences. We've seen that English, German, Welsh, and Japanese use different word orders. How can Universal Grammar (or UG) explain these differences? One could think that a UG is exactly what we *don't* want. Except then we'd have to say that different word orders mean different mental capacities, and that doesn't seem promising. The solution to this conundrum is to say that UG lays down the basic **principles**, but that each language is free to pick and choose the **parameters** along which those principles are realized. We'll see, for example, that

UG makes certain demands on word order in all languages (so that you can't just reverse the order of words as I did in (2)), but that the principles of word order allow languages a bit of leeway – hence the differences in (1) and (3). The twin concepts of principles and parameters are so important (and so powerful) that the theory is often known by them: we'll follow this practice and refer to it henceforth as Principles and Parameters (P&P) theory.

So this book is about P&P theory, the developing theory of comparative syntax. We'll look at the central components of that theory, how they can account for the nature of language, and the ways in which languages differ. We'll look at four main topics: the make-up of constituents, the ways in which constituents agree with each other and 'mark' each other (this is known as Case theory), how constituents can relate semantically to each other (**anaphora**), and how far away from each other interacting constituents can be (the theory of locality). There's also a fifth topic at the end: the P&P view of how children acquire the syntax of their native language. If the terms in brackets seem strange or daunting now, don't worry. All will be revealed in due course. Before getting into the heart of the matter, though, there are one or two preliminaries that it would be useful to clear up. Depending on how much syntax and how much linguistics you've done before, you may be able to skip the rest of this introduction and go straight on to Chapter 1.

Concepts of Language

The first preliminary point concerns the nature of the object of our study. What is a language? A moment's reflection should reveal that this innocuous-looking question is not an easy one to answer: language and languages are so pervasive in all our activities that it's not a straightforward matter to give a simple definition of what they are. Giving a definition means circumscribing something, and it's very difficult to separate language from the rest of human life. And in any case, we can't do everything – we have to restrict our study to a manageable subject. What we need to do, as in any scientific investigation, is give a clear definition of what we take the object of our investigation to be. This means that we should replace our loose everyday notion of language with a properly defined technical notion. Then we use the technical notion as a basis for constructing our theory and our hypotheses.

Chomsky (1986a: 19–24) does this. He points out that one can, in principle, study language as either an 'external' or an 'internal' phenomenon. 'External' here means 'external to speakers'. Viewed 'externally', in this sense, the study of language involves no claim about the minds, brains, knowledge, or mental states of users of language. Viewed 'internally', on the other hand, the ability to speak and use a language is regarded as a function of some mental capacity, and the study of language necessarily involves claims about the mental states of speakers.

Chomsky considers that the 'external' and the 'internal' approaches really involve different conceptions of the object of study. So he calls the former

'E(xternal)-language' and the latter 'I(nternal)-language'. An E-language is a collection of actual or potential linguistic objects associated with some population of users; it could be, for example, a corpus of tape recordings and transcriptions. An I-language, on the other hand, is taken to be 'some element of the mind of the person who knows the language, acquired by the learner and used by the speaker/hearer' (Chomsky (1986a: 22)). As you can probably guess from what I said at the beginning, the focus of this book, like all generative studies, is firmly on I-language. On the other hand, to a large extent, our everyday conception of language views it as E-language (to the extent that it is not normative, a view which I simply discard here). The words for languages – 'English', 'French', etc. – really refer to E-language concepts; in fact English, French, and so on are socio-political entities rather than mental entities. Atkinson (1992: 23) gives the following characterization of the everyday notion of 'English speaker' in these terms:

> the person in question has an internal system of representation (an I-language), the overt products of which (utterance production and interpretation, grammaticality judgements), in conjunction with other mental capacities, are such that that person is judged (by those deemed capable of judging) to be a speaker of English.

So, really, whenever we use the terms 'English', 'English speaker', etc., we should bear in mind that these are terms with no import for linguistic theory. What we're really talking about are the mental states of people who are conventionally referred to as 'English speakers', etc. The term 'English', if it really refers to anything, refers to an E-language.

You couldn't have E-language without I-language. Recordings of speakers, socio-political constructs like 'the French language', etc., couldn't exist if we didn't have an I-language in our heads. In this sense, I-language is logically prior to E-language.

I-language, then, is the mental faculty that underlies the knowledge and use of language. Of course, many other mental faculties are involved in the use of language. Usually, when you say something, your beliefs and desires (which philosophers call your 'propositional attitudes') are involved. Your beliefs and desires are somewhere in your head, too, but they're distinct from your language. Also, to actually speak (or sign or write), certain nerves and muscles have to be activated. By and large, these nerves and muscles aren't dedicated solely to language, but are also used for other activities. There is no doubt, then, that language *use* combines several mental capacities. I-language is the particular one that we're interested in. I-language, as the knowledge that an adult native speaker has of his or her language, is taken to be the final state of a process of development of the language faculty from an initial state. This initial state is a species-characteristic of humans, and is present at birth. In other words, the initial state is an innate capacity; I'll take up this point in detail in Chapter 5.

The goal of theoretical linguistics is the characterization of the properties of I-language and of the initial state. Linguists' theories of given I-languages (for example, the I-language in the mind of individuals commonly referred to as 'English speakers', 'French speakers', etc.) are grammars (of 'English', 'French', etc.). The theory of the initial state is UG, which I've already introduced.

If we want to work out what UG really consists of, we have to reconcile two seemingly contradictory requirements: on the one hand, UG must be 'rich', in the sense that it must be able to explain how small children develop competence (the unconscious mastery of one's native language that I illustrated earlier) in their native language so rapidly and easily – this is dealt with in Chapter 5. Language acquisition suggests that much of the final state is determined by the initial state, and so UG must have much in common with particular I-languages. On the other hand, the observed diversity of the world's languages – which we've already seen a little example of in (4) – poses a challenge for any UG: it must be sufficiently 'impoverished' to allow for the attested variation. The basic appeal of the principles and parameters theory is that it gives us a way of resolving the tension between these requirements. The principles are the invariant core of UG; however, distinct languages emerge from the parametric variation associated with these principles. A small analogy might help: think of a restaurant which offers a three-course menu. The fact that a meal has three courses and that these come in a certain order defines the meal. This is like the principles of UG. For each course there is a choice among perhaps three or four different dishes. This is somewhat like the parametric variation associated with UG principles. Like all analogies, the above shouldn't be taken too literally. It is intended to help clarify the concepts of principles and parameters, but of course the real force of the idea will only become apparent once we've looked at some real examples.

What You Ought to Know

I'm going to presuppose some knowledge of syntax. If you've never studied any syntax before, I suspect you'll find this book too advanced. However, I'm not going to presuppose a lot – if you've had one or two semesters of basic syntax, that should be enough for you to follow everything. Also, concepts which are **bold-faced** when introduced for the first time are defined in the Glossary at the end of the book.

Ideally, you should be familiar with the following things:

- *basic grammatical terminology* like noun, adjective, verb, preposition, auxiliary, subject, object, clause, and so on. If you're not familiar with these, a good source is Hurford (1994)
- *basic notions of logic and set theory*; it will help if you know something about propositional logic, in particular the ways in which the connectives are defined, and have a basic understanding of set-theoretic notions such as union, intersection, subset, etc. A good introduction to this area, designed explicitly for linguists, is Allwood, Andersson, and Dahl (1977)

- *basic notions of phrase structure*; it will help enormously if you're familiar with the idea that sentences can be diagrammed so as to show how they are constructed from their constituent parts. A simple sentence like (5) can be diagrammed roughly as in (6a), or, equivalently, its structure can be shown by **labelled bracketing** as in (6b):

(5) Andy kissed Lou

(6a)

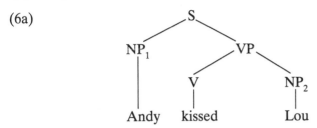

(6b)   [$_S$ [$_{NP1}$ Andy] [$_{VP}$ [$_V$ kissed] [$_{NP2}$ Lou]]]

You should also be familiar with the usual concepts of dominance and constituency, as follows (the Xs and Ys here stand for any category):

  (i) *Dominance*: if there is a continuous set of branches going down the tree from a higher category to a lower category, then the higher category dominates the lower category. In (6a), for example, S dominates everything, while VP dominates V and NP$_2$ but not NP$_1$ (you have to go up the tree to get from VP to NP$_1$ along a continuous line of branches).
 (ii) *Constituency*: if a category X is dominated by another category Y, then X is a constituent of Y. This means that VP is a constituent of S in (6a), and V and NP$_2$ are also constituents of S – but not of NP$_1$.

Immediate dominance and immediate constituency are just like dominance and constituency, respectively, with one refinement. The definition of immediate dominance makes this clear:

(iii) *Immediate dominance*: if there is a continuous set of branches going down the tree from a higher category X to a lower category Y, *and no other category intervenes on the branch connecting X and Y*, then X immediately dominates Y.

So, in (6a), S dominates everything, but immediately dominates just NP$_1$ and VP. We can define immediate constituency in terms of immediate dominance, along the lines of (ii):

(iv) *Immediate constituency*: if a category X is immediately dominated by another category Y, then X is a immediate constituent of Y.

This means that NP$_1$ and VP are the immediate constituents of S in (6a), for example. These notions are discussed at greater length in Borsley (1991, chapter 2), Ouhalla (1994, chapter 2). The ideal background for this book would be the first four chapters of Ouhalla (1994).

If the above areas (grammatical terminology, basics of phrase structure, and elements of logic and set theory) are wholly unfamiliar to you, then you should probably take a look at the references I've given before going any further. If you feel completely comfortable with them, then go on to Chapter 1 (where I briefly go over some of the basics of phrase structure). If you're not sure how much phrase structure and grammatical terminology you know, then try the exercise below. If you're not sure how much logic and set theory you know, try the exercises in Chapters 1 and 2 of Allwood, Andersson, and Dahl (1977).

Exercises

Exercise 1
Give a labelled bracketing and a tree diagram for the following sentences:

   (a) The boy saw the girl

   (b) John said that the boy saw the girl

   (c) Mary took the dog to the park

Exercise 2
Give two sentences that can have their structure diagrammed by this tree:

What are the relations of dominance and immediate dominance in this tree?

1

Categories and Constituents

1.0 Introduction

Universal Grammar must have principles that specify how words can be combined to make phrases, how phrases can be combined to make sentences, and how sentences can be combined to make larger sentences. Given the word-order variation that we find in the world's languages, we might also want these principles to tell us how different languages have different possible word orders. This chapter outlines the usual conception of the part of the grammar that, more than any other, tells us what the permitted combinations of elements are. X'-theory (pronounced 'ex-bar' theory) is the slightly exotic name that is given to the theory of the 'categorial component' of the grammar. That is, X'-theory defines the elements that can be combined to make up syntactic representations, and the ways in which they can be combined. The elements that are combined are the categories of grammar; the ways in which they are combined define constituency relations of various sorts.

Generative grammar, and thus P&P theory, has inherited from American structuralism a conception of language that takes the notions of category and constituency as fundamental. Among many other things, this very general view implies that 'functional' notions of various types, such as subject, topic, etc., are not considered *primitives* of language. Instead, they are *defined* using definitions based on relations of category and constituency. We can illustrate this point with a very simple sentence like the one we used towards the end of the introduction:

(1) Andy kissed Lou

Here, *Andy* is an NP in a given structural position; *Lou* is another NP in a different structural position. The fact that *Andy* is the subject of *kiss* and *Lou* is its object can be stated in these terms. For example, Chomsky defines 'subject-of' as the 'NP immediately dominated by S' in *Aspects of the Theory of Syntax* (71). This is a very clear example of how a functional notion is reduced to a structural notion. It represents an important aspect of generative grammar, and one way in which theories based on generative grammar (of which principles and parameters theory is just one) differ profoundly from many other syntactic theories.

This chapter begins by sketching the original motivation for the X'-theory (and at the same time we see why it has such an odd name). We then give a sketch of the theory of categories. We next move on to the question of the relations between linear order and hierarchical structure. Finally, we consider the structure of the clause. Aside from the first, all of these topics are hotly debated at the time of writing, and so we will immediately enter into areas that are at the forefront of research. There's nothing as invigorating as plunging in at the deep end!

1.1 The Motivation for X'-Theory

1.1.1 Phrase Structure Rules

The early versions of generative grammar that were developed in the 1960s assumed that the basic notions of category and constituency were given by **phrase structure rules** (PS-rules). These rules specify the constituency relations directly, in terms of 'rewriting instructions'. So, for example, (2) states that a sentence S should be rewritten as the sequence *NP–Aux–VP*; in other words, that NP, Aux, and VP are the immediate constituents of S, and that they appear in the left-to-right linear order given:

(2) S → NP Aux VP

Thus, (2) specifies (or generates) a structure that can be diagrammed as follows:

(3a)

$$
\begin{array}{c}
S \\
\diagup \mid \diagdown \\
\text{NP} \quad \text{Aux} \quad \text{VP}
\end{array}
$$

This has been argued to be the structure for simple sentences like *Andy is smoking*, namely:

(3b)

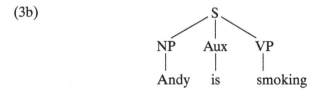

(However, we'll see another hypothesis about the structure of this kind of sentence in 1.4.) Such diagrams are technically known as **phrase markers**, less technically as 'trees'. Other phrase structure rules are those in (4), which, in conjunction with (3) allow a range of familiar English sentences to be generated (here the parentheses indicate optionality, so (4a) should be read as 'a VP consists of a Verb, an optional NP, and an optional Sentence'):

(4a) VP → V (NP) (S)

(4b) NP → Det (AP) N

The fact that S appears on the right of the arrow allows rule (3) to be reapplied, opening up the possibility of repeated, or **recursive**, application of the rules. For example, if V in (4a) is *saying*, then S could be the S of (3). Combining the rule in (4a) with the rule in (2) we can generate *Lou is saying Andy is smoking*. And we could apply rules (2) and (4a) once more, and generate *John is thinking Lou is saying Andy is smoking*. In fact, there is no limit, in principle, to the length of the sentences we can generate by recursively applying rules (2) and (4a) in this way. Because of this, PS-rules can capture the very important insight that natural languages make 'infinite use of finite means' (incidentally, it is this facet of languages which means that you cannot in principle devise a shopping list of all the sentences of a language – even if you wanted to).

Categories like VP and NP are usually called **phrasal categories** (but later we'll introduce a different term for them in the context of X'-theory proper); those like V or N, which dominate only words are called **lexical categories**. Both lexical and phrasal categories are **non-terminals**. **Terminals** are syntactic entities that cannot dominate anything, and hence they 'terminate' their branch of the tree. The lexical categories N and V are the respective **heads** of the phrasal categories NP and VP; these are the most important members of those categories, the elements that essentially define the nature of the phrasal categories.

1.1.2 Problems with Phrase Structure Rules

It is now generally recognized that the approach based on PS-rules of the type just sketched is a bit of a non-starter. On the one hand, it does not generate structures that we find. On the other hand, it generates structures that we don't find. We'll look at examples of each of these below. But first I want to emphasize that there's an important point at stake here. Of course, we want our theory to be able to describe what is found. Also, we don't want a theory which allows us to say things about languages that aren't true. We can't afford to overlook any empirical shortcomings just by shrugging our shoulders and saying 'Well, I predict that, but I don't find it.' Instead, we want our theory to give as precise a characterization as possible of the syntactic properties of natural languages, and so we want it to be unable even to countenance syntactic systems of the sort we don't find. If we can pull that off across the board, then we have some chance of being able to claim that our theory is modelling accurately whatever it is in our brains that turns shopping lists into news. Unfortunately, the kind of PS-rules that were posited in the 1960s seemed to fall short on both of the above counts, and so they were abandoned.

What is the evidence that PS-rules like (2) and (4) do not generate everything we find? The evidence is that we need something intermediate between phrasal categories and lexical categories. We can see this if we consider a simple nominal phrase which contains a modifier, like (5):

(5) this very beautiful girl

It is clear enough that *this* is a Determiner, *very beautiful* is an AP, and *girl* is a Noun. The PS-rule in (4b) gives an analysis of (5), as follows:

(6)

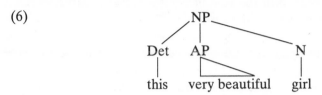

However, a variety of evidence shows that (6) is not the correct structure for (5), but that AP and N (i.e. *very beautiful* and *girl*) form a constituent which excludes the Determiner *this*. This emerges if we apply standard **constituency tests**, syntactic manipulations that are sensitive to the presence of constituents. There are several of these; in general they are the stuff of more elementary textbooks than this one, and so we won't linger over how they work, but just show how they isolate a constituent containing AP and N.

- The first piece of evidence comes from *coordination*. In general, there is good reason to think that only constituents can be coordinated, and, sure enough, we find that *AP+N* can be coordinated:

(7) These VERY BEAUTIFUL GIRLS and VERY UGLY MEN don't like each other

- *Pronominalization* is another classic way of spotting constituents. Again *AP+N* comes out as a constituent on this test:

(8) I like this very beautiful girl more than that ONE

Here, we can add an interesting cross-linguistic confirmation. Italian has a pronoun *ne*. This word translates roughly as 'of it/them' when used with a quantifier (a word which introduces **quantification**). *Ne* belongs to a class of pronouns in Italian that can only show up immediately to the left of the inflected verb; it must appear here instead of in its logical, post-quantifier position (these pronouns are called 'clitic pronouns', because they have to 'cliticize to' something else – the root of 'clitic' comes from the Greek for 'lean on', so clitics are elements which can't stand alone but which have to lean on something else). So we get sentences like (9), for example in the rather plausible dialogue: 'How many beautiful girls do you like?' Answer:

(9) Me ne   piacciono molte
     Me of-them please   many
     'Many of them please me'

Here *ne* can be understood as pronominalizing *AP+N*.

The above tests alone are good enough to show us that *very beautiful girl* is a constituent in (5) (either that, or we drop coordination and pronominalization as tests for constituents). This constituent is obviously smaller than the whole NP, and equally obviously bigger than N. It's neither a big, phrasal version of a Noun, an NP, nor a little, word-level N. Conclusion: it's a *middle-sized* version of a Noun. The middle-sized Nouns are more technically known as **intermediate projections,** and are written as N' (pronounced 'N-bar'). Instead of (6), then, the structure of (5) is more like (10):

(10)

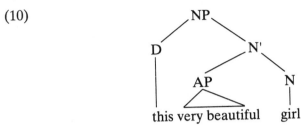

So, by adding an intermediate projection of lexical categories, we can remedy the first problem we noticed with PS-rules. There's an important point here: the intermediate projection must be *a projection of the lexical category*. Every N will 'project' an N', every V a V', etc. Of course, sometimes the N' will contain only N, as in a simple NP like John, and in that case we don't write the N' because it doesn't really do any work. Nevertheless, the general principle holds that intermediate projections of lexical categories correspond categorially to the lexical categories. An economical way to state this is as follows, where we use 'X' as a **category variable**: a symbol that stands for any lexical category (just as, in school algebra, x can represent any number):

(11) Every X projects an X'

Now you know why we call it X'-theory.

The other big problem with the original PS-rule approach emerges when we consider the kinds of things that it allows us to say. In particular it allows us, if we want, to posit rules like (12a) which give structures like (12b):

(12a)   AP → V

(12b)   AP
          |
          V

That is, PS-rules allow us to generate structures that we don't find. Rule (12a) says that we have an Adjective Phrase that contains only a Verb. But surely, anything that contains only a Verb is a Verb Phrase, and, conversely, any AP that contains just one thing will contain an Adjective (we hinted at this a couple of pages back, when we said that a head determines the nature of its phrasal category). In that case, how can a verb determine the nature of an AP? If we allow rules like (12a) we effectively abandon the whole idea that words are organized into phrases which have labels that correspond in any systematic way at all to the labels the words have. Now, here's where the theoretical point made above comes in: we could just be sporting and use the

PS-rule framework without ever postulating nonsense like (12a and b); after all, you may ask, what sensible person *would* postulate a structure like (12)? What kind of bizarre language would lead you to think that this structure exists? Very well; but if we never use certain possibilities of the system, then we're really working with a more restricted system. And that more restricted system is closer to the linguistic reality (which is what we're interested in – we don't just do this for fun). So let's develop the more restricted system into *the* theory of phrase structure. Obviously, what's needed here is a general principle of phrase-structure rules and representations which looks like this:

(13) Every lexical category X corresponds to a phrasal category XP

(13) ensures that (12a) is not a possible PS-rule. It also bears a more-than-passing resemblance to (11). In fact, (11) and (13) together make up the essence of X'-theory, and it's time we laid the system out in full . . .

1.2 The Theory of Categories

1.2.1 Introduction

X'-theory is the theory of how words are built up into larger units such as phrases and sentences. To put it another way, X'-theory takes words, things out of the lexicon, and turns them into syntactic objects capable of combining in such a way as to make some kind of sense.

Because of its absolutely fundamental role in the syntax, X'-theory has to do quite a bit of work for us. In particular, we want it to give us the following information:

- what the possible syntactic categories are
- what the possible hierarchical and linear structures associated with each category are.

In this section, we'll concentrate on the first point: the theory of categories. The next section is devoted to linear order and hierarchical structure.

It is generally recognized now that there are two types of category: **lexical categories** and **functional categories**. This distinction corresponds to the traditional distinction between 'content words' (*television, eat, drink, happy, fat, asteroid*, and so on) and 'grammatical words' (*if, not, will*, and so on), or to that between 'open-class items' and 'closed-class items' – the idea here being that if you invent a new gizmo you can invent a new Noun for it, if you invent a new activity you can invent a new Verb for it, but it's hard to invent a new word like *if* or *not* (unless you're Wittgenstein). I'll say more about this distinction as we go along; for now, I hope that this rather sketchy first pass will suffice.

1.2.2 Lexical Categories

The lexical categories are those that correspond to the content words, or open-class items. These are elements that have a full lexical and semantic life. It's clear that the lexicon functions in part just like a familiar dictionary in that it tells you that associated with the word *asteroid*, for example, there are certain phonetic properties (it's pronounced /æstərɔid or similar), some kind of definition telling you its semantic content (which should somehow relate the linguistic and the non-linguistic), and relevant syntactic information, namely that it's a countable Noun. This information, including the syntactic specification, is idiosyncratic to that particular word, and so must be associated with that word in its lexical entry: where else would you put it?

What we're interested in here is the syntactic information. We assume that there are four lexical categories: N(oun), V(erb), A(djective), and P(reposition) (adverbs are taken to be a variant kind of adjective); these are based on a subset of the syntactic information in the lexical entry, like *asteroid*, which is a countable Noun and so a Noun. These categories can be further broken down into combinations of the 'categorial distinctive features' (a bit like the distinctive features of phonology, but much less elaborate) [± N] and [± V]. Example (14) shows how this is done:

(14) A = +N +V

N = +N −V

V = −N +V

P = −N −V

Again like phonology, this feature system creates natural classes of categories. We can talk about the [+N] categories – Adjective and Noun – or the [+V] categories, Verb and Adjective:

(15) [+N] = N, A   [− N] = V, P

[+V] = V, A   [− V] = N, P

As we'll see in the next chapter in particular, this way of breaking down categories can be useful in various ways, and so there seems to be some reality to it.

So, in the syntax, each word projects its particular combination of [± N] and [± V] features to (maybe) an intermediate projection and (definitely) a phrasal projection. We can see, then, that 'X' in (11) and (13) above refers to values of [± N] and [± V]. This is the theory of lexical categories: a restricted subset of the lexical information associated with words 'projects' into the syntax, and in this way syntactic categories are created. Finer distinctions like that between countable Nouns (like *asteroid*) and uncountable Nouns (like *pasta*) are taken to be irrelevant for the basic combinatorial operations that the syntactic projection is for.

1.2.3 Functional Categories

What about the functional categories? The basic idea is that certain kinds of grammatical information must also be categorially projected into the syntax; the most obvious case of this concerns information about clauses. In (2) above, I introduced the category S for Sentence, following 1960s practice. You might have noticed that S doesn't figure among the list of lexical categories, and can't be derived by combining [± N] and [± V]. So what are sentences? One possibility is that they don't exist, but I think we can dismiss that one. Another, much more sensible, is that sentences are big verbs. Certainly there is a strong intuition that the main verb is the most important thing in a sentence. But sentences contain kinds of information that aren't readily associated with verbs, in particular speech-act information (Is this a question? An order! Or just a statement.). Another thing is the actual position of the clause: subordinate clauses of various types are marked in various ways. These markers are traditionally known as 'subordinating conjunctions' and include, in English, words like *that, if,* and *for* in examples like the following:

> (16a) I think THAT Phil is a genius

> (16b) I wonder IF there's life on Mars

> (16c) We planned FOR there to be a party

You can't have the subordinating conjunctions marking main clauses:

> (17a) *THAT Phil is a genius

> (17b) *IF there's life on Mars

> (17c) *FOR there to be a party

This kind of thing seems to be independent of verbs; any verb can appear in a main or a subordinate clause. Because this is not idiosyncratic information about a particular verb, but a common feature of all Verbs, we don't want to put anything about it in the lexical entry of a particular verb. So we need a new category: the functional category C for Complementizer (a term largely synonymous with 'subordinating conjunction', since the prime function of complementizers is to introduce complement clauses).

It seems pretty clear that the members of C lead rather more impoverished semantic lives than members of lexical categories: does the lexicon have to tell us the content of *that* in (16a) in the way it has to tell us the content of *asteroid, fat,* or *eat*? It doesn't seem as though the 'meaning' of *that* really has much to do with non-linguistic stuff at all. It's much more plausible to suppose that the lexical entry of a word like *that* is limited to phonological information and basically syntactic, information along the lines of 'introduces a finite subordinate clause'. It's perhaps also worth remarking that functional elements are often phonologically 'weak': you can't stress *that* in (16a) (!!*I think THAT Phil is a genius*), and you can reduce it from / ðæt/ to / ðət/; but you can't, say, reduce *fat* from /fæt/ to /fət/. So it appears that functional elements have syntactic properties, but are defective in their semantic (and probably also their phonological) properties. In a way, then, functional categories are almost purely syntactic entities. So, the natural assumption to make is that C projects into the syntax into a C' and a CP in accordance with (11) and (13). CP corresponds to the traditional category of 'clause'.

A host of other functional categories have been proposed in the research of the last 10 years or so. The most important of these are Determiners, Tense, Negation, and Agreement (of various types). Determiners are clearly associated with Nouns, but are in principle independent of them. If we don't want to encode information about **definiteness** and **quantification** in the lexical entry of every Noun, then we should postulate a separate category of Determiners, which projects a D' and a DP. Again, Determiners, although they obviously have a semantic interpretation, lack lexico-semantic content in the sense that ordinary Nouns like *asteroid, television,* and *pasta* have it. Broadly the same can be said about Tense or Negation: although often associated with Verbs, we don't want to say of every Verb in its lexical entry that it can be present or past (etc.) or that it can be positive or negative – this is not idiosyncratic information and so shouldn't be in lexical entries. If we propose separate categories for tense-markers and negative words like *not,* then these entries will lack the specification of lexico-semantic content that we find with verbs. In particular, a tense-marker like *will* and the negator *not* don't contain information about who did what to whom the way that typical verbs do (this is called thematic information; we'll see more about it in Chapter 2). So we postulate the functional categories T and Neg, which project T' and TP, Neg' and NegP, respectively.

Unlike the lexical categories, it has not been possible (yet!) to reduce the functional categories to a more primitive feature system. However, one thing is clear: functional categories usually relate to a particular lexical category. So, as we mentioned above, D is associated with N, T with V, Neg arguably with V, etc. In fact, this association often takes the form of the functional category appearing affixed to the lexical category. You can see this in English past-tense forms, where the affix *-ed* is the tense marker, and it is attached to V. Similarly, many languages have Determiners that attach to Nouns: for example, in Swedish *huset* is 'the house' while *hus* is 'house'. It is clear that *-et* is D here. Also, in Turkish, negation is an affix attached to V, as in (18):

(18) Hasan kitab-*ı*   oku-ma-du
     Hasan book-ACC   read-NEG-PST
     'Hasan hasn't read   the book'

It makes sense, then, to think of different functional elements as 'N-related' (D), 'V-related' (T), and so forth. Functional categories that are related to lexical categories in the way just sketched are L-related. Not all functional categories are L-related; in particular, it's usually thought that C isn't.

This last point raises another very important issue. Comparing different

languages, we can quite easily point to instances of functional categories that
are realized in one language as a separate word, in another as an affix, and
in still another not at all. A simple case is Determiners. In English these are
separate words from Nouns, like *the* and *a(n)*. In Swedish, as we just saw, the
definite article is affixed to the Noun. In Latin or Russian, there are no articles at all, and so we might think that D is either absent or always empty.
This kind of variation in the realization of functional categories, although usually described in purely morphological terms, may turn out to be a fundamental dimension of syntactic differentiation among languages, or parametric
variation. This is another idea you'll be hearing more about.

Anyway, here's a diagram that shows how the theory of categories is
organized:

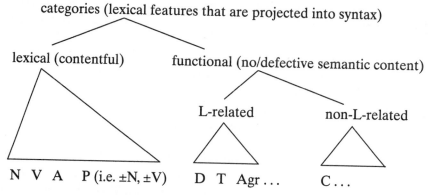

Every category, whether functional or lexical, projects to X' and XP. Now it's
time to see exactly what kinds of structures are projected. What else is in X'
and XP?

1.3 Linear and Hierarchical Structure

1.3.1 Principles and Parameters Across Categories

One of the central ideas of X'-theory is that hierarchical structure is assumed
to be the same for all categories, both lexical and functional. Moreover, we
will assume from now on that branches are always binary. Thus we allow
structures like (19a) and (19b), but not (19c):

(19a)
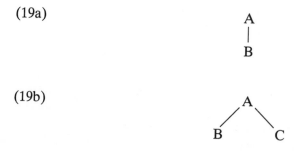

(19b)

(19c)

$$*\quad \overset{\displaystyle A}{\underset{\displaystyle B \quad C \quad D}{\bigwedge}}$$

A consequence of restricting ourselves to binary-branching structures is that each projection of X can contain at most one sister of X. One way to present how this works (borrowed from Rizzi (1988)) is to say the following (from now on, I adopt the convention of using Greek letters to refer to syntactic categories in definitions of structural relations):

(20) XP dominates {α, X'}

X' dominates {β, X}

Here we use the curly-bracket notation of set theory to indicate that the order of the elements is irrelevant (remember that in set theory $\{a, b\} \equiv \{b, a\}$). From now on, we refer to XP as the **maximal projection** of X; X' as the **intermediate projection** of X; and X (or X°) as the **head**. More terminology: α is known as the **Specifier** of X', and β as the **complement** of X. The presence of the complement of X is largely determined by the lexical properties of X, as we will see in more detail in the next chapter. The presence of the specifier depends in part on lexical properties of X, but specifiers can also function as modifiers of X'. Both specifiers and complements are themselves maximal projections, so they have the same structure inside them (this is another instance of recursion). Example (20) gives what we take to be the internal structure of all categories in all languages. These are inviolate principles of UG. P&P theory thus assumes that languages differ very little in their hierarchical organization.

Now it's time to see how principles and parameters can interact. We know that different languages have different orders of words (or constituents). The simplest assumption is that different word orders are a reflection of different linearizations of the same hierarchical structure, i.e. the one in (20). So we might think that the principles in (20) are parametrized along the following lines:

(21a) X' [$_{parameter}$ precedes/follows] α

(21b) X [$_{parameter}$ precedes/follows] β

Each language takes its pick of the bracketed options in (21). You can see straight away that this gives rise to quite a few different possible orders; these are the result of the parametric variation in the invariant principles in (20).

So let's see how this works. We begin with English, in part because we need to get a sense of what the various complements and specifiers are. In English, X' follows its specifier and X precedes its complement. So the general internal structure of categories is as in (22):

(22)

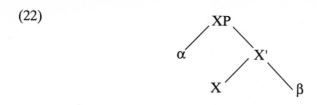

Now let's look at some examples of this general structural schema for different values of X. We begin with APs:

(23) X=A:

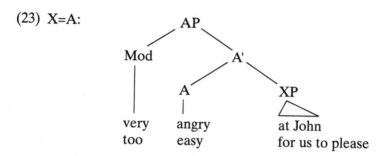

Here we take 'Mod' (short for 'Modifier') as a general cover term for various kinds of elements that are associated with Adjectives. We might think of Mod as an A-related functional category, in which case we might expect it to be a ModP (this would also entail a rather different structure, in all likelihood, but we'll leave that matter aside). Adjectives can take PP or CP complements, as (23) shows.

Next, consider the internal structure of PP:

(24) X=P:

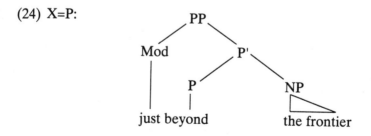

The 'Mod' here is functionally parallel to the one seen above, but somewhat different as far as its membership is concerned. It typically contains 'measure phrases' of various sorts. Again, there is certainly a possibility that these elements are P-related functional categories, but let's leave that to one side. Prepositions usually take NP complements, although some take CPs, like *before* in *before he went home (John finished his work)*. They can also take other PPs as complements, as in *out from under the table* (this happens twice here).

One possible internal structure for VP is this:

(25) X=V:

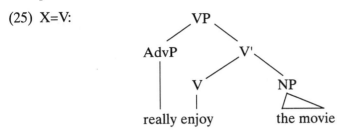

In the next chapter, we'll give reasons to think that the subject occupies the Specifier of VP, at least in an abstract sense (see 2.3.4). Verbs, of course, take a full range of complements: NPs, CPs, PPs, and APs. In fact, some can take all of these categories as complements, like *get* in the following examples:

(26a) get [NP the money]

(26b) get [CP to know someone]

(26c) get [PP into the final]

(26d) get [AP angry]

We see that the internal structure of AP, PP, and VP is quite parallel in English.

So much for English. What about other languages? The Romance languages all have essentially the same parameter values as English, as (27) illustrates using French examples:

(27)

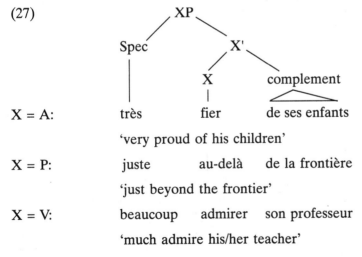

So English and the Romance languages have the parameter values for (21) given in (28):

(28a) X' FOLLOWS its specifier

(28b)   X PRECEDES its complement

These languages are head-initial (in X') and Spec-initial (in XP). Now let's look at some other possibilities.

Japanese is a good example of a language where X FOLLOWS its complement. The following examples illustrate this (I've left out APs, as Adjectives are rather hard to distinguish from Verbs in Japanese):

(29a)   X = P: Nihon   kara
                 Japan   from
                 'from   Japan'

(29b)   X = V: Sensei   wa [$_{VP}$ Taroo o   sikata]
                 Teacher-TOP   Taro-ACC   scolded
                 'The teacher scolded Taro'

(29c)   X = N: Taroo no   hon
                 Taroo GEN   book
                 'Taroo's book'

These examples show that Japanese is a head-final language: it chooses *follows* as the value of the parameter in (21b). We can handle the large differences in word order between Japanese and English (or French) by just choosing a different option in (21b). This is an example of the utility and the power of the principles and parameters approach.

1.3.2 The Structure of Nominals: DP

Let's take a look at the slightly more complicated case of nominals. One possible structure is the following:

(30) X = N:

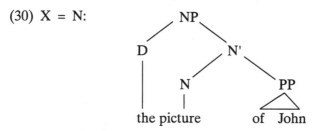

However, (30) glosses over the possibility that D projects a DP. This was originally proposed by Abney (1987) and by Fukui and Speas (1986).

Abney (1987) motivated the postulation of DP for the analysis of an English construction known as **POSS-*ing* gerundives**, as in *John's building a spaceship* in a sentence like (31):

(31) [John's building a spaceship] upset the neighbours

POSS-*ing* gerundives have the external distribution of a nominal phrase, but an internal structure that appears to contain the VP *building a spaceship*. The nominal-like external distribution is shown by the fact that these gerundives can appear in positions where true clauses cannot appear, such as subject position and object of preposition:

(32a)   *Did [that John built a spaceship] upset you?

(32b)   Did [John's building a spaceship] upset you?

(33a)   *I told you about [that John had built a spaceship]

(33b)   I told you about [John's building a spaceship]

Examples (32a) and (33a) show that a true clause, introduced by *that*, cannot appear in subject and object-of-Preposition position respectively. Examples (32b) and (33b), on the other hand, show that POSS-*ing* gerundives can appear in these positions. This in turn shows that POSS-*ing* gerundives aren't clauses. And since, of course, an ordinary nominal *can* appear in these positions, this implies that POSS-*ing* gerundives are ordinary nominals.

However, if we look inside the gerundive we can find evidence that the gerund itself and its object (*building a spaceship* in (31)) is a VP: it has a number of syntactic properties that are typical of VPs rather than nominals, and it allows complements of a type that nouns don't usually allow but verbs do. Some of these are listed in (34):

Nominal objects:

(34a)   John's destroying the spaceship

(34b)   *John's destruction the spaceship

Certain kinds of infinitival sentences ('raising infinitives': see 2.3.3):

(34c)   John's appearing to be dead

(34d)   *John's appearance to be dead

'Double-object' constructions:

(34e)   John's giving Mary a Fiat

(34f)   *John's gift Mary a Fiat

Also, gerundives are like VPs in being modified by adverbs, while nouns are typically modified by adjectives:

(35a)   John's DELIBERATELY building a spaceship

(35b)   John's DELIBERATE building of a spaceship

So the evidence is that gerundives are nominal elements which contain a VP.

However, we can't analyse POSS-*ing* gerundives by simply positing a structure like (36), because here NP$_1$ lacks a corresponding N' and N (it is **exocentric** – lacking a head; X'-theory claims that all syntactic categories are **endocentric**):

(36)

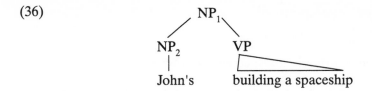

Structures like (36) are ruled out by X'-theory. Instead, though, we can posit the following structure:

(37)

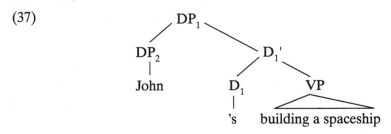

The DP-structure allows us to retain the idea that POSS-*ing* gerundives are nominal categories containing a VP, and satisfy the requirement that all categories must be endocentric. In this construction, the complement of D is VP. Note that I've put possessive *'s* in D.

If the complement of D is NP, we have a standard nominal. So we have (38) rather than (30):

(38) X=D:

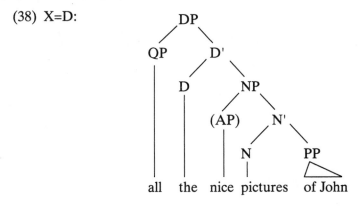

QP is a category projected by the functional head Q(uantifier); it might be possible to identify QP with DP, but we'll leave that question aside. We see here that QPs can modify D'. The DP-structure also has the advantage of creating a natural position for prenominal APs. In this position, they function as modifiers of NP. The complements to Nouns can be PPs, as in (38), or CPs (as in *the attempt* [*CP* *to save the ship*]).

1.3.3 Parameters and Typology

In fact, the idea that X'-theory consists of the principles and parameters we've described opens up the possibility of accounting for word-order typologies of

he kind developed from a very different theoretical point of view, starting
vith Greenberg (1963). Greenberg took a sample of about thirty languages
rom different families and different parts of the world. He observed that,
*l*though there was considerable variation in word order, the variation was
tructured in the sense that certain properties varied together. Two important
tatements of this kind are:

- Universal 3: Languages with predominant VSO order are always prepositional
- Universal 4: With overwhelmingly greater than chance frequency, languages with normal SOV order are postpositional.

'Postpositional' here refers to the order complement – P; strictly speaking,
' can't be a *Pre*position when it follows its complement, so such Ps are called
*Post*positions. The cover term for Pre- and Postpositions that is sometimes
ised is 'Adpositions'.) Universals 3 and 4 together imply that there is a ten-
lency for VO languages (we will conflate SVO and VSO here – see Chapter
* for justification) to be prepositional and for OV languages to be postposi-
ional. In terms of the principles and parameters of X'-theory as we've pre-
ented them, this would be expected: OV and OP arises when a language opts
or *follows* in (21b), and VO and PO where a language opts for *precedes*.

In this way, the principles and parameters of X'-theory might be able to
;ive a theoretical underpinning to the observations made by Greenberg and
)thers developing word-order typologies. Naturally, our theory of syntax has
o be able to account for real cross-linguistic generalizations. It also predicts
hem. Another important point is that the generalizations themselves need
;ome theoretical explanation, unless we just take them to be fantastic coin-
:idences. What we have seen up to now strongly suggests that a parametrized
X'-theory might be able to provide us with a theoretical basis for word-order
ypologies.

However, there are a number of serious difficulties. First, Greenberg and
is followers extended the correlations to include 'noun–possessor' and
noun–adjective' order. OV-OP languages typically have PossN and AN
)rders; VO-PO languages have NPoss and NA. These conclusions are slightly
ricky for the principles and parameters of X'-theory as I've presented them
o far, since possessors and adnominal adjectives are not complements to N;
)ossessors occupy the Specifier of DP and adnominal APs are modifiers
*i*rguably occupying the Specifier of NP (see (37) and (38)). PossN and AN
)rder should therefore be independent of order within X' (namely (21b)),
*i*lthough the evidence from language typology is that there is a relation.
;o it's doubtful that the parameters in (21) can handle all the results of typo-
ogical work.

One might think that the choice of PossN and AN over NPoss and NA is
i reflection of (21a), the choice of Spec – X' order against X' – Spec.
Jowever, languages that are NPoss and NA (such as Romance languages)
lo not have general Specifier-final order; this would involve putting all PP,

AP, and VP modifiers after the head they modify, patterns that we don't find in these languages. In fact, and this is the second problem for relating the parameters in (21) to the results of language typology, no clear case of a generally Specifier-final language has been discovered. Now, it is possible that there are a few languages like this lurking in the Amazonian rain forest or the New Guinea highlands, or even lying unobserved in less exotic locales. But what seems clear is that there is less variation in the Spec-X' parameter than in the head-complement parameter. Look at it like this: the parametrized principles in (21) define four possible language types (to borrow Greenbergian terminology), which we list in (39):

(39a) (21a) = precede; (21b) = precede: a Spec-initial, head-initial language

(39b) (21a) = precede; (21b) = follow: a Spec-initial, head-final language

(39c) (21a) = follow;   (21b) = precede: a Spec-final, head-initial language

(39d) (21a) = follow;   (21b) = follow: a Spec-final, head-final (in XP) language

We have seen examples of (39a) (English is one), and Japanese patterns like (39b) (there is evidence that Japanese is a Specifier-initial language, but I won't go into that here). But (39c) and (39d) are at best very rare. We might very well be back in the situation where we are really using fewer options than our theory allows, so that we should restrict the theory. Or perhaps we should just abandon (21a), and say that only head-complement order is parametrized. This seems to be closer to the truth, but we now have a partially parametrized X'-theory of a kind that is rather unsatisfactory. Our choice of what to parametrize here is being dictated purely by empirical considerations, and the result is a dissatisfyingly lopsided theory (why *should* just part of X'-theory be parametrized?). And we still can't account for the correlations involving NA and NPoss orders.

   Things are actually worse than this. There is some evidence that the parameters in (21) should be enriched. I've been presenting and discussing them up to now in a purely category-neutral fashion. In other words, I've been assuming that all categories (or at least all lexical categories) go the same way in (21). And for English, Romance, and Japanese this works fine. However, there is at least one language fairly close to home which is PO and OV, namely German (note that this is awkward for Greenberg, too).

(40a) auf   dem Tisch   P O
      on   the table

(40b) den Film genießen   O V
      the film enjoy

(There's a major complication in German: in main clauses the finite verb must come immediately after the first constituent. This is the infamous 'verb second constraint', which I'll discuss at greater length in 1.4.2.4). It's conceivable that German can be analysed as being head-final in X' [+V] (here we exploit the feature system of (14)). This idea would predict that Adjectives follow their complements, but that Nouns precede their complements, which (with some complications in nominals that I won't go into here) is basically correct:

(41a) ein [AP seinen   Freunden   treuer] Mann
      a   his-DAT friends-DAT   true   man
      'a man faithful to his friends'

(41b) Karls Betreuung seines Vaters
      Karl's care   of-his   father
      'Karl's looking after his father'

In this way, we might arrive at a description of German word order that fits with what we've proposed so far. However, this move has a price: now we're predicting lots more different types of languages: instead of the four options in (39), we would have sixteen. And if [+V] categories can choose differently from [−V], then we should expect [+N] to do the same. This squares the number of options once again, to give 256 language types. Now, it's possible that these 256 language types exist, but remember that we couldn't find two out of the original four .... The alternative is to create an arbitrary parametrization driven by data (one option for head-complement order, another for Specifier-X'; only [+V] categories can do this and only [−V] can do that, and so on). As I said above, this gives you a lopsided, unprincipled theory in the end; if you're not careful, you end up just listing differences between languages.

1.3.4 A Universal Word Order?

Partly as a response to problems of this kind, and partly for much more general reasons, Richard Kayne (1993, 1994) has recently proposed an entirely different approach. Kayne's idea, quite simply, is that UG cannot contain the parameters in (21). The parametrized X'-theory that we have described here dissociates linear order and hierarchical structure entirely, as I hope I have shown. Kayne takes exactly the opposite tack. He proposes a theory of phrase structure which is based on the central idea that hierarchical structure determines linear order. The hierarchical relation that determines linear order is asymmetric c-command; and to see what asymmetric c-command is, we first need to see what **c-command** is. The definition of c-command that he adopts is (42):

> *C-command:*
> (42) α c-commands β iff α does not dominate β and every category dominating α dominates β

'Iff' here is an abbreviation for 'if and only if', the relation of logical equivalence. If the statement on one side of 'iff' holds, then the statement on the other side must hold. Similarly, if one side of 'iff' doesn't hold, neither can the other.

Try this definition on a made-up structure, such as (43):

(43)

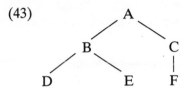

Here, A dominates everything, and so c-commands nothing. For the same reason, B cannot c-command D or E. However, B c-commands F and C; C c-commands B, D, and E, and D and E c-command each other (a moment's checking of (43) against (42) will show you that this is true).

Now for asymmetric c-command. The notion of asymmetry used here is the standard logical one: an asymmetric relation between two things is one which holds in one direction but not in the other, e.g. 'taller than' (if John is taller than Bill, then Bill is not taller than John). So, C *asymmetrically* c-commands D and E because it c-commands them and they don't c-command C; similarly, B asymmetrically c-commands F, by the definition in (42).

We can now phrase Kayne's central constraint as follows:

The Linear Correspondence Axiom (LCA):
(44) If a non-terminal node A asymmetrically c-commands another non-terminal node B then all terminals *a* ... dominated by A precede all terminals *b* ... dominated by B

The statement in (44) doesn't correspond to how Kayne puts it – I've simplified it somewhat. Kayne's exact statement of the LCA is given in the Appendix to this chapter.

The best thing to do with rather abstract proposals like that in (44) is see how they work 'in practice'. So, let's take a pretty simple VP (and I'm briefly ignoring the DP-structure for simplicity's sake):

(45)

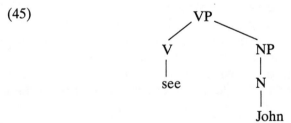

Here V asymmetrically c-commands N (this is analogous to the relation between B and F in (43)). So what the LCA says is: *see* must precede *John*. There are no ifs and buts about it: that just has to be the order. This conclusion would follow even if we chose to draw the phrase-marker the other way around. If the LCA is right, then, it implies that there can be no parametric variation as regards head–complement order; heads precede their complements in all languages. For this conclusion to follow, we must respect the X'-structure of the object; it is the fact that the object has internal structure that makes it impossible for N to c-command V in (45).

Kayne's theory has the interesting and – at first sight – astonishing consequence that all languages are underlyingly head-initial. What, you may well ask, about Japanese (and German)? Kayne's approach implies that superficial OV patterns, or, more generally, head-final typologies, must be **derived structures**. That is, the only way that OV patterns can conform to X'-theory is by proposing that a **movement rule** places the object to the left of the verb; this happens in the syntax as part of the **syntactic derivation**. Very roughly, what must happen is schematized in (46):

(46) Object$_i$ [$_{v'}$ V   t$_i$]

(Here I've indicated the starting point of the movement with *t*, the symbol for a trace, and I've indicated the relationship between the moved object and the trace by co-indexing them with the index *i*; we'll see much more on traces, indices, and movement in the chapters to follow, especially Chapter 4.) We are not at present in a position to know what this really means, although I hope the next chapter will shed some light on the matter. I should point out that, at the time of writing, Kayne's proposals are somewhat contested. What is sorely needed is an analysis of a classic head-final language like Japanese which shows us whether Kayne's approach is likely to prove feasible or not. For the moment, all I can do here is to leave word-order typology in something of a limbo (although we haven't seen the last of it).

In this section we've seen that X'-theory imposes the hierarchical structure in (22) on all categories in all languages. Let's see (22) again:

(22)

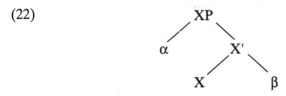

We saw that (22) might be parametrized as in (21), and some of the advantages and disadvantages of this idea. Finally, we briefly discussed the proposal that (22) isn't parametrized at all, and that word-order typologies are the result of differing orders, all derived from (22). As I said at the outset, some of these issues are currently much debated. Now let's move on to the equally debated question of clause structure.

1.4 Clause Structure and Head-Movement

1.4.0 Introduction
Up to now, we haven't looked much beyond the lexical categories, except for a brief discussion of DP. But we mentioned in Section 1.2 that clauses are

CPs, and also briefly introduced V-related functional categories like Tense and Negation. In this section, I want to introduce some of the issues that arise in the analysis of basic clause structure. In this way, we'll meet the V-related functional categories again, and see what they really do. I'll also introduce an important word-order difference between English and French, and show how it can be accounted for by assuming that heads can move in the course of the syntactic derivation. The differences between English and French also give us another example of the interaction of principles and parameters. We next consider CP; here we see that English and French are rather alike, but that they pattern differently from German. This is where we discuss and analyse the German verb-second rule in detail, showing how extending the X'-theory to CP can provide the crucial elements of an analysis of this striking phenomenon. The final topic in this section is the 'split-Infl' hypothesis; this permits us to establish, at least for the purposes of the next chapter, a definitive clause structure.

1.4.1 Verb Movement and the V-related Projection

1.4.1.1 Verb Positions in English and French
Joe Emonds (1978) was the first to notice that finite verbs in simple clauses in French can be thought of as occupying a different position in the structure of the clause from that of their English counterparts. The basic form of the observation is as follows: there is a class of elements, call it *VP-Mods* for now, which is ordered differently in relation to main verbs in the two languages. These elements include VP-adverbs, clausal negation, and floated quantifiers (quantifiers that have 'floated' away from the rest of the nominal they quantify). In French, we always have the order *finite main verb–VP-Mods*, and the opposite is impossible. This is shown in (47):

(47a) Adverb:
　　　Jean EMBRASSE SOUVENT Marie
　　　*Jean SOUVENT EMBRASSE Marie

(47b) Negation:
　　　Jean (ne) MANGE PAS de chocolat
　　　*Jean (ne) PAS MANGE de chocolat

(47c) Floated quantifiers:
　　　Les enfants MANGENT TOUS le chocolat
　　　*Les enfants TOUS MANGENT le chocolat

(As (47b) shows, French has a double-barrelled negation *ne ... pas*; we ignore *ne* here, as do many French speakers in colloquial speech. It seems that *pas* is the real negation, and that's the word we translate consistently as *not*.)

In English, we always have the opposite order, that of *VP-Mods–finite main verb*, as (48) shows:

(48a) Adverb:
    *John KISSES OFTEN Mary
    John OFTEN KISSES Mary

(48b) Negation:
    *John EATS NOT chocolate
    John does NOT EAT chocolate

(48c) Floated quantifiers:
    *The children EAT ALL chocolate
    The children all eat chocolate

It seems very reasonable to assume that the class VP-Mods is the same in the two languages. We certainly have no particular reason to imagine that negation or adverbs or floated quantifiers are different in English and French; they are, for example, semantically the same in both languages. If we say that VP-Mods is structurally the same in the two languages, then the different orders in (47) and (48) show that finite verbs are in different positions in both languages.

English auxiliary verbs like *have* and *be* differ syntactically from main verbs in that they seem to be able to precede VP-Mods (they can also follow VP-Mods, but that's not so important just now). We illustrate with the *have* that marks the perfect tense:

(49a) Pete HAS OFTEN played the marimba

(49b) John has not played the marimba in his whole life

(49c) The kids have all played the marimba for years

If we compare (47), (48), and (49), we see that perfect *have* occupies the same position in relation to VP-Mods as French main verbs. (And note the position of the English dummy auxiliary *do* in (48b), which is the same as that of perfect *have* in (49b), or of the French verb in (47b).)

Now, remember what we said in Section 1.2 about functional categories not having any primary semantic content (not saying anything about who did what to whom – this is also called 'thematic content', as we'll see in Chapter 2). Perfect *have* doesn't seem to have any thematic structure either: the examples in (49) are all about people playing the marimba – *have* just gives us a specification of the tense and aspect of the marimba-playing. So we should think of perfect *have* as a functional category.

Another important consideration here is that it is only *finite* French verbs
that precede VP-Mods; infinitives follow VP-Mods. We illustrate with
negation:

(50a) Ne PAS MANGER   de chocolat   est une honte
      Not to-eat   chocolate   is a   disgrace

(50b) *Ne MANGER PAS   de chocolat   est une honte
      To-eat not   chocolate   is a   disgrace
      'It's a disgrace not to eat chocolate'

(Remember what we said above about ignoring *ne*.) A still further consideration is that we need to bring in stems directly from what we saw in the
previous section. How can X'-theory allow the VP-Mods-type elements
to intervene between the verb and its complement in the French examples
in (47)? We certainly don't want to say that X'-theory allows French to
have a different hierarchical structure inside VP as compared to English.
Whatever the final verdict is on parameters of linear order, everyone
agrees that hierarchical structure should not differ across languages. The
natural thing to say is that finite French verbs occupy the same functional
position as English auxiliaries, while French infinitives occupy the same
position as English main verbs. This idea has a number of things going for
it: first, it captures the distributional observations in (47–49); second, it allows
us to maintain that VP-Mods is the same in both languages; third, it
means that we're not led to posit hierarchical differences between the two
languages. However, we don't want to say either that French verbs are functional heads – that would be far too silly. We obviously can't maintain for a
moment that French verbs don't have thematic content: *embrasser* has just as
much thematic content as *kiss, manger* as *eat*, and so on (of course, you're
quite free to invest these French verbs with whatever extra *cultural* content
you like). Moreover, French infinitives, like English main verbs, *follow* VP-
Mods.

We are thus led to the conclusion that French verbs move to the functional
head in question during the syntactic derivation. In other words, the relevant
part of the structure of an example like (47a) looks like this:

(51) ... [$_I$ embrasse$_i$] [$_{VP\text{-}Mod}$ souvent] [$_{VP}$ t$_i$ Marie]

Here, as in (46), we indicate the starting-point of movement with *t* and
the relation between the starting-point and the moved element with the
index *i*. I've followed a fairly common practice in calling the functional
head I, for Inflection, since it is the position where 'inflectional' information
about Tense and Agreement is located (although this idea will be revised in
1.4.3).

1.4.1.2 The Structure of the Clause
We require I to conform to the X'-schema in (22). The full structure of (47a)
is something like:

(52)

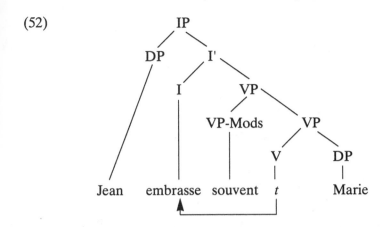

As (52) shows, we can locate the subject in the Specifier of IP, and the VP in the complement of I. Let's take this as a first pass at the structure of a simple clause (we'll get back to CP in the next subsection). We can now also see an important difference between English and French: in French, finite main verbs move to I, while in English this doesn't happen (although English auxiliaries, being functional, appear in I). The effect of the V-to-I rule is to place the finite verb in a position preceding VP-Mods. The operation of this rule in French thus derives the orders seen in (47) above, and its non-operation in English derives the English orders seen in (48). Moreover, the movement operation only applies to *finite* main verbs in French. Infinitives stay in V, as their position in (50) shows.

1.4.1.3 Word-Order Variation at Clause Level
Before going on to look at CP, let's look again at some observations about cross-linguistic patterns made by Greenberg. Greenberg's observations amount to the following implicational statements:

(53a) If a language has VO order, then it will have Aux V order

(53b) If a language has OV, then it will have V Aux order

Table 1.1 gives a little more detail, showing how the languages in Greenberg's sample patterned, and Table 1.2 shows the comparable relation with PO and OP orders. We also name the offending languages which do not appear to fit the typology.

Table 1.1 Synopsis of some of Greenberg's Universals (1)

	VSO	*SVO*	*SOV*
Aux V	3	7	0
V Aux	0	1 (Guarani)	8

Table 1.2 Synopsis of some of Greenberg's Universals (2)

	Prepositional	*Postpositional*
Aux V	9	1 (Finnish)
V Aux	0	9

Japanese is a clear example of an OV-V Aux language, as (54) shows:

(54) Taroo ga   taima   o   utte iru
     Taroo-NOM marijuana-ACC   sell AUX
     'Taroo sells marijuana'

Similarly, German embedded clauses have V-Aux order (as well as OV):

(55) Die Polizei vermutet, daß Tommy Marijuana verkauft hat
     the police   suppose   that Tommy marijuana sold   has
     'The police suppose that Tommy has sold marijuana'

It would be natural to suggest that this is a further instance where these languages choose the head-final option of the head-complement parameter in (21). In that case, German and Japanese would have IPs like this:

(56)

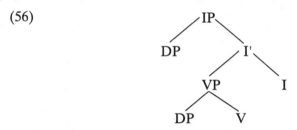

We discussed the pros and cons of the parametrized X'-theory in general in the previous section. If we assume that X'-theory can indeed be parametrized along the lines of (21), then the correlations given in Tables 1.1 and 1.2 are very suggestive evidence in favour of the type of clause structure proposed in (50).

In this section, we've seen the evidence for a V-movement rule in French that places V in a V-related functional category called I. We've seen evidence for the existence of I in English, in the form of the positions occupied by auxiliaries. Consequently, we've adopted (41) as the basic clause structure. Now it's time to look at CP.

1.4.2 CP

1.4.2.1 Complementizers

We said in section 1.2 that complementizers like *that*, *if*, and *for* are members of the functional category C, which projects a C' and a CP. CP is the category of subordinate clauses at least, as we pointed out. What is the relation between CP and IP? A glance at a simple finite subordinate clause will give us the answer:

(57a) I think [CP that John often kisses Mary]

(57b) Je crois [CP que Jean embrasse souvent Marie] (= (53a))

It seems pretty clear that the structure of the embedded clause (the bracketed part) of (57) should be as in (58):

(58)

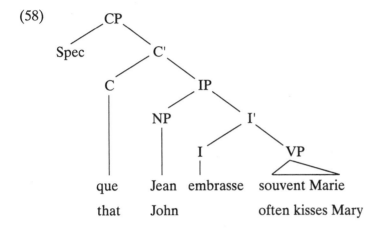

So C takes IP as its complement.

What is in CP's Specifier? In an example like (58), the answer appears to be 'nothing at all'. In other kinds of embedded clauses, though, this position is filled. To see this, we first need to introduce an important condition on movement, the Structure Preservation Constraint:

Structure Preservation Constraint:
(59) Maximal projections can only move to Specifier positions; heads can only move to head positions

Now, let's look at another kind of subordinate clause, indirect questions:

(60a) I wonder [CP which girl John often kisses]

(60b) Je me demande [CP quelle fille Jean embrasse souvent]

In indirect questions of this type, where the question bears on a particular constituent in the subordinate clause which is marked with a *wh*-word, the constituent in question (known as the *wh*-constituent) is moved to the front of the clause by an operation known, imaginatively enough, as *wh*-movement. In (60) *which girl/quelle fille* undergoes *wh*-movement. Since this constituent is the direct object of the main verb of the subordinate clause, it's clear enough that the starting point of movement is the postverbal position that would be occupied by a normal object (since both French and English are VO languages). What, though, is the landing site? Since the *wh*-constituent precedes the subject of the subordinate clause, this position must be higher than IP in (58). Since it follows the verb of the main clause, the *wh*-constituent must be lower than the upper V. There isn't much choice other than to say it's in the region of C, then. Now, the *wh*-constituent is a DP, a maximal projection, and so the Structure Preservation Constraint of (59) prevents it from moving to C. And so it must be in the Specifier of CP (or 'SpecCP' for short). Example (61a) gives the structure of the embedded clause in (60):

(61a)

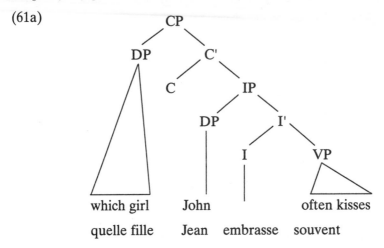

Here, C is empty. However, in some languages, C is filled with an element somewhat like *that* in indirect questions. This is the situation in Dutch, as the following example shows:

(62) Ik vraag me af welk   meisje dat Jan   gekust heeft
      I ask   me of which girl   that John kissed has
      'I wonder which girl John has kissed'

We conclude that the Specifier of CP can be filled by a fronted XP.

1.4.2.2 Root CPs and Root-Embedded Asymmetries

It's clear that CP is present in subordinate clauses. What about main clauses? Is there any reason to think that there is any structure above IP in sentences like those in (47–49), to which we gave the general structure in (52)? Perhaps not, but we have some reason to think that, at least in some kinds of main clauses, there is a CP above IP. A case in point is direct questions:

(63a) Which girl has he kissed?

(63b) Quelle fille a-t-il embrassée?   (= (63a))

As in the embedded clauses of (60), the direct object has undergone *wh*-movement in both of these examples. Parallel with (60–61), we take it that the object moves to SpecCP here. These examples also illustrate the inversion of the auxiliary over the subject. Assuming that French *avoir*, like its English counterpart *have*, is a functional element in I, we can analyse these inversion processes as movement from I to C. So the structure of (63) is:

(64)

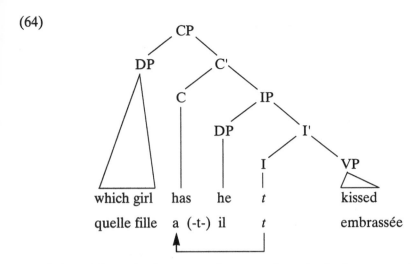

In English and French, direct questions are the principal context where I-to-C movement takes place.

There is a striking asymmetry between direct and indirect questions, in that I-to-C movement takes place in the former, but not in the latter, as a comparison of (60) and (63) shows (although I should point out that I-to-C movement is not obligatory in direct questions in French: *Quelle fille il a embrassée?*). This is an example of what is often called a **root-embedded asymmetry**, a case where embedded clauses pattern differently from main (or root) clauses. Various accounts of this particular root-embedded asymmetry have been proposed. Perhaps the simplest relies on the idea that the presence of a complementizer in C blocks I-to-C movement (since it effectively takes up the space that I is trying to move into) and that English and French are covertly like Dutch, in that there is a silent complementizer – call it ø – present in indirect questions which blocks I-to-C movement. In that case, the structure of (61) should really be (61b):

(61b)

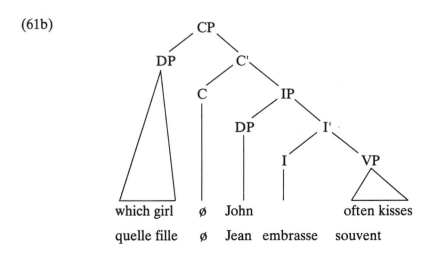

Here ø blocks I-to-C movement. Like other complementizers, ø is not present in main clauses (remember that complementizers introduce subordinate clauses), and so I-to-C movement can take place.

1.4.2.3 The Head Movement Constraint

We've now seen the IP structure for the clause, and the operation of V-to-I movement, as well as the CP-structure for embedded clauses and the I-to-C operation. The next thing to look at is how V-to-I and I-to-C interact. We begin by looking at another notable difference between French and English, the fact that main verbs can undergo inversion in French but not in English. This fact can be seen by simply putting the examples in (63) and (64) into the present tense:

(65a) Quelle fille embrasse-t-il?

(65b) *Which girl kisses he?

In English, the grammatical version of (65b) is of course (66):

(66) Which girl does he kiss?

As we mentioned above, *do* seems like a good candidate for a functional element. In fact, it seems to only mark the 'I-properties', as we might call them, of Tense (here, present) and subject-verb agreement (here, third person singular); it is plainly lacking in any kind of thematic content. The presence of *do* in C in (66) is the result of I-to-C movement, just as is the presence of *has* in (63b).

The ungrammaticality of (65b) seems to show us that V can't move to C in English. Comparing (65b) with (65a), then, we'd have to say that V *can* move to C in French. Putting this conclusion together with our previous results, we arrive at the following list of differences between English and French:

Table 1.3   V- and I-movement patterns in English and French

	V-to-I	I-to-C	V-to-C
English	No (48)	Yes (63a)	No (65b)
French	Yes (47)	Yes (63b)	Yes (65a)

There's an obvious redundancy here. The V-to-I column and the V-to-C column replicate each other exactly. We can reduce the two apparent differences between French and English to just one if we can set up a syntactic correspondence between V-to-I movement and the appearance of V in C. In this way, we can reduce the V-to-C column of (67) to the V-to-I column. We can do this with the following very important constraint:

The Head Movement Constraint:

(67) A head X can only move to the minimally c-commanding head-position.

The definition of c-command was given in (42). We can define minimal c-command as follows:

Minimal C-command:

(68) β minimally c-commands α iff β c-commands α and there is no γ, such that γ c-commands α and does not c-command β.

As ever with such abstract definitions, let's see what (68) does in practice. We can do this by looking again at the clause structure we've proposed:

(69)

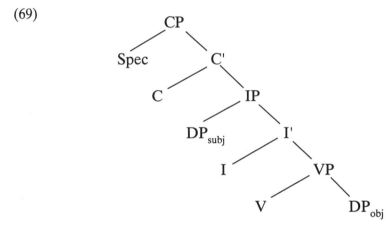

The minimal c-commander of V here is DP_{obj}. However, the Head Movement Constraint in (67) refers to the minimally c-commanding **head** position, which would be the head that c-commands V without c-commanding another head that c-commands V. In (69), the minimal c-commanding head for V in this sense is I. It can't be C, because there is another head, I, which c-commands V without c-commanding C. Thus, V-to-C movement (in one hop) is ruled out by the Head Movement Constraint. In general, the Head Movement Constraint (HMC) stops heads from 'skipping' over other c-commanding heads as they move up the tree, so here it stops V from skipping I on its way to C. (We'll see other constraints on movement rules that bear a general family resemblance to the HMC in Chapter 4.)

Of course, we don't want to rule out V-to-C movement as such, because (65a) shows us that it appears to exist in French. But the Head Movement Constraint doesn't in fact stop V moving to C altogether, it only stops V moving *directly* to C. Movement rules can be iterated (they are 'cyclic'), and as long as V moves to I *en route* to C, the HMC is satisfied; each step of movement then goes to the most local c-commanding head. This is what happens in French sentences like (65a). The HMC thus implies that a language will have V-to-C movement only if it has V-to-I movement. Now we can see why English lacks V-to-C movement while French has it, and, in fact, why there is a redundancy in Table 1.3. Neither English nor French has direct V-to-C movement – no language does, because the HMC rules it out. However, French verbs *can* get to C *via* I. Since English lacks V-to-I movement, English verbs can't get to C at all; this is true quite irrespective of whether English has I-to-C. Of course, the position of *have* in (65a) and of *do* in (66) shows us that English in fact has I-to-C movement.

Although both English and French have I-to-C movement in main-clause interrogatives, whether we say the CP structure is present in main-clause *declaratives* in English and French is something of a moot point, which we won't fully address here. However, the CP structure gives us a way to analyse the German verb-second constraint, which we alluded to earlier. It's now time to look at this phenomenon in more detail.

1.4.2.4 Verb Second

The verb-second (or V2) constraint is in fact found in all Germanic languages (except for Modern English). This constraint requires the finite verb to appear immediately after the first constituent in a finite declarative main clause. The precise nature of the first constituent is immaterial as long as it's an XP; it may be the subject, a complement, or an adverbial element. The following German sentences (from Tomaselli (1989)) illustrate:

(70a) ICH LAS   schon   letztes Jahr diesen   Roman
       I   read   already last   year   this   book

(70b) ICH HABE schon   letztes Jahr diesen   Roman gelesen
       I   have   already last   year   this   book read

(71a) DIESEN   ROMAN LAS   ich   schon   letztes Jahr
       This   book   read I   already last   year

(71b) DIESEN   ROMAN HABE ich   schon   letztes Jahr   gelesen
       This   book   have I   already last   year   read

(72a) SCHON   LETZTES JAHR LAS   ich   diesen   Roman
       Already last   year read I   this   book

(72b) SCHON   LETZTES JAHR HABE ich   diesen   Roman gelesen
       Already last   year have I   this   book read

Using the clause structure in (69), we can propose that the inflected verb moves to the C-position in matrix declaratives in V2 languages. We must then assume that German has V-to-I movement, given the HMC. So V2 involves V-to-I-to-C movement. This operation is associated with the fronting of some XP to SpecCP (presumably a kind of non-interrogative *wh*-movement). The structure of a V2 clause like (71a) would then be as follows:

(73)

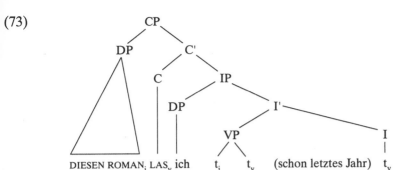

In (73), I've given the direct object *diesen Roman* the index i, and so its starting-point is marked by the trace t_i. The verb *las* has the index v (appropriately enough), and I've marked its starting point with t_v. I've adopted, for the sake of illustration, the idea that I is final in German (as also shown in (56)) – remember that this implies a parametrized X'-theory of the sort we discussed in 1.3. The order of the traces in VP shows that German is OV – this is a good example of how the 'true' word order of a language can be disguised by movement processes. And I'm being quiet about where the adverbial phrase *schon letztes Jahr* goes.

The analysis of V2 shown in (73) can capture another thing about this phenomenon. V2, like I-to-C movement in English or French, is restricted to main clauses (it is a 'root phenomenon', in the terminology we introduced above). The root nature of the phenomenon is explained if we recognize that embedded C-positions are usually filled and so cannot serve as the landing site for the fronted verb. German seems to confirm this idea, because some verbs allow V2 in their complements, but with the important proviso that where the complement is V2 the complementizer *daβ* can't appear (and the verb is usually in the subjunctive mood):

(74a) Er sagte, GESTERN   SEI   er   schon   angekommen
      (embedded V2)
      He said, yesterday have he already arrived

(74b) Er sagte DAß   er   gestern   schon   angekommen   IST
      (C filled, no embedded V2)
      He said that   he   yesterday already   arrived   has
      'He said he'd already arrived yesterday'

It would be natural to say that this a case where I-to-C can take place in an embedded clause, since the C of the embedded clause is empty.

In this subsection, we've seen that the postulation of CP gives us a regular structure for embedded clauses and for many types of main clauses, including V2 clauses. It can also handle root-embedded asymmetries involving verb-movement.

1.4.3 The 'Split-Infl' Hypothesis

1.4.3.1 TP and AgrP

Now let's look again at the structure of IP. There is evidence that the structure is more complex than the one we gave in (52). This evidence leads to the 'split-Infl' hypothesis, originated by Pollock (1989), and to a consequent dramatic elaboration of clause structure.

One important piece of evidence for the split-Infl hypothesis comes from the behaviour of French infinitives. We have already seen that French infinitives do not move over negative *pas* (see (50)). In fact, though, things are more complicated and more intriguing. While infinitives cannot raise over negation, they can precede some adverbs, such as:

(75a) À PEINE PARLER l'italien après cinq ans   d'étude est une honte
      Hardly   to-speak Italian after   five years of study is   a disgrace

(75b) PARLER À PEINE l'italien après cinq ans   d'étude est une honte
      To-speak hardly   Italian after   five years of study is   a disgrace
      'To hardly speak   Italian after   five years of study is   a disgrace'

Pollock accounts for this by proposing a 'short' movement of main-verb infinitives, to a position closer to VP than that of the finite main verbs. The Structure Preservation Constraint (see (59)) tells us that this position must be a head. But (52) has no room for another head in between I and V. Now, the functional category I that we introduced in 1.4.1.1 is a rather uncomfortable combination of Tense (T) and Agreement (Agr). So let's suppose instead that these two kinds of feature, each representing a functional head that projects its own X-bar structure. This means that we split IP into two separate functional projections TP and AgrP. Given this 'split-Infl' structure, we can analyse the 'short' movement of main-verb infinitives in French as movement to the lower of these two heads, while the longer movement of tensed main verbs in French is to the higher of them. We also have to split up the VP-Mods elements: Negation, in the form of *pas*, sits between the higher and the lower of these projections, while adverbs like *souvent* and *à peine* sit between the lower one and VP. If AgrP dominates TP (although Pollock initially assumed the opposite, Belletti (1990) suggested this order), we have the following clause structure:

(76)

Here I've indicated possible positions for the adverbs and for Neg; although, if Neg is a functional category, then we should put NegP in between Agr and TP. This means that *pas* in French, which probably occupies Spec,NegP, always precedes main-verb infinitives – even when they undergo 'short' movement over a VP-adverb as in (75b). Finite verbs move all the way to Agr, and so always precede *pas*.

1.4.3.2 AgrOP

A further elaboration of clause structure stems from Kayne's (1989b) work on past-participle agreement in Romance languages. In French, past participles agree with the object in number and gender when the object is a clitic pronoun that moves from the object position to a position in front of the participle. The following example illustrates this, where the pronoun *les* refers to an object of feminine gender (such as *tables*):

(77) Jean les (F.Pl.)   a   peintEs (F. Pl.)
     John them (F.Pl.) has painted
     'John has painted them'

The same agreement process is seen (although, in the pronunciation of Standard French, not heard) in (63b), where a direct object is wh-moved across the participle; the agreement marking here is *-e*, the mark of the feminine singular.

    Kayne urged that we should have a general characterization of the structural environment in which agreement takes place. We know that agreement between subject and verb is a relation between a Specifier (Spec, AgrP), and the head Agr in (76), and so we can unify participle agreement with this by assuming that there is a further AgrP lower down in the clause, and that fronted categories pass through this position, giving rise to participle agreement in a Spec-head configuration. Let's call the AgrP which relates to the object AgrOP (Object Agreement Phrase). Then the structure of the clause is (78), where we rename the earlier AgrP AgrSP (Subject Agreement Phrase):

(78)

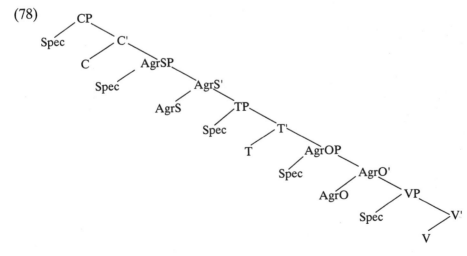

Pollock's 'split-Infl' hypothesis has given rise to an enormous amount of research on basic clause structure and functional categories. Almost any property that can be reasonably ascribed to an auxiliary system – Aspect, Modality, Voice, and so on – has been associated with its own functional category. Thus, just as it is unclear what the inventory of 'possible auxiliary notions' is, it is unclear what the full inventory of functional categories might be (see the discussion of this in 1.2). From now on, however, I'll take (78) to be the structure of the clause. However, whenever it's not really necessary to give the entire 'split' structure I'll just abbreviate it with IP. 'IP' should be taken as standing for all the functional structure between C and VP.

1.4.4 Conclusion

In this section, we have developed an X'-theory of the clause. In doing this, we have seen a range of cross-linguistic differences connected to verb placement: it seems that different languages put V in different functional heads in different kinds of clauses. We haven't given any real rationale for these differences, though, or actually formulated any parameters (the way we did in (21)). Instead, we've been using the different verb positions as evidence for clause structure and, given the strictures of X'-theory, for the presence of functional heads. In the next chapter, we'll present the P&P approach to case and agreement. Among many other things, this will go some way towards making possible a statement of the parameters connected to verb placement.

1.5 Conclusion

In this chapter, we've introduced the theory of categories and constituents. We've seen the following principal points:

- lexical *vs* functional categories: 1.2
- a feature system for lexical categories: (14)
- principles of hierarchical structure: (20)
- parameters of linear order: (21)
- the DP-hypothesis: 1.3.2
- the LCA: (44)
- the functional structure of the clause: 1.4.1
- V-movement to I and I-movement to C: 1.4
- the Head Movement Constraint: 1.4.2.3
- the split-Infl hypothesis: 1.4.3.

As I've mentioned several times, almost all these ideas are the subject of research and controversy at the time of writing. I've tried to indicate what some of these controversies involve, but what this chapter has really tried to do is to give you enough of a grasp of X'-theory that (a) you'll be able to follow what comes in later chapters and (b) you'll be able to understand what the various controversial issues are. And, I hope, you'll be able to make your own contribution to ongoing research on these issues.

The next chapter will build very directly on what we've seen here. Its principal focus is on the conditions governing the external distribution of categories.

Parameters Discussed in this Chapter

At the end of each chapter, I'll give a brief summary of the cases of cross-linguistic variation that are mentioned as parametrized properties in the text. The purpose of this is twofold. On the one hand, it should be a useful revision/synopsis of certain important points in the chapter. On the other hand, it should give you a sense of the kinds of things parameters are, or might be. We'll return to this question in Chapter 5; there we'll also look at the related question of what kinds of experience can fix parameter values in the course of language acquisition.

1. Functional categories may be realized as a separate word, an affix, or zero, such as D in English (*the*), Swedish (*-et*), and Latin (ø). See 1.2.3.
2. X'-linearization:

   (21a) X' $[_{parameter}$ precedes/follows $]$ α

   (21b) X $[_{parameter}$ precedes/follows $]$ β

   English/Romance choose *follow* for (21a), *precede* for (21b). Japanese chooses *follow* for both (see (28)). More generally, *precede* in (21a) gives VO-PO typology and *follow* gives OV-OP typology: see 1.3.1. Related to this may be the fact that English/Romance have I-VP order in IP; Japanese/German have VP-I – see 1.4.1.2.
3. Finite main verbs move to I in French, but not in English: see 1.4.1.1. We come back to the nature of this parameter in 2.6.
4. In main clauses in German(ic), V moves to C and some XP moves to Spec,CP: see 1.4.2.4. It is very unclear whether this is a single parameter or a 'conspiracy' of independent principles and parameters.

Further Reading

The first discussion of X'-theory is in Chomsky (1970), although the idea is sketched in a rather rough fashion at the end of a long discussion of the differences between derived and gerundive nominals (which is relevant for our discussion of the DP-hypothesis in 1.3.2). The most comprehensive discussion and illustration of X'-theory is Jackendoff (1977); although this is rather out-of-date, particularly in its treatment of functional categories, the range of English data discussed is impressive. Jackendoff also discusses an alternative to the feature system for lexical categories given in (14). Chomsky (1955, 1957) introduces the concept of PS-rules, and indeed the whole modern concept of phrase structure. The former is a very difficult text, and certainly not recommended for beginners. The latter is a classic of the field; although, naturally, out of date and with a strong emphasis on formal languages, it is worth perusing since it is effectively the founding text of the field. Another fundamental text is Chomsky (1965). The nature of PS-rules is discussed here, as is the idea of structurally defining functional notions like subject, along with an unparalleled discussion of the goals of linguistic theory and the nature of Universal Grammar. Stowell (1981) provides an extended argument that PS-rules are superfluous to requirements in a theory which makes use of abstract Case – read this (if you can get hold of it) after reading Chapter 2. Other variants of generative theory, that are not really the focus of this book, make PS-rules the central mechanism. Unsurprisingly, these theories are collectively known as Phrase Structure Grammar. A good introduction is Gazdar *et al.* (1985); more recent introductions are Pollard and Sag (1991) and Borsley (forthcoming). Phrase Structure Grammars explicitly distinguish Linear Precedence rules from Immediate Dominance rules, in a way that parallels the discussion in 1.3.1.

The idea of functional categories is an old one, but the idea of explicitly distinguishing these elements from lexical categories in the context of X'-theory was first proposed by Fukui and Speas (1986) and developed by Abney (1987). These authors also originated the DP-hypothesis. The idea that I is the head of the clause originates with Hale, Jeanne, and Platero (1977), although the X'-structure of IP and CP was first proposed in Chomsky (1986b) – read the latter only after reading 4.4 of this book. Rizzi (1988) has a very clear discussion of the principles and parameters of X'-theory, which also takes into account some of Greenberg's results. Although it doesn't adopt the DP-hypothesis, Giorgi and Longobardi (1991) is a very thorough discussion of the cross-linguistic properties of nominals.

The classic work which began the field of language typology is Greenberg (1963). Good introductions to this kind of work are Comrie (1981), Hawkins (1983, 1988), and Croft (1990). Many of the results of this kind of approach are given in Shopen (1985). A rather different slant on language typology can be found in the essays collected in Keenan (1988).

The LCA is presented and discussed at length in Kayne (1994). Chomsky (1995) adopts a slightly different version of the LCA. These works are the kind of thing that I hope you'll be able to grapple with after finishing this book – I wouldn't recommend that you try to manage them after just this chapter.

The original observations about differences in verb positions between English and French are in Emonds (1978). The central article in this connection is Pollock (1989). Bresnan (1972) is the first discussion of the C-position (as we now call it). Den Besten (1983) is the classic discussion of root-embedded asymmetries, although see also Emonds (1976) and Rizzi and Roberts (1989). Other important works on verb movement are Koopman (1984) and Zagona (1992).

The Head Movement Constraint was originally proposed by Travis (1984)

– this is also a good discussion of verb-movement and verb second in Germanic languages, and a nice example of the principles and parameters approach in action (a more readily obtainable work is Travis (1991), which contains many of the ideas of the earlier work). Chomsky (1986b) and Rizzi (1990) discuss the Head Movement Constraint in the context of the general theory of locality – again, you need to read Chapter 4 before you can fully appreciate these. M. Baker (1988) is the fullest statement of both theoretical and empirical aspects of head movement to date.

As mentioned in the text, TP and AgrP are introduced in Pollock (1989). Alternative interpretations of Pollock's data are proposed by Iatridou (1990), L. Baker (1991) and Williams (1994). Pollock's ideas have been extremely influential. In addition to work already mentioned, just a few of the works that build on Pollock are Belletti (1990), Kayne (1989a, 1991), Vikner (1994) and the papers in Lightfoot and Hornstein (1994). Haegeman (1995) is an extended study of NegP in a cross-linguistic perspective. Pollock's work also contributed to the development of checking theory, on which see 2.6.

Kayne (1989b) introduces AgrOP (although not under that name – the term is first used by Chomsky (1991)).

More generally, the collection in Webelhuth (1995) gives an advanced introduction to all areas of GB theory, along with an introduction to minimalism by Alec Marantz. Chapter 1 deals with X'-theory and Case theory. Other chapters cover material dealt with later in this book, and in more depth. This collection would probably be the ideal thing to read immediately after this book – then you can try the primary material.

Exercises

A word of caution:
Don't look at the back of the book for the answers – there aren't any there. This is because most of the exercises raise genuine problems for which there are no good solutions at present. The goal of these exercises is to get you thinking.

Exercise 1
Here are some basic word orders of Welsh:

1. VO: Naeth Siôn golli dwy bunt
        Did   John lose   two   pounds
        'John lost two pounds'

2. PO: gyda Sioned
       with Sioned
       'with Sioned'

3. NA: ysgol   fawr
       school big
       'big school'

4. NPoss: tŷ   Dafydd
            house Dafydd
            'Dafydd's house'

Do these patterns fit the Greenbergian typology as described in 1.3.3? What is the relevant generalization? How, if at all, can the generalization be accommodated in the X'-typology proposed in (21)?

Try to put together the ideas about head-movement in IP from 1.4, the DP-hypothesis of 1.3.2 and the general idea that all categories have symmetrical internal properties. What might one suggest as an account of the NA and NPoss orders in (3 and 4) here?

Exercise 2
Here's a synopsis of three more of Greenberg's universals. These universals correlate the positions of *wh*-elements with basic word order:

Table 1.4 Synopsis of some of Greenberg's Universals (3)

	VSO	*SVO*	*SOV*
Initial Q-particle	5	0	0
Final Q-particle	0	2 (Thai, Yoruba)	5
Initial *wh*	6	10	0

Table 1.5 Synopsis of some of Greenberg's Universals (4)

	Prepositional	*Postpositional*
Initial *wh*	14	2 (Finnish, Guarani)

Leaving aside the badly-behaved exceptions (as usual), we see a correlation between initial *vs* final Q-particles and VP–PO *vs* OV–OP orders. How might we account for this correlation using the parameters in (21)? Do these correlations support an approach like that based on (21) or not?

Exercise 3
We've seen that English is a head-initial language – there's no doubt that it is VO and PO. What about the other two properties that Greenbergians claim to correlate with this? What are the basic word orders inside DP in English? You should consider data such as the following:

1 red bus
2. John's house
3. *a faithful to his friends man
4. a man faithful to his friends
5. an easy-to-solve problem

6. ?a problem easy to solve
7. ??an eager-to-please student
8. a student eager to please
9. ?*the house of John
10. the house of fun
11. *fun's house
12. the destruction of the city
13. the city's destruction
14. Bill's destruction of the city
15. Bill's destruction (Note the meaning of this example)
16. those photographs of John's

Looking at data like this (and you should try to come up with more if you're a native speaker of English), it emerges that it is very difficult to tell whether English is NA or AN, NPoss or PossN. What general tendencies can you isolate? What conclusions does this lead you to draw regarding the correlations discussed in 1.3?

Exercise 4
In 1.4, we saw that English *have* can raise to I. We said that this was connected to the fact that it's a functional element. While it's reasonable to regard perfect *have* as a functional element for the reasons we gave, and it's true that it always raises, consider the following three kinds of *have*.

1. Modal *have*:
   I have to find the man called Duran Duran
2. Possessive *have*:
   I have my car and my TV
3. Causative *have*:
   I have Jeeves wash the Rolls every morning

Which of these allows inversion over the subject in your dialect? (There's quite a bit of dialectal variation on this point – you should also try variants with (*have*) *got*.) Which ones allow or require *do*-insertion? How do your observations fit with the idea that only functional elements can raise to I? Which of the notional categories modal, possessive, and causative are functional and which not, according to the behaviour of English *have*?

Two other things might pattern with inversion. One is clausal negation with *n't* – try that. Another is reduction to *'ve* – try that. How do the patterns work? Can you make any clear generalizations?

Exercise 5
We saw in 1.4 that French main-verb infinitives don't raise over negation. Now look at the following contrasts with auxiliaries, observed by Pollock:

1. N'être pas content est une condition pour écrire
   'To be not happy is a condition for writing'

2. *Ne sembler pas content est une condition pour écrire
   'To seem not happy is a condition for writing'

3. N'avoir pas de voiture en banlieue rend la vie difficile
   'To have not a car in the suburbs makes life difficult'

4. *Ne posséder pas de voiture en banlieue rend la vie difficile
   'To possess not a car in the suburbs makes life difficult'

What generalization can be made here? With regard to possessive *avoir* in (c), how does this relate to your conclusions about possessive *have* in the previous exercise?

Exercise 6
One of the original motivations for X'-theory was the observation that the internal structure of complex nominals is rather like the internal structure of clauses (see Chomsky (1970), Jackendoff (1977)). We mentioned in 1.3 that possessor DPs in English, like *John* in *John's hat*, are rather like subjects. So there's a parallel between SpecDP and SpecIP, we might think. In the light of this, what do you make of Turkish evidence that possessor DPs agree with the Noun, both in simple possessive and in the equivalent of POSS-*ing* gerundives:

1. on-un   el   -I
   he-GEN   hand   -3Sg
   'his hand'

2. Halil'-in   kedi-ye   yemek-0   er-me   -diğ   -I
   Halil-GEN   cat-DAT   food-ACC   give-NEG   GER   -3SG
   'Halil's not giving food to the cat'

Could we postulate a 'split-DP' structure? What might it look like? Can you connect your answer here to your answer to Exercise 1?

Appendix: Kayne's Linear Correspondence Algorithm (LCA)

In 1.3.4, I gave a simplified version of Kayne's LCA (see (44)). Here I want to give a more detailed technical presentation of Kayne's approach. Kayne begins his discussion by noting certain logical properties of linear order. Linear order is transitive (in the logical sense): if x precedes y and y precedes z, then x precedes z. Second, linear order is total: for all pairs of elements x and y in a linearly ordered string, either x precedes y or y precedes x. Finally, linear order is antisymmetric: it is impossible for x to precede y and y to precede x. (I've used 'precede' here as the example of linear order, but you can see that the same logical properties hold if you substitute 'follow' – these are not just properties of the precedence relation, but of any linear ordering relation.)

In order to derive linear order from asymmetric c-command, Kayne introduces two formal notions. The first is the function $d(X)$, which defines, for X a non-terminal node, the set of terminal nodes X dominates. The second is the set A, which gives all pairs of non-terminals such that the first asymmetrically c-commands the second (i.e. A is a set of ordered pairs). With these two notions under our belt, we can give the LCA as follows:

> *Linear Correspondence Axiom (LCA):*
> (A1) For a given phrase marker P, with T the set of terminals, $d(A)$ is a linear ordering of T.
>
> As usual, let's see how this works in practice. Or not quite in practice; let's begin by looking at a made-up tree, where the non-terminals are given in capital letters and the terminals are given in lower-case letters:

(A2)

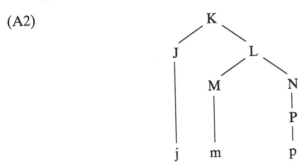

Here, A is {<J, M> <J, N> <J, P> <M, P>}. Therefore, $d(A)$ is {<j, m>, <j, p>, <m, p>} (you should be able to verify both of these claims for yourself by applying the definition of c-command in (42) and the definition of $d(X)$ and A just given). This tree satisfies the LCA, as $d(A)$ is transitive, antisymmetric, and total.

Compare (A2) with (A3):

(A3)

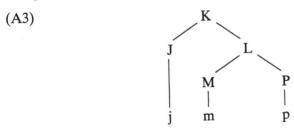

Here, A is {<J, M> <J, P>} and $d(A)$ is therefore {<j, m>, <j, p>}. This tree fails the LCA since the ordering defined is not total: there is no ordering of m with respect to p. So the LCA rules out trees like (A3). As Kayne points out, this result derives two important claims of X'-theory, namely (i) that no head can have a head as its complement and (ii) that each category must have a unique head. The tree that violates (i) looks like (A4):

(A4)

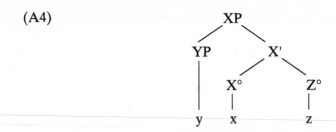

As you can see, this tree is isomorphic with (A3) and violates the LCA for the same reason as (A3). Similarly, the tree that violates (ii) looks like (A5):

(A5)

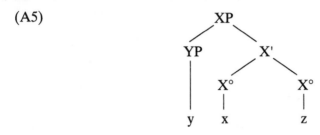

Just like (A3) and (A4), this tree violates the LCA because it cannot yield a total ordering of terminals. Kayne goes on to show how a number of other aspects of X'-theory can be derived from the LCA (with some auxiliary hypotheses, but I won't go into that aspect of his work here – again I refer you to Kayne (1994)).

An important consequence of the difference between (A2) and (A3) is that, as mentioned in 1.3.4 in connection with (45), we have to assume that simple XPs that dominate a single terminal contain both an X node and an XP node. That is, the LCA rejects a DP like (A6), but allows (A7):

(A6)

(A7)

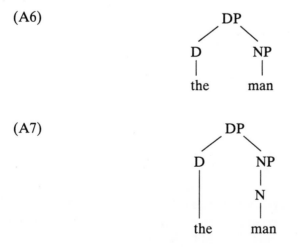

Now let's look at how the LCA can derive a universal ordering of elements within XP, as discussed in 1.3.4. Consider the internal structure of XP:

(A8)

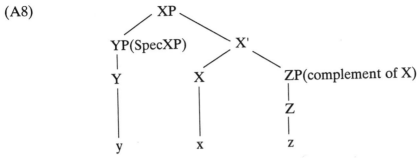

Here, *A* includes <YP, X>, <X,Z> and <YP, ZP> and so *d(A)* includes <y, x>, <x, z>, and <y, z>. (You may notice that *A* will also include <YP, ZP> and <X', Y> which gives *d(A)* including <y, z> and <z, y>; we can avoid this problem by assuming that X' does not count for the determination of these relations – Kayne proposes a more principled and more complex solution to this problem which I won't go into here.) (A8) is an example of *Specifier–Head–Complement* order, as you can see. Compare this with (A9), where the order of head and complement is reversed:

(A9)

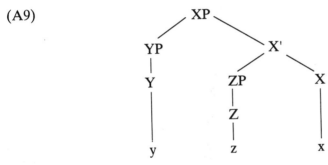

In (A9), *A* and *d(A)* are as in (A8), since the asymmetric c-command relations are the same. However, suppose we tighten up the LCA so that it requires a uniform mapping from *d(A)* to *a given linear order*, either precedence or subsequence. In that case, (A9) is not allowed, since <y, x> is a precedence relation and <x, z> a subsequence relation here. (A8), on the other hand, is allowed, since <y, x> and <x, z> both map onto precedence. So the tightened up LCA predicts that we can only have *Specifier–Head–Complement* order or *Complement–Head–Specifier* order. Of these, it is quite clear that *Specifier–Head–Complement* is more usually found among the world's languages. *Complement–Head–Specifier* order corresponds to having the subject on the right and *wh*-movement to the right (you should be able to see these consequences from your reading of 1.4), both of which are rather rarely attested. For this reason, we can tighten the LCA still further and require that *d(A)* map onto precedence. Hence (A8) is the only possible ordering in XP. This result is encapsulated in our less formal presentation of the LCA in (44). Although this is a very interesting result with potentially enormous empirical consequences, as we pointed out in 1.3.4, we haven't eliminated order from the system since the 'tightened up' LCA must make direct reference to precedence. We'll come back to the idea that all OV orders are derived by movement in the next chapter (see Section 2.7.2).

2

Case and Agreement

2.0 Introduction

In the previous chapter I presented the theory of constituent structure, so now you know what the *internal* structure of syntactic categories is supposed to be, as well as the general inventory of possible categories (to the extent that the inventory of functional categories is at all determined at present). I also introduced, somewhat inconclusively, the parametrized X'-theory, with its potential for accounting for the different word-order patterns that we observe across languages.

This chapter is about the principles determining the *external* distribution of categories, particularly DPs. The basic idea, which has its roots in traditional grammar, is that all DPs must be syntactically 'marked' for their function. In many languages, this 'marking' takes the form of **morphological case**. For example, in Latin every Noun has six cases, and each of these cases is typically marked with an inflectional ending on the Noun. Example (1), which gives the singular forms of the Noun *dominus*, meaning 'master', may bring a shudder of recognition to those of you who have studied some Latin:

(1) Nominative: dominUS
    Vocative: dominE
    Accusative: dominUM
    Genitive: dominI
    Dative: dominO
    Ablative: dominO

Traditional manuals of Latin will tell you that the Nominative case is usually the case of the subject; Accusative is typically the case of the direct object, Dative of the indirect object, and Genitive of possessors, while the Ablative is usually associated with various Prepositions. The Vocative is the form of address – as in *Et tu, BrutE?* – and so is arguably less directly concerned with the syntactic functions of a DP within a sentence.

Now, remember that generative grammar – and so P&P theory – continues the structuralist tradition of reducing function to structure. In that case, we would rephrase the traditional idea that Accusative is the case of the direct object, for example, by saying that it is the case of the structural complement of V (in the X'-theoretic sense of the previous chapter). More generally, we would say that in Latin *the structural position of a DP must correspond to particular morphological mark on the Noun* (and on other constituents of DPs, such as adnominal adjectives).

Many languages work basically like Latin in this respect: Greek, Russian, Polish, German, Old English, Finnish, Sanskrit, Basque, Eskimo, Georgian, Classical Arabic, many Australian languages, and hosts of others from all over the world and from many different language families. But not all languages do. The position of an English Noun (or DP) is not marked in this way, except for pronouns: there is at least a Nominative–*vs*–Non-Nominative contrast in some pronouns (*I* against *me*; *he* against *him*, and so on). Chinese, Vietnamese, Thai, and most creoles simply have no morphological case at all. However, the tack that P&P theory has taken has been to assume that the *morphological* marking is a parameter (since some languages have it and others don't), but that *syntactic* marking of function is a principle, and so universally required. 'Syntactic marking' simply means that DPs in *designated structural positions* have to be associated with designated functions like subject, object, and so on. And, conversely, if a DP wants to have a particular function, it has to be in the designated structural position for that function. This is the essence of the theory of **abstract Case**, which forms the principal subject matter of this chapter. From here on in, we write 'Case' (capital 'C') for abstract Case and 'case' (small 'c') for morphological case. Abstract Case is a theoretical construct; morphological case is a particular kind of nominal inflection. They are very different things; for example, we could be completely wrong about abstract Case (perish the thought!), and it might simply not exist; but morphological case undoubtedly does exist, as anyone who has studied Latin can testify.

The marking of syntactic functions can be thought of as giving particular morphological shapes to the constituents of DPs that occupy given positions. The paramount notion here is the fact that DPs must occupy certain positions in order to have certain grammatical functions. Here we see something we saw before: some languages do it with affixes (Latin and company); some languages do it with little markers that are not affixes, because they are not part of the Noun (both Japanese and Hindi do this; note also that in English indirect objects are often marked with the all-but-meaningless Preposition *to*); and some languages don't do anything morphological at all (such as Chinese). What these observations suggest is that functional heads are involved, given that this kind of morphological variation is the characteristic way in which functional heads vary from language to language.

Moreover, there is no doubt that case and agreement are related. For example, in Latin, only DPs that are Nominative agree with a Verb in person and number. Since Nominative is the case of the subject, this implies that, if a DP agrees with the Verb, then it is the subject. If we're going to connect case to functional heads, then, it's natural to think that Nominative is associated with AgrS. We might extend this to AgrO, and propose that Accusative Case is linked to this functional head. And so we tie abstract Case to the functional categories, in particular to various kinds of AgrP.

The theory of abstract Case, then, is a theory of how DPs are marked in designated positions for various grammatical functions, such as subject, direct object, indirect object, possessor, and so on. In this chapter, I'll summarize the main elements of Case theory, a number of its consequences, and some recent developments and extensions. We will see that Case theory is a very important locus of parametric variation.

In Section 2.2 I present the 'government theory of Case', basically as proposed in Chomsky (1981), following an original suggestion by Jean-Roger Vergnaud. Section 2.3 deals with how Case theory can explain why certain DPs have to undergo syntactic movement – and it will allow us to develop more fully the technical notions relevant to movement that we briefly introduced in Chapter 1. Section 2.4 continues this theme by being all about traces and other types of syntactically present but phonetically silent DPs – **empty categories**. In Section 2.5 we introduce the distinction between two kinds of abstract Case, structural and inherent. Section 2.6 picks up more recent developments concerning the relation between Case and functional categories, and shows how Case theory has been developed into a more general theory, known as **checking theory**. Finally, Section 2.7 relates functional heads, checking, and movement, and shows how many aspects of word-order variation can be thought of as derived from quasi-morphological features of functional heads.

But first, we have to clarify what the notion of 'grammatical function' which I slipped in above really means. What are the functions of DPs that Case theory marks?

2.1 Thematic Roles and Grammatical Functions

In Chapter 1, we briefly introduced the idea that lexical verbs have a thematic structure which is specified as part of each verb's entry in the lexicon. Let's begin by looking a bit more closely at thematic structure. This will shed some light on the notion of grammatical functions.

A typical verb like *eat* contains in its lexical meaning the scenario for an eating event involving an Agent consuming an unfortunate Patient in a particular way. Eve eating an apple, me eating pasta, or a shark eating a surfer all instantiate this general eating scenario in different ways. Part of knowing what *eat* means involves knowing this. So we say that *eat* has two **thematic roles** (or **θ-roles**, for short): Agent and Patient.

Other verbs clearly have a different thematic structure from *eat*. *Run* seems to imply just a runner, the Agent. So *run* has one θ-role while *eat* has two. *Enjoy* is like *eat* in having two θ-roles, but they are of a rather different nature from those of *eat*. In the event described by the sentence *John enjoyed the concert*, John, who obviously has the role of the Enjoyer, doesn't really *do* anything. He merely undergoes a psychological effect of a rather pleasant kind. For this reason this role is often referred to as the Experiencer. Similarly, nothing happens to the concert as a consequence of John's enjoying it. Unless John is given to extreme manifestations of displeasure, we can think that the concert itself would have been exactly the same if John had hated it. Being enjoyed isn't like being eaten; the Enjoyed Object does not really undergo anything. In fact the Enjoyed Object is really the *cause* of John's enviable psychological state, so that this θ-role can be called the Cause role. We see then that DPs bearing different θ-roles can appear in the same syntactic position. This fact is exploited in the following bad joke (for which I apologize in advance):

> (2) A: My dog's got no nose.
>   B: Oh really, how does he smell?
>   A: Awful.

B intends *he* to be the Agent (or perhaps Recipient, since it's not clear that sensory impressions are something we pick up voluntarily) of *smell*; but A's answer reveals that A interprets *he* as the Cause of *smell*. This brings us to the matter of how the thematic structure is realized in the syntactic structure.

The two θ-roles of *eat* are realized syntactically by the DPs that function as the subject and direct object respectively of *eat*. Clearly, this is quite a normal state of affairs; in fact, this is what is found with most transitive verbs that denote an action. However, as our bad joke above tells us, it is possible that in different sentences different θ-roles can be associated with a single grammatical function; this is a matter that depends primarily on the verb.

Agent and Patient are θ-roles; subject and direct object are grammatical functions. We take θ-roles to be a lexical primitive, something that makes up part of the lexico-semantics of verbs (and other lexical categories, too, although verbs are by far the thematically richest category, so I'm just going to talk about them). Grammatical functions are neither lexical nor primitive: they are syntactically defined notions, as we mentioned earlier. However, it is clear that there is a relation between θ-roles and grammatical functions. For example, it seems that Agents are always subjects. However, subjects are not always Agents – the subject of a stative Verb like *know* doesn't actually *do* anything. Similarly, for my dog to smell on the Cause interpretation, he doesn't have to actually do anything – that's just how he is. The same goes for direct objects and Patients: the object of a psychological verb like *enjoy* doesn't undergo anything, as we saw.

Nevertheless, we want to be able to say that, for each verb, a given θ-role is associated with a given grammatical function. This is why *dog bites man* is not news but *man bites dog* is (and why the ambiguity of *my dog smells* depends on that particular verb). The obvious place to put this information is in the lexical entries of verbs (although I should point out that there are clearly defined lexical classes of verbs, and so we don't want to say that the connection between θ-roles and grammatical functions is entirely idiosyncratic). Now, how does the syntax determine when a given DP has a given grammatical function? Our traditional Latin grammar gives us the answer: subjects are Nominative (usually), direct objects are Accusative (usually), and so on. Grammatical functions, then, are *defined by abstract Case*.

So abstract Case ultimately permits you to recover from the position of a DP its particular place in the scheme of who's doing what to whom. Depending on the language, this may be morphologically marked on the DP; we regard the morphological marking as a reflection of the DP's syntactic position. Obviously, to understand how this works in detail we need to know what the principles of Case theory are, and that's what the next few sections are going to be about. However, there's one rather crucial thing which we need first: a way of making sure that the θ-roles have some kind of syntactic realization in the first place. This is achieved by the Projection Principle:

The Projection Principle:
(3) All θ-roles associated with all lexical heads present in the structure must be realized by arguments at all points in the syntactic derivation

Here we refer to 'arguments' rather than DPs, since other categories can bear θ-roles (CPs, for example); an argument is a category that bears a θ-role. We will say more about the nature of syntactic derivation in later subsections of this chapter.

Let's suppose that lexical categories assign θ-roles only to arguments that are within their minimal m-command domain. We define this notion by first defining m-command, thus:

M-command:
(4) α m-commands β iff α does not dominate β and some projection of α dominates β

(Remember that we are using Greek letters as symbols for positions of any kind.) Minimal m-command is defined in (5):

Minimal M-command:
(5) α minimally m-commands β if and only if α m-commands β and there is no γ that both m-commands β and does not m-command α

(You might want to compare (5) with the definition of minimal c-command given in Section 1.4.2; there is a clear formal similarity.) These definitions mean that β can be assigned a θ-role by α just where α^n (some projection of α) contains β and there is no maximal projection γP, also in the minimal m-command domain of α, that contains β. In other words, β must be α's Specifier or complement. To see this, let us look at the following tree:

(6a)

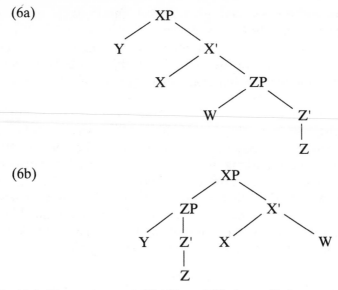

(6b)

In (6a), X m-commands Y, ZP, and W, since all these categories occupy positions inside projections of X. X also minimally m-commands Y and ZP. However, X does not *minimally* m-command W, because there is another maximal category – namely ZP – which m-commands W (since W is contained in a projection of Z, ZP) and does not m-command X since X is *not* contained in a projection of ZP. In (6b), on the other hand, X minimally m-commands ZP and W, but not Y. Here Y is m-commanded by a category that does not m-command X – Z again. You should be able to see that the only way a category can be minimally m-commanded by X is by being either its complement or its Specifier. So, in order to be assigned a θ-role by V, a DP must be either its complement or its Specifier.

One consequence of the Projection Principle of (3) is that when a DP undergoes movement from out of VP, for example, there must be a trace of DP left behind to, as it were, continue to receive the relevant θ-role. This is a point that we will come back to when we discuss movement in more depth in Section 2.3.

One final point on θ-roles. There's an important biuniqueness condition on the assignment of θ-roles, usually called the θ-criterion:

> *The θ-criterion:*
> (7) Each θ-role is assigned to exactly one argument and each argument receives exactly one θ-role

In fact, if it wasn't for (7), the lousy joke in (2) wouldn't even elicit a groan. The simple fact is that *My dog smells* cannot mean 'My dog is a Cause and a Recipient of odour'. The joke in (2) is ambiguous between the Cause and the Recipient interpretations, but it cannot have both interpretations at once – it's either one or the other, and it trades on this ambiguity. Condition (7) also rules out nonsensical sentences like those in (8):

(8a) *John sneezed Mary

(8b) *There ate

Sneeze can have just one argument, the Sneezer, which is the Agent, and so the subject. This means that *sneeze* has no θ-role to assign to a direct object. Condition (7) then tells us that (8a) is ungrammatical; it contains an argument DP, *Mary*, which has no θ-role. Conversely, (8b) is ruled out because *eat* has two θ-roles to assign, but here it has no arguments in its minimal m-command domain (or anywhere else) – *there* is an expletive pronoun, a kind of pronoun which is not an argument – and so the sentence falls foul of (7).

In this section we have given some details of the theory of θ-roles and grammatical functions. The most important thing about θ-roles is that each θ-role in the lexical entry of a lexical category corresponds to exactly one argument in the syntax; this is ensured by the Projection Principle of (3) and the θ-criterion of (7). These are usually argument DPs which occupy positions that are designated for grammatical functions. As we said in the introduction to this chapter, abstract Case is what defines the grammatical-function positions. It's now time to look in more detail at how this is done.

2.2 The Government-Based Case Theory

2.2.1 The Subjects of Infinitives

The initial motivation for Case theory came from looking at positions in which overt DP arguments are not allowed, although covert ones clearly are. This observation led to the idea that Case was connected to the availability of an overt DP argument in a given position. The principal position in question is the subject position of infinitives. Infinitives generally cannot have overt subjects, as the following examples show (in each example, the infinitive is bracketed):

(9a) In the complement to Nouns:
     *Alan's plan [Tommy to sell marijuana]

(9b) In the complement to Adjectives:
     *It's illegal [Tommy to sell marijuana]

(9c) Initially in a sentential subject:
     *[Bill to be president] is nice

(9d) After many (but not all – see below) classes of Verbs:
     *Phil tried [Steve to play the marimba]

However, it's very clear that these infinitives have argumental subjects. We can see this if we take out the overt subject of the infinitive in the above examples:

(10a) In the complement to Nouns:
       Alan's plan [— to sell marijuana]

(10b) In the complement to Adjectives:
       It's illegal [— to sell marijuana]

(10c) Initially in a sentential subject:
       [— to be president] is nice

(10d) After many (but not all) classes of Verbs:
       Phil tried [— to play the marimba]

We could paraphrase the (a–c) examples in roughly the following way:

(11a) In the complement to Nouns:
       Alan's plan [that he would sell marijuana]

(11b) In the complement to Adjectives:
       It's illegal [if one sells marijuana]

(11c) Initially in a sentential subject:
       [That I'm president] is nice

This kind of paraphrase is impossible with example (d), but it's clear that the subject of *play* must be *Phil* here (the subject arguments of both *play* and *try* must have distinct syntactic realizations, given the Projection Principle and the θ-criterion, introduced in the previous subsection). In (11a–c) the subject argument of the embedded clause is a pronoun. Given the general closeness in meaning to (10), and the fact that we know from the Projection Principle and the θ-criterion that the subject argument of the lower clause must be syntactically present, we conclude that the subject of the infinitive in (10) is a phonetically silent pronoun: PRO. PRO has a rather restricted distribution; in fact, it can only occur as the subject of an infinitive. In Chapter 3, we will see one account of why this restriction holds. Here our main concern is the converse question: why can only PRO appear as the subject of the infinitives in (10)? In other words, why are the sentences in (9) ungrammatical?

The answer to this question emerges from the following observation: if we insert *for* in front of the infinitives in (9a–c), they become grammatical:

(12a) In the complement to Nouns:
       Alan's plan FOR [Tommy to sell marijuana]

(12b) In the complement to Adjectives:
       It's illegal FOR [Tommy to sell marijuana]

(12c) Initially in a sentential subject:
       FOR [Bill to be president] is nice

And if we change *try* to *want* or *believe* in (9d), the resulting sentences are grammatical:

(13a) Phil wants [Steve to play the marimba]

(13b) Phil believes [Steve to play the marimba]

Now, our traditional Latin grammars tell us that Verbs and Prepositions 'govern certain cases' (Verbs typically govern the Accusative; Prepositions vary between the Accusative, Dative, and Ablative). We can capture the contrast between (9) and (12 and 13) if we say that all overt DPs require Case, and that Verbs and Prepositions – but not Nouns or Adjectives – can govern Case (or, in a more commonly used terminology, assign Case to a DP which they govern). In (9), the subjects of the infinitives are not assigned a Case, while in (12) – thanks to the presence of the Preposition *for* – they are. In a similar way, the difference between (9d) and (13) can be thought of as a difference in the Case-governing properties of the different Verbs (although we'll come back to this point below).

So, as a first pass, let's formulate the Case Filter roughly as in Chomsky (1981):

> *The Case Filter:*
> (14) *DP if DP is phonologically realized and not Case-marked

The subject of an infinitive is not a Case-marked position (unless *for* or V is present). Therefore only empty categories like PRO can appear there; this explains the contrast between (9) and (10), and, more generally, why subjects of infinitives are typically empty. Another advantage of Case theory is that we do not have to specify that Nouns and Adjectives cannot have DP complements (in a language like English); if we exclude Nouns and Adjectives from the class of Case-assigners, then no DP complement will ever pass the Case Filter.

Abstract Case may or may not be morphologically realized; this is something that varies from language to language, as we saw above. The presence of morphological case is secondary to the syntactic definition of Case-assignment contexts. What we have to do next is see precisely what the Case-assignment contexts are.

2.2.2 Contexts of Case-Assignment

Two of the principal Case-assignment contexts are defined below:

(15a) DP is Accusative when governed by V

(15b) DP is Dative when governed by P

The term 'government' here is intended to recall the usage in traditional grammar. However, we need a structurally precise definition; we cannot content ourselves with the intuitive notion used in traditional grammars. So we now introduce a technical notion of government. Many definitions of this relation have been proposed in research literature. Here is one which is approximately based on Chomsky (1986b) (although it is slightly simpler than the one Chomsky actually proposes there):

Government:
α, a head, governs β if and only if

(16a) α c-commands β

(16b) no barrier dominates β but not α

C-command came up in the discussion of the Head Movement Constraint in Chapter 1. Here, for convenience, is the definition again:

C-command:
(17) α c-commands β iff α does not dominate β and every category dominating α dominates β

Condition (16a) puts an upper bound on government; no category can c-command 'outside' the category that immediately dominates it and therefore no category can govern outside that category. In this respect, the relations of government and c-command are identical.

Condition (16b) places a lower bound on government, preventing the relation from 'reaching too far down'. To see how this is done, we need to know what barriers are. In Chomsky (1986b) this is quite a complex matter, as we'll see in 4.4. However, for now we can live with the following simplified definition:

Barrier:
(18) any XP except IP

All maximal projections are barriers to government, except for IP. We can take 'IP' to include the various functional categories that make up the 'split-Infl' clause structure we discussed in Section 1.4.3 of Chapter 1. Let's just stipulate that these categories are 'defective', and so they do not block government. Then, (18) means that no head α can govern into the maximal projection of another head β, unless β is in the I-system. This is the lower bound that we impose on government.

Now we can see what the definitions of the Case-assignment contexts in (15) amount to. (15a) defines the following as the typical Accusative-Case-assigning context:

(19)

```
          V'
        /    \
       V      DP[ACC]
       |      |
      see     me
```

Analogously, (22) gives the context for Dative Case defined by (15b):

(20)

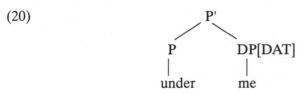

(By the way, (19) and (20) show us that, even in the pronominal system, English doesn't distinguish Accusative and Dative morphologically.) The usual way of looking at things in the government-based Case theory is to say that Case features like [ACC] or [DAT] are assigned by the Verb and Preposition to the relevant DPs. However, at least in languages with a lot of morphological case-marking, it's reasonable to think that a DP with a given form – such as the Accusative *dominum* of (1) – intrinsically has a Case feature, here ACC, which has to be 'matched' or 'checked' against the relevant head under government. For the moment, it doesn't really make any difference how you think about it. However, in Section 2.6 we'll see that the matching or checking idea plays a central role in the recent extension of Case theory known, appropriately enough, as 'checking theory'.

Now let's look at the context for Nominative Case. Here we must distinguish finite from non-finite clauses, since, in English and many other languages, subjects of infinitives cannot be Nominative. Also, I mentioned above that there is an intrinsic connection between Nominative Case and subject–verb agreement. So it's natural to say that AgrS is the category that assigns Nominative Case. Now, subject-verb agreement is impossible in infinitives in English and many other languages, so we can say that AgrS lacks the morphological features for agreement in this context. For convenience, even though it may seem strange, let's say that the AgrS of infinitives is [–Agr]. What we're really saying here is that AgrS is 'deactivated' in non-finite clauses. Now we can state the context of Nominative Case assignment as follows:

(21) DP is Nominative when in Spec of AgrSP, where AgrS is [+Agr].

To put it more succinctly, we say that Nominative Case is assigned under 'Spec-head agreement' between the subject and AgrS. This captures the intrinsic relation between Nominative Case and agreement. We see, then, that there are two ways of assigning Case: under government, and under Spec-head agreement. In both configurations, the head assigning the Case is the central element.

Statement (21) defines the following as the context of Nominative Case:

(22)

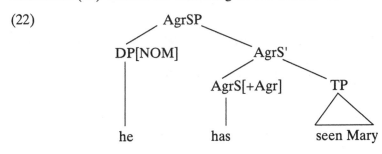

We can define Spec-head agreement as follows:

Specifier-head Agreement;

(23) α, a head, agrees with β iff α minimally m-commands β and does not govern β

Definition (23) uses the notions of government and minimal m-command that we defined earlier in this chapter. In the Appendix to this chapter there is a synopsis of the various structural relations which shows how they are related and how they are built up from relatively simple primitives.

Infinitives like those in (9) look like this:

(24)

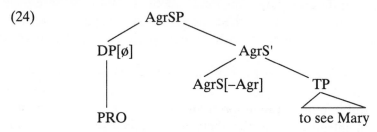

Here we can think of [–Agr] AgrS as having a ø-feature, so it agrees with PRO. Only empty categories can appear in SpecAgrS here, given the Case Filter, as only empty categories can go without Case. Of course, if we take literally the idea that Case defines grammatical functions, then we want to say that PRO has a grammatical function here. One possibility is to say that the absence of Case itself marks a grammatical function; another is to say that PRO bears a special kind of Case: 'zero Case'. For the moment, either of these is acceptable; this is a point we'll come back to in Section 2.4, when we look in more detail at the relationship between Case and empty categories.

The idea that AgrS is deactivated in English infinitives seems to be a parameter. In Portuguese, infinitives show person and number agreement with an overt subject, and this subject is clearly Nominative. So we find examples like the following:

(25a) Sera   difícil [eles aprovar**EM**   a   proposta]
       Will-be difficult they to-approve-**3Pl** the proposal
       'It will be difficult for them to approve the proposal'

(Compare (9b))

(25b) Eu   lamento [os deputados ter**EM**   trabalhado pouco]
       I   regret   the M.P.s   to-have-**3Pl** worked   little
       'I regret that the M.P.s have worked little'

(Compare (9d))

Here, it seems as though AgrS remains 'active' in infinitives. If we simply say this, that AgrS can be [+Agr] in Portuguese infinitives, then our definition of the context of Nominative Case assignment in (22) will allow Nominative DPs in the SpecAgrS position. (I should point out that there are a number of complexities surrounding inflected infinitives in Portuguese; it's clear that the higher Verb plays a role in allowing AgrS to be 'active', but we will put these further details aside here.)

Genitive Case is assigned under Spec-head agreement with D in English. The structure of (26a) is as in (26b):

(26a) the cat's miaow

(26b)

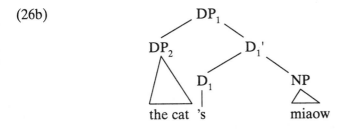

The genitive marker *'s* is not an inflection on *cat*, but is attached to the whole DP in the Specifier position here. We can see this if we put a more complex DP in the possessor position:

(27a) [$_{DP}$ the man I met yesterday] 's dog

(27b) *[$_{DP}$ the man's I met yesterday] dog

While (27a) may not exactly be a choice example of elegant English, it is certainly grammatical, which is more than you can say for (27b). The fact that you can't put the *'s* on the head Noun (*man* is the head of the relative in (27)), but can put it on the whole DP shows that *'s* is not a Noun inflection. A natural thing to think is that it is in D; in fact, we can draw an interesting parallel with Nominative Case assignment and say that *'s* is the mark of an 'active' D, just as agreement is the mark of an 'active' AgrS.

2.2.3 'Exceptional' Contexts

Going back to the definitions of Accusative and Dative assignment in (15), the structures in (19) and (20) are not the only possible contexts that (15) allows. The crucial thing is the definition of government, of course (see (16)), and in particular the lower bound to government, defined by the notion of barrier as in (18). The 'barrier clause' in the definition of government prevents a Verb or Preposition governing anything inside its complement *unless that complement is an 'IP'* (remember that IP means any element of the I-system). So, it is possible for Verbs and Prepositions with 'IP' (AgrSP) complements to govern into that AgrSP and to assign Case to a DP inside it, as long as the DP is a subject (the object position is inside VP, and so 'protected' from outside government by the barrier VP).

This possibility is what explains the grammaticality of the versions of (9) where *for* appears before the infinitive, as in (12). The relevant part of the structure of the complement clause in (12a), for example, is:

(28)

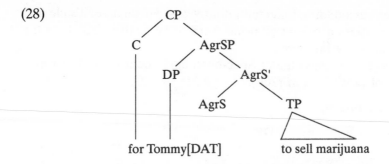

for Tommy[DAT]   to sell marijuana

Here *for* is a prepositional complementizer. Since AgrSP is not a barrier, and since C c-commands the DP in SpecAgrSP, *for* governs *Tommy*. Hence *for* assigns (Dative) Case to *Tommy* here. We can see it's Dative, since if we put in a pronoun, it cannot have the Nominative form: *for *he/him to sell marijuana* (and remember that English does not have distinct Accusative and Dative forms even of pronouns).

A similar situation arises in complements to Verbs of a certain class, known as 'exceptional Case-marking' (or ECM) Verbs (the term is actually a misnomer, since there is nothing exceptional about the way in which these Verbs assign Case). The class includes Verbs like *believe, consider, know,* and others. These Verbs have AgrSP complements (rather than CPs) and are able to assign Accusative to the subjects of those complements. Here are some examples:

(29a) I believe Phil to be a genius

(29b) Andy considers Lou to be a good singer

(29c) We know him to have sold marijuana on many occasions

(29d) We understand them to be able to play the glockenspiel

(29e) Everyone acknowledges George to be best

The forms of the pronouns in (29c and d) show us that these subjects are not Nominative (this and the lack of subject–verb agreement in the infinitive). The relevant parts of the structure for these examples is (30):

(30)

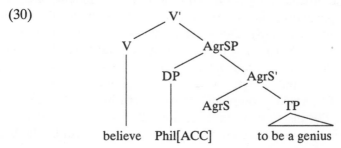

believe   Phil[ACC]   to be a genius

Our definitions of Case-assignment contexts and of government tell us that, where V has an AgrSP infinitival complement, the subject of that complement must be Accusative.

However, this system has one very strange general property. There are four abstract Cases, and two basic modes of Case-assignment: government and Spec-head agreement. Why should things fall out this way? Are we not just following the facts too slavishly, and so positing a lopsided theory again? Or can we make sense of the situation, as it stands? One interesting observation is that the two Cases that are assigned under Spec-head agreement (Nominative and Genitive) are assigned by functional heads, while the two Cases that are assigned under government (Accusative and Dative) are assigned by lexical heads. Below, we'll see how this observation plays a very central role in checking theory. For the moment, we can simply note that the Case-assignment rules are formally a little odd.

In this section, I've presented the basic mechanisms of the government-based Case theory, very much along the lines proposed in Chomsky (1981, 1986a). We saw the inventory of Cases (Nominative, Accusative, Dative, and Genitive) and their contexts of assignment. I also introduced the notions of government, Spec-head agreement, and barrier, all of which are needed in the characterization of the contexts of Case assignment. We also saw that empty categories do not require Case, and raised the question of determining the grammatical function for PRO. The contexts of Case-assignment can be seen as definitions of grammatical functions like subject, direct object, and so on.

With these basics under our belt, we can start to look at some of the work Case theory does for us. The next two sections are primarily devoted to this, beginning with a discussion of what Case can tell us about movement.

2.3 Case and Movement

2.3.1 Movement of the Object I: Passives

If Case theory defines grammatical functions, then we expect it to tell us something about the various processes languages have that change grammatical functions. The best-known and most discussed process of this kind is the passive. It is clear that pairs of active and passive sentences like the ones in (31) describe basically the same unpleasant situation, while what distinguishes the two sentences are the grammatical functions of the arguments:

(31a) The police beat up the students

(31b) The students were beaten up by the police

The passive sentence in (31b) is related to the active one in (31a) by a change in grammatical functions: the DP which is the subject of (31a) is inside the PP headed by *by* in (31b), and the DP which is the object of (31a) is the subject of (31b).

Any theory of syntax has to provide an account of passives and other grammatical-function-changing processes. Many theories take either grammatical functions themselves or the processes that change them as primitives. You won't be surprised to learn by now, though, that P&P doesn't. Just as grammatical functions are seen as structurally defined, so the operations that change grammatical functions are seen as manipulations of structure. More precisely, these operations are taken to involve syntactic movement, and the Case Filter is the principal condition that triggers the movement.

There is a strong intuition that the passive sentence (31b) is somehow parasitic on the active one in (31a). Earlier theories captured this by deriving (31b) directly from (31a). We won't quite follow this approach here, but stay closer to the proposals in Chomsky (1981) and Burzio (1986) by deriving (31b) from something intermediate between (31a) and (31b). Comparing these two sentences, we see that there are three principal differences:

(32a) The DP which is the subject of the active (31a) is the complement of *by* in (31b). Moreover, the *by*-phrase is optional

(32b) The DP which is the object of the active (31a) is the subject of the passive (31b)

(32c) The verb of (31a) is a participle in (31b), and *be* appears in (31b)

Beat up, although two separate words, is usually regarded as a single Verb, a so-called 'phrasal verb'. The lexical entry of the verb *beat up* includes two θ-roles: Agent and Patient. According to the normal way in which θ-roles are mapped into grammatical functions (see Section 2.1), we expect the Patient to correspond to the object of *beat up* and the Agent to its subject. This will give us the active sentence. How do we get the passive?

Let us suppose, for the sake of keeping things as simple as we can, that there exists a general possibility for Agents and other θ-roles that are realized as subjects to be 'demoted'. This 'demotion' may involve the θ-roles in question just not being in the syntax at all, or it may involve their being realized in special ways, such as in a *by*-phrase. 'Demotion' in passives is connected to the appearance of the Verb in its passive form. If we simply assume that the object is projected normally, then we will get a representation like (33) for (31b):

(33) *e* was beaten up the students (by the police)

(I've put the *by*-phrase in parentheses, as it won't play much of a role in the subsequent discussion, and is optional anyway.) As it stands, (33) is ungrammatical. We can get to the grammatical passive sentence in (31b) if we move the object to the subject position (conveniently empty, given the 'demotion' process):

(34) The students$_i$ were beaten up t$_i$ (by the police)

This movement is clearly obligatory, as the ungrammaticality of (33) shows (although it's true that (33) could be ungrammatical because it lacks an overt subject, since English requires all finite clauses to have an overt subject; however, the sentence doesn't improve at all if you add an expletive pronoun:

There were beaten up the students (by the police)). The Case Filter can force this movement for us, if we say that the object position of a passive verb is not a position that the Verb can assign Case to (since *beat up* is a phrasal verb, *up* can't do anything on its own, and so it can't assign Case to the object either). The subject of a finite clause is assigned Nominative Case by AgrS, in the way described in the previous section. The trace in the object position tells us that the subject bears an object's θ-role.

Now, our discussion of the context of Accusative Case assignment in the previous section defined the direct-object position as the position of Accusative Case *par excellence*. So why should direct objects of passive Verbs suddenly not be able to be assigned Accusative? The answer must have to do with the differences in the form of the Verb between active and passive sentences. In other words, we can bring the factor in (32c) into the story by saying something like the following:

(35) Passive participles (even of transitive verbs) are unable to assign Case

Statement (35) is enough to make the object in (33) move in order to seek the Case it needs elsewhere. It ends up in subject position, and so receives Nominative Case from AgrS. Thus, it has all the hallmarks of a subject, and the effect of a change in grammatical function emerges. If the subject is demoted and the Verb unable to assign Accusative Case, the fact that the DP which has the 'object θ-role' appears in the subject position becomes an automatic consequence of the Case Filter. At least one property of passives does not have to be stipulated, in that case. (If you want more of this sort of thing, read Baker (1988).)

The Case-based account of how objects turn into subjects in passives depends entirely on the statement in (35). But why should (35) hold? One possibility is to reason as follows. First, we have said that only the [–N] lexical categories (of V and P) can assign Case. This means that Adjectives, since they are [+N, +V] (see Section 1.2) cannot assign Case. Now, it's well known that participles are quite like Adjectives in various ways. So perhaps passive participles lack the [±N] feature. In that case, they'd be simply [+V]; this would neatly capture the idea that they are half-verb, half-adjective. Since only [–N] categories assign Case, saying that participles are only [+V] means that they are not [–N], and so makes sense of (35). Given these assumptions, we don't expect participles to be Case-assigners. (This line of reasoning was first proposed in Rouveret and Vergnaud (1980).)

Another possibility is to propose that passive participles don't so much lack the capacity to assign Case as they 'absorb' a Case. This idea, originally due to Jaeggli (1986), fares a bit better than the one described above in that we can claim that 'Case-absorption' only takes away one Case from the Verb. So, where a Verb normally has two Cases to assign, 'Case absorption' in passives means that the participle is left with one Case. This seems right for passives of so-called 'double-object' Verbs in English (and other languages, including Swedish):

(36a) John sent Mary flowers

(36b) Mary was sent flowers (by John)

Here it's clear that the first object in the active (36a) can be passivized, to give (36b). The analysis of passives given above applies nicely here. However, it looks as though *send* still has a Case left for the other object in (36b). In this respect, it seems that the Case-absorption idea does better than the approach outlined above. However, we are then left with the question of what 'Case-absorption' might really be. We will leave this matter aside here.

We can find support for the idea that object moves to subject position in passives for Case reasons in languages like Italian and Spanish. In these languages, we find that there is a rather general possibility of 'postverbal subjects' (despite the fact that these are generally thought of as essentially SVO languages). Like all subjects, the postverbal ones agree with the verb in person and number. Here are some Italian examples:

(37a) È   arrivato Gianni
       Is-**3Sg** arrived   John (**Sg**)
       'John has arrived'

(37b) Hanno   telefonato molti studenti
       Have-**3Pl** phoned   many students (**Pl**)
       'Many students have phoned'

(37c) Vinceremo   noi
       Will-win-**1Pl** we (**1Pl**)
       'We will win'

The natural thing to say is that in these languages, it is possible to assign Nominative Case to DPs inside VP. We will come back to what exactly makes this kind of Nominative-assignment possible later; for now, it suffices to note that it must be connected to a parameter of some sort, since we do not find sentences like those in (37) in English.

Now, if Nominative Case can, by whatever means, be assigned to DPs inside VP in Italian, then we should expect that objects don't have to move to the (preverbal) subject position in passives. The object of a passive participle won't be able to be assigned Accusative Case inside VP, assuming that (35) holds in Italian just as it does in English (and there is no particular reason to think otherwise); but it should be able to be Nominative. And this is precisely what we find:

(38) È   stato ucciso Cesare
      Is-**3Sg** been   killed Caesar (**3Sg**)
      'Caesar has been killed'

We can explain the possibility of postverbal subjects in the various contexts in (37) and (38) in terms of the idea that Nominative Case can be assigned to

DPs inside VP in Italian. An important implication of this idea is that there is a position for subjects inside VP where the head of the VP is an active Verb like those in (37). Let's now leave passives and look at this idea more closely.

2.3.2 Movement of the Object II: Unaccusatives

It is possible to show that the subject argument is in a different place in VP in (37a), as compared to (37b) or (37c). This can be shown by the different possibilities of fronting the clitic pronoun *ne* ('of it/them') that we briefly met in the previous chapter. We can take *ne* out of the subject DP where the Verb is *arrivare* ('arrive'), but not where it is *telefonare* ('telephone'):

(39a) NE$_i$ sono arrivati molti t$_i$
      Of-them are   arrived many
      'Many of them have arrived'

(39b) *NE$_i$ hanno telefonato molti t$_i$
      Of-them have   telephoned many

The Verbs in (39) are both intransitives. If we look at transitives, we find that *ne* can only be taken out of the object, never from the subject:

(40a) I   bambini NE$_i$ mangiano molti t$_i$
      The children of-them eat   many
      'The children eat many/a lot of them'

(40b) *Molti t$_i$ NE$_i$ mangiano gli spaghetti
      Many   of-them eat   the spaghetti

The natural conclusion is that the 'subject' of intransitives like *arrivare* is a kind of object, while the subject of intransitives like *telefonare* is a true, if postverbal, subject. This idea has become known as the **unaccusative hypothesis**, and is associated with Perlmutter (1978, 1983) and Burzio (1986).

Let's state the unaccusative hypothesis more succinctly, and then we'll see why it has the name it has. Intransitive verbs are verbs which have just one argument; that is, they assign just one θ-role. We are used to thinking of this one argument as being the subject, and hence that intransitives differ from transitives in having no object. However, the unaccusative hypothesis states that *the single argument of some intransitive verbs is an underlying object*. The intransitives with a single-object argument are known as 'unaccusatives' (like *arrive*), while those that have a single-subject argument are usually called 'unergatives' (like *telephone*). Unaccusatives are like passive participles in that they are unable to assign Accusative Case to their object; they are literally unaccusative. Because of this peculiarity, which must be a lexical property, the object must undergo movement to find a Case somewhere, or else it will violate the Case Filter. This is just like what happens with the object of a passive participle. So, the sentence *John has arrived* involves movement of *John* from the underlying object-position to the superficial subject-position:

(41) John$_i$ has arrived t$_i$

The single argument of an unaccusative is both a subject and an object. It is a subject in terms of its syntactic position and morphological markings (as in subject–verb agreement in English), but it bears an object θ-role which is indicated by the trace in the object position.

And now we see why we can have sentences like (37a) in Italian: here *Gianni* is able to stay in its object position because, in Italian, Nominative Case can be assigned to subjects in VP. In this regard, (37a) is directly comparable to a passive like (38). What's more, since this really is an object position, *ne* can be extracted from here. Verbs like *telefonare*, on the other hand, are unergatives, and so the postverbal subject is not in an object position. Hence they do not allow *ne* to be extracted. For the moment, let's leave aside the question of where the postverbal subject actually is in (37b and c).

Unaccusative verbs have a number of other properties. Typically, their single argument is not an Agent. You can see this by comparing *arrive* with *telephone*; arriving is not something you do, it's really something that happens to you. Telephoning, on the other hand, is very much a voluntary, agent-driven activity. The single argument of an unaccusative usually denotes an entity that undergoes a change of state or location: *come, go, die, grow, fade, redden*, and so on. If unaccusatives form a more or less well-defined lexical class in this way, then it follows that they should be found in every language. This is now generally admitted.

Certain things correlate with unaccusativity. In Italian, for example, there is a choice in compound tenses between the auxiliary 'have' (*avere*) and the auxiliary 'be' (*essere*). As you can see from (37a and b) and (39), *arrivare* takes *essere* as its auxiliary and *telefonare* takes *avere*. This is quite a general correlation: unaccusative Verbs have *essere* as their auxiliary in compound tenses in Italian, while all others have *avere*.

In English, only unaccusative Verbs can appear in 'presentational' sentences like (42):

(42a) After a long delay, there arrived an extremely old, beaten-up train

(42b) *Five minutes later, there telephoned a man with a funny accent

Also, only compound adjectives formed using the participles of unaccusatives can be prenominal:

(43a) a newly arrived recruit

(43b) *a recently telephoned boy

(You might notice that (43b) can mean 'a boy who has recently been telephoned'; however, it cannot mean 'a boy who has recently telephoned (someone else)'. The first interpretation is the passive interpretation of *telephoned* – so this is another parallel between unaccusatives and passives.)

Another important point that arises as a direct consequence of what we've just been saying is that unaccusative verbs can't have subjects – if they did, there'd be nowhere for their object to move to in order to satisfy the Case Filter. This is summed up by Burzio's generalization:

(44) If a Verb has no Accusative Case, it has no subject θ-role

Given (44), it's enough to say that the lexical property of unaccusatives is that they can't assign an Accusative Case to their object – they are literally unaccusative. Also, if we think of the 'demotion' of subjects that is characteristic of passives as being a kind of lack of a subject θ-role, then (44), read from right to left, gives us another reason for the lack of Accusative Case assignment by passive participles (see (35)). In passives, the subject is demoted (or 'lacking') and so there is no Accusative Case available for the object.

2.3.3 Movement of the Subject I: Raising

There is a third class of movements triggered by the Case Filter. These are the various **raising constructions**. Compare the following sentences:

(45a) It seems [that John speaks Chinese]

(45b) *It seems [John to speak Chinese]

(45c) John seems [to speak Chinese]

Sentences (45a) and (45c) are very nearly synonymous. In each example, there are three θ-roles: the Speaker (Agent of *speak*), the Spoken (Patient of *speak*) and the Situation That Seems (arguably a kind of Cause argument of *seem*). The first two are realized by DPs and the third by the CP-complement of *seem*. It's clear that *John* bears the Agent role in all three sentences.

Now let's look at the Case relations here. In (45a), *John* appears as the subject of a finite CP, and clearly receives Nominative Case from the AgrS of the lower clause (we can even see the subject–verb agreement that is the morphological mark of this). In (45b), the lower clause is infinitival, however. *Seem* neither selects *for* as a complement, nor assigns Accusative to the subject of its complement (unlike *believe*, and others: – see 2.2.3). Hence *John* has no way to receive Case here, and the sentence is ruled out. Sentence (45c), of course, is grammatical. Here *John* receives Nominative Case from the higher AgrS; again we can see this in the subject–verb agreement on *seems*. It's clear, however, that *John* bears the θ-role assigned to it by *speak*. So we want to represent the fact that *John* is thematically the subject of *speak*. The obvious way to do this is by proposing that *John* has moved in (45c), as follows:

(46) John$_i$ seems [t$_i$ to speak Chinese]

The trace in the subject position of the lower clause tells us that *John* is the subject of *speak*, in the sense that it receives a θ-role from *speak*. *John* cannot stay in that position, since no Case is assigned there, and so the Case Filter requires it to move to a position which is assigned Case: the subject position of the main clause.

Raising verbs like *seem* are actually a kind of unaccusative. They have no subject θ-role of their own (no person or thing can 'do the seeming' in examples like (45)), and, as we just mentioned, they do not assign Accusative Case. It is also reasonable to think that the infinitival complements of these Verbs are AgrSPs rather than CPs, given the complete impossibility of *for* here: *It seems for John to speak Chinese*. In the previous section, we saw that some Verbs can assign Accusative to the subject of their AgrSP complements, the inaptly named ECM Verbs like *believe*, and others. Now, if unaccusatives with DP arguments are like passives of ordinary transitives, as we just saw above, then we might expect Verbs like *seem* to be like passives of ECM Verbs. This is in fact what we find. The passives of *believe* and the other Verbs in (29) are raising structures:

(47a) Phil$_i$ is believed [t$_i$ to be a genius]

(47b) Lou$_i$ is considered [t$_i$ to be a good singer]

(47c) He$_i$ is known [t$_i$ to have sold marijuana on many occasions]

(47d) They$_i$ are understood [t$_i$ to be able to play the glockenspiel]

(47e) George$_i$ is acknowledged [t$_i$ to be best]

In each of these examples, the moved DP has the subject θ-role of the lower clause, but cannot receive Case in that position, and so moves to the higher subject position where it is assigned Nominative by the higher AgrS.

Raising verbs like *seem* have two main properties, then:

- they have no subject θ-role of their own
- their subject is also the subject of the predicate of the lower clause.

The second of these points implies that, if the predicate of the lower clause is also a raising predicate, then the surface subject of *seem* can be either an expletive pronoun or a DP that has raised twice:

(48a) It$_i$ seems [t$_i$ to be likely that the train is late]

(48b) The train$_i$ seems [t'$_i$ to be likely [t$_i$ to be late]]

Example (48a) shows us that even DPs that have no θ-role of their own, expletive pronouns, are subject to the Case Filter. This shows that Case-assignment and θ-role-assignment are distinct things. Example (48b) shows us that raising can take place 'cyclically'; *the train* here moves first from the lowest to the intermediate subject position, and from there to the highest one. Both movements are caused by the Case Filter. The cyclic movement shows that a DP which is looking for Case moves to the nearest available potential Case position, looks for Case, and, if it can't find it, moves to the *next* nearest position, and so on. In Section (4.5) we'll see in detail how 'nearest' is defined here.

Another thing you should be expecting at this point is that passive and unaccusative movements can interact cyclically with raising. Look at the following examples:

(49a) The money$_i$ seems [t'$_i$ to have been stolen t$_i$]

(49b) The train$_i$ is expected [t'$_i$ to arrive t$_i$ an hour late]

(49c) The weeds$_i$ appear [t'$_i$ to have grown t$_i$ while we were on holiday]

(49d) The patient$_i$ seems [t'$_i$ to be expected [t'$_i$ to die t$_i$]]

In (49a), *the money* is moved from the object position of passive participle *stolen* to the subject position of the lower clause, and thence to the subject position of the higher clause. This is a combination of passive and raising. In (49b), *the train* moves from the object position of *arrive* to the lower-subject and from there to the higher-subject position. This is a combination of an unaccusative and the passive of an ECM Verb. In (49c), *the weeds* move from the object position of *grow* (an unaccusative Verb) to the lower-subject position and then to the higher-subject position. Finally, (49d) combines all three kinds of movement: *the patient* moves from the object position of *die* to the subject-position of the lower clause, from there to the subject-position of the intermediate clause and, finally, to the subject-position of the main clause.

2.3.4 Movement of the Subject II: the VP–Internal Subject Hypothesis

A very important recent development in our conception of clause structure follows on naturally from the discussion of raising. This is the 'VP–internal subject hypothesis' – the idea that subjects are moved to their superficial positions from a position inside VP. In fact, we have to propose something like this if we want to maintain that subjects are assigned their θ-role under minimal m-command as defined in Section 2.1, since SpecAgrSP is not minimally m-commanded by V (you can check this as an exercise). A version of the VP–internal subject hypothesis was originally proposed by Fillmore (1968), and it has been developed in recent theories by Fukui and Speas (1986), Koopmann and Sportiche (1991), Kuroda (1988), and others. The central idea, as Koopmann and Sportiche put it, is that one can show that I (to revert to the 'non-split' Infl for ease of presentation) has the properties of a raising predicate just given. This emerges if we compare the modal *will*, which is usually taken to be an I-element, with *seem*:

(50a) It will be likely [that the train is late]

(50b) The train$_i$ will be likely [t$_i$ to be late]

(50c) John will speak Chinese (after his holiday in Harbin)

Example (50a) shows that *will* has no subject θ-role of its own; (50b) and (50c) show that the 'subject' of *will* can be anything that can be the subject of the predicate following *will*. So we see that *will* is just like *seem*.

However, there are good reasons to think that *will* is not a Verb, but part of the I-system, or a functional head. First, *will* has no θ-roles at all to assign;

in fact, the semantic content of *will* is practically limited to the expression of future time. Second, *will* obligatorily precedes *not* in negatives, and moves to C in main-clause questions:

(51a) John will not be famous

(51b) Will John be famous one day?

Do-insertion is impossible with *will*:

(52a) *John doesn't will be famous

(52b) *Does John will be famous?

Similarly, *will* can precede VP-adverbs and floated quantifiers:

(53a) John will always be famous

(53b) The kids will all be there

It is quite clear from this that *will* is part of the I-system (see 1.4.1), and yet it is a raising trigger. So we are led to the following conclusion:

(54) The I-system contains raising triggers

Statement (54) combines with the general definition of the domain of θ-role-assignment in terms of minimal m-command as in 2.1(5) to give the conclusion that *subjects are raised from a VP-internal position.*

We take this conclusion to be completely general (it doesn't make sense to adopt it only partially). So we would take even the simplest sentence to involve raising of the subject, such as:

(55) John$_i$ [$_{VP}$ t$_i$ ate his dinner]

The position that the subject raises from is SpecVP, we assume (the authors cited above have differing ideas about this point, but we gloss over that). Consequently, we reformulate the X'-structure of VP that we gave in Chapter 1 (1.3.1) along the following lines:

(56)

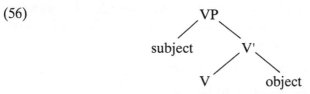

SpecVP is not a position where a DP can receive Case, and the Case Filter dictates that movement from this position is always obligatory. Thus the 'subject' and 'object' positions in (56) are the positions where subjects and objects typically receive their θ-roles, not necessarily those where Case-assignment identifies these grammatical functions.

To get the full picture, we should now combine the VP–internal subject hypothesis with the elaborated functional structure of the clause that we gave at the end of the previous chapter. We give the structure of (55) after movement of the subject has taken place:

(57)

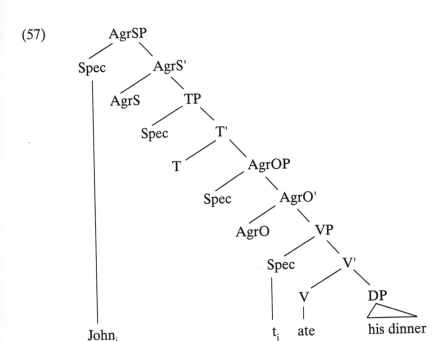

John raises from SpecVP to SpecAgrSP in order to receive Nominative Case from AgrS. SpecAgrS is the nearest available Case position to SpecVP, we assume. Whether *John* must or may pass through the other Specifier positions (SpecTP, SpecAgrOP) on its way to SpecAgrSP is a matter for debate at present and we won't go into it here.

The VP–internal subject hypothesis has many consequences. One very striking one from a comparative perspective is that it offers the possibility of a fairly novel account of VSO languages. VSO languages are those in which the normal order in a declarative sentence is Verb–Subject–Object. Welsh is a good example of a VSO language, as the following sentence illustrates:

(58) Mi welais i Megan
Prt saw(V) I(S) Megan(O)
'I saw Megan'

Other VSO languages include Irish (and indeed all the other Celtic languages), Classical Arabic, Biblical Hebrew and other Semitic languages, some Mayan languages, and many of the languages of Polynesia.

It is tempting to think that the Verb has moved to one of the V-related functional heads in (58), rather as French Verbs do (as we saw in 1.4.1.1), and that the subject stays in VP. In that case, the parameter which distinguishes Welsh from French would be one which determines whether or not the subject is able to be assigned Case in SpecVP. In French the subject must raise to SpecAgrSP, with the result that it always precedes the Verb (unless of course the Verb raises to C). In Welsh, on the other hand, Case is available for the subject in SpecVP, and hence the subject does not raise. The effect of Verb-movement is then to create the VSO order.

There are certainly good reasons to think that VSO order results from the Verb moving over the subject, at least in Welsh (and the same has been suggested for many VSO languages – see Emonds (1980)). Welsh has a kind of *do* auxiliary, which, like English *do*, can carry tense and agreement marking but is totally devoid of meaning of its own. Unlike English *do*, however, the Welsh equivalent can appear freely in any kind of finite clause. So, alongside (58), we have (59):

(59) Mi wnes i [weld   Megan]
      Prt did   I   see(-fin) Megan
      'I saw Megan'

When something carries the tense and agreement, the main Verb (the thing that assigns the θ-roles) follows the subject and has a non-finite form (known as the 'verbal noun'). It is thus very natural to argue that the Verb raises to the V-related functional positions when there is no other element available to 'pick up' the marking of tense and agreement.

If such an analysis is correct, then all we need to do in order to fully account for VSO word order is to find out what the parameter is that lets Nominative Case be assigned to the subject in SpecVP. In Section 2.7, we will see one proposal about this.

2.3.5 Conclusion

In this section, we've seen the connection between Case theory and the kind of movement operation which moves DPs from a position to which Case cannot be assigned to a position which can be assigned Case. This operation takes place in passives, with unaccusative verbs, and in raising constructions. In connection with passives and unaccusatives, we saw how this operation has the effect of changing the grammatical function of a DP from object to subject. In connection with raising, we developed the VP–internal subject hypothesis. We also saw how these kinds of DP-movement can interact in the derivation of a single sentence, and also that DP-movement can be cyclic.

DP-movement is the second kind of movement that I've introduced. The first was head-movement, which we saw in Chapter 1. Now it's time to look at what distinguishes the various types of movement, and also at some of the properties of traces, a little more closely.

2.4 Empty Categories and Types of Movement

Now that we've seen a number of examples we can look more closely at the nitty-gritty of movement, and also say a bit more about the traces that are left behind by movement. We'll also see what distinguishes traces from empty pronominals. 'Empty categories' is the cover term for traces and null pronominals. It's actually a misnomer, in the sense that empty categories do have content, as we'll see. What empty categories always lack is *phonological* content; they generally have syntactic and semantic content. For this reason, a better term would really be 'silent categories' – however, as usual, we stick to the standard term here. (By the way, some people find the concept of empty categories rather abstract and hard to justify, but it isn't at all. If we distinguish syntax and phonology, as all linguistic theories do, then it's reasonable to find things that are present in one and absent in the other. Phonologists happily posit epenthetic segments that exist only in the phonology; empty categories are just the inverse – they exist in the syntax but not in the phonology. If we take the division between phonology and syntax seriously, then we should expect to find empty categories in the syntax.)

In the 1960s and 1970s many different kinds of movement rules were posited. In the P&P theory, these are reduced to three principal kinds of movement operations: head-movement, DP-movement, and *wh*-movement. We've seen the first two of these, and will talk about the third at great length in Chapter 4. Let's now compare them with each other (and in the process I'll introduce *wh*-movement).

I introduced head-movement in Chapter 1 (1.4.1.1). This operation takes an X°-element (a head, as defined by X'-theory) and places it in the nearest c-commanding head position, leaving a trace in the position that it vacates. The Head Movement Constraint says that heads only move to the minimally c-commanding head position (minimal c-command is defined in 1.4.2.3). This constraint is independent of the movement operation itself, and so we can look at head-movement as being just the movement of a head, and assume that movement leaves a trace in the vacated position. In fact, the Head Movement Constraint contains two components: the idea that the 'landing site' of movement (the position moved to, in other words) must c-command the starting point of movement, and the idea that the movement must be as short as possible, taking the head to the *minimal* c-commanding head position. And of course, we know from our discussion of the Structure Preservation Constraint in Chapter 1 (1.4.2.1) that the landing-site of head-movement must be a head. So, we can sum up the properties of head movement as follows:

> *Head-movement:*

(60a) moves a head

(60b) leaves a trace in the starting position

(60c) moves to a position c-commanding the trace

(60d) moves to the closest possible position to the trace

(60e) obeys the Structure Preservation Constraint

This much is (hopefully) useful revision of Chapter 1, even if I've put things slightly differently here. Now let's compare the movement operations we saw in the previous section.

What are the properties of DP-movement as in passives, unaccusatives, and raising? First, it always moves a DP – this should be pretty obvious. Second, it leaves a trace in the vacated position (this is arguably forced by the Projection Principle, as we mentioned in 2.1). Third, it always moves a DP from either a complement position (in fact, a direct-object position in all the examples we've looked at) as in passives or unaccusatives, or, in the case of raising, from a lower-subject to a higher-subject position. In fact, the landing site of DP-movement always c-commands the trace of movement, as a cursory inspection of the following two trees will reveal (I've left out various Specifier positions here for the sake of simplicity):

(61a) Passive/unaccusative:

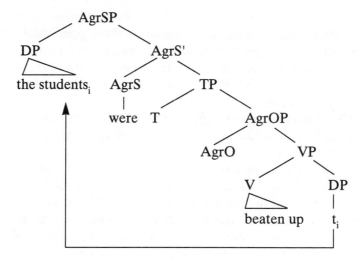

(61b) Raising (from a lower clause):

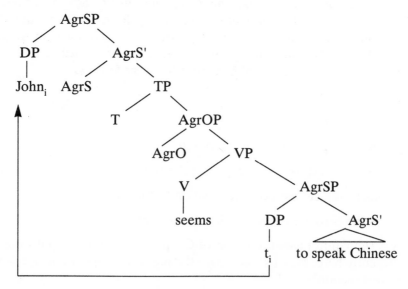

Fourth, we can show that DP-movement always goes to the closest possible position. Remember that DP-movement is always motivated by the Case Filter – that was the subject-matter of the previous section. If, say, raising skips an 'available' subject position and goes into the next clause up, then you get gobbledygook (or 'word salad', as some people call it) like the following:

(62) *$[_{AgrSP_1}$The train$_i$ seems that $[_{AgrSP_2}$ it is likely $[_{AgrSP_3}$ t$_i$ to be late]]]

What's happened here is that *the train* has undergone perfectly normal raising, in search of Case as usual (the subject position of the lower infinitive – AgrSP$_3$ - is Caseless, as usual). However, the movement has gone too far: there's an available subject position in the middle clause, AgrSP$_2$. If the movement stops there, we get the perfectly grammatical:

(63) $[_{AgrSP_1}$ It seems that $[_{AgrSP_2}$ the train$_i$ is likely $[_{AgrSP_3}$ t$_i$ to be late]]]

One step too far, and the result is trash like (62). This phenomenon, known as super-raising, shows that DP-movement too, can only go to the nearest available position.

The fifth property of DP-movement is that it obeys the Structure Preservation Constraint. This means that you can't move DPs to head positions. In fact, you can only move DPs to Case positions (since the movement is always motivated by the Case Filter). Moreover, since the Projection Principle requires that DP-movement leaves traces to 'keep track' of thematic relations (which θ-roles have been assigned where, so we know who's doing what to whom), the landing-site of DP-movement can't be a θ-position. This effectively means that DP-movement puts DPs in Specifier positions of functional heads – in fact, in all the examples we've seen, the landing-site is SpecAgrSP (we'll see some examples of other landing-sites in 2.6 and 2.7).

By now you should have spotted where all this is leading. Let's list the properties of DP-movement that I've just discussed and illustrated:

    DP-movement:
(64a) moves a DP

(64b) leaves a trace in the starting position

(64c) moves to a position c-commanding the trace

(64d) moves to the closest possible position to the trace

(64e) obeys the Structure Preservation Constraint

(64f) only ever moves to Specifiers of functional heads

If you compare (64) with the properties of head-movement listed in (60), the similarities ought to be obvious. Indeed, the only differences are in property (a) – which is basically definitional of the two different kinds of movement – and property (64f). Let's leave (64f) aside for now (we'll come back to it when we look at checking theory later in this chapter). In that case, it rather clearly emerges that head-movement and DP-movement are really the same operation, applied to different X'-entities (heads in one case, maximal projections in the other). Properties (b) to (e) are definitional properties of the generalized movement operation, usually known as Move-α (where α means any category, remember).

What's all this got to do with empty categories? The answer will emerge if we look at the third type of movement, *wh*-movement. This is the operation which places interrogative phrases (which in English usually contain a word beginning with *wh-* like *who, what, when, where, why* and ... uh ... *how*) at the beginning of the clause. We already saw *wh*-movement when I introduced the structure of CP in Chapter 1 (1.4.2.1). Let's look again at the examples we had there:

(65a) I wonder [$_{CP}$ which girl John often kisses]

(65b) Je me demande [$_{CP}$ quelle fille Jean embrasse souvent]

These are indirect questions. In the embedded clause, the *wh*-phrase (*which girl* in English, *quelle fille* in French) is moved to SpecCP. It is clear from the meaning of the sentence that the girl referred to in *wh*-phrase is the Kissee, or the Patient of *kiss*. As a typical Patient, this phrase is the direct object (*kiss* is a pretty typical transitive Verb in this and most other respects). The Projection Principle requires this information to be recorded, and the natural way to do this is with a trace. So the proper representation for the embedded clause in (65a) ought to be:

(65a) ... [$_{CP}$ [$_i$ which girl] C [$_{AgrSP}$ John often kisses t$_i$]]

(I've put the index on the whole DP *which girl* to make it clear that it does in fact belong to this DP and not just to the Noun *girl*.) Direct questions are much the same, so we have a representation like (66b) for (66a):

(66a) Which girl has he kissed?

(66b) [$_{CP}$ [$_i$ which girl] [$_{C'}$ [$_C$ has] [$_{AgrSP}$ he kissed t$_i$]]]

What are the properties of *wh*-movement? First, we've seen that it moves a DP which contains a particular kind of Determiner, a *wh*-word. In fact, it can move other categories as well, as long as they (a) are maximal projections, and (b) contain a *wh*-word:

(67a) [$_i$ How tall] is John t$_i$?   (AP)

(67b) [$_i$ Where] does he live t$_i$? (PP)

Curiously, there are no VP *wh*-words.

Second, *wh*-movement leaves a trace in its starting position, as we've just seen. Third, it always moves the *wh*-phrase to a c-commanding SpecCP.

Fourth, locality. Here in fact things are very complex and interesting. For the moment, we can just observe that *wh*-movement appears to be able make arbitrarily long leaps, as in:

(68a) What$_i$ did Bill buy t$_i$?

(68b) What$_i$ did you force Bill to buy t$_i$?

(68c) What$_i$ did Harry say you had forced Bill to buy t$_i$?

(68d) What$_i$ was it obvious that Harry said you had forced Bill to buy t$_i$?

$\qquad\qquad\qquad\qquad$ (These examples are from Ross (1967:5))

These arbitrarily long leaps are known as **unbounded dependencies**. *wh*-movement dependencies, unlike head-movement and DP-movement, apparently hold across syntactic distances of unlimited length. In Chapter 4, we'll see that this isn't quite true, despite appearances, but for now I'm just going to duck the question of the local nature of *wh*-movement. This topic is of such importance and complexity that it gets practically the whole of Chapter 4 to itself later.

wh-movement clearly obeys the Structure Preservation Constraint, and in fact only moves *wh*-phrases to SpecCP. So, to sum up the properties of *wh*-movement, we see:

wh-*movement:*

(69a) moves a *wh*-XP

(69b) leaves a trace in the starting position

(69c) moves to a position c-commanding the trace

(69d) does NOT move to the closest possible position to its trace (or so it appears)

(69e) obeys the Structure Preservation Constraint

(69f) only ever moves to Specifiers of CP

So there's no doubt that *wh*-movement is a further variant of Move-α.

Now, what are the differences among the variants of Move-α? Head-movement is obviously distinct from both *wh*-movement and DP-movement because it affects a different X' entity – namely, heads as opposed to maximal projections. But what distinguishes *wh*-movement from DP-movement? There's clearly a difference in landing sites: *wh*-movement moves things to SpecCP while DP-movement moves things to Specifiers of other functional heads, notably SpecAgrSP. *wh*-movement moves any category, as long as it has a *wh*-element in it. DP-movement just moves DPs. And here's the most important difference: DP-movement, as we saw in the previous section, is caused by the Case Filter: DPs move *to* Case-positions. *wh*-movement, on the other hand, is movement *from* Case positions when it moves a *wh*-DP. *wh*-movement of a DP from a position that does not receive Case is impossible, as the following sentences illustrate:

(70a) *Who$_i$ does it seem [t$_i$ to speak Chinese] ?

(70b) *Who$_i$ was it believed [t$_i$ to speak Chinese] ?

(70c) Who$_i$ do you believe [t$_i$ to speak Chinese] ?

Wherever the trace of *wh*-movement, the *wh*-trace, is not in a Case position the sentence is ungrammatical; this is the situation in (70a) and (70b). In (70a), the *wh*-trace is the subject of the infinitival complement of *seem*, which we know is not a Case position. In (70b), the *wh*-trace is the subject of the infinitival complement of the passive participle of *believe*; although *believe* can assign Case to this position, we saw in Section 2.3.1 that passive participles cannot assign Case, and so the *wh*-trace is not in a Case position here either. In (70c), on the other hand, the *wh*-trace *is* in a Case position – the subject of the infinitival complement of *believe* – and the sentence is grammatical.

So we can see that *wh*-traces must have Case, exactly the opposite of traces of DP-movement (DP-traces). Another important feature of *wh*-movement may be related to this. Think of the meaning of a typical question such as (66). What it really means is something like 'Tell me what the value of *x* is, where *x* is the girl such that John kissed *x*'. The relationship between the moved *wh*-phrase and the *wh*-trace is like the relationship between a quantifier and a variable in standard kinds of predicate logic: the quantifier tells you where to look for the value of the variable (if you're not familiar with the concept of variable-binding, look at the Appendix to Chapter 3). *wh*-movement does not change grammatical functions, but places the *wh*-phrase in a position which permits the variable-binding relation to be set up. DP-movement, on the other hand, changes grammatical functions, as we saw. The fact that DP-traces don't have Case, but *wh*-traces do, is linked to this, as is the difference in the landing-sites of the two kinds of movement: SpecCP is an 'operator position', a position from which a quantificational element can bind a variable in a grammatical-function position, while SpecAgrSP (and other landing-sites for DP-movement) are Case positions in which grammatical functions can be defined. We'll say more about this fundamental distinction among Specifier positions later (3.3.2.3). These are the two ways in which maximal projections can be moved: to change grammatical function or to bind a variable.

We now have two XP-level empty categories: *wh*-trace and DP-trace (there's also the trace of head-movement, but that is clearly a different thing, being a different X'-entity). In fact, we saw a third empty category in Section 2.2: the empty pronoun PRO. PRO, as we saw, only appears in the subject position of infinitives where, due to the Case Filter, ordinary (phonetically realized) DPs can't appear. As I said in the earlier discussion, we can either regard PRO as exempt from the Case Filter (being an empty category) or as requiring a particular Case, one that only the subjects of certain kinds of infinitives can get. Either way, PRO has a special kind of grammatical function, that of 'controlled subject', 'control' being the relation between a grammatical function in the main clause and the embedded PRO subject in examples like the following (indicated here by coindexing):

(71a) Andy convinced Lou$_i$ [PRO$_i$ to write some new songs]

(71b) Lou$_i$ tried [PRO$_i$ to think of a new idea]

(71c) Tommy$_i$ promised Alan [PRO$_i$ to behave better in future]

Control relations can be quite complex, but they are often lexically determined by the Verb of the main clause. This is what appears to be going on here (see Section 3.2.2.2.).

So we have three XP-level empty categories, which we can distinguish in terms of Case. The following table sums up the situation:

Table 2.1 The XP-level empty categories

PRO	*DP-trace*	wh-*trace*
Null or no Case	No Case	Case
Special grammatical function	Change in grammatical function	No change in grammatical function
Content fixed by control	Content from moved DP	Bound variable

There's plenty more to say about empty categories, but most of that falls under the heading of Binding Theory, so we'll leave it to Chapter 3.

In this section we've seen three of the empty categories (there's a fourth one to come later), and how they can be distinguished in terms of Case. We've also had a close look at the different kinds of movement; we've seen that all three of these are variants of a single operation, Move-α. One kind of movement of maximal projections is Case-driven (DP-movement) and the other, *wh*-movement, is connected to setting up variable-binding relations. In the next section, we'll look at the idea that there are two distinct kinds of Case which DPs may have.

2.5 Categories and Case

2.5.1 Case-Assignment by Adjectives and Nouns

Up to now we've been looking at Case as a relationship between certain kinds of heads and DPs. In section 2.6, we'll entertain the idea that other categories can receive a kind of 'Case'. Here, however, I want to look at the different kinds of things that can *assign* Case.

We suggested in Section 2.3.1 that only [–N] categories can assign Case (remember that we used this as a possible way of accounting for the fact that passive participles don't assign Case). This means that Adjectives and Nouns (the [+N] categories in terms of the feature-system for lexical categories – see Section 1.2.2) can't assign Case. Hence the ungrammaticality of examples like (72); the Case Filter rules them out:

(72a) *John is proud his children (Adjective: [+V, +N])

(72b) *the destruction the city   (Noun: [–V, +N])

Of course, these examples become correct if we place *of* before the Caseless DP:

(73a) John is proud of his children

(73b) the destruction of the city

Of is a Preposition, and so [–N, –V]. Being a [–N] category, it can assign Case to the DP it governs. So in (73), the complements of *of* are Case-marked, and the examples are grammatical. There appears, then, to be a little fix-up rule of *of*-insertion which 'saves' DPs in certain positions from the Case Filter.

However, there are at least two reasons to be suspicious of the *of*-insertion scenario. First, it's clear that the DPs governed by *of* in (73) get their θ-roles from the Adjective *proud* and the Noun *destruction* respectively. In (73a), *his children* is clearly the object of the pride (in fact, the Cause of the pride). Similarly, in (73b) *the city* denotes the Patient of *destruction*, the thing destroyed. We have seen that lexical heads assign their θ-roles under minimal m-command. This means that, in the examples in (73), *of* should be the element that assigns a θ-role to the following DP. However, *of* appears to be quite 'inert' as far as θ-roles are concerned (in fact, it appears to be rather like a functional element in this respect).

Second, some languages appear to have transitive Adjectives, Adjectives that can have a direct object. In German, for example, *überdrüssig* ('tired') can have a direct object, as in the following example:

(74) Er ist seiner Freundin   überdrüssig
      He is his   girlfriend-GEN tired
      'He is tired of his girlfriend'

Of course, not all Adjectives are transitive (any more than all Verbs are transitive). The possibility of taking a direct object is restricted to certain Adjectives. However, the fact that transitive Adjectives exist in some languages poses a problem for the idea that only [–N] categories assign Case. And in fact it's a problem of a particularly tricky kind; we don't simply want to change the theory and allow Adjectives to assign Case, because they don't appear to be able to do so in English (or French, or plenty of other languages). But we do need to account for what we observe about German, preferably in a way that leaves as intact as possible what we have said about English. In other words, we need to find a way of parametrizing the idea that only [–N] categories assign Case.

If we cast our net a bit wider crosslinguistically we find that things get worse, if anything. For instance, many languages – including a number of the Semitic and Celtic languages – have what is known as a 'construct state' construction. This is a construction which expresses a possessor–possessee relation by apparently juxtaposing the possessee and the possessor, in that order. Here are some Welsh examples:

(75a) llyfr Siôn
      book John
      'John's book'

(75b) tŷ   y   hen wraig
      house the old wife
      'the old wife's house'

It might look as though two Nouns are being stuck together here, but (75b) demonstrates that it is in fact the sequence N–DP. In (75b) the possessor is a full DP, complete with article and a prenominal AP (prenominal APs are rare in Welsh; *hen* ('old') is one of very few cases – see Exercise 1, Chapter 1).

Without delving any further into the best way of accounting for construct states (and, as you might expect, there are interesting and subtle differences among the languages that have this construction), what we see is an apparent example of a Noun being able to assign Case: the post-nominal DP is grammatical, and so it must be Case-marked, but there is no obvious candidate Case-assigner aside from N. This adds to the problem raised by the German kind of example just discussed, because the apparent ability of Nouns to assign Case in languages like Welsh is not lexically governed in the way that transitive Adjectives are; instead, pretty much any Noun that refers to something that can be possessed can appear in a construct-state construction. It's clear that we need some kind of parametrization of the idea that [–N] categories can be assigners.

One way to cope with the problems about defining the class of Case-assigners is to make a distinction between structural and inherent Case (this was proposed by Chomsky (1986a)). Nominative and Accusative are structural Cases – in fact, we can maintain pretty much intact what we've said about them up to now. Verbs, then, typically assign Accusative Case to their direct objects in the way I described in Section 2.2.2. On the other hand, instead of saying that Nouns and Adjectives ([+N] categories) do not assign Case, this point of view states that they assign inherent Genitive Case. In English one morphosyntactic marker of this Case is *of*. In Welsh, there is no morphosyntactic marker of inherent Genitive (in fact, Welsh entirely lacks any morphological case, even on pronouns).

The inherent Case idea can get around the problems mentioned above. The ungrammaticality of examples like (72) is quite simply due to the fact that the Case-marker *of* is missing (this was the first problem mentioned above). The fact that the Noun and Adjective, rather than *of*, assign the θ-roles in (73) is connected to the idea that *of* is just a mark of Case, rather like a Latin ending (this was the second problem mentioned above). In other words, we assimilate a 'dummy' Preposition like *of* to the declensional endings that are found in languages like Latin. The structural position of certain DPs (object of a Noun or Adjective) must correspond to a given 'morphological' mark: in English, this is the presence of *of*. *Of* here is the marker of an inherent Genitive Case. In this connection, it is interesting to note that the majority of transitive Adjectives in German require their objects to be morphologically marked as Genitive. The approach that I'm sketching effectively reduces the difference between English and German to a morphological one, whether inherent Genitive is marked by an ending, as in German, or by a 'dummy' Preposition, as in English.

There's more to the notion of inherent Case than this, though. Inherent Case is assigned in a different structural configuration from structural Case. In fact, inherent Case can only be assigned to a given DP by a category that also assigns a θ-role to that DP. Now, remember that θ-roles are assigned under minimal m-command while Case, as far as we have seen up to now, is assigned under government. If you study the definitions of these relations that we have given, you'll see that there are just two differences between them. The first is that a head does not govern but does m-command its Specifier. The second is that a head can govern into its complement, if that complement is an 'IP', while minimal m-command implies (by definition) that the m-commanding head cannot 'see' into its complement. (The Appendix to this chapter gives a succinct overview of the various structural relations that we're using and shows what the connections among them are.)

Let's take a closer look at the second of these differences. What are really at issue here are so-called 'exceptional' Case-marking contexts (which I introduced in Section 2.2.3). These are contexts defined by Verbs with clausal complements that are AgrSPs rather than CPs. Because the complements are AgrSPs, the Verbs can assign (Accusative) Case to the subject of an infinitival complement. The following examples, which are repeated from Section 2.2.3, illustrate this:

(76a) I believe [$_{AgrSP}$ Phil to be a genius]

(76b) Andy considers [$_{AgrSP}$ Lou to be a good singer]

(76c) We know [$_{AgrSP}$ him to have sold marijuana on many occasions]

(76d) We understand [$_{AgrSP}$ them to be able to play the glockenspiel]

(76e) Everyone acknowledges [$_{AgrSP}$ George to be best]

Here the Verb of the main clause governs the subject of the lower clause, and so is able to assign Case to it, but does not minimally m-command it (the subject of the lower clause is in fact in the minimal m-command domain of AgrS, not that of the higher Verb). Given what we've said about θ-role assignment, we expect that the Verb of the main clause cannot assign a θ-role to the subject of the lower clause either. This is clearly true: in an example like (76c), *him* is in no sense a Patient or Cause (or anything else) of *know*. Instead, this DP is clearly the Agent of *sell*. Similar observations can be made about the other examples in (76). The subjects of the infinitivals in (76) receive Case from one head (the higher Verb) and a θ-role from another one (the lower Verb – remember that this subject has been raised from inside the lower VP, like any other subject).

Now, if inherent Case is only assigned under minimal m-command, or in exactly the same structural relation as θ-roles, then there can be no 'exceptional Case-marking' involving inherent Case. This appears to be true. We find that [+N] categories – those that are restricted to inherent Case – never appear in exceptional Case-marking contexts. So we find that, in English, the Nouns that correspond to the Verbs of (76) are totally unable to appear in the comparable syntactic context (with or without *of*; the presence or absence of this element makes absolutely no difference):

(77a) *the belief [$_{\text{AgrSP}}$ (of) Phil to be a genius]

(77b) *Andy's consideration [$_{\text{AgrSP}}$ (of) Lou to be a good singer]

(77c) *our knowledge [$_{\text{AgrSP}}$ (of) him to have sold marijuana on many occasions]

(77d) *our understanding [$_{\text{AgrSP}}$ (of) them to be able to play the glockenspiel]

(77e) *everyone's acknowledgement [$_{\text{AgrSP}}$ (of) George to be best]

Similarly, although *proud*, like many an Adjective, can have both a finite CP and a gerund as its complement, it cannot have a complement parallel to that of the Verbs in (78):

(78a) John is proud [that his son can speak Chinese]

(78b) John is proud [of his son speaking Chinese]

(78c) *John is proud [(of) his son to speak Chinese]

The idea that inherent Case is assigned exactly where θ-roles are assigned explains an interesting fact about complementation in English. Adjectives are just like Verbs in having both raising and control infinitives as their complements:

(79a) John$_i$ is eager [PRO$_i$ to go on vacation next week]

(79b) John$_i$ is likely [t$_i$ to go on vacation next week]

We can see that *eager* has a control infinitive complement because (a) *eager* assigns a θ-role to *John* here (the sentence is interpreted as implying, among other things, that John has the property of being eager) and (b) you can't have an expletive subject even if the lower clause requires one (**There is eager to be trouble tonight*); this means that the subject of the lower clause is not the same element as that of the higher clause. On the other hand, *likely* assigns no θ-role of its own (no property of 'likeliness' is attributed to John in (79b)) and can take whatever is the subject of the lower clause as its own subject (as in *There is likely to be trouble tonight*). As far as raising and control properties are concerned then, Adjectives are just like Verbs. However, Adjectives never assign Case to the subject of an infinitival complement: there are no 'exceptional Case-marking' Adjectives, as (78c) shows. The fact that Adjectives are

[+N] lies behind this: because Adjectives are [+N], they assign inherent Case to their complements; inherent Case is assigned under minimal m-command (unlike structural Case, which is assigned either under government or under Spec-head agreement); and a higher predicate X does not minimally m-command the subject of its infinitival complement, as (80) illustrates:

(80)

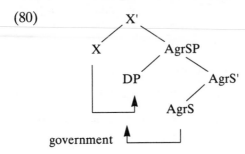

m-command, therefore X cannot minimally m-command DP

Therefore, Adjectives cannot have 'exceptional Case-marking' complements of the type seen in (76).

To arrive at the above conclusion, we don't need to say anything about the lexical or categorial properties of Adjectives and their infinitival complements, beyond the fact that they are [+N]. The rest follows from Case theory. This kind of thing is what is known as 'rich deductive structure' – and it is what you want a good theory to have. Here, ordinary logic allows us to deduce a significant consequence from premises that are stated in theoretical terms. Basically if our theory is tight enough, we will be able to do this a lot, and thus account for a lot of facts using just a few theoretical statements. What we're after is the set of theoretical statements that will give us the richest set of consequences for the least possible effort (other than ordinary deduction) on our part.

2.5.2 Passives Again

Another important facet of the inherent-Case idea has to do with the analysis of passives that I sketched in Section 2.3.1. Remember that the basic idea about passives was the statement we made in (35), which I now repeat:

(35) Passive participles (even of transitive Verbs) are unable to assign Case

Statement (35) forces the object of a transitive Verb to move to subject position in search of Case, as we saw. As to why (35) should hold, we saw that Rouveret and Vergnaud (1980) had suggested that passive participles are [+V] only (as opposed to real Verbs which are, of course, [+V, –N]). Since only [–N] categories assign structural Case, and [+N] ones assign inherent Case, we might think that a category which has no value for [±N] just can' assign a Case. That would be exactly what we want for passive participles.

However, there's some reason to think that passive participles *can* assign inherent Case. In some languages, there are Verbs which assign an inherent Case to a particular argument. German and Latin are good examples of this

For example, (81) gives an inherent Dative assignment to the Goal argument (the person towards whom help or envy is directed):

(81a) Caesar mihi   invidet   (Latin)
      Caesar me-DAT envies
      'Caesar envies me'

(81b) Johann hilft seinem Freund   (German)
      John   helps his-DAT friend
      'John helps his friend'

This kind of property of certain Verbs really is just lexical (although once again, we find that the lexica of different languages are remarkably similar in that the same semantic classes of Verbs tend to show the same inherent-Case requirements; psychological Verbs in particular very often have an inherent Dative). In fact, the link between inherent Case and θ-roles is particularly close here: if an argument requires inherent Dative, it is almost always the Goal argument. One reason to think of this Case as inherent, then, is the fact that it is lexically determined.

Another reason comes from the fact that *inherent Case is totally unaffected by passivizing the Verb.* If we turn the Verbs in (81) into passives, we find that the Dative Case remains:

(82a) Mihi   invidetur
      Me-DAT is-envied
      'I am envied'

(82b) Seinem Freund wurde geholfen
      His-DAT friend was   helped
      'His friend was helped'

The conclusion should be clear: passive forms of Verbs that assign inherent Case retain the ability to assign inherent Case. So we can't claim that (35) derives directly from the distinction between inherent and structural Case. (It's worth pointing out, in passing, that Latin shows us that 'passive Verbs' aren't just participles: Latin, like many languages, has entire conjugations of finite passive forms, as those who have been subjected to learning them will know.) To phrase the conclusion in terms of Jaeggli's Case-absorption idea, we can say that passive participles only 'absorb' structural Case.

2.5.3 Types of Abstract Case

All the examples of inherent Case that we've seen in this Section involve either Dative or Genitive. Are some Cases 'inherently inherent', as it were? Certainly our discussion up to now implies this, and suggests that Nominative and Accusative are always structural, while all other Cases are inherent. If you look back to the presentation of the basic mechanisms of Case-assignment in Section 2.2, however, you'll see that this isn't quite consistent with what we said there.

If we revise what we said in Section 2.2.2 about Prepositions assigning

Dative, it turns out that Dative is always inherent. So let's do that, and say instead that some Prepositions assign Dative and some assign Accusative. In fact, some assign both, with a corresponding difference in θ-role assignment. German *in*, for example, assigns either accusative or dative. When it assigns accusative it denotes a Path (roughly like English *into*); when it assigns dative it denotes a Position (like English *in*). So Prepositions come out looking like Verbs: they're basically assigners of structural Case, but some are lexically marked as Dative-assigners.

Genitive Case as assigned by [+N] lexical categories is always inherent. However, there is also the structural Genitive assigned by D to its Specifier, discussed in Section 2.2.2. It's worth noting that the structural Genitive is assigned by a functional head, while the inherent Genitive is assigned by a lexical head.

Accusative Case is almost always structural, being assigned as described in Section 2.2.2. There are some examples of inherent Accusative, lexically selected by particular Verbs, however. In German, the Verb *lehren* ('teach') appears to behave like this. You can see that the Accusative assigned to *Deutsch* is inherent because it's unaffected by passivizing the Verb in (83b), while the Accusative to *mich* in (83a) is structural as this argument becomes Nominative in the passive sentence (83b):

(83a) ...daß er mich   Deutsch   gelehrt hat
      ...that he me-ACC German-ACC taught has
      '...that he taught me German.'

(83b) ...daß ich von ihm Deutsch gelehrt worden bin
      ...that I   by   him German taught been   have
      '...that I have been taught German by him'

On the other hand, Nominative Case is always structural; it is assigned by AgrS to its Specifier in the way we described in Section 2.2.2.

When I introduced the concept of abstract Case at the beginning of this chapter, I said that some languages mark it morphologically and some don't. However, inherent Case shows a far greater cross-linguistic tendency to be morphologically marked than structural Case. English, as we saw, is a good example of a language in which morphological nominative and accusative case is generally not marked. However, inherent Genitive must be marked by *of*. Kayne (1984) has suggested, moreover, that English entirely lacks inherent Dative: Verbs and Prepositions always assign Accusative to their complements in English. Kayne proposed that the lack of Dative Case in English is due to the lack of any manifestation of morphological dative case, even in the pronominal system (English pronouns have 'nominative', 'accusative', and 'genitive' forms only). Conversely, the languages that we have been using to exemplify abstract Dative Case are languages with plenty of morphological case marking: Latin and German. It may be, then, that the inventory of possible abstract inherent Cases is parametrized, and that the parameters are connected to the morphological case system fairly directly.

On the other hand, structural Nominative and Accusative, at least, do not seem to be parametrized in this way (although it's not clear quite what one should say about structural Genitive).

2.5.4 Conclusion

In this section I've introduced the distinction between structural and inherent Case. To summarize:

Inherent Case:
- is assigned by [+N] categories (and lexically marked Verbs and Prepositions)
- is restricted to the domain of θ-role assignment of the assigner
- is unaffected by 'passivization' of a Verb
- may be parametrized, and as such may be connected fairly directly to morphological case.

If we put together the above with the observation we made at the end of Section 2.2.2 about the two kinds of structural Case, we see that quite a complex picture emerges. The following table attempts to summarize it (I'm leaving out the rather rare inherent Accusative).

Table 2.2 Cases and Case Assignment

Case	Mode of assignment	Assigner
Nominative	Spec-head agreement	AgrS (functional)
Accusative	Government	V, P (lexical)
Genitive (structural)	Spec-head agreement	D (functional)
Genitive (inherent)	Minimal m-command	A, N
Dative	Minimal m-command	V, P (lexical)

We've got more options than we really need here, surely. If we were to cut anything out, the natural candidate would be Accusative. If we could group (structural) Accusative where it surely belongs, with the other structural Cases, then we'd have a very nice division between structural and inherent Case. To do this, we'd need to find a functional head that could assign Accusative Case under Spec-head agreement. The inherent Cases would then be those Cases that are assigned by lexical categories under minimal m-command; the link to θ-role assignment would be natural, since lexical categories are those that assign θ-roles. The structural Cases would all be assigned under Spec-head agreement by functional heads.

And in fact, we have already seen, in Chapter 1 (Section 1.4.3.2) the natural candidate for the role of functional head that assigns Accusative Case: AgrO (we mentioned this in Section 2.0). We've now reached the point where we can take a look at a theory of Case that works in the way outlined in the previous paragraph: the checking theory.

2.6 Checking Theory

2.6.1 Case Checking

The checking theory is quite a recent development, having been put forward in Chomsky (1993). Because of this, it is very much the object of current research and ongoing refinements, so in this section more than most you should bear in mind that the ideas I'm presenting are hypotheses that are in the process of being fully worked out. Nevertheless, it's worth introducing checking theory since it is claimed to be the locus of much, if not all, crosslinguistic variation, a point that I'll develop more fully in Section 2.7.

Checking theory is at once a simplification and a generalization of the government-based Case theory that I've presented in the preceding sections of this chapter. Checking theory simplifies the earlier Case theory by eliminating Case-assignment under government, and treating Accusative Case, like Nominative Case, as assigned under Specifier-head agreement (the elimination of government here is part of Chomsky's 'minimalist program', which aims at eliminating all superfluous notions from the theory of language, stripping it down to the absolute bare essentials). We'll see the details of how this is done below.

Checking theory generalizes the government-based Case theory in three principal ways. First, it extends the idea of Case-assignment as a mode of 'licensing' DPs that is implicit in the Case Filter, becoming a theory of how functional heads license lexical categories. Second, it extends the idea that many instances of movement (DP-movement, in fact: see Section 2.4) are the result of DPs looking for a Case – checking theory implies that *all* movement is motivated by the need for the moved element to be licensed by a functional head. Third, all lexical categories are assumed to require licensing by functional heads; thus there is a kind of 'Case Filter' for Verbs as well (and, presumably, for Adjectives and Prepositions). Here, of course, we begin to depart rather radically from traditional notions of case, although the conceptual foundation still lies in intuitions that are expressed in traditional grammar.

Checking theory gets its name from the mechanics of the way functional heads license lexical categories. Up to now we have talked in terms of Case-assignment; for example, we said that AgrS assigns Nominative Case to a DP in its Specifier. However, as I briefly mentioned in 2.2.2, it is perfectly possible (and was advocated by some researchers such as Jaeggli (1982), Sportiche (1983), and Brody (1984)) to substitute *Case-checking* for Case-assignment. Then we would say that AgrS has a Nominative feature and the subject DP has a Nominative feature. This feature is checked, by a kind of cancellation operation like school maths, when AgrS and the subject DP are in the relevant structural relation. If the features are not all checked then the sentence is ungrammatical. Chomsky proposes that this is so because Case features do not have a semantic interpretation. All material in syntactic structures which lacks a semantic interpretation must be eliminated, because the endpoint of the syntactic derivation is the level which interfaces with the semantics (this level is known as Logical Form). Material which survives to this point and lacks semantic properties will interfere with the semantic interpretation and thereby make the sentence ungrammatical. More recently, Chomsky (1995) has refined this idea a little, suggesting that certain kinds of features, such as the agreement features of nominals, may be interpretable at LF; in the case of relations like agreement, there is an asymmetry in the checking relation in that Agr's feature is not interpretable ([–Interpretable]) and so must be eliminated by LF, while the DP's feature is [+Interpretable] and so is not eliminated at LF. Case features are always [–Interpretable], Chomsky suggests. This idea has a number of ramifications that are still being worked out at the time of writing.

The functional heads that have features that are relevant for checking theory were all introduced in Chapter 1: AgrS, AgrO, T, C, and D. The content of these heads includes abstract morphosyntactic features that enter into checking relations with features of lexical categories: AgrS has a Nominative feature (when the clause is finite; because of this sensitivity to finiteness that we discussed in Section 2.2.2 Chomsky (1993) in fact proposes that Nominative is a feature of T and T moves to AgrS; I'm going to gloss over this point here, however), AgrO has an Accusative feature, and so on.

The checking operation takes place in the **checking domain** of a functional head. As far as the checking of DPs (and other XPs) goes, the checking domain of a functional head is equivalent to the definition of Specifier-head agreement that I gave in (23), to wit:

Specifier-head Agreement:
(23) α, a head, agrees with β iff α minimally m-commands β and does not
      govern β.

For example, Nominative Case assignment in English is construed as a checking relation between a DP in Spec of AgrSP and AgrS. The element checked is a Case feature (or N feature, in Chomsky's terminology) associated with the functional head AgrS. AgrS's Case feature causes the subject DP to raise from its VP-internal position to Spec of AgrS. This much is really just a restatement of what we saw in connection with the VP–internal subject hypothesis in Section 2.3.4. The Case feature of AgrS makes the subject move out of VP and into the position where we see it.

The point about checking theory is that what goes for Nominative Case also goes for other Case-relations; so Accusative Case is assigned by AgrO under Spec-head agreement with the object. Just like subjects, objects have to move in order to be licensed by a checking relation with a functional head. As we said at the end of the previous section, this eliminates the option of Case-assignment under government in general, which is all to the good. (By the way, it's not clear how inherent Case fits into the checking theory; I'm just going to assume that inherent Case is assigned by lexical heads pretty much as described at the end of Section 2.5).

At this point you should have noticed that something's slightly amiss. Let's look at the clause structure that I gave at the end of Chapter 1:

(84)

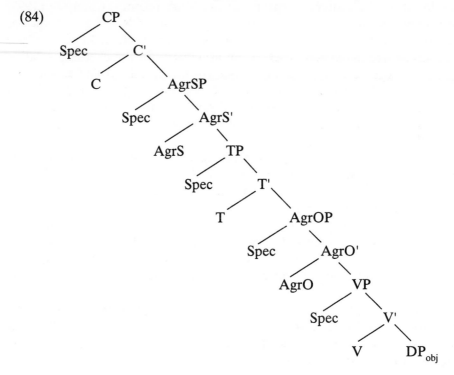

To have its Case features checked, the object DP must move out of VP to the Specifier of AgrO, giving a structure whose relevant parts look like this:

(85)

Remember that V doesn't move in English (see Section 1.4.1.1). This means that the object should end up preceding the Verb. In other words, the adoption of the idea that objects are Case-checked in a Spec-head relation with AgrO seems to lead us to the embarassing prediction that English is an SOV language! Clearly we have to add something, if we want to keep the checking theory in the form presented so far.

2.6.2 The Organization of the Derivation

At this point, it's time to make rather more precise what syntactic derivations are. We've seen that there are three kinds of movement, and we know that DP-movement at least is always triggered by Case (we'd now say that this is a question of the need to check features rather than the Case Filter as such). The view of the derivation put forward by Chomsky (1993) is as follows:

(86)

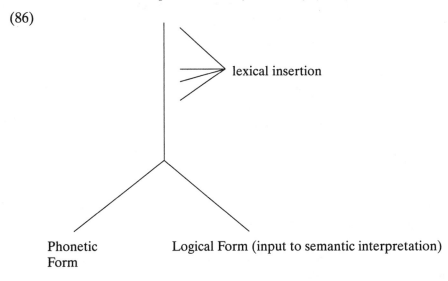

Syntactic trees are built up by lexical insertion, in conformity with the requirements of X'-theory. The derivation branches at a point known as Spell Out. This point corresponds roughly to Surface Structure or S-Structure of earlier theories, although it is not quite the same thing in that it is defined as the place where the derivation branches, rather than being a primitive level of representation with a list of specific properties, as in earlier theories. If you are familiar with earlier models you will also notice that Deep Structure, or D-Structure, is absent, and that lexical insertion can take place at several points in the derivation. This elimination of levels is part of the minimalist programme of stripping down the theory to its bare essentials. Phonetic Form (PF) and Logical Form (LF) are still needed, since they provide the inputs to, respectively, the phonetics/phonology and the semantics.

A very important feature of the kind of derivation illustrated in (86) is that *movement takes place everywhere*. Most importantly, this implies that there are cases of movement after the point of Spell Out which can rearrange the order of elements without this being 'seen' by the PF component. In other words, this approach countenances the possibility of covert movement, movement which has no effect on the phonetics/phonology, and so is invisible and inaudible, though real.

Now you should be able to see the way out of our dilemma. *Objects raise for checking after Spell Out*. And so English is 'spelt out' as an SVO language, despite the existence of covert object movement. The object moves after Spell Out has taken place. This idea permits us to retain the idea that Accusative Case is checked in just the same way as Nominative Case, without getting us into hot water regarding the correct word order.

2.6.3 Parameters of Feature Checking

In English, then, objects move after, but subjects move before Spell Out (since we can see that the subject precedes functional material which is external to VP like auxiliaries and negation). What's the difference? Here, Chomsky introduces an important concept for comparative syntax: the idea that the features used for checking can vary in 'strength'. The basic idea is this: remember that we said that Case features have to be checked by LF, because they have no semantic interpretation and so must be eliminated by that level (which, as (86) shows us, is essentially the end of the derivation). What about PF? Well, Chomsky suggests that one type of feature can be 'seen' by the phonology, and so must be eliminated before Spell Out – or else it will interfere with the phonology just as all features interfere with the semantics. These features are 'strong', and are prone to have some kind of morphological or phonological realization. Other features are completely invisible to the phonology, and so they don't have to be eliminated by Spell Out – these are 'weak' features. Of course, these still have to be eliminated by LF. The basic difference between strong and weak features is that *strong features always trigger overt, visible movement*. Weak features always trigger movement, but this movement may be covert. In fact, movement usually is covert, triggered by weak features; this is ensured by the strange but aptly-named Procrastinate Principle, which we can formulate as follows:

Procrastinate:
(87) Movement is delayed whenever possible

So: in English AgrS has a strong Case feature, triggering overt movement of the subject, while AgrO has a weak Case feature, and so object-movement is covert. There's a connection to morphology, too, in that English has subject-verb agreement (a manifestation of AgrS's strong Case feature), but does not have object-verb agreement.

The next thought that naturally springs to mind at this point is: some languages do have object–verb agreement (Georgian, Basque, Pashto, and lots of Amerindian languages, for example.). So AgrO might have a strong Case feature in these languages. More generally, since we know that languages vary quite a bit in their morphological properties, we expect feature strength to vary. The checking theory implies that there will be a certain amount of co-variation between morphological properties and word order. This is a matter for ongoing research (and a good deal of controversy), but it's an extremely interesting idea, and one that I want to explore in more depth in Section 2.7.

For now, though, the essential point is that *abstract morphosyntactic features of functional heads are the principal domain of parametrization*. The minimalist approach attempts to restrict cross-linguistic differences to this area; if this can be achieved, it will clearly be a major simplification of the theory.

Now, we said above that checking theory goes beyond Case theory (and beyond traditional notions of case) in extending to other categories and to the other types of movement. Let's take a look at this, starting with *wh*-movement.

It's quite natural to think of *wh*-categories as having a specific morphosyntactic feature, which we might as well call [*wh*]. An interrogative C can be thought of as having a strong *wh*-feature, which must be checked against a *wh*-constituent. Hence *wh*-movement to the SpecCP. May (1985) and Rizzi (1991) both formulated a general requirement, the *wh*-Criterion, which states that a [*wh*] head must have a [*wh*] XP in its Specifier, and a [*wh*] XP must appear in the Specifier of a [*wh*] head. In terms of checking, the *wh*-Criterion is an instance of the very general requirement that features must be checked.

wh-movement differs from DP-movement in that the feature is checked in a different position from Case features (SpecCP, as opposed to SpecAgrSP or SpecAgrOP), and also in that it seems to be associated with a semantic value connected to quantification. Also, *wh*-traces must check for Case, as we saw in Section 2.4. Despite these differences, we can still maintain that *wh*-movement is triggered by a morphosyntactic feature of C.

If *wh*-movement is triggered by checking requirements, then we expect that there will be languages where *wh*-movement is covert. This idea was in fact proposed by Jim Huang (in his 1982 doctoral dissertation) quite some time before checking theory was introduced. In Chinese, as in many Oriental languages, *wh*-movement does indeed seem to be absent. The following examples illustrate this:

(88a) Zhangsan yiwei Lisi mai-le shenme?
Zhangsan thinks Lisi buy-ASP what
'What does Zhangsan think Lisi bought?'

(88b) Zhangsan xiang-zhidao Lisi mai-le shenme
Zhangsan wonder Lisi buy-ASP what
'Zhangsan wonders what Lisi bought'

In Chinese and similar languages, then, we can say that an interrogative C has a weak WH feature. For this reason, *wh*-movement is 'delayed' until after Spell Out. We'll look in more detail at the nature of covert *wh*-movement in Chapter 4 (4.3.1). (I should point out in this connection that recent work by Watanabe (1992) suggests that *wh*-movement is universally pre-Spell-Out, but that what is moved is a silent *wh* quantifier; we won't go into this here, though.)

What about head-movement (the third type of movement, remember)? Here most of the research that has been done has concentrated on Verb-movement of the type that we discussed in Section 1.4 of Chapter 1. The proposal is that, in addition to Case features (or N-features), functional heads can have V-features. These are tense and agreement features, and are associated with the functional heads which make up the clausal system (AgrO, AgrS, and T in particular, or the V-related functional heads). Just like Case-features, V-features can be weak or strong, triggering covert or overt verb-movement respectively. The parallels with Case features (and maybe *wh*-features) should be reasonably clear.

One technical point needs clearing up, though: what is the checking domain for head-movement? Here we have to be a bit more precise about the kind of structure that results from head-movement. Let's say that head-movement *adjoins* a head $X°$ to the minimally c-commanding head $Y°$. This gives the derived structure in (89):

(89)

$$
\begin{array}{c}
X° \\
\diagup \quad \diagdown \\
Y° \qquad X°
\end{array}
$$

More generally, movement by **adjunction** gives rise to configurations like (89). So adjunction of a maximal projection, such as YP, to another maximal projection XP will give (90):

(90)

$$
\begin{array}{c}
XP \\
\diagup \quad \diagdown \\
YP \qquad XP
\end{array}
$$

Movement by adjunction obeys the Structure Preservation Constraint, which we should now reformulate as follows:

> *Structure Preservation Constraint (revised):*
> (91) *Movement of X^n to Y^m, where $n \neq m$ for X'-theory

(91) says that a category of one X'-level (such as a head, an intermediate projection, or a maximal projection) cannot move to the position of a category of another X'-level. The upshot of this is that a maximal projection can only move to a Specifier position or to a position adjoined to another maximal projection, as in (90), and a head can only move to a position adjoined to another head.

In the adjunction configuration in (89), $Y°$ is the checking domain of $X°$. More generally, whenever a head is moved to another head-position the moved head will be in the checking domain of the target head. In other words, when V is raised to I-type positions, in the way we described for French in Chapter 1, Section 1.4.1, V will be in the checking domain of the I-type heads it raises to. So we can think of head-movement as movement that checks the abstract features of the moved head.

2.6.4 Checking Domains

Our notion of checking domain now has two distinct parts: one for maximal projections (Spec-head agreement, as in (23)) and one for heads (adjunction, as in (89)). This is not a good situation, as it suggests that checking domain is not a unified entity, and so that checking the features of heads and checking the features of maximal projections is a fundamentally different business. But that, of course, is exactly what checking theory sets out to deny. So we have to say a bit more (even if this gets rather technical) about what checking domains are.

One possibility is to say that Specifiers are really adjoined categories. This means that the X'-structure of a category would be (92a), rather than (92b), as we proposed in Chapter 1 (the crucial difference is bold-faced):

(92a)

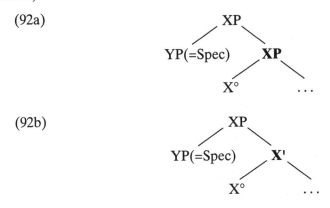

(92b)

In other words, this view entails the disappearance of the X'-node. If we say this, then the checking domain of any category α, is the set of categories adjoined to α. For reasons that are quite independent of the definition of checking domains, Kayne (1993, 1994) proposes that the intermediate category X' should be done away with, and therefore that Specifiers are adjoined maximal projections.

Another possibility is to say that the checking domain of α corresponds to the 'agreement domain' of α. The agreement domain can be defined as in (23), which I repeat once again:

Specifier-head Agreement:
(23) α, a head, agrees with β iff α minimally m-commands β and does not govern β

β here could be extended to include heads adjoined to α. We can see this if we look again at (89). Here, it's obvious that X° minimally m-commands Y° (the definition of minimal m-command is given in (5) and in the Appendix to this chapter), so one of the conditions for 'agreement' in this sense is met. Does X° govern Y° in (89)? The definition of government was given in (16):

Government:
α, a head, governs β if and only if
(16a)   α c-commands β

(16b)   no barrier dominates β but not α

It's clear that no barrier intervenes between X° and Y° in (89). However, the question now is whether X° c-commands Y° or not. Here's the definition of c-command, repeated from Section 2.2:

C-command:
(17)   α c-commands β iff α does not dominate β and every category dominating α dominates β

Everything dominating X° also dominates Y° in (89) – that much is clear. But what is the relation between X° itself and Y°? It certainly looks as though a piece of X° (or a 'segment' of X°, in the usual terminology) dominates Y° – does this mean that, as it were, *all* of X° dominates Y°? Let's say it doesn't, which seems reasonable. Then we can conclude that X° agrees with Y°, and so we have a unified notion of checking domain which we can define as follows:

Checking Domain:
(93)   The checking domain of α, a head, is the set of categories that α agrees with, where agreement is defined as in (23)

How did we arrive at this conclusion? It goes like this:

Assumption: A segment of X° dominates Y° in (89)
Step 1:   Therefore X° doesn't c-command Y° in (89) (definition of c-command in (17))
Step 2:   Therefore X° doesn't govern Y° in (89) (definition of government in (16))
Step 3:   Therefore X° agrees with Y° in (89) (definition of agreement in (23) and definition of minimal m-command in (5))

All this technical discussion illustrates again that the theory has some 'deductive structure'. It also shows us that, despite initial appearances, the two kinds of checking domain are the manifestations of a single, more abstract, structural relation.

2.6.5 Verb Movement Again

Back to V-movement. In Chapter 1 (Section 1.4.1.1), we saw that English and French differ in that V moves to 'I' in French but not in English. Here's the French example (52) from that chapter, alongside the structure for its English counterpart:

(94a)

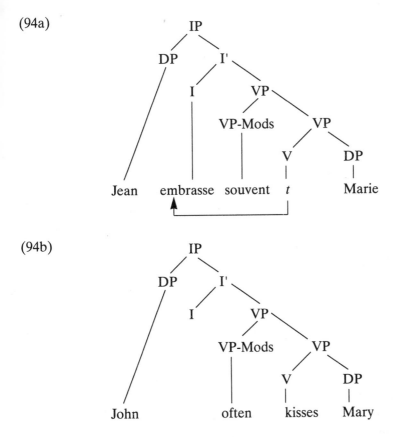

(94b)

Checking theory gives us a very simple way of capturing these differences between English and French. We can simply say that English 'I' has weak V-features, while French 'I' has strong V-features (in finite clauses). Again, we find that there is a correlation of sorts with morphological factors. English Verbs have very few different forms in their conjugations (usually either four or five: V, V+s, V+ed and V+ing, with some Verbs, such as *sing* or *swim*, having separate forms for the past tense and the past participle). French Verbs, on the other hand, have a very large number of different forms: present, imperfect, past, future, and conditional tenses, each with four or five different person forms. There's no doubt, then, that 'I' in French has more morphological realizations than I in English. And this seems to be connected to its having strong V-features (although the precise nature of this connection becomes harder to state when one takes a number of different languages into consideration).

I'm using 'I' here as a cover term for the V-related functional categories. Really, I should say 'AgrO, T and AgrS' every time I say 'I'. That complicates things slightly, but only really in degree – the essential idea is just the same. There's a technical complication in that when V moves from AgrO to T in a tree like that in (84) above, it's really AgrO, containing V that moves. That is, what is moved at this step of the derivation is the object in (95):

(95)

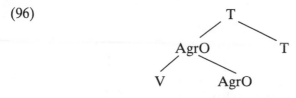

And what is moved from T to AgrS is the object in (96):

(96)

However, it is the fact that these heads are V-related that triggers the movement of the categories containing the Verb. There may be further complications for the technical characterization of checking domain here, but we leave those to one side. The V-features are properties of the V-related functional categories, an idea which appears to be very simple and natural.

Thus the checking theory is behind head-movement, too, and cross-linguistic differences in Verb-movement, for example, can be captured by different 'feature strengths' of V-features of V-related functional heads. The 'feature strength' idea implies that all languages are the same by LF; so we would conclude that English Verbs move covertly, since the English I-system contains weak V-features. By now, checking theory has gone far beyond the earlier Case theory and traditional notions of case: nevertheless, it is a powerful and principled system for accounting for the movement and licensing of lexical categories. Ultimately, we can think of it as a way of marking grammatical functions, just like the government-based Case theory. One of the functions which it marks is that of 'predicate', a category, such as a lexical Verb, which assigns θ-roles.

I should end this section by stressing again that checking theory is very much at the forefront of research, and many aspects of what I've presented here are likely to undergo revision in the near future. Nevertheless, the two basic ideas are clear enough. One is that functional heads license lexical heads by a feature-checking relation which subsumes the earlier notion of abstract Case, but also extends to Verbs (and other lexical heads) and to *wh*-movement. The other is that the features which are checked can vary parametrically in such a way as to give rise to different visible word-orders across languages. I now want to develop this last point a bit more in the final section of this chapter.

2.7 Case and Word Order

In this section I want to come back to questions connected to word-order typologies that I discussed rather inconclusively in Chapter 1, Section 1.3.3 and 1.3.4. Not that the discussion here will necessarily be any more conclusive than the earlier one; however, what I want to do here is show how checking theory can be combined with Kayne's proposal that there are no X'-theory parameters in such a way as to give an account of both VSO and SOV orders. Since the other logically possible orders (OVS, OSV, and VOS) are either extremely rare or nonexistent, I will leave them aside in our discussion (although of course we ultimately do need an account of these orders too).

2.7.1 VSO

Let's look first at VSO orders. When I introduced the VP-internal subject hypothesis in Section 2.3.4, I sketched out an idea that various authors (notably Chomsky (1993)) have proposed for analysing this kind of order, namely that the verb moves to some functional head while the subject remains inside VP. If we gloss over the 'split-Infl' structure once again for the sake of exposition, what we are saying is that a Welsh sentence like (58) (repeated below) has the structure given in (97):

(58) Mi welais   i   Megan
     Prt saw(V) I(S) Megan(O)
     'I saw Megan'

(97)

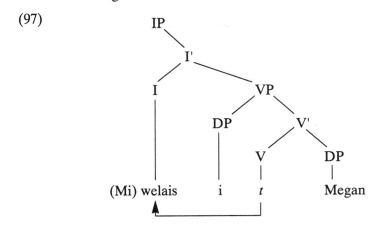

As I said in Section 2.3.4, the Verb-movement here resembles what is found in French, while the basic difference between Welsh and French would be that subjects can be Case-marked inside VP in Welsh, while in French they have to move to SpecIP. In terms of checking theory, as I presented it in Section 2.6, the analysis should be plain to see: Welsh 'I' has strong V-features, but weak N-features. Hence the Verb moves out of VP, but the subject doesn't. If we accept Kayne's idea that all categories are really head-initial, then the inevitable result is VSO order.

Appealing and rather neat though this account of VSO word order is, it faces a number of problems. The most important of these was already noticed by Koopman and Sportiche (1991) in their original article on the VP-internal subject hypothesis. If we think back, once again, to the discussion of Verb-movement in English and French of Chapter 1, Section 1.4.1.1, the structure in (97) implies that adverbs and negation will appear between the Verb and the subject, since these elements appear in VP-external positions. However, this is not true: in Welsh (and in Irish) the subject must appear adjacent to the finite Verb. The ungrammaticality of the following examples illustrates this:

(98a) *Dúirt sí   go   dtabharfadh amárach   a   mac turas orm
      said   she that would-give   tomorrow her son visit on-me
                                                              (Irish)

(98b) *Mi welith   yfory   Emrys ddraig   (Welsh)
      PRT will-see tomorrow Emrys dragon

Koopman and Sportiche also point out that the clausal negation, an element which is syntactically rather similar to English *not* or to French *pas*, follows the subject in Welsh:

(99) Ddarllenodd Emrys mo   'r   llyfr
      Read   Emrys neg+of the book
      'Emrys hasn't read the book'

If we say that this negative element is in NegP, and place NegP in the split-Infl system (as we would naturally do), then (99) shows us that the subject is outside of VP in Welsh.

Of course, the split-Infl system offers us a solution to the problem posed by the above data; in fact, it offers us quite a range of solutions. All we have to do to get VSO order is put the Verb in the next functional head above the specifier position where the subject is. This will go a long way towards capturing the adjacency requirement between the verb and the subject (how far depends on further questions about adverb positions that I don't want to get into here). The abstract structure of VSO clauses should thus be as follows:

(100)

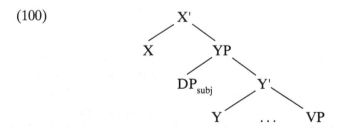

In checking terms, X has a strong V-feature and a weak N-feature, while Y has a strong N-feature.

The question now becomes: What are the identities of X and Y in 'split-Infl' terms? There are basically two possibilities if we stick to the clause structure of (84): X is C and YP is AgrSP, or X is AgrS and Y is TP. Now, if we say that X is C, then we are saying that VSO languages have an important feature in common with V2 languages (see 1.4.2.4). However, VSO languages allow Verb-movement in all finite clauses, while, as you may recall from

Section 1.4.2.4, V2 languages typically don't allow V-movement in embedded clauses. There's a major comparative issue here which at present is unresolved.

If we adopt the second approach (X = AgrS, YP = TP in (100)), we have to explain why SpecTP can be a subject position in some languages and not in others. This is a problem if, following Chomsky (1993), we suppose that T always has the Nominative feature. The hypothesis we're entertaining is that T has a strong Nominative feature, and so then we have to explain why moving T to AgrS with V (which must happen, since the Head Movement Constraint requires V to move through T on its way up to AgrS) does not also cause SpecAgrS to become the position in which Nominative Case is checked. Despite this technical problem, there is one fact which is found in a range of VSO languages (although not all) that many people have taken as support for the idea that X is AgrS and YP is TP in (100): this is the so-called anti-agreement effect. The effect is this: when a subject follows the verb in a VSO language, *it cannot agree in all morphological features with the verb*. I illustrate with Irish:

(101a) D'   imíodar
        PRT left-3Pl
        'They left'

(101b) D'   imigh na   fir
        PRT left   the men
        'The men left'

(101c) *D'   imíodar na   fir/siad
        PRT left-3Pl the men/they
        'The men/they left'

As you can see, the Verb cannot show 3Pl agreement when it precedes a 3Pl subject. The same fact shows up in Classical Arabic, another VSO language. Here things are more interesting, in that Classical Arabic also allows subjects to precede the verb, and when they do, they show full agreement. On the other hand, in VSO order, the subject can only agree with the verb in gender, but not in person or number. (102) shows the relevant facts:

(102a) ganna   Ɂal Ɂawlaad-uu
        sang-M.Sg the children
        'The children sang'

(102b) Ɂal Ɂawlaad-uu gannuu
        the children sang-3M.Pl
        'The children sang'

The anti-agreement effect can naturally be linked to the weak Case features of the head to which the Verb moves in VSO orders (such as X in (100)).

Of course, if we allow for a more complex clause structure than that in (84), and particularly if there are further functional heads between C and

AgrS, then the possible analyses of VSO multiply. Also, one might think that the subject can move to SpecAgrOP, with V in T in these languages (this sounds rather odd, but it has been proposed). As I write, all I can say is that the only consensus among those who have looked at VSO languages is that it is very likely that a range of possibilities is required. On close comparative inspection, VSO turns out to be a rather crude designation of a class of different structures. I can briefly illustrate this with another Celtic language, Breton. In Breton, the subject follows the negation element equivalent to *pas* or *not*; the order of this element and the subject is exactly the opposite of what we saw in Welsh in (99). Compare (103) with (99):

(103) Ne   lenn KET AR VUGALE levrioù
      PRT read not the children books
      'The children do not read books'

Although this is an inconclusive discussion, with a large number of unresolved detailed questions, the basic issues are clear: a subpart of the clause structure of VSO languages looks like (100), and this is due to the fact that, in this structure, X has a weak N-feature and a strong V-feature.

2.7.2 SOV

Now let's look at SOV orders. If we adopt Kayne's idea that all categories have head–complement order, then we are obliged to say that the object moves out of VP. In other words, we must assume at least a partial structure like that given in (46) of Chapter 1, which I repeat as (104):

(104) Object$_i$ [$_{VP}$ V   t$_i$]

In fact, we are now in a position to put a bit more functional flesh on this skeleton. The obvious landing-site for movement of the object is SpecAgrOP, so instead of (104), we can say that the relevant part of the structure of OV clauses is (105) (here I'm completely ignoring the trace of the subject in SpecVP):

(105)

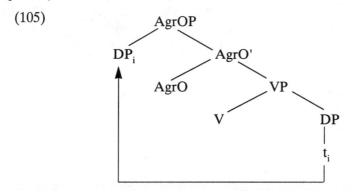

In other words, the basic property of OV languages is that AgrO has a strong Case feature, which causes overt movement of the object to SpecAgrOP. If V doesn't move, then we have SOV order.

We saw in Chapter 1 that German has been analysed as an OV language in which the Verb is fronted to second position in main clauses. You won't be surprised to learn that a similar analysis works for Dutch. However, Zwart (1993) has shown that an approach of the type just sketched for OV orders yields positive results in the analysis of Dutch (and, because Dutch is so similar to German, this approach can be fairly readily carried over to German).

Zwart claims three principal advantages for his approach. The first is very simple. If we treat Dutch as being OV, then we are obliged to say that it is in effect a 'mixed branching' language. This is because there is absolutely no doubt that some projections have the head–complement order. For example, it is quite clear that AgrSP follows C and that NP follows D:

(106a) ... dat [$_{AgrSP}$ het regent buiten]   C–AgrSP
     ... that   it   rains outside

(106b) de vader van Jan   D–NP
     the father of John

So, if we wanted to maintain that Dutch chose *complement–head* order in VP (and perhaps elsewhere), then we'd have to say that some categories went one way (head–complement) and some went the other (complement–head). We saw the problems that this kind of thing poses for language typology in Chapter 1 (Section 1.3.3). It is clearly an inelegant and unduly data-driven kind of analysis. The approach we've just sketched, however, avoids this problem by saying that Dutch in fact uniformly chooses *head–complement* order. And if Kayne is right, of course, this isn't in fact a choice.

The second advantage of Zwart's approach is that it can neatly capture the following generalization about Dutch: 'When a head allows its complement to appear on one side only, the complement always follows the head.' D and C only allow their complements to be on the right, and these complements cannot be separated from the heads which select them. So the only possible relationship between D and its complement and between C and its complement is the one seen in (106). Among the lexical categories, the same goes for the complements of N. These can only appear immediately adjacent and to the right of N, as the contrast between the following examples shows:

(107a) de verwoesting van de stad
      the destruction of   the city
      'the destruction of the city'

(107b) *de van de stad verwoesting
      the of   the city destruction

If we say that C, D, and N do not allow their complements to move, then these facts have a straightforward analysis.

The third advantage concerns another generalization that is related to the one we just looked at. We can phrase this as follows: when a head allows its complement to appear on both sides, the head and the complement do not have to be adjacent when the complement precedes the head. This is true of the complements of A, P, and V. (108) illustrates this:

(108a) ... dat Jan ZIJN RIJBEWIJS NOOIT HAALT (object–X–Verb)
     ... that John his driving licence never gets
     '... that John will never get his driving licence'

(108b) Hij was HET AMHAARS VOLLEDIG MACHTIG
                                       (complement–X–Adjective)
     He was the Amharic completely in-command-of
     'He knew Amharic perfectly'

(108c) de weg HET BOOS WEER IN (complement–X–P)
     the road the forest back into
     'the road back into the forest'

Zwart proposes that APs, VPs, and PPs are head-initial (like all categories in Dutch), and that DP complements of A, V, and P move leftward during the derivation essentially in the way illustrated in (105). (You might notice that this idea implies that even DPs that are assigned inherent Case – objects of Adjectives – move leftward for Case-checking. This goes against what we said about inherent Case and checking theory in Section 2.6, which needs sorting out.)

So the idea that the Germanic OV languages might really be quite uniformly head-initial, with apparent head-final orders derived by an operation of the kind in (105), has something going for it. However, as Zwart himself notes, this approach leaves two very big questions open.

The first concerns 'rigidly OV languages'. Nobody who has looked at word-order typology has ever regarded Dutch and German as typical OV languages. The really nice, well-behaved OV languages are those like Japanese, Basque, and Turkish. In these languages it is pretty difficult to put anything at all after the Verb. These languages differ from Dutch and German in three main ways: first, their complement clauses are always preverbal, whereas finite CP complements must be postverbal in Dutch and German:

(109) Taroo wa Takasi kara [$_{CP}$ Yosiko ga zibun o nikundeiro
     Taroo TOP Takasi from Yosiko NOM self ACC be-hating
         to] kiita
         that heard
     'Taroo heard from Takasi that Yosiko hated him'

Second, D follows NP. This can only really be seen in Basque, as Japanese and Turkish lack anything that is very obviously a Determiner:

(110) etche-a
     house-the
     'the house'

Third, AgrSP appears to precede C, at least in Japanese. We can see this in (109), of which I repeat the relevant part here as (111):

(111) ... [$_{CP}$ [$_{AgrSP}$ Yosiko ga   zibun o   nikundeiro] to] ...
           ...   Yosiko NOM self   ACC be-hating   that ...
    '... that Yosiko hated him ...'

As I said in Chapter 1, we really need an analysis of languages like these that uses Kayne's ideas about head-complement orders. Until then, it's hard to say whether OV orders in general can be accounted for along the lines that Zwart proposes for Dutch, following the schema in (105).

The second issue concerns the kind of word-order correlations that we discussed in Section 1.3.3. Remember that we saw in Chapter 1, on the basis of a discussion of Greenberg's Universals 3 and 4, that VO languages tend to be prepositional and OV languages tend to be postpositional. We want to be able to capture these generalizations in our theory of comparative syntax. However, it is not very clear how checking theory can do this. One way might be for groups of Agrs (AgrO and, say, AgrPrep – the Agr associated with Prepositions) always to pattern together in having weak or strong N-features. For example, Roberts and Shlonsky (1996) propose that VSO languages are such that X has weak Case features and strong V-features.

After all of these loose ends and open questions you might be wondering what this section was really for. The point of it was to show how the checking theory offers us avenues of research in accounting for different word-order patterns. Current work is taking some more or less tentative steps down these avenues, but, as ongoing research often does, it may be getting lost on the way. One of the fundamental things about research is that you don't have a map of where you're going. When you get there it is often easy to see how you did it, but on the way things are often, well, inconclusive.

2.8 Conclusion

We've covered quite a bit of ground in this chapter, so it's worth giving something of a synoptic overview of it all. The two basic sets of theoretical ideas that I wanted to present are, first, the government-based Case theory, and, second, the checking theory. As a preamble to the whole discussion, it was necessary to introduce the ideas of grammatical functions and θ-roles. That was the subject matter of Section 2.1. After presenting the government-based Case theory in Section 2.2, I then showed how the need for DPs to have Case can explain a number of instances of movement, particularly movement that creates the appearance of a change in grammatical functions. Section 2.4 systematized our notion of movement, by showing that there are three distinct types: DP-movement, *wh*-movement, and head-movement, all of which are subspecies of the very general operation of move-α. Here I also showed that there are three different empty (or silent) categories, which can be distinguished in terms of Case theory. The subject matter of Section 2.5 was the distinction between structural and inherent Case: here we saw that inherent Case is assigned in a distinct structural configuration from structural Case, by different categories from structural Case, and that it may be missing in some languages, perhaps as a function of morphological properties.

Section 2.6 involved quite a shifting of gears as we moved into areas of more recent research, in which there are many more open questions and contested issues. I presented the two fundamental ideas of checking theory: that functional heads have abstract features which license lexical categories, and that these features are parametrized as strong and weak in such a way that there is a direct link between their 'strength' and the visible word orders in a given language. This also entailed sharpening up our conception of a syntactic derivation and the levels of representation, which had been left open until then. And finally, Section 2.7 was a kind of marriage of checking theory with Kayne's ideas about word order that we discussed in Chapter 1 (Section 1.3.4). Here I tried to show what may be at stake in analysing VSO and SOV word-orders using the techniques that we have developed. Perhaps the clearest conclusion of this section was that notions like 'VSO language' are too crude to be really useful; they describe rather gross properties of certain linguistic systems, but closer inspection and comparison always reveal that there are further distinctions to be made.

Chapters 1 and 2 have looked at the internal structure of categories (X'-theory) and some principles governing the external distribution of certain categories – Case theory and checking theory. Now it's time to consider how categories can relate to each other in different kinds of dependencies, beginning with the semantic dependencies that make up binding theory.

Parameters Discussed in this Chapter

We've seen quite a bit of cross-linguistic variation in this chapter. Roughly, we can group the parameters we've mentioned into three groups: those concerning the relationship between morphology and abstract Case, those concerning Nominative Case assignment, and those concerning the abstract features of functional heads (although, if the proposals described in Section 2.6 are right, then this kind subsumes the others).

1. a. Morphological marking of abstract Case: Thai (no); English (pronouns only); Latin (all Nouns) – see 2.0. See also (3) below.
   b. Morphological marking of *inherent* abstract Case: Latin and German have abstract and morphological Dative; English doesn't. Because of this, English Prepositions only assign Accusative: see 2.5.3.
2. a. AgrS assigns Nominative in infinitives in Portuguese, but not in English (or in other Romance languages). See 2.2.2; this is a well-known feature of Portuguese that has never been successfully reduced to a deeper property.

b. Can postverbal subjects get Nominative Case? In Italian they can; in English they can't. See 2.3.1. In Chapter 3 (3.3.3) we'll see that this is part of the **null-subject parameter.**

c. Can Nominative Case be assigned to SpecVP? In Welsh (and possibly other VSO languages), it can; in non-VSO languages it cannot. See also under (3) below.

3. The 'strength' (or the ability to trigger overt movement) of abstract features of functional heads may be the only domain of parametrization: see 2.6. Examples include:

a. The French I-system has strong V-features; English does not (see also 1.4.1.1).

b. Part of the I-system has strong V-features but weak N-features in VSO systems (see 2.7.1).

c. AgrO has a strong N-feature in SOV systems (see 2.7.2).

Further Reading

There's a vast literature on thematic roles and grammatical functions. A major debate within generative grammar has been whether to regard grammatical functions as derived (as in Chomsky (1965) and all subsequent 'mainstream' generative work, including the theory described here) or primitive. Theories that explicitly adopt the latter view include relational grammar (see Perlmutter (1983), Perlmutter and Rosen (1984)) and lexical-functional Grammar (see Bresnan (1982a)). A hybrid theory is developed by Marantz (1984). Baker (1988) argues that all operations which change grammatical functions (passive and many others) can be reduced to the interaction of head-movement and Case theory.

Thematic roles were first discussed in the context of generative grammar by Gruber (1965). Jackendoff (1972) is a very important early work. Fillmore (1968) developed an early theory of thematic roles (which he called 'case relations', as have other researchers working outside the framework described here, such as Anderson (1971)). The θ-criterion and the Projection Principle are put forward for the first time in Chomsky (1981, Ch. 2). Other important references on the nature of thematic roles, their representation in lexical semantics and their relation to grammatical functions are Williams (1980, 1981), Borer (1984), Keyser and Roeper (1984), Higginbotham (1985), Burzio (1986), Jaeggli (1986), Levin and Rappaport-Hotav (1986), Roberts (1987), Zubizarreta (1987), Belletti and Rizzi (1988), and Grimshaw (1990). The most important recent work, which is somewhat in the spirit of the minimalist programme, is Hale and Keyser (1993).

The 'Government-based Case Theory' of Section 2.2 is more or less that of Chomsky (1981, ch. 2) (although I've taken various technical liberties in the interests of exposition); this theory was inspired by Rouveret and Vergnaud (1980). It is further developed in a number of important ways in Stowell (1981). A movement approach to ECM constructions is argued for by Postal (1974), Koster (1984) and, assuming a clause structure containing AgrO, Lasnik and Saito (1991).

On passives, see Chomsky (1981, ch. 2), Burzio (1986), Jaeggli (1986), and Baker, Johnson and Roberts (1989). For approaches in other frameworks, see Perlmutter and Postal (1984) (relational grammar), Postal (1986) (arc-pair grammar, a development of relational grammar), and Bresnan (1982b) (lexical-functional grammar). Several of the essays in Keenan (1988) also discuss passives.

On unaccusatives, see Perlmutter (1978), Burzio (1986), Keyser and Roeper (1984), and Levin and Rappaport-Hotav (1995). The VP-Internal Subject Hypothesis has a long history in various guises. The earliest version of it is in Fillmore (1968). In the mid-1980s, the idea was developed by Fukui and Speas (1986), Kitagawa (1986), Koopman and Sportiche (1991), and Kuroda (1988).

Early typologies of empty categories and movement are in Chomsky (1981, 1982) and Brody (1984). We'll come back to this question in Chapters 3 and 4, and give fuller references there. Inherent Case is discussed in Chomsky (1981, 1986a). Several of the papers in Kayne (1984) develop the implications of the idea that English lacks abstract Dative Case. Belletti (1988) is an interesting extension of the theory of inherent Case. Checking Theory is discussed and developed in Chomsky (1993, 1995). Watanabe (1993) is a development of Chomsky's 1993 theory.

The analysis of VSO languages in terms of the verb moving over the subject was first proposed in Emonds (1980), and was applied to Irish by McCloskey (1983) and Welsh by Sproat (1985) (although see Jones and Thomas (1977)). Benmamoun (1991), Koopman and Sportiche (1991), and Mohammad (1988) discuss VSO order in Semitic languages. McCloskey (1991, forthcoming) develops analyses for Irish (see also Duffield (1995)). On VSO in Celtic more generally, see the papers in Borsley and Roberts (1996). The analysis of SOV order discussed in 2.7.2 is argued for in detail by Zwart (1993).

Exercises

Exercise 1

Show how DP-movement and *wh*-movement combine in the following examples and identify where the different traces are:

1. How many students were arrested last night?
2. Who did they say was believed to have done it?
3. What did they say was believed to have been done?

Exercise 2

Construct examples of 'super-passive' and 'super-unaccusative', analogous to the example of super-raising in Section 2.4.

Can you explain why the relation between *John* and the empty category that is the subject of the lower clause in (1) is not super-raising?

1. John exclaimed that it was time [— to leave]

Exercise 3

Why is 'exceptional Case-marking' (assignment of Accusative from the higher Verb to the lower subject) impossible in the following contexts?

1. *John tried [$_{CP}$ [$_{AgrsP}$ Mary to leave]]

2. *It seemed [John to be a nice guy]

3. *I assure you [John to be a nice guy]

Examples (1) and (2) are easy – just read Sections 2.2 and 2.3 again. Example (3) isn't so easy.

Exercise 4

There are at least two words in English that have both adjectival and prepositional behaviour. These are *near* and *worth*. *Near* is like an adjective in that (a) it has comparative and superlative forms, (b) it can follow adjectival intensifiers like *very*, and (c) it can follow raising verbs. None of these are properties of standard Prepositions like *in*, as the following contrasts show:

1a. John lives nearer the park than the bank
1b. *John lives inner the city than the country
2a. John lives very near me
2b. *John lives very in London
3a. John seems near to an answer to the question that's been on his mind
3b. ?*John seems in London

However, as (1a) and (2a) show, *near* takes a direct object, like a Preposition. In this respect, *near* contrasts with the semantically very similar Adjective *close*, as you can see if you try substituting *close* in (1a) and (2a) ((3a) is suspiciously different, in fact, in that it deteriorates without *to*, at least to my ear). What might we say about all of this in terms of the government-based Case theory?

Exercise 5

Everything that we said about Case (and case) in this chapter was based on the assumption that there is a particular Case (or case) associated with the subject (Nominative) and a particular Case (or case) associated with the direct object (Accusative). A great deal of crosslinguistic work, particularly that done by typologists, implicitly or explicitly rejects this idea. The reason for this is the existence of ergative languages, in which there appears to be one case (usually called ergative) for the subject of a transitive verb and another case (usually called absolutive) for both the subject of an intransitive and the object of a transitive. The following examples from the North-East Caucasian language Avar illustrate:

1. W-as   w-ekér-ula
   M-child-ABS M-run-PRES
   'The boy runs'

2. Inssu-cca   j-as   j-écc-ula
   (M)father-ERG F-child-ABS F-praise-PRES
   'Father praises the girl'

(Blake (1994: 122))

These examples also illustrate something that is very frequently found in ergative languages: the absolutive case is morphologically unmarked, while the ergative case has a special marker.

What issues arise in trying to formulate an analysis for an ergative system in terms of abstract Case? What parameters might distinguish a case/Case system like that of Avar from that of Latin or English? I'm not asking you to actually give an analysis of Avar, but just to consider what the issues are that phenomena of this type raise.

Exercise 6
In Section 2.1, we adopted the supposition that lexical categories can assign θ-roles only to arguments that are within their minimal m-command domain. As I showed in the discussion in that section (around examples (5) and (6), if you want to refer back to it), this effectively means that θ-roles can only be assigned by to the Specifier or complement of a lexical category. Now, if you look back to Section 1.3.1, you'll see that we've also assumed that all branching in phrase structure is binary. This means that each head can have at most one Specifier and one complement. If θ-roles are assigned under minimal m-command, that in turn implies that each head can have at most two θ-roles to assign, one to its complement and one to its Specifier. Or does it? The fact is that this appears to be an incorrect claim. Most languages have classes of verbs which have three arguments. In English, many three-argument Verbs can appear in two different kinds of syntactic frame. *Give* is a good example, as the following shows:

1. John gave Mary a flower
2. John gave a flower to Mary

There are at least two ways that we might allow for three-argument Verbs, while retaining some version of the minimal m-command idea. One of them should come to mind if you reread Section 2.5. The other is less obvious. Here's a hint: any maximal projection can in principle take another version of itself as a complement.

Appendix: Formal Relations

In Chapters 1 and 2, I've introduced a number of different formal relations among syntactic positions. The goal of this Appendix is threefold: first, to summarize what these are; second, to show how these definitions are all built up from a small number of more primitive relations, and, finally, to show how, following Chomsky (1993), these relations can be reduced to set-theoretic definitions.

Here, then, are the various structural relations that we have introduced so far:

C-command:
(A1) α c-commands β iff α does not dominate β and every category dominating α dominates β (see Chapter 1, (42))

Minimal c-command:
(A2) β minimally c-commands α iff β c-commands α and there is no γ, such that γ c-commands α and does not c-command β (see Chapter 1, (68))

M-command:
(A3) α m-commands β iff α does not dominate β and some projection of α dominates β (see (4))

Minimal m-command:
(A4) α minimally m-commands β iff α m-commands β and there is no γ that both m-commands β and does not m-command α (see (5))

Government:
(A5) α, a head, governs β iff
(a) α c-commands β
(b)   no barrier dominates β but not α (see (16))

Barrier:
(A6)   any XP except IP (see (18))

Agreement:
(A7) α, a head, agrees with β iff α minimally m-commands β and does not govern β (see (23))

Checking Domain:
(A8)   The checking domain of α, a head, is the set of categories that α agrees with, where agreement is defined as in (A7) (see (93))

It should be reasonably clear how these definitions are connected to one another, once you see them all together. Let's look at how they're built up.

(A1–A4) are all explicitly based on the notion of *command*. The intuition behind this notion could apply to any kind of hierarchy: positions higher in the hierarchy command those lower down. Command relations are therefore intended to formalize in various ways the fact that one category is higher up the tree than another. Now, the basic relations of dominance and constituency define the simplest case where one category is higher than another: in this case, the upper category contains the lower. The command definitions are explicitly formulated so as to apply only where the upper category does not dominate the lower one; so command relations define what it means for a category α to be higher in the tree than another category β where α does not dominate β.

Command relations define an upper and sometimes a lower limit. The relation does not hold beyond that limit. In this command relations define a kind of syntactic locality. Since we know that syntactic structures are potentially infinite, owing to their property of recursion (see 1.1), some kind of locality requirement must be imposed in order to make structures manageable. If not, we could allow for processes that refer to the 1,205,894th DP on the left of β, for example. (Movement and other dependencies are also subject to locality requirements which, as we shall see in Chapters 3 and 4, are parasitic on the relations being discussed here.)

C-command and m-command are distinguished by the upper limit they refer to. For c-command, this is simply the first category above α. For m-command, it is a projection of α. M-command is therefore the more liberal relation, as it allows α, a head, to m-command its Specifier. We can see the difference in (A9):

(A9)

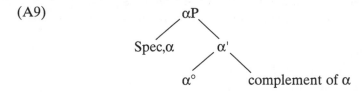

The upper limit on c-command, the first category dominating α, is α'. So α c-commands its complement but not its Specifier. On the other hand, since a projection of α, namely αP, dominates Spec,α, α m-commands this element, as well as its complement, since that category is dominated by α', a projection of α. α' both c-commands and m-commands Spec,α: it c-commands Spec,α because the first category dominating it dominates Spec,α and it m-commands Spec,α because a projection of it dominates Spec,α. Maximal projections can't m-command anything, since by definition they aren't dominated by further projections. On the other hand, they can c-command, although in (A9) we have not shown any category c-commanded by αP.

As they stand, the relations of c-command in (A1) and m-command in (A3) go right to the bottom of the tree. That is, however much structure there might be inside Spec,α in (A9), α' both c-commands and m-commands all of it. So there is no locality restriction 'going down the tree', as it were. There are two principal ways of imposing a lower limit on locality relations. One is by adding a 'minimality clause' to the definition of command. As you can see from (A2) and (A4), such a clause says that α must be the closest head which fulfils the relevant command criteria to the head it minimally commands. If there's a closer one which fulfils the same criteria (where 'closeness' can also be defined in terms of the relevant command relation, as in (A2) and (A4)), then α doesn't count. We discussed instances of the minimality clause in 1.4.2.3 for c-command and in 2.1 for m-command, so I won't go over it further here. We'll be seeing minimality again in Chapter 4, 4.4 and 4.5.

The other way of imposing 'downward locality' is by means of barriers. For the moment, until 4.4, we stick to the crude definition in (A6). In 4.4, we'll see a more sophisticated definition of barrier. We'll also see that barriers and minimality are central for defining locality for movement relations.

The definition of government in (A5) makes use of barrier as the downward locality requirement and c-command as the upward one. It also imposes a further restriction, stating that only heads can be governors; and we'll see further cases of this type of restriction in 4.3, 4.4, and 4.5. This seems like a legitimate restriction, as heads are independently needed entities in X'-theory – so this is not some *ad hoc* invention. In (A9), α governs its complement. If its complement is IP, it will also govern positions inside the complement. If the complement is not IP, α will not be able to 'look inside' it.

Finally, the definition of 'agreement' in (A7) uses a negative property. The categories that α agrees with are those which it m-commands but does not govern. These include the Specifier of αP and categories adjoined both to αP and to $\alpha°$ (as we saw in 2.6.4). Because of the negative clause in the definition, the categories with which α agrees, the set of categories that make up α's checking domain in (A8), are the set-theoretic complement of the categories that it governs. We thus have:

(A10)

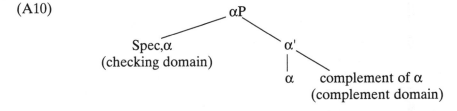

Chomsky (1993) develops this kind of thinking and provides definitions of important structural relations that are based purely on the primitives of X'-theory and set theory. Let's see how this is done. Following Chomsky's presentation, let's look at the following structure:

(A11)

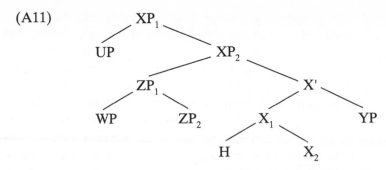

(Here the subscripts are just a convenient way of distinguishing segments of categories in the sense of 2.6.4.) Chomsky distinguishes dominance and containment as follows:

(A12) α **dominates** β iff every segment of α dominates β

(A13) α **contains** β iff some segment of α dominates β

We can then define MAX(α) as the smallest maximal projection dominating α. In (A11), then, MAX(X) is XP. In terms of MAX(α), we can define the notion of **domain** of a category, or DOM(α), as follows:

(A14) The domain of α, α an X°, is the set of nodes contained in MAX(α) that are distinct from and do not contain α

This definition means that DOM(X) in (A11) is the following set of nodes: UP and everything it dominates, ZP and everything it dominates, WP and everything it dominates, YP and everything it dominates, and H and everything it dominates. DOM(X) corresponds to the basic command relation.

Chomsky next divides DOM(X) into two subsets. First, there is the **complement** domain. The complement domain of α is the subset of DOM(α) reflexively dominated by the complement of α. In (A11), this corresponds to YP and everything it dominates. You should be able to see that the difference between domain and complement domain corresponds to the difference between m-command and c-command. Second, there is the **residue**, RES(X), which is everything in DOM(α) which isn't in the complement domain as just defined, of UP and everything it dominates, ZP and everything it dominates, WP and everything it dominates, and H and everything it dominates. Since RES is negatively defined, it is similar (but not identical) to the notion of agreement in (A7).

Finally, Chomsky introduces a general notion of MIN(S), for any set S of nodes. MIN(S) defines the smallest possible subset K of S, such that, for any node α in S, there is a node in K that reflexively dominates α. For example, applying MIN to the complement domain of X in (A11), we need to find the smallest set of nodes among YP and all the nodes YP dominates such that there is a node that reflexively dominates any node we choose as being in MIN. If you think about it, the only possibility here is YP itself. YP reflexively dominates itself, as well as everything else in the complement domain of X. So the smallest set of nodes in the complement domain of X that satisfies MIN(S) must be just YP. More generally, MIN(S) will always pick out the 'highest' nodes in any domain. (In this way it imposes a 'downward locality' restriction of the type we discussed above). Similarly, we can define MIN(RES(X)). This will give, in (A11), the set {UP, ZP, WP, H}. MIN(RES(X)) defines the checking domain of X. As you can see, MIN(RES(X)) is very close to the notion of agreement defined as in (A7), which we used to define checking domain in 2.6. The differences lie in the adjunction structures, which we glossed over in our text presentation; I did not take a view on whether a category adjoined to XP is minimally m-commanded by X or not. However, if we adopt the definition of dominance in (A11), then we see that categories adjoined to XP are not dominated by XP. Hence they are c-commanded by XP, according to (A1), and minimally m-commanded by XP according to (A4) (you can work through these definitions for yourself). Whether such a category agrees with X in the sense of (A7) depends on whether X governs it, and that in turn depends on whether XP is a barrier. IP is not a barrier, so I agrees with categories adjoined to it; other categories are barriers (for now), and here there is a difference between (A7) and Chomsky's notion of MIN(RES(α)). A good exercise is to see whether this difference has any empirical consequences.

Leaving aside these points of detail, I hope you can see that Chomsky attempts to derive the various notions that enter into formal relations from set theory. DOM gives the basic command relation, MIN the 'downward locality' relation, and RES the negative relation. These relations are thus derived from the combination of X'-theory and set theory. If we take X'-theory as primitive (although this is challenged both by Kayne (1994) and Chomsky (1994, 1995)), then we deduce these relations to the barest conceptually necessary primitives of phrase structure and set theory.

3

Binding

3.0 Introduction

Now you've seen the conditions on the internal structure of syntactic categories (X'-theory) and one set of well-formedness conditions on the external distribution of categories (Case theory and checking theory). The next step is to look at how categories can be related to each other in a syntactic representation. In general terms, then, the next two chapters are concerned with dependencies among positions in a syntactic structure. This chapter deals with dependencies that do not appear to involve movement, while Chapter 4 is concerned with movement relations.

The kinds of dependencies I'll be concerned with here are those that hold between certain kinds of DPs that appear to be able to 'stand for' other DPs. The theory that classifies which can stand for others, and explains the syntactic domains in which the 'stand-for' relation can hold, is **binding theory**. In Section 3.1, I'll present the basic facts concerning the distribution of different types of pronouns – these are, of course, the DPs that stand for others most readily. Section 3.2 gives a simplified version of the binding theory that was presented in *Lectures on Government and Binding* (Chomsky (1981)). In Section 3.3, we extend the approach to look at non-pronouns and empty categories. Sections 3.4 and 3.5 deal with more recent developments. In Section 3.4 I look at the 'movement theory' of some kinds of binding (this approach treats some kinds of binding as the effect of covert move-α, and so effectively claim that this kind of dependency is due to movement, contrary to the way I divided things up in the previous paragraph). We'll see how this approach can capture some interesting crosslinguistic differences in binding relations. Finally, Section 3.5 outlines a rather different approach that has recently been developed by Reinhart and Reuland (1991, 1993).

3.1 Anaphors and Pronouns

Traditional grammars tell us that pronouns can stand for nouns. Actually, this isn't quite true: in terms of the theory we're discussing here, we'd say that pronouns stand for DPs. If a pronoun stands for a DP, we say that the DP in question is the **antecedent** of the pronoun. So, *Phil* can be interpreted as the antecedent of *he* in (1) (although it doesn't have to be):

(1) Phil thinks he is a genius

In the interpretation of (1) where *Phil* is the antecedent of *he, he* is understood as standing for *Phil*, and so the sentence means 'Phil thinks that he, Phil, is a genius'. And (1) allows another interpretation, where *he* just refers to any male in the context.

From now on, we'll indicate antecedence relations with coindexing. (1a), then, only means that *Phil* is the antecedent of *he*, since the two are coindexed:

(1a) Phil$_i$ thinks he$_i$ is a genius

Among the traditionally recognized pronouns there are in fact two main classes. We'll refer to these, following fairly standard practice, as **anaphors** and **pronouns** (so we're using the term 'pronoun' in a slightly more restricted way than in traditional grammar). The two classes are distinguished in terms of the syntactic domains in which they can or must connect to their antecedents. Let's look at them in turn.

3.1.1 Anaphors

Anaphors include reflexives (like *myself, yourself, himself*) and reciprocals (*each other*). Anaphors are subject to three main requirements. First, they must have an antecedent. The ungrammaticality of the sentences in (2) shows this:

(2a) *Himself left

(2b) *Each other left

These sentences are bad because the anaphor has no antecedent.

Second, the anaphor's antecedent must c-command it. You can see this by comparing (3a) and (3b):

(3a) Brian hates himself$_i$

(3b) *Brian$_i$'s mother hates himself$_i$

Sentence (3a) is fine, and means 'Brian hates Brian'; (3b), on the other hand, can't mean 'Brian's mother hates Brian' (it could mean 'Brian's mother hates Brian's mother', but only if Brian's mother is masculine, since *himself* has to agree in gender with its antecedent). In other words, *Brian* can't be the antecedent of *himself* in this example; *himself* can't 'stand for' *Brian*. We can see why this is if we look more closely at the structure of (3b), which is given (with the clause structure once again reduced to IP, as in most of the structures in this chapter) in (4):

(4)

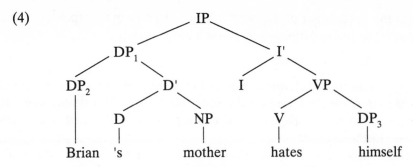

Let's look (once again) at the definition of c-command that we gave in Chapter 1:

C-command:
(5) α c-commands β iff α does not dominate β and every category dominating α dominates β

If we take DP_2 to be α and DP_3 to be β in (4), we can immediately see that not every category dominating DP_2 dominates DP_3. This is because DP_1 dominates DP_2 but does not dominate DP_3. For this reason, *Brian* cannot be the antecedent of *himself*, and so the sentence is ungrammatical.

Compare the structure of (3b), given in (4), with that of (3a):

(6)

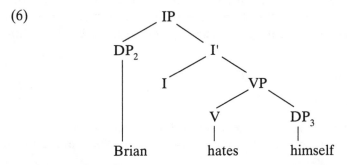

This time, if DP_2 is α in terms of the definition of c-command, it certainly does c-command DP_3 (which would be β): every category dominating DP_2 (namely IP) also dominates DP_3, and, of course, DP_2 does not dominate DP_3. So in this example *Brian* can be the antecedent of *himself*. So reflexives and reciprocals must be c-commanded by their antecedents. The same is true for reciprocals, as you can see if you substitute *John and Mary* for *Brian* and *each other* for *himself* in (3a).

Now let's define **syntactic binding**. This notion is related to but distinct from logical binding, which is discussed in the Appendix to this chapter: from now on, when I use the term 'binding' on its own, you should take it to mean 'syntactic binding'. The definition of binding is as follows:

Binding:
(7) α binds β iff α c-commands β and α is coindexed with β

If a category is not bound, it is 'free'.

Regarding anaphors, then, we can now say that:

(8) Anaphors must be bound

In fact, not only must anaphors be bound, but – and here's the really interesting thing – *they must be bound in a particular kind of syntactic domain.* There are two basic conditions on the syntactic domain of anaphor-binding.

The first condition is: no binding into a tensed clause. You can see this condition at work in (9):

(9a) *Mick and Keith$_i$ always thought [$_{tensed\ clause}$ that each other$_i$ were weird]

(9b) *Phil$_i$ said [$_{tensed\ clause}$ that himself$_i$ was a genius]

This constraint is very interesting, because it is not at all difficult to see what these sentences are trying to mean. Sentence (9a) would mean something like 'Mick always thought that Keith was weird and Keith always thought that Mick was weird', if only it were grammatical. Similarly, (9b) would mean 'Phil said that he, Phil, was a genius', if the syntax would let it. We can perfectly well imagine how we'd interpret these sentences, how the anaphors could be seen as standing for their antecedents. And there's nothing semantically ill-formed about the meanings that we imagine. But there's a syntactic constraint which, in some sense, prevents the anaphors from linking up with their antecedents. The result is that the anaphors act as though they had no antecedents, and the sentences are bad.

This last point is borne out by the fact that swapping the tensed clauses in (9) for infinitives, and holding everything else constant (well, I've changed the verbs into ones which more readily accept infinitival complements), gives perfectly good results:

(10a) Mick and Keith$_i$ always believed [$_{infinitival\ clause}$ each other$_i$ to be weird]

(10b) Phil$_i$ believed [$_{infinitival\ clause}$ himself$_i$ to be a genius]

And here the meanings are exactly those that we imagined for (9). So the syntax is imposing some kind of a ban on binding into finite clauses. Chomsky (1973) called this the 'Tensed-S Condition'.

The second constraint is: no binding across an intervening subject. This constraint is at work in the examples in (11), where the relevant subject is in small capitals:

(11a) *Mick and Keith$_i$ believe [CHARLIE to like each other$_i$]

(11b) *Phil$_i$ believes [LORETTA to admire himself$_i$]

Here the binding goes into an embedded clause, but that clause is an infinitive, and so the Tensed-S Constraint doesn't apply. As with the examples in (9), it's fairly easy to see what these sentences would mean, if only they could. Example (11a) would mean 'Mick believes Charlie to like Keith and Keith believes Charlie to like Mick', and (11b) would mean 'Phil believes that Loretta admires him, Phil'. The syntactic condition that makes these sentences ungrammatical was called the 'Specified Subject Condition' in Chomsky (1973).

We can combine Tensed-S and Specified Subject Condition violations. The resulting sentences are, of course, ungrammatical:

(12a) *Mick and Keith$_i$ think [$_{tensed\ clause}$ that CHARLIE likes each other$_i$]

(12b) *Phil$_i$ thinks [$_{tensed\ clause}$ that LORETTA admires himself$_i$]

Here we have seen that there are three main things to say about how anaphors are connected to their antecedents:

- anaphors need antecedents
- anaphors must be c-commanded by their antecedents
- the syntactic relation between an anaphor and its antecedent is constrained by the Tensed-S Condition and the Specified Subject Condition.

Now let's compare anaphors with ordinary pronouns.

3.1.2 Pronouns

In many major respects, ordinary personal pronouns (*I, me, you, he, she, him, her, they*, and so on) are the opposite of anaphors, aside from the general point that they can stand for another DP.

First, unlike anaphors, pronouns don't actually *need* antecedents, although of course they can have them:

(13a) He wrote an opera

(13b) Phil said he wrote an opera

Example (13a) is grammatical, with *he* referring to some contextually given male individual (the context can 'give' the reference of *he* in all kinds of ways: the speaker could point at someone, there might have been some earlier discussion of someone, or it might just be that someone is 'on the mind' of both the speaker and the hearer, and the speaker knows it). Similarly, (13b), without indices, is ambiguous: *he* could be either *Phil* or some contextually given male individual.

Second, the antecedent of a pronoun does not have to c-command that pronoun. Compare (14) with (3b):

(14) Johnny$_i$'s manager exploited him$_i$

It is perfectly grammatical to interpret *him* as standing for *Johnny* here, so the sentence can mean 'Johnny's manager exploited Johnny'. The structure of this sentence is exactly like that of (3b), given in (4), and so Johnny does not c-command *him* here. Nevertheless, *Johnny* can be the antecedent of *him*. This is just the opposite of what we saw with the anaphors in (3).

Third, the antecedent of a pronoun can be quite far away from the pronoun. The antecedent–pronoun relation does not at first sight appear to be subject either to the Tensed-S Condition or the Specified Subject Condition. Example (15), which contrasts directly with the comparable anaphor case in (12), shows this:

(15) Andy$_i$ thinks [$_{tensed\ clause}$ that LOU hates him$_i$]

The antecedent–pronoun relation goes into a tensed clause, and across the subject of that clause. Nevertheless, the relation is allowed; the syntax lets you interpret this example as meaning 'Andy thinks that Lou hates Andy'.

In the three ways given above, then, pronouns are different from anaphors. Each time, we've seen that pronouns are more 'liberal' than anaphors, in that they can have a wider range of structural relations with their antecedents than anaphors can.

However, there is another difference between anaphors and pronouns, this time one which limits the possibilities of pronouns. This is: *the antecedent of a pronoun cannot be too close to that pronoun*. If the antecedent c-commands the pronoun, and is in the same clause as the pronoun, with no intervening subject of any kind, the sentence is bad:

(16) *Brian$_i$ hates him$_i$

This sentence is at best a very odd way of expressing 'Brian hates Brian', and at worst is just ungrammatical.

In fact, the constraint on pronouns is that they must be free in a particular syntactic domain. In other words, they and their antecedent cannot both be in the same syntactic domain. The domain in question is parallel to that which constrains the binding of anaphors. So the Tensed-S Condition and the Specified Subject Condition are relevant to pronouns too, but this time a pronoun requires that there must be a finite-clause boundary or a subject between the pronoun and a c-commanding antecedent (it's OK if the antecedent doesn't c-command the pronoun, as in (14)). So we find the following:

(17a) Mick and Keith$_i$ said [$_{tensed\ clause}$ they$_i$ are the best] (Tensed-S)

(17b) *Mick and Keith$_i$ believe $_{[tensed\ clause}$ them$_i$ to be the best]

(Compare these examples with the anaphor ones in (9) and (10).)

(18a) Mick and Keith$_i$ believe [ANDY to like them$_i$] (Specified Subject)

(18b) Mick and Keith$_i$ think [$_{tensed\ clause}$ ANDY likes them$_i$] (Specified Subject and Tensed S)

(Compare these examples with the anaphor ones in (11) and (12).)

On the basis of what we've seen so far, then, we've reached the following generalization:

(19) Pronouns must be free wherever anaphors must be bound.

This is sometimes called the 'Disjoint Reference Condition'.

I've devoted this subsection to showing how pronouns are, in a way, the inverse of anaphors. Now it's time to look at how we can make a theory which accounts for the observations we've made in this section.

3.2 The Binding Theory

3.2.1 Two Binding Principles

Having seen some of the basic data regarding the distribution of anaphors and pronouns, we can now take a look at a (rather simplified) version of the binding theory as it was developed in the early 1980s. This theory consists of two main parts: a statement of the binding principles and a definition of binding domain. The former says something about the complementarity between anaphors and pronouns, while the latter subsumes the Tensed-S Condition and the Specified Subject Condition.

The binding principles are as follows:

The Binding Principles:
(20) Principle A: an anaphor must be bound in its binding domain
      Principle B: a pronoun must be free in its binding domain

These principles directly state the basic differences between anaphors and pronouns that we saw in the preceding sections. Obviously, the binding conditions don't say very much unless we can give a workable definition of binding domain. This is not a trivial matter; in fact, quite a research effort was devoted to this in the late 1970s and early 1980s. Example (21) will suffice for our needs here:

Binding Domain:
(21) The binding domain (BD) of α is the smallest XP containing α and:
    either (a) a subject (distinct from α)
    or   (b) an I that assigns Nominative Case to α

There are three principal configurations that we need to look at in order to see how the definition in (21) works:

(a) where α is the subject of a finite clause

(b) where α is a complement

(c) where α is the subject of an infinitive.

So let's take each one of these in turn, and see how (21), combined with the statement of the binding conditions in (20), gives the right result. Then we can look at some more complicated examples.

In Case (a): subject of a finite clause, as the Tensed-S Condition states, pronouns are good and anaphors are bad. We saw this in examples (9) and (17a), which I repeat here:

(9a) *Mick and Keith$_i$ always thought [$_{tensed\ clause}$ that each other$_i$ were weird]

(9b) *Phil$_i$ said [$_{tensed\ clause}$ that himself$_i$ was a genius]

(17a) Mick and Keith$_i$ said [$_{tensed\ clause}$ they$_i$ are the best]

The relevant parts of the structure of these examples are as follows (*t* here is the trace of the VP-internal subject of the higher clause):

(22)

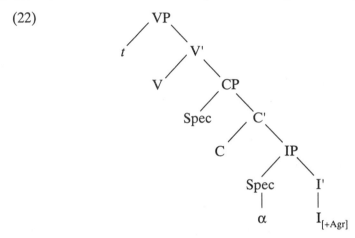

Applying option (a) of (21), the smallest XP containing α and a subject distinct from α in (22) is the matrix VP (the subject in question is the trace of the VP-internal subject). This would appear to give the wrong result, since α is bound in this domain, and so we expect the anaphor to be allowed and the pronoun to be bad – exactly the opposite of what we see in (9) and in (17a). However, let's try option (b) of (21). The smallest XP containing α and an I that assigns Nominative Case to α is IP. Since IP is smaller than VP here (in the straightforward sense that it is contained in VP), then this is the category that counts as the BD for α. So option (b) is the one that must be taken, since it gives us a smaller binding domain than option (a). Since IP contains no binder for α, α is free in its binding domain. Hence, if α is an anaphor (as in (9)), Principle A of (20) is violated. And if α is a pronoun (as in (17a)) Principle B is satisfied.

In Case (b), where α is a complement, the Specified Subject Condition states that an anaphor will only be allowed if it is bound by the subject and that a pronoun will be allowed unless it is bound by the subject. The examples which illustrate this are (11) and (18a):

(11a) *Mick and Keith$_i$ believe [CHARLIE to like each other$_i$]

(11b) *Phil$_i$ believes [LORETTA to admire himself$_i$]

(18a) Mick and Keith$_i$ believe [ANDY to like them$_i$]

Glossing over the VP-internal trace of subject, the structure of the complement clauses here is as follows:

(23)

```
            IP
          /    \
        DP      I'
              /    \
            I       VP
                  /    \
                 V      DP
                        |
                        α
```

The smallest XP containing α and a subject is IP, hence IP is the BD for α in this structure. This is the result whichever option we take in (21). If α is an anaphor, Principle A says that it must be bound in IP; the only candidate is the DP in subject position, and so we see that an anaphor will only be allowed in complement position when it is bound by the subject. Conversely (as usual), if α is a pronoun, then it cannot be bound by the subject, as Principle B says that it must be free in its BD. If we take the VP-internal subject hypothesis seriously, and allow the subject trace (which would be in Spec,VP) to count as an antecedent, then really the BD for α in (23) is VP, and the only available antecedent is the VP-internal trace of the subject. It should be clear that this doesn't really change anything in terms of the account of (11) and (18a), however, although we see that only option (a) of (21) is the relevant one.

In Case (c), when α is the subject of an infinitive, both the Tensed-S Condition and the Specified Subject Condition allow an anaphor to be bound from the next clause up, and prevent a pronoun from being bound in this way. The following examples illustrate:

(10a) Mick and Keith$_i$ always believed [$_{infinitival\ clause}$ each other$_i$ to be weird]

(10b) Phil$_i$ believed [$_{infinitival\ clause}$ himself$_i$ to be a genius]

(17b) *Mick and Keith$_i$ believe [$_{tensed\ clause}$ them$_i$ to be the best]

Here the relevant portion of the structure is as follows:

(24)

```
              IP
            /    \
        DP_i      I'
                /    \
            I_{[+Agr]}  VP
              |       /   \
             t_i     V'
                   /    \
                  V      IP
                       /    \
                    Spec     I'
                     |      /  \
                     α   I_{[-Agr]}
```

We saw in 2.2.3 that it is usual to assume that in Exceptional Case-marking infinitives there is simply no CP level, so there's no CP here. We also saw in Section 2.2.2 that infinitival I lacks the ability to assign Nominative Case. Because of this, option (b) of (21) cannot define the lower IP as the BD for α. Option (a) stipulates that α itself cannot be the subject that is relevant for defining its own BD, and so we conclude that there is no way for the lower IP to be the BD for α. The BD for α must therefore be the next smallest category that satisfies one of the options in (21). The next smallest category is VP. By option (b) of (21), the VP-internal trace of the higher subject makes VP the binding domain for α. So if α is an anaphor it can be bound by the higher subject, and if α is a pronoun it cannot be bound by the higher subject. This corresponds to the data in (10) and (17b).

You might want to go over the preceding paragraphs more than once, in order to fully grasp fully how the definitions in (20) and (21) explain all the facts.

Let's look next at a trickier case, which will lead us to make a slight refinement to (21). Compare the following:

(25a) *Mick and Keith$_i$ always thought [that each other$_i$ were weird] (= (9a))

(25b) Mick and Keith$_i$ think [that [$_{DP}$ songs about each other$_i$] would sell well]

Example (25a) is (9a) once again, and we saw above (under case (a)) that (20) and (21) account for the ungrammaticality of this example. Example (25b) is rather surprising, given that we have an anaphor – *each other* – inside the subject of a tensed clause. The anaphor appears to violate the Tensed-S condition, and moreover appears in an intuitive sense to be further away from its antecedent than its counterpart in (25a).

Let's look at the structure of the embedded clause, and we'll see how the definitions apply:

(26)

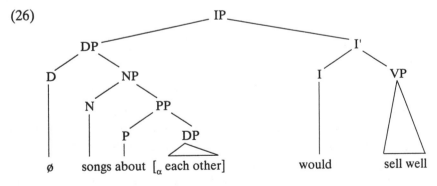

The definition of binding domain in (21) requires us to look for the smallest XP containing α and either (a) a subject distinct from α or (b) an I that assigns Nominative to α. We can immediately discount option (b), as α in (26) is not Nominative, being the object of a Preposition. So we are looking for a subject, option (a). PP, the smallest XP containing the anaphor, contains no subject. Neither NP nor DP contain a subject either. IP, of course, contains a subject, the whole DP containing α: *songs about each other*. Applying option (a) of (21) strictly, then, we arrive at the wrong result: the lower IP contains α and a subject. In that case, the anaphor *each other* is not in the same binding domain as its antecedent, and so Principle A should be violated, exactly as in (25a). But we observe that this is not so.

The trick here is to specify more carefully what counts as a subject for option (a) of (21). We can rephrase (21a) like this:

(21a') a subject distinct from α which does not contain α

Rephrasing (21a) in this way prevents the subject DP of the lower clause from counting, and so the lower IP cannot be the binding domain for the anaphor. The smallest category containing the anaphor, an m-commander, and a subject which does not contain the anaphor, is then the higher VP (again assuming the VP-internal subject trace counts). This means that *each other* can be bound by the matrix subject without violating Principle A, as (25b) shows. The contrast between (25a) and (25b) is due to the fact that in (25a) *each other* receives Nominative Case from the lower I, which means that the lower IP is a binding domain by option (21b) (as we saw above under case (a)). In (25b), however, *each other* receives (Accusative) Case from *about*.

A crucial step in the above reasoning about (25b) was that neither NP nor DP in the lower clause contain a subject. If they did, they would form a binding domain (by (21a)) and the anaphor would be unable to be bound from the matrix clause. This deduction is correct, as the following example shows:

(27) ??Mick and Keith$_i$ think [that [$_{DP}$ Charlie's songs about each other$_i$] won't sell]

There is a clear contrast between (27) and (25b) – although (27) is perhaps not quite as bad as we have predicted.

The binding theory given in (20) and (21) can be used as evidence for the presence of PRO. This element is needed in order to account for the impossibility of examples like:

(28) *Sid$_i$ permitted his children$_j$ [(PRO$_j$) to mutilate himself$_i$]

If there were no subject in the lower clause, then we would have to drastically modify (21) in order to explain the ungrammaticality of the anaphor here; as it stands, (21a) would in that case falsely predict that the matrix clause is the binding domain for the anaphor, since this is the smallest category containing a subject as well as the anaphor itself. However, if PRO is present in the lower clause, the same definition gives us the correct result, since that clause now contains a subject and the anaphor – and, of course, it is smaller than the matrix clause. We know that PRO cannot be the antecedent of the anaphor, since it must bear the index of the object of *permit*, i.e. it is controlled by the object of *permit* (see 3.2.2.2 for more on control). This emerges clearly from examples like the following:

(29a) Sid permitted his children$_i$ [PRO$_i$ to mutilate the cat]

(29b) Sid permitted his children$_j$ [PRO$_j$ to mutilate themselves$_j$]

(29c) Sid permitted his children$_i$ [PRO$_i$ to mutilate each other$_i$]

You should be able to see that the anaphors in (29b and c) are bound in accordance with Principle A of the binding theory. *Permit* contrasts with a subject-control verb like *promise*:

(30a) Sid$_i$ promised his children [PRO$_i$ to mutilate the cat]

(30b) Sid$_i$ promised his children [PRO$_i$ to mutilate himself$_i$]   (see (28))

(30c) *Sid$_i$ promised his children$_j$ [PRO$_i$ to mutilate themselves$_j$]
$\qquad\qquad\qquad\qquad\qquad\qquad\qquad\qquad\qquad\qquad$ (see (29b))

(30d) *Sid$_i$ promised his children$_j$ [PRO$_i$ to mutilate each other$_j$]
$\qquad\qquad\qquad\qquad\qquad\qquad\qquad\qquad\qquad\qquad$ (see (29c))

The single statement that the subject of *promise* controls the PRO of its infinitival complement makes it possible for (20) and (21) to account straightforwardly for these examples. If you substitute pronouns for the anaphors in (28), (29b and c), and (30b, c and d), you'll see that the judgements switch around exactly as predicted by (20).

3.2.2 The Distribution and Interpretation of PRO

3.2.2.1 The PRO Theorem

It's now time to look a bit more carefully at PRO, its distribution, and its interpretation. We've seen that it appears as the subject of an infinitive, and it has an interpretation similar to that of a pronoun. In infinitival complements it is usually controlled by an argument of the matrix verb. In other contexts, such as infinitivals in subject position, it has an 'arbitrary' interpretation meaning approximately 'someone or other' (often with a weak implication that the speaker and hearer are included in the 'someone or other'), like this:

(31) [PRO to make a new record now] would be a good idea

PRO cannot appear anywhere other than in the subject position of an infinitive (this was mentioned in Section 2.2.1):

(32a) *John met PRO

(32b) *PRO left

Why can't these examples mean 'John met someone or other' and 'someone or other left' respectively? Another observation is that PRO cannot appear in ECM infinitives or in *for-to* infinitives:

(33a) *Mick believes [PRO to be the best]

(33b) *[For PRO to make a new record] would be a good idea

What can we say about these distributional restrictions?

Working with slightly different technical assumptions from those I have been adopting here, the *Lectures on Government and Binding* version of the binding theory could give an interesting account of the distribution of PRO (remember, what I'm presenting here is a simplified version of that theory.). This became known as the 'PRO theorem', and we can summarize the reasoning as follows:

- *Assumption 1*:   PRO is a pronominal anaphor.
  This is arguably a reasonable characterization of PRO's interpretive properties. The phenomenon of control certainly involves the imposition of an anaphoric dependency as a consequence of lexical properties of the matrix verb, and arbitrary PRO is very similar in interpretation to pronouns like *one* (or French *on*, German *man*, Italian *si*, and others.).
- *Consequence*: PRO is subject to Principle A of the binding theory, as an anaphor, and to Principle B, as a pronoun.
  However, these Principles impose contradictory requirements, in that PRO must be both free and bound in its BD (see (20)), and 'free' is defined as 'not bound' (see (7)); so PRO must be bound and not bound in its BD. We have thus reached a contradiction (this kind of reasoning is known as *reductio ad absurdum*, 'reduction to the absurd') and must abandon one of our assumptions.
- *Conclusion*: PRO cannot have a BD.
  This is clearly one way to retain our initial assumption (PRO is a pronominal anaphor) and the binding principles of (20).
- *Assumption 2*: BDs are defined so that any category with a BD is governed.
  This is one of the important divergences between the *Lectures on Government and Binding* (Chomsky (1981)) approach and the version of binding theory I've been summarizing here. Another one is Assumption 3.
- *Assumption 3*: government is defined so that all Case-marked DPs are governed.
  The important consequence here is that the subject of a finite clause is a governed position but not the subject position of an infinitive, except for ECM and *for-to* infinitives.
- *The PRO Theorem*: PRO is neither governed nor Case-marked.
  This is an important, and empirically correct, conclusion. It was a very nice result to be able to deduce this from the initial statement that PRO is a pronominal anaphor, combined with the other assumptions (which were not adopted especially for PRO, but did other work in the context of the government-based Case theory). In this way, PRO's distribution was derived purely from its status as a pronominal

anaphor – a further example of desirable deductive structure in the theory.

More recent work does not retain this result, however, as the developments in Case theory that I described in Chapter 2 should make clear. The checking theory, as described in 2.6, abandons Assumption 3 ('all Case-marked DPs are governed'), and, in consequence, it is possible to define BDs as in (21), without mentioning government. So Assumption 2 can be abandoned. If we define BDs without reference to government, as in (21), then PRO will have a binding domain (in fact, it will have the binding domain of the subject of an infinitive, case (c) above). As a consequence, it cannot be a pronominal anaphor, as this characterization will always lead to ungrammaticality: it will inevitably violate Principle A exactly when it satisfies Principle B, and vice versa. In other words, by making different assumptions about the relation between Case-marking, government, and the definition of binding domains, we see that the chain of reasoning that led to the PRO theorem unravels, and we must abandon the initial assumption.

The alternative to the PRO theorem in accounting for the definition of PRO is, as I mentioned in Chapter 2 (see 2.2.2 and 2.4), that PRO requires a special Case which is only available in the subject position of an infinitive which receives no other Case. This approach suffers from the consequence that PRO's distribution cannot be derived from the statement that it is a pronominal anaphor, however.

3.2.2.2 Control

I've already mentioned that the interpretation of PRO is determined by control. Control is a phenomenon that has resisted being fully integrated into the theory; a lot of facts are known, but they do not seem to fall into patterns that we can explain using known theoretical precepts. Since control involves antecedence relations (in its interpretation, PRO 'stands for' its controller, much as any pronoun or anaphor stands for its antecedent), the natural move would be to reduce control to binding. This was proposed by Manzini (1983), and certainly looks like the most promising avenue to pursue.

I mentioned above that if PRO has a BD, then it would fall under case (c), and act like the subject of an infinitive in taking the higher clause as its BD. For PRO in many classes of complement infinitival this is true, as the following examples show:

(34a) Ryan$_i$ tried [PRO$_i$ to play better]

(34b) Eric$_i$ promised Alex [PRO$_i$ to behave in future]

(34c) Eric persuaded Alex$_i$ [PRO$_i$ to give him more money]

Examples (34b and c) illustrate that we need to add a lexical component to control theory, in that *promise* requires its subject to control PRO while *persuade* requires its object to do so. In fact, *promise* is exceptional here; many

Verbs obey the Minimal Distance Principle (originally proposed by Rosenbaum (1967)), which requires the structurally nearest argument to PRO to be the controller. This is the case with *ask*, for example:

(35a) John$_i$ asked [PRO$_i$ to leave]

(35b) John asked Bill$_i$ [PRO$_i$ to leave]

PRO is also like an anaphor in these cases in requiring an antecedent that c-commands it. This can be most clearly seen in passive examples like the following:

(36) *Alex was promised (by Eric$_i$) [PRO$_i$ to behave better]

If the *by*-phrase is left out here, there is no antecedent for PRO and the sentence is bad. If the *by*-phrase is included, the antecedent of PRO, *Eric*, fails to c-command it. This example also shows that it is the lexically determined subject argument (the Agent) that is the controller for PRO with *promise*; the subject that is derived by the operation of passive cannot be the controller. Where an object-control verb is passivized, on the other hand, the derived subject is the controller:

(37) Alex$_i$ was persuaded (by Eric) [PRO$_i$ to give him more money]

This is consistent with the observation that control verbs lexically determine which of their arguments is the controller. In these contexts, PRO acts like an anaphor in accordance with (21).

However, in complement clauses with a [+*wh*] C, PRO does not act like an anaphor for (21). In this context, it doesn't require a controller. In (38) this is shown by the fact that it can be the antecedent for *oneself*, which cannot take a definite DP like *John* as its antecedent:

(38) John asked [$_{CP}$ how [$_{IP}$ PRO to shave oneself]]

Infinitival relatives are a similar case:

(39a) This is the guru [$_{CP}$ who$_i$ [$_{IP}$ we$_j$ should prostrate ourselves$_j$ before t$_i$]]

(39b) This is the guru [$_{CP}$ Op$_i$ [$_{IP}$ PRO$_j$ to prostrate oneself$_j$ before t$_i$]]

In (39b) there is a *wh*-movement relation inside the relative clause, just as in (39a). Here, unlike (39a), the *wh*-element is null (these are known as 'null operators'). We see a further occurrence of PRO without an antecedent here; in the relevant respect this example is like (38). *wh*-infinitivals are a context of 'non-obligatory control', unlike complement clauses.

There are two other principal contexts of non-obligatory control: subject clauses and complements to certain kinds of adjectives and nouns. Both of these also allow optional 'long-distance control' (as do *wh*-clauses – PRO can be controlled by *John* in (38) if *oneself* is changed to *himself*). These contexts, and the possibility of long-distance control, are illustrated in (40):

(40a) [PRO$_{i/j}$ to mutilate himself$_i$/oneself$_j$] would amuse Sid$_i$

(subject clause)

(40b) Sid$_i$ thinks [$_{CP}$ that [$_{IP}$ it's nice [$_{CP}$ PRO$_{i/j}$ to mutilate himself$_i$/oneself$_j$]]]

(complement to adjective)

Here PRO is more like a pronoun, in that it takes an optional, long-distance antecedent.

Aside from the *wh*-complements, the complements which allow optional, long-distance control are those where PRO has no antecedent in its BD, according to option (a) of (21). In (40a), there is no XP that contains PRO, and a subject not containing PRO, and so there is simply no BD for PRO at all. In (40b), the BD for PRO is IP; this category contains no antecedent for PRO. In a sense, then, it seems that PRO, must be an anaphor if it is in a context where it can be one (complement to a control verb), and otherwise acts as a pronoun. Because of this, the original idea that PRO is a pronominal anaphor is partly correct, but the truth seems to be that PRO is either an anaphor or a pronoun, depending on complex conditions in the context, rather than being both at once. As I said at the beginning of this section, the precise nature of control is not at present understood; what I've offered here is an indication of the issues involved.

3.2.3 Conclusion

In this section, we've seen Principles A and B of the binding theory, and how they account for the distribution of anaphors, pronouns, and, finally, PRO. The central element of the binding theory is the definition of binding domains, which we finally arrive at as (21'), as follows:

Binding Domain (Revised):

(21') The binding domain (BD) of α is the smallest XP containing α and:

EITHER (a) a subject (distinct from α and which does not contain α)

OR (b) an I that assigns Nominative Case to α

Now it's time to see what the binding theory says about non-pronominal, non-anaphoric DPs.

3.3 Referential Expressions and Empty Categories

3.3.1 Referential Expressions and Principle C

As you've probably realized, Principles A and B only apply to a rather restricted range of DPs: anaphors, pronouns, and pronominal anaphors. Many, in fact most, DPs aren't in these classes. In this section we'll look at how binding theory applies to non-pronominal, non-anaphoric DPs, and how it applies to empty categories.

To start off, we can sum up the situation so far by positing the existence of two binary features that are associated with DPs: [± anaphor] and [± pronoun]. These features are just a useful device for restating what we've already seen; for now at least, there's no reason to think that they have any further content. So a [+ anaphor] DP is an anaphor, including PRO, and [+ pronoun] DP is a pronoun, including PRO. Table 3.1 illustrates:

Table 3.1. DP types as classified by [± anaphor] and [± pronoun]

	Anaphor	Pronoun
reflexives, reciprocals	+	–
pronouns	–	+
PRO	+	+
all other (non-empty) DPs	–	–

The first three rows of Table 3.1 are familiar, and I'll say no more about them. What I want to discuss now is the fourth row: 'the rest' (by the way, I added the proviso 'non-empty DPs' there, as we'll see that some empty categories appear to belong in the other rows).

What is 'the rest' referred to in Table 3.1? This class includes all non-pronominal, non-anaphoric DPs. In other words, it includes the great mass of DPs that do not require antecedents of any type, that do not 'stand for' something else, but which have their own semantic content. We might think of such DPs as 'semantically complete', in the sense that they do not require further elucidation from other linguistic material or from context for their basic descriptive content to be clear. So we're talking about DPs like *my dog, the King of France's toupee, John, the asteroid, a pizza, lots of pasta*, and so on. Because such DPs have their own descriptive content, they're known as referring expressions or R-expressions, the latter term being more neutral with respect to the difficult semantic notion of reference. The quasi-semantic definition of R-expressions given is rather rough and ready and isn't intended to have serious content for semantic theory; nevertheless, it seems to capture a clear intuitive distinction between the anaphors and pronouns which we looked at in Section 3.2 and the 'rest' of the DPs.

What are the binding properties of R-expressions? The logical thing to do is to put them in the same syntactic contexts as those in which we have seen anaphors and pronouns and see how they fare. From this, we should be able to deduce whether they follow Principle A, Principle B, or some other principle.

The first thing to note is that R-expressions, like pronouns and unlike anaphors, can stand alone without an antecedent:

(41a) Every good boy deserves favour

(41b) Pasta is nice

Second, R-expressions are ill-formed in the contexts where anaphors are well-formed, as the following examples show (compare (3), (10a)):

(42a) *He$_i$/Brian$_i$ hates Brian$_i$

(42b) *Mick$_i$ believes Mick$_i$ to be the greatest

C-command is relevant to the distribution of R-expressions, as a non-c-commanding coindexed DP is allowed:

(43) His$_i$ manager exploited Johnny$_i$

So we can see that R-expressions are quite distinct from anaphors as regards their binding properties.

Now let's compare R-expressions with pronouns. Given that they are so different from anaphors, we might expect R-expressions to pattern more similarly to pronouns, and up to a point this is true. R-expressions are clearly like pronouns in that they do not require an antecedent (compare (13) and (41)). Secondly, R-expressions resemble pronouns in allowing non-c-commanding antecedents: compare (14) and (42). And third, neither R-expressions nor pronouns allow antecedents in their BD: compare (16) and (42). At this point, one might be tempted to think that R-expressions were like pronouns in being subject to Principle B of the binding theory.

However, although it is true that R-expressions are subject to a 'freedom' requirement (a negative binding requirement, or a Disjoint Reference requirement), like pronouns, they differ from pronouns in that they cannot be bound *even in the contexts where pronouns can be bound*. We can see this if we look at the contexts where pronouns are bound by a c-commanding antecedent which is outside their BD, in conformity with Principle B, and compare these examples with what happens when we substitute R-expressions. Here once again are the relevant sentences with pronouns:

(17a) Mick and Keith$_i$ said [THEY$_i$ are the best]

(18a) Mick and Keith$_i$ believe [ANDY to like them$_i$]

(18b) Mick and Keith$_i$ think [ANDY likes them$_i$]

Now we substitute R-expressions for the pronouns:

(44) *Mick and Keith$_i$ said [Mick and Keith$_i$ are the best]

(45a) *Mick and Keith$_i$ believe [ANDY to like Mick and Keith$_i$]

(45b) *Mick and Keith$_i$ think [ANDY likes Mick and Keith$_i$]

The conclusion, then, is that R-expressions cannot be bound either where anaphors are bound or where pronouns are bound. So:

(46) R-expressions must be free

Condition (46) is usually added to the conditions in (20) as Principle C of the binding theory. The full binding theory is thus as follows, where I repeat the definition of BD in (21') once more:

The Binding Principles:
(20')   Principle A: an anaphor must be bound in its binding domain
          Principle B: a pronoun must be free in its binding domain
          Principle C: an R-expression must be free

Binding Domain (Revised):
(21')   The binding domain (BD) of α is the smallest XP containing α and:
          EITHER   (a)   a subject (distinct from α and which does not contain α)
          OR   (b)   the I that assigns Nominative Case to α

Definitions (20') and (21') will now account for all the data that we've discussed here and more. Among the further phenomena that binding theory can handle are a range of facts about empty categories. This is our next topic.

3.3.2 Empty Categories

In this subsection, I want to show how (20') and (21') can account for many aspects of the distribution of empty categories. Ideally, we want the empty categories to be no different from phonologically realized categories: this would be consistent with the idea that there's really nothing special about empty categories aside from the fact that they don't have a phonological realization. We'll see that this point of view can be largely maintained if the fact that empty categories are not necessarily Case-marked is taken into account (remember that the definition of BD in (21') only applies to Case-marked categories).

I already introduced three of the four commonly recognized XP-level empty categories in Section 2.4 (there's also the trace of head-movement, but we'll leave that aside here, as binding theory is only concerned with XPs; in fact, really only with DPs). Let's take another look at Table 2.1 from that section (repeated here as Table 3.2):

Table 3.2 The XP-level empty categories

PRO	*DP-trace*	wh-*trace*
Null or no Case	No Case	Case
Special grammatical function	Change in grammatical function	No change in grammatical function
Content fixed by control	Content from moved DP	Bound variable

Let's look at each of these in turn. What we really want to do is to try to relate the information about empty categories given in Table 3.2 to the subdivision of all DPs into [± anaphor, ± pronoun] given in Table 3.1.

3.3.2.1 PRO

We saw in the previous section that the fact that PRO has no Case might follow from defining it as a pronominal anaphor; alternatively, PRO might have a special, null, or zero Case). At this stage, I have nothing further to add to this, which we have covered in the previous section.

3.3.2.2 DP-trace

DP-traces are created by DP-movement, which has the properties listed in Chapter 2 (see 2.4). I repeat these here as (47):

> *DP-movement:*

(47a) moves a DP

(47b) leaves a trace in the starting position

(47c) moves to a position c-commanding the trace

(47d) moves to the closest possible position to the trace

(47e) obeys the Structure Preservation Constraint

(47f) only ever moves to Specifiers of functional heads

If we look at the properties listed here 'from the trace's point of view', we see that a DP-trace will always be associated with a moved DP (47a and b), will be c-commanded by that DP (47c) and will be in the closest possible position (47d), which will be the Specifier position of a functional head (47e and f). An obvious way to sharpen up the idea of an 'associated DP' is to say that the trace is coindexed with that DP. Since the DP also c-commands the trace (47c), then we conclude that *the moved DP binds its trace*. What we now need to do is to see which, if any, of the binding conditions apply to DP-traces.

Property (47d) should give us a clue. If movement must be to the closest possible position to the trace then we might expect it to take place within the DP's binding domain. Let's in fact look at the contexts of DP-movement which were discussed in Section 2.4 in the light of the definition of BD. Here I repeat (61) from Chapter 2 as (48):

(48a) Passive/unaccusative:

(48b) Raising (from a lower clause):

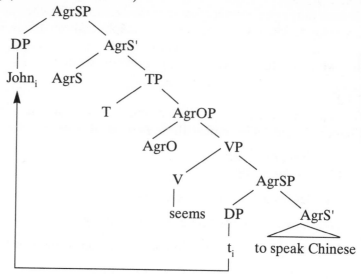

Passive/unaccusative movement, as in (48a), involves movement from a complement position to the local subject. By the definition of binding domain in (21'a) the local subject is in the BD of the complement position. This kind of movement cannot cross an intervening subject:

(49a) *Many students$_i$ seem that there were beaten up t$_i$ (by the police)

(49b) *A train$_i$ seems that there arrived t$_i$

Let's look at the DP-trace in (49) in the light of our discussion of anaphors and pronouns earlier in this chapter. Compare (49) with the examples with reflexives and reciprocals that we gave Section 3.1.1:

(12) *Mick and Keith$_i$ think [$_{tensed\ clause}$ that CHARLIE likes each other$_i$]

*Phil$_i$ thinks [$_{tensed\ clause}$ that LORETTA admires himself$_i$]

In both (12) and (49), we have a situation that we can schematize as follows (where α is the position of the reflexive, reciprocal, or DP-trace):

(50) [$_{AgrSP1}$ DP$_i$ ... [$_{AgrSP2}$ Subject ... α$_i$]

Since AgrSP$_2$ contains a subject, it forms a binding domain for α. Where α is a reflexive or reciprocal, Principle A and the definition of BD tell us immediately why (50) is ill-formed, as we have seen. We could explain the ungrammaticality of (49) – the case of (50) where α is a DP-trace – in the same way, if we assume that DP-traces are anaphors. So we might consider putting DP-traces in Table 3.1 in the row for [+ anaphor, – pronoun] elements.

Some support for this idea comes from the super-raising phenomenon that we looked at in Section 2.4. Here are the relevant examples again:

(51) *[$_{AgrSP1}$The train$_i$ seems that [$_{AgrSP2}$ it is likely [$_{AgrSP3}$ t$_i$ to be late]]]

(52) [$_{AgrSP1}$ It seems that [$_{AgrSP2}$ the train$_i$ is likely [$_{AgrSP3}$ t$_i$ to be late]]]

Again, the movement passes over an intervening subject, and we're dealing with an instance of (50) again, only here the trace is not in a complement position but a subject position. Finally, it's worth observing that raising only ever takes place from the subject position of an infinitive; raising from the subject position of a finite clause is impossible:

(53a) John$_i$ seems [t$_i$ to speak Chinese]

(53b) *John$_i$ seems [t$_i$ speaks Chinese]

We have seen that anaphors are impossible in the subject position of a finite clause; the examples in (9) – which I repeat once again – showed this:

(9a) *Mick and Keith$_i$ always thought [that each other$_i$ were weird]

(9b) *Phil$_i$ said [that himself$_i$ was a genius]

So we can perhaps regard (53b) as comparable to (9). In that case, (53a) would be comparable to (10):

(10a) Mick and Keith$_i$ always believed [each other$_i$ to be weird]

(10b) Phil$_i$ believed [himself$_i$ to be a genius]

It looks as though there's a real parallel between the distribution of DP-traces and that of reflexives and reciprocals. Therefore, we could include DP-traces in the [+ anaphor, – pronoun] category.

The idea that DP-traces and reflexives or reciprocals have essentially the same distribution, which is controlled by Principle A of the binding theory, was originally put forward in Chomsky (1973) and incorporated into the *Lectures on Government and Binding* version of binding theory more or less in the way I've just described.

In conclusion, we see that there's a striking similarity between the distribution of DP-traces and that of reflexives and reciprocals. We can account for this by classifying DP-traces as [+ anaphor, – pronoun].

3.3.2.3 wh-traces, Crossover, and L-relatedness
We saw in Section 2.4 that *wh*-traces are Case-marked (this is also stated in Table 3.2 above). The relevant evidence is that *wh*-movement cannot take place out of Caseless positions, as in the following examples (repeated from Chapter 2):

(55a) *Who$_i$ does it seem [t$_i$ to speak Chinese] ?

(54b) *Who$_i$ was it believed [t$_i$ to speak Chinese] ?

(54c) Who$_i$ do you believe [t$_i$ to speak Chinese] ?

So there is no question about *wh*-traces being subject to the binding theory. The question is, then, to which principle of the binding theory are they subject?

Let's look again at the properties of *wh*-movement that we gave in 2.4:

wh-*movement:*

(55a) moves a *wh*-XP

(55b) leaves a trace in the starting position

(55c) moves to a position c-commanding the trace

(55d) does NOT move to the closest possible position to its trace (or so it appears)

(55e) obeys the Structure Preservation Constraint

(55f) only ever moves to Specifiers of CP

Just as with DP-traces above, let's consider these properties from the point of view of the *wh*-trace. The trace will be c-commanded by 'its' *wh*-XP (actually here we are only concerned with DPs, as binding theory only applies to DPs), which is (55c). As with DP-traces, we can assume that the *wh*-DP is coindexed with the trace and therefore binds it. Let's leave aside the fact that the *wh*-DP can apparently be arbitrarily far away from the trace; as we said, this issue will be dealt with in Chapter 4. The other important thing to note is that the *wh*-DP is always in SpecCP, and so the trace is always bound from this position. This means that *wh*-traces are always in a configuration like (56):

(56) $[_{CP}$ *wh*-DP$_i$ ... $[_{AgrSP}$ ... t_i ... $]]$

Here there are two possibilities to consider. If the *wh*-trace is not a subject, then there will be a subject in SpecAgrSP which, by (21'a), will mean that AgrSP is a BD, and so the *wh*-trace will not be in the same BD as the *wh*-DP. Alternatively, the *wh*-trace may be a subject. If it is Case-marked by I (remember that *wh*-traces must be Case-marked), (21'b) makes the smallest AgrSP containing the trace a BD, and so again the *wh*-trace is in a different binding domain from the WH. The only remaining possibility is that the trace is the (Case-marked) subject of an ECM or *for-to* infinitive; however, these infinitives do not allow *wh*-elements in their SpecCP (in the case of ECM infinitives this is because they simply lack CP altogether: see Chapter 2, 2.2.3):

(57a) *We believe who$_i$ John to like t$_i$

(57b) *We prefer which one$_i$ for John to see t$_i$

The conclusion is, then, that the *wh*-DP is outside the *wh*-trace's binding domain. So we can see that *wh*-traces are not anaphors. In fact, since they can be bound by a c-commanding element (the *wh*-DP) which must be outside their binding domain, *wh*-traces look rather like pronouns.

However, there is important evidence that *wh*-traces are *not* subject to Principle B. This comes from so-called 'crossover phenomena', originally discovered by Postal (1971). The phenomenon of crossover is illustrated by contrasts like the one in (58):

(58a) Which manager$_i$ t$_i$ thinks the players hate him$_i$?

(58b) *Which manager$_i$ does he$_i$ think the players hate t$_i$?

The contrast here is very sharp: (58a) is a quite innocuous sentence, whose meaning is very clear. Sentence (58b), on the other hand, is sharply ungrammatical (with the intended interpretation: it's fine if *he* is taken to mean someone other than the manager, but of course then *he* would have a different index). What goes wrong in (58b) is captured by the term 'crossover'; the *wh*-DP *which manager* 'crosses over' a coindexed pronoun on its way to SpecCP. Postal's original Crossover Constraint said something more or less to this effect.

However, if we look at (58b) in the light of the binding theory we can see something else. Applying (21'), we find that the *wh*-DP, *he*, and the trace are all in different binding domains:

(59) *[$_{CP1}$ Which manager$_i$ does [$_{AgrSP1}$ he$_i$ think [$_{CP2}$ [$_{AgrSP2}$ the players hate t$_i$]]]] ?

AgrSP$_1$ is a binding domain by (21'b), and AgrSP$_2$ by (21'a). So we see that *he* satisfies Principle B (as *him* does in the well-formed (58a)). The *wh*-movement meets all the defining criteria in (56a–f), so it must be the trace that's causing the ungrammaticality here. If the trace were subject to Principle B, it would be well-formed (like *him* in (58a) – there is no binder in its BD).

What seems to be the crucial difference between (58a) and (58b) is that, while in (58a) it is the trace that binds the pronoun, in (58b) *it is the pronoun that binds the trace*. In both cases, the trace is bound by the *wh*-DP, so that can't make the difference. The pronoun is not in the same BD as the trace in (58b), and so the only way that the pronoun binding the trace can lead to ungrammaticality is if the trace is subject to Principle C. Remember, Principle C requires R-expressions to be free, and so the pronoun binding the trace will violate this Principle. This happens in (58b) but not in (58a), and so that seems to make the difference.

You can only reach the conclusion that *wh*-traces are subject to Principle C by blithely ignoring the fact that *wh*-DPs themselves bind *wh*-traces. However, there is a principled way of leaving *wh*-phrases out of the picture. All the cases of binding relations we have considered so far have involved subject positions and complement positions. In other words, these are positions in which arguments of lexical heads (in almost all our examples, arguments of verbs) carry grammatical functions (see Section 2.1). Spec,CP is not such a position, and, as (57) states, Spec,CP is *the* position for categories that have undergone *wh*-movement. So, if we restrict the binding conditions to holding amongst grammatical-function positions, then we can exclude *wh*-DPs from the binding conditions altogether. And this means that *wh*-traces can be regarded as subject to Principle C.

The simplest way to make the moves described in the above paragraph is to define a class of argument positions, as follows:

(60a) A(rgument)-position: any position capable of bearing a grammatical function

(60b) Non-argument position (Á-position): the rest

Then we can say that binding theory is a theory of binding from A-positions. To make this clear, we can restate (20') as follows:

The Binding Principles (Revised):
(20') Principle A: an anaphor must be A-bound in its binding domain
Principle B: a pronoun must be A-free in its binding domain
Principle C: an R-expression must be A-free

Here 'A-bound' means 'coindexed with a c-commanding category in an A-position', and 'A-free' means 'not so coindexed' (without saying anything about the possibility of being bound from an Á-position, notice).

In Chapter 1 (1.2.3) I introduced the idea that some functional categories are L-related while others aren't. I didn't really define L-relatedness beyond alluding to some notion of 'association' with a lexical category. In 2.6 we saw that V-related functional heads have V-features that trigger movement and checking. Chomsky and Lasnik (1993) suggest that the notion of L-relatedness can be used to define A-positions. They propose that an A-position would be the Specifier of an L-related head; so Spec,AgrSP and Spec,AgrOP, for example, would be L-related positions. C, on the other hand, would not be. *wh*-phrases always move to Spec,CP and so never occupy an L-related Specifier. We can connect this idea with the definition of A-position in (60) in terms of the proposal we made in Chapter 2 (2.1) that grammatical functions are defined by Case theory, that is, as the Specifiers of categories which have features which can license arguments of a given head. Since AgrS and AgrO have features which license arguments of V, they are V-related (in addition to being able to license V itself). Again, C can't license either an argument of V or V itself, and so it's not L-related. A-binding can now be defined as binding from an L-related position, and the binding principles stated as in (20') above.

3.3.2.4 Conclusion

A consideration of the properties of *wh*-traces has led us, via the notion of L-relatedness, to the conclusion that *wh*-traces are R-expressions. We have now looked at the three XP-level empty categories introduced in Section 2.4 and seen how they obey the binding principles (which has led to certain further refinements of those principles along the way). So let's make the relevant modifications to Table 3.1:

Table 3.3 DP types as classified by [± anaphor] and [± pronoun] (revised)

	Anaphor	*Pronoun*
reflexives, reciprocals, DP-traces	+	−
pronouns	−	+
PRO	+	+
R-expressions, *wh*-traces	−	−

The nice thing about Table 3.3 is that we see that the empty categories are mostly nothing special from the perspective of binding theory, which is what we want, since – as I've already said – the only special thing about empty categories is phonological: they aren't pronounced. Ideally, then, for each class of overt DPs as defined by [± anaphor] and [± pronoun], there should be both empty and overt DPs. As Table 3.3 shows, this is true for [+ anaphor, – pronoun] and for [– anaphor, – pronoun]. It is not true for the other two classes. Let's try to see what's going on here.

In fact, we already have all the elements in place to deduce why this is so for [+ anaphor, + pronominal]. The empty category in this class is PRO. Our version of the PRO theorem, given in 3.2.2, tells us that any category with these features can have no BD and so no Case. But overt DPs require Case, as we saw in Chapter 2. So there can be no overt pronominal anaphors.

We have no such good reason to suppose that there are no empty counterparts of 'pure' pronouns, however. Obviously, there can be overt [– anaphor, + pronoun] elements, so why not empty ones? In fact, there is good evidence for an empty element of this type. This element is quite important from a comparative perspective, and so it deserves a whole section to itself.

3.3.3 Pro and Null Subjects

3.3.3.1 Pro

The evidence for an empty [– anaphor, + pronoun] element is comparative (which is all to the good, since comparative considerations have up until now taken something of a back seat in this chapter). Empty pronouns clearly exist in some languages, but not, apparently, in English. The empty element which is [– anaphor, + pronoun], is written *pro* (known as 'little *pro*' to distinguish it from the larger PRO – 'big PRO').

The main evidence that *pro* exists in some languages comes from the fact that overt pronouns are not always required where they would be in a language like English. Let's restrict attention here to subject pronouns, although there's been plenty of work on empty object pronouns. The basic fact is really quite well known, and very easy to state: in some languages subject pronouns can be apparently omitted, while in others this is not possible. The following examples illustrate this:

(61a) — parla italiano (Italian)
      he/she speaks Italian

(61b) — habla español (Spanish)
he/she speaks Spanish

(61c) * — parle français (French; OK as an imperative, bad as a declara
tive) he/she speaks French

(61d) * — speaks English

Languages like Italian and Spanish are known as 'null-subject languages', for the rather obvious reason that they allow pronominal subjects of finite clauses to be null. Lots of languages are like Italian and Spanish: Portuguese, Rumanian, Catalan, Latin, Greek, Bulgarian, Serbo-Croatian, Chinese, Japanese, Thai, Korean – indeed the majority of the world's languages.

There are a number of reasons to suppose that there is an empty pronoun in subject position in examples like (61a and b). One is the simple cross-linguistic observation that some languages, like English and French, require such pronouns to be overtly present. Another is that the interpretation of the subject here is clearly pronominal: examples like (61a and b) are understood as having subjects that refer to any contextually relevant individual, where, as with overt pronouns, 'contextually relevant' covers a range of possibilities (see the discussion of English pronouns in 3.1.2). Third, and most important, the null subject interacts with the binding principles. Since it is a pronoun which always appears in the subject position of a finite clause, we expect that it can have an antecedent in another clause (and (61a and b) show that it does not require an antecedent):

(62) Gianni$_i$ ha detto che *pro$_i$* parla italiano
John has said that — speaks Italian
'John$_i$ said that he$_i$ speaks Italian'

We can't directly illustrate the effects of Principle B, however, in that this variety of *pro* is restricted to the subject position of finite clauses, and so can never have a c-commanding antecedent in its binding domain. Nevertheless, we can further illustrate how *pro* interacts with the binding theory by showing how it creates contexts of crossover, just like its overt counterpart in English examples like (58). If we translate (58a and b) into Italian, using null subjects where possible, the results are as in English:

(63a) Che allenatore$_i$ t$_i$ pensa che i giocatori lo$_i$ odiano ? (= (59a))
'Which manager$_i$ thinks the players hate him$_i$?'

(63b) *Che allenatore$_i$ *pro$_i$* pensa che i giocatori odiano t$_i$? (= (59b))
'Which manager$_i$ does he$_i$ think the players hate t$_i$?'

Null subjects seem, then, to have the syntactic and semantic properties of overt pronouns. Obviously, they lack the phonological property of being pronounced, but that is a secondary concern. We have every reason, aside from a superficial phonological detail, to consider that null subjects are *bona fide* pronouns. So we have a [– anaphor, + pronoun] empty category.

3.3.3.2 *The Crosslinguistic Occurrence of* Pro

I have been tacitly assuming that the other empty categories are universal. At least for traces, this seems justified: DP-traces appear wherever there are grammatical-function changing operations like passive, and the vast majority of languages seem to have this kind of possibility. Of course, if we adopt the checking theory outlined in Section 2.6, then all languages have DP-traces either overtly or covertly. Similarly, all languages have *wh*-movement; in many languages this is clearly an overt process, and indeed it may be in all languages (as Watanabe (1992) argueS). On the other hand, it is not certain that PRO is universal. Certainly, many languages lack infinitives (Modern Greek, Serbo-Croatian, Bulgarian and Albanian are well-known examples), although this may not directly entail their lacking PRO (PRO appears in gerunds in English, as well, like *John quit [PRO smoking]*, and languages lacking infinitives often seem to have this kind of construction). And, as we have seen, not all languages have *pro*, English being among them. In fact, it is rather natural to think that traces are universal – because movement is universal; but that the inventory of pronouns can vary from one language to another. In the case of overt pronouns this is clearly true; for example, some languages have dual pronouns (like Old English *wit, git* 'we two, you two') and many others don't.

If the above speculation is true, we have to ask what determines whether a given language has *pro*. The naïve observation is that languages like Italian and Portuguese have enough information in their verbal morphology to permit the person and number of *pro* to be recognized, while a language such as English does not. We can see how this idea works if we compare some simple verbal paradigms of English and Italian:

(64) *Italian*   *English*

Present tense:

parl-o   I speak
parl-i   you speak
parl-a   he/she/it speak-s
parl-iamo   we speak
parl-ate   you speak
parl-ano   they speak

Past tense:

parl-ai   I spoke
parl-asti   you spoke
parl-ò   he/she/it spoke
parl-ammo   we spoke
parl-aste   you spoke
parl-arono   they spoke

In both tenses here, the Italian verb has a distinct ending for every person.

English, on the other hand, only distinguishes the third singular present form in terms of person (although the *speak* – *spoke* distinction, of course, marks tense). It's immediately obvious, then, that any given Italian verb form can give enough information to make the person/number specification of *pro* clear, while this is just not possible with English verbs.

Luigi Rizzi (1986a) proposed that this intuition be incorporated into the theory by imposing two requirements on *pro*. The first is a 'formal licensing' requirement, which basically states that *pro* must be in a position that can be Case-marked by its licensing head. Clearly, if *pro* is in SpecAgrSP it will be in a position capable of being Case-marked by AgrS. The second requirement is that *pro*'s content can be recovered from the features of its Case-marker (the identification requirement). Since we're dealing with null subjects, the licenser/Case-marker for *pro* is AgrS. The Case requirement excludes *pro* from infinitives (although we predict that it would be available in agreeing infinitives in European Portuguese (see 2.2.2); this is the correct prediction). The second requirement is met where AgrS has a rich enough overt specification to permit the recovery of *pro*'s content, as in Italian, though not in English. So we see why Italian allows *pro* to appear in subject position of finite clauses, while English doesn't.

This approach directly takes up the naïve observation that the possibility of null subjects correlates with the richness of subject agreement marking. And, when we compare English and Italian, things seem pretty black and white. However, a large grey area emerges when we bring in other languages. Compare the following paradigms, and see if you can guess which might be the null-subject languages and which not:

(65)

German	Icelandic	French	Rumanian
werf-e	kast-a	jett-e	dorm
wirf-st	kast-ar	jett-es	dorm-i
wirf-t	kast-ar	jett-e	doarm-e
werf-en	köst-um	jet-ons	dorm-im
werf-t	kast-ið	jet-ez	dorm-iţi
werf-en	kast-a	jett-ent	dorm
'throw'	'throw'	'throw'	'sleep'

Out of a maximum of six forms and a minimum of one, German and French both appear to have five here, and neither are null-subject languages. In fact, the counting here may be a little off. Most German verbs have four forms rather than five, as the third singular and second plural are the same (such as *er/ihr arbeitet* 'he/you (Pl) work(s)'). Similarly, French phonology notoriously differs from its orthography, so that the second singular is pronounced exactly the same as the first and third singular (/ʒɛt/) and the third plural is also pronounced this way in all except liaison contexts. On the other hand, the Rumanian verb has five forms and *is* a null-subject language, while Icelandic has five and isn't. It may be that in the grey area there's simply indeterminacy, and languages simply opt to license *pro* in subject position or not. This, however, would seriously weaken the theory sketched above (note that we then ultimately end up listing which languages in the grey area allow null subjects and which do not; and lists are anathema to theory, as you should have gathered by now). Alternatively, and more interestingly, it may be that the naïve theory only tells part of the story. This wouldn't be surprising, since it is based on a very simple pre-theoretical observation.

Let me just mention two factors that probably intervene here. One is whether a language has overt expletive pronouns like *it* and *there*. English of course does, as do French (*il*), German (*es*), and Icelandic (það). Italian, Spanish, and Rumanian don't, however. Here are the sentences for 'it's raining' in all these languages (I should point out that the 'meteorological expletive' that appears in sentences like these is not quite typical of expletives in various ways, but I'm using it here since these sentences readily illustrate this particular fact):

(66a) Il pleut   (French)

(66b) Es regnet   (German)

(66c) það rigndi (Icelandic)

(66d) – piove   (Italian)

(66e) – llueve   (Spanish)

There is no possibility of leaving out the pronoun in French, German, or Icelandic, since these are not null-subject languages. Conversely, in this case, Italian, Spanish, and Rumanian do not allow a pronoun: the word-for-word literal translation of *il pleut* in Italian, for example, would be the ungrammatical **ciò piove*. This is different to the situation that obtains with examples like those in (61a and b), where a pronoun can be included, like: *lui parla italiano* 'he speaks Italian'. So perhaps the simple presence of overt expletive pronouns is correlated with the impossibility of null subjects. This is an avenue which has been pursued by many researchers trying to make sense of the grey area.

The second factor is the verb-second constraint (see Chapter 1, 1.4.2.4). All the non-English Germanic languages are verb second, and none of them allow null subjects. In fact, it seems that we can generalize as follows:

(67) No verb-second language is a fully null-subject language

(We have to specify a '*fully* verb-second language' because there are some interesting halfway cases, notably Old French, but I won't go into that here.) Nobody really knows why this generalization holds, but, in any case, it opens up the possibility that German and Icelandic have enough morphology to be null-subject languages, but that their verb-second nature prevents this.

The previous two paragraphs have touched on some of the comparative issues connected with predicting whether a given language will allow *pro* in subject position or not. Once again, these matters are all highly inconclusive, but I think that they make clear the extent to which it is probably necessary to go beyond the naïve theory.

One last point on the naïve theory, which represents the biggest challenge of all for this approach. Many languages, mostly spoken in East Asia (although from many different language families), lack agreement morphology entirely – or anything that is recognizably agreement morphology in the European sense – and yet allow null subjects quite readily. Chinese is a case in point, as the following example shows (see Huang (1984)):

(68a) Zhangsan shuo – mingtian   bu   bi   lai
      Zhangsan say   he tomorrow not need come
      'Zhangsan says he need not come tomorrow'

This appears to fly in the face of the naïve theory entirely, and many people have taken these facts to be the final nail in the coffin of that approach. However, there are two points to be made here.

One possibility is that these languages do not allow null subjects by the theory I've just sketched, but that they have some other property – Factor X – which does allow them. In a seminal paper Huang (1984), following an idea due to Haj Ross, points out that it's possible to distinguish at least informally between 'hot' languages – those which supply the consumer with all the information required in an upfront way – and 'cool' ones, which require that the consumer put some effort into getting the information. (This distinction between 'hot' and 'cool' media goes back to McLuhan (1964).) The European languages we've been discussing here would be hot languages, so if you don't phonologically specify a subject pronoun you have to be able to recover its content from the verbal inflection – the naïve theory. East Asian languages, on the other hand, are cool, and permit the 'dropping', or lack of phonological specification, of all kinds of material, not least pronominal subjects. This idea is supported by the fact that these languages allow null objects (but lack object agreement). The 'coolness' of Chinese can be illustrated by the following discourse (again taken from Huang (1984)):

(68b) Speaker A: Zhangsan kanjian Lisi le   ma?
                 Zhangsan see   Lisi ASP Q?
                 'Did Zhangsan see Lisi?'

      Speaker B: (a) ta   kanjian   ta   le
                      he   see   he   ASP
                 (b) –   kanjian   ta   le
                                see   he   ASP
                 (c) ta   kanjian   –   le
                      he   see   ASP
                 (d) –   kanjian   –   le
                                see   ASP
                 'He saw him'

> (e) wo cai [– kanjian – le]
> I guess – saw – ASP
> 'I guess he saw him'
>
> (f) Zhangsan shuo [– kanjian – le]
> Zhangsan say he saw him

In other words, there may be an overarching distinction, internal to which the naïve theory sits quite happily.

The second possibility is similar, in that it posits a superordinate distinction to be made between East-Asian-type languages and the European ones discussed earlier. Then, internal to the European languages, a version of the naïve theory described above can be maintained. This approach is essentially based on the idea that nothing follows from nothing. That is, the complete absence of agreement marking in a language tells you nothing about whether abstract agreement can license *pro*. In this context, it's important to see that non-null-subject European languages like English and French, do have agreement marking – they just don't have enough. In East Asian languages, on the other hand, agreement is completely 'switched off', and so anything goes as far as the possibility of *pro* is concerned. This proposal was made by Rizzi in the appendix to his 1986a paper, and it seems like a reasonable way of making sense of what is going on in the East Asian languages. Needless to say, though, the idea is controversial.

3.3.3.3 The Null Subject Parameter

The presence of null subjects has been argued – by Rizzi (1982) – to correlate with other variant possibilities. I'll mention just one here, a phenomenon that has become known (rather misleadingly) as **free inversion**. We already mentioned in Section 2.3.1 that languages like Italian and Spanish allow the subject to appear in a postverbal position. Here are the examples from (37) in Chapter 2:

> (69a) È arrivato Gianni
> Is-**3Sg** arrived John (**Sg**)
> 'John has arrived'

> (69b) Hanno telefonato molti studenti
> Have-**3Pl** phoned many students (**pl**)
> 'Many students have phoned'

> (69c) Vinceremo noi
> Will-win-**1Pl** we (**1Pl**)
> 'We will win'

In that section, we also saw that the subject in (69a) is in fact in the direct-object position. This was one of the arguments for the unaccusative hypothesis. So let's leave aside (69a) here.

The kind of inversion seen in (69b and c) is different from the AgrS-to-C movement that we looked at in Chapter 1 (1.4.2.2) in two important respects.

First, it is not subject to root-embedded asymmetries. Examples (69b and c) can easily be embedded in any kind of subordinate clause:

(70a) il giorno in cui hanno telefonato molti studenti
the day in which have telephoned many students
'the day that many students telephoned'

(70b) l'idea che vinceremo noi (è sbagliata)
the idea that will-win we (is mistaken)
'the idea that we'll win (is mistaken)'

In Section 1.4.2.2 we saw that root-embedded asymmetries are characteristic of AgrS-to-C movement. The lack of such asymmetries with free inversion implies that this operation does not involve AgrS-to-C movement.

Second, when AgrS-to-C movement takes place with a compound tense, only the auxiliary moves to a position preceding the subject. The English and French examples in (52) of Chapter 1 – which I repeat here as (71) – show this:

(71a) Which girl has he kissed?

(71b) Quelle fille a-t-il embrassée?   (= (71a))

The derived order is *auxiliary–subject–main verb*. If you compare this with the examples in (69b), however, you'll see that the order is *auxiliary–main verb–subject*.

Rather than posit some kind of AgrS-movement, then, the usual analysis of free inversion places the subject in a special postverbal position. AgrS is in its usual position. This, of course, will account for the fact that there are no root-embedded asymmetries–there is no AgrS-to-C movement. Both the exact nature of the postverbal position and the mechanism which gives case to the DP in it (we can see that this is Nominative Case because it agrees with V) are unclear. We'll leave these points aside here.

The link between 'free inversion' and null subjects is this: there's a general principle that says that SpecAgrSP must be filled. This principle is usually called the Extended Projection Principle, or EPP. The EPP appears to be violated in (70b and c). What occupies SpecAgrSP here? The answer is *pro*. In fact, this is expletive *pro*, similar to the one that appears in sentences like (67d–f). Because *pro* appears in SpecAgrSP, the subject is able to appear in its special postverbal position. I mentioned that the postverbal subject receives Nominative Case, as we can see from the fact that it agrees with the verb. What about *pro*? It seems that it is enough for it to be in a context of potential Case-marking by its licenser (AgrS) – this is why the formal licensing condition on *pro* was stated in a slightly tortuous way above.

In a non-null-subject language, an overt expletive pronoun would appear here and require Nominative Case, and then a postverbal subject wouldn't get Nominative Case. This is why the French and English examples corresponding to (69b and c) are ungrammatical:

(72a) *There have telephoned many students   (= (69b))

(72b) ??Il a téléphoné trois amis
     'There have telephoned three friends'

(73a) *There will win we   (= (69c))

(73b) *Il va vaincre nous

(The English and French equivalents of (69a) are better, as long as the postverbal subject is indefinite – we briefly looked at the relevant English examples in 2.3.2.) So we can see that the possibility of 'free inversion' is related to the possibility of *pro* occupying Spec,AgrSP, the null subject parameter. In Chapter 4 (4.3.2) we'll see another correlate of the null-subject parameter that is important for the theory of locality.

3.3.4 Conclusion

In this section we've seen the *Lectures on Government and Binding* version of binding theory and a number of its ramifications. The key points are:

- the binding principles: (20')
- the definition of binding domain: (21')
- the distribution of DPs according to [± anaphor, ± pronoun]: Table 3.1
- the distribution of empty categories according to [± anaphor, ± pronoun]: Table 3.3

In fact, we should revise Table 3.3 so that it includes *pro:*

Table 3.4 DP types as classified by [± anaphor] and [± pronoun]
(2nd revision)

	Anaphor	*Pronoun*
reflexives, reciprocals, DP-traces	+	–
pronouns, *pro*	–	+
PRO	+	+
R-expressions, *wh*-traces	–	–

The principal issue for comparative linguistics that we discussed here concerns the crosslinguistic distribution of *pro* (although I suggested that the crosslinguistic distribution of PRO is probably also an issue, but one which seems to have received less attention). Nevertheless, you may have noticed that all the examples that I gave in the basic discussion of binding theory were in English. This is because anaphors in particular appear to have a rather varied crosslinguistic distribution, one which, at least at first sight, doesn't accord very well with Principle A. Now it's time to look at this. At the same time, for reasons that I hope will become apparent, I want to take up again the issue of the relationship between DP-traces and anaphors.

3.4 Movement and Long-Distance Anaphora

In the previous section (3.3.2) we saw that DP-traces have a very similar distribution to reflexives and reciprocals. This is the justification for putting them in the [+ anaphor, – pronominal] category in Table 3.3. However, I mentioned that there might be another approach to accounting for the distributional similarities. Table 3.3 assimilates DP-traces to anaphors, but why shouldn't we try assimilating anaphors to DP-traces? We know that DP-traces are subject to a general locality requirement, as seen in the fact that DP-movement can only move a DP to the nearest possible landing site (see (47d)), although the locality requirement won't be revealed in full until Chapter 4 (see 4.5.1). The possibility that opens up, then, is that the distribution of anaphors can be accounted for by a locality condition on movement. This would imply that English reflexives and reciprocals, at least, undergo covert movement and is one idea that I want to discuss here.

A related question has to do with the typology of reflexives: there is clear evidence that reflexives in many languages seem to be able to have antecedents that are outside their BD. This phenomenon has become known as 'long-distance' (LD) anaphora. Since we know that movement possibilities of various kinds can vary crosslinguistically (see in particular the discussion of checking theory in 2.6) we might think that LD anaphora is connected to different movement possibilities for anaphors. In this section, I want to look at the crosslinguistic evidence that the distribution of at least some anaphors in some languages can be explained in terms of movement. At the same time, this survey will give at least some idea of the kinds of crosslinguistic variation that are found in the area of anaphora.

3.4.1 A Movement Analysis of English Reflexives

Let's start by looking at the French counterparts of simple English sentences like (3a):

(74) Jean-Paul se   déteste
     Jean-Paul SE   hates
     'Jean-Paul hates himself'

Here, instead of a postverbal anaphor of the sort found in English, French has the preverbal clitic reflexive *se*. Now, French is an SVO language, and so it's reasonable to think that *se*, which obviously has the grammatical function of direct object here, has moved from object position. So (74) has a representation something like (74'):

(74') Jean-Paul$_i$ se$_i$ déteste t$_i$

In his seminal work on French syntax, Kayne (1975) showed that the relation between pronominal clitics and their traces is subject to the Specified Subject Condition (as well as arguing in detail for a clitic-movement rule).

So French provides direct evidence that reflexives can move and thereby create an anaphoric relation with their traces.

Chomsky (1986a) proposes that English reflexives may be like *se* at LF. So the LF representation for (3a) would be (3a'):

(3a) Brian$_i$ hates himself$_i$

(3a') Brian$_i$ himself$_i$-hates t$_i$

(Remember that French verbs overtly move to AgrS, but English ones don't (see 1.4.1.1), and so *se* is attached to the verb in AgrS in (74'); if English verbs also raise to AgrS at LF (see 2.6.5), then *himself* may be in a precisely analogous configuration in (3a').) Chomsky suggests that there are really two locality conditions at work in (3a'): one is the condition on movement, and the other is the constraint that, at LF, a reflexive must agree with the Specifier to whose head it is attached (Chomsky puts this in terms of government, but that's because he was working with a different definition of government from the one adopted here).

The implication of the first condition is that the 'distance' between a reflexive and its antecedent is completely deducible from constraints on movement. I've been assuming that the movement in question is DP-movement, but you may have spotted that adjoining the reflexive DP to AgrS, a head, would violate the Structure Preservation Constraint (see (47e)). If we treat the movement in question as head-movement, we run into problems with the Head Movement Constraint (see (67) of 1.4.2.3). Although these points are problematic, we have exactly the same problems with movement of *se* in (74), and so they are not artefacts of the LF-movement analysis of reflexives. Clitic-movement seems to combine properties of DP-movement and head-movement; this fact suggests that it is a composite operation, but I won't go further into this here.

The second condition – that the reflexive's antecedent be in the Specifier of the head to which the reflexive attaches – has two interesting consequences. The first is that we can immediately understand why reflexives must agree in person, number, and gender with their antecedents. The Specifier-head relation is the structural correlate *par excellence* of agreement. Moreover, we saw in 2.6.4 that when a head X adjoins to another head Y, X is also in an abstract agreement relation with Y. So the reflexive must agree in number and person with AgrS (AgrS has no gender features in English) and in person, number and gender with the DP in Spec, AgrSP. This is why sentences like (75) are bad, even though they satisfy Principle A:

(75) *I$_i$ hate themselves$_i$

In short, this proposal makes it possible to capture the agreement component in anaphoric relations.

Second, Chomsky's proposal can capture the 'subject-orientation' of anaphors. In many languages, as we shall see in the next section, there are reflexives that can only have subjects as antecedents. In fact, this is not the case for English reflexives, as examples like (76) show:

(76a) We spoke to Brian$_i$ about himself$_i$

(76b) We showed Mick$_i$ some photographs of himself$_i$

Here, we have to say that the reflexives attach to a lower position. If we adopt the clause structure put forward in 1.4.3.2, then AgrO would be a natural suggestion. However, if a given reflexive in a given language is subject-orientated, then we can straightforwardly capture this by saying that it must attach to AgrS – either overtly or covertly. Again, we know that clitics vary in their placement properties from language to language, so it's not outlandish to think that reflexive pronouns may vary in a similar way.

3.4.2 Long-Distance Anaphora

Now it's time to see how the ideas that I've been discussing so far in this chapter can do some crosslinguistic work in accounting for some of the variation in the distribution of reflexives that is found in various languages. My presentation follows that of Koster and Reuland (1991:10ff.).

LD anaphors seem to have five main properties crosslinguistically. I'll now take them one by one.

First property: LD anaphors allow an antecedent outside their binding domain. Clearly, this is defining property of LD anaphors, and it is what gives them their name. We can illustrate this with the examples in (77):

(77a) Anna$_i$ telur [þig$_j$ hafa svikið sig$_{i/j}$]   (Icelandic)
  Anna believes you to-have betrayed self
  'Anna believes you to have betrayed {your/her}self'

(77b) Jan$_i$ liet [mij voor zich$_i$ werken]   (Dutch)
  John made me for self work
  'John made me work for himself'

(77c) Zhangsan$_i$ renwei [Lisi$_j$ hai-le ziji$_{i/j}$]   (Chinese)
  Zhangsan think   Lisi   hurt   self
  'Zhangsan (m.) thinks Lisi (f.) hurt {him/her}self'

To see how these examples are problematic, let's look again at the relevant English translations:

(78a) *Anna$_i$ believes [you to have betrayed herself$_i$]

(78b) *John$_i$ made [me work for himself$_i$]

(78c) *Zhangsan$_i$ thinks [Lisi hurt himself$_i$]

All of the sentences in (78) are quite clearly ungrammatical in English. And the binding theory that I described in the previous section tells us why: in each case the lower clause (bracketed in (78)) is a binding domain by the definition in (21') (option (a)), while reflexives are subject to Principle A of

(20'), which requires anaphors to have an antecedent in an A-position in their binding domain. So the Icelandic, Dutch, and Chinese data in (77) present a problem for the binding theory as we've seen it so far. The question is: what is the difference between English and these other languages that underlies the contrast between (77) and (78)? Quite a few other languages have some kind of LD anaphora: Norwegian, Danish, Latin, Italian, Polish, Hungarian, Finnish, Japanese, and Korean, to name but a few. In fact, it's beginning to look as if English is rather untypical in not admitting sentences like (77).

One possibility is to suppose that what we've seen up to now is the *English* binding theory, and that there are others which permit LD anaphora. One version of this idea would deny that any of the binding theory is universal: perhaps it's all just a weird idiosyncracy of English. However, especially after all our effort in the earlier sections, it makes more sense to be conservative: something isn't universal about the binding theory that I've presented, as the differences between English and the other languages show. But let's try and restrict that something as much as we can. In doing this, of course, we'll really be developing further the principles and parameters approach: we've got the **principles** of binding (we think), now we need to look for the parameters. In the next few paragraphs, we'll see good empirical reasons to suppose that much of the binding theory as we've presented it up to now can stay intact: the locus of the parametric variation that we're interested in seems to lie with morphological properties of reflexives (note how this accords with the general view of parameters associated with minimalism that we discussed in 2.6).

Second property: LD anaphors tend to be subject-orientated. I introduced the concept of a subject-orientated anaphor in the previous subsection. To quickly recap: a subject-orientated anaphor can only have a subject as its antecedent. English reflexives aren't restricted to subject-orientation, as the sentences in (76) show. On the other hand, the reflexives in (77) are subject-orientated in the sense that, although they can have antecedents that are apparently outside their BD, these antecedents can only be subjects. This is illustrated in (79) (there is no Dutch example here because in Dutch it is very hard to have an LD anaphor in the complement of the right kind of verb, probably for independent reasons):

(79a) *Eg_i lofaði $Önnu_j$ [PRO_i að kyssa sig_j]   (Icelandic)
  I   promised Anna   to kiss   self
  'I promised Anna to kiss herself'

(79b) $Wangwu_i$ shuo Zhangsan$_j$ zengsong gei Lisi$_k$ yipian guanyu
   Wangwu   say Zhangsan give   to Lisi   one   about
   $ziji_{i/j/*k}$ de   wenchang
   self   DE   article
   'Wangwu says that Zhangsan gave an article about him/himself to Lisi'

As I suggested in the previous section, subject-orientation can be handled by a movement analysis of reflexives which requires them to attach to AgrS at LF. LD anaphors, therefore, would be required to attach to the AgrS of a higher clause. For example, in (77a), where *sig* takes *Anna* as its antecedent, there would be an LF that looks like (80) (in relevant respects):

(80) $Anna_i$ .. sig_i-$AgrS_1$ .. $[_{AgrSP2}$ .... $AgrS_2$ ... t_i]

Example (80) can get the interpretation right, if we adopt Chomsky's (1986a) assumptions as described in the previous subsection. However, the problem of LD-anaphora has now become the problem of long-distance movement of reflexives. Why is *sig* able to move out of its clause in (80)? Whether we regard reflexive-movement as DP-movement, head-movement, or a composite of these operations, such a 'long' movement shouldn't be possible. In general, clitic pronouns in Romance cannot undergo this kind of 'long' movement, and so the correspondence with that kind of movement appears to break down. So the reflexive-movement approach here seems to solve one problem at the cost of creating another one.

Third property: LD-anaphora is restricted to reflexives, while reciprocals do not allow it. This is a very interesting, and somewhat mysterious, fact about LD anaphora. The examples in (81) show the contrasts that are found in the languages in question (I've left Chinese out, as reciprocal expressions don't seem to involve bound anaphora in quite the same way in this language):

(81a) $*þeir_i$ skipuðu $mér_j$ [PRO_j að raka hvorn $annan_i$]   (Icelandic)
       They   ordered me   to shave each other
       '$They_i$ ordered me_j [PRO_j to shave each $other_i$]'

(81b) $*Zij_i$ lieten [mij voor $elkaar_i$ werken]   (Dutch)
       They made   me for each-other work
       '$They_i$ made me work for each $other_i$.'

As you can immediately see, the sentences in (81) are ungrammatical in exactly the same way as their English counterparts (look at the English translations). There have been no clearly reported cases of LD-reciprocals. So, whatever the special property of LD anaphors is, we know it must be restricted to reflexives. Incidentally, the absence of LD-reciprocals shows that something very like the 'English' kind of binding domain, the one defined in (21'), is operative in these languages. The ungrammaticality of (81) can readily be accounted for by saying that the reciprocals fail to be bound in their binding domain: they do not satisfy Principle A with respect to a binding domain defined as in (21').

Reflexives, then, seem to have some special ability to 'escape' this BD. We've entertained the hypothesis that this special dispensation for reflexives consists in their ability to move out of their BD and form a Spec-head relation with a higher subject, although we've also noted that this idea has its problems. Rather than speculate further, let's look at some more properties of LD reflexives (as we can now confidently call them).

Fourth property: LD reflexives are morphologically simple. This very important observation is sometimes known as Pica's Generalization, after the linguist who first noticed it (see Pica (1987); although see also Faltz (1977)).
The first thing we can note is that the LD reflexives in the examples in (77)
are all monomorphemic: Icelandic *sig*, Dutch *zich*, and Chinese *ziji* are, as the
glosses to (77) indicate, single morphemes meaning basically 'self'. This is also
true of the LD reflexives in many of the other languages that I mentioned
above: Norwegian *seg*, Danish *sig*, Italian *sè*, Japanese *zibun*, and Korean *caki*.
Some of these, as well as those in languages like Latin and Polish, have case
morphology; but the important point is that these reflexive forms are simple
in the sense that their stem consists exclusively of a morpheme meaning
roughly 'self', rather than being compound in the way that English reflexives
are.

A second point is that, if this kind of morphological simplicity plays a role
in allowing reflexives to be LD-bound, then we can see why English lacks
LD-reflexives: there is no 'pure' reflexive form *self* in English that can stand
alone.

Third, and this is very important given that we want the most conservative
parametrization of binding theory possible, most of the languages which have
LD reflexives that consist just of the 'self' morpheme also have compound
reflexives that are morphologically much more like English reflexives. So
Icelandic has forms such as *sjálfur sig* ('self's self') and *hann sjálfur* ('himself') alongside *sig*; Dutch has *zichzelf* (self's self) as well as simple *zich*;
Chinese has *taziji* ('himself') in addition to *ziji*, and so on. This state of affairs
is fairly typical.

Now here comes the good part: *the compound reflexives are typically not
LD.* We can illustrate this with the following examples, which should be compared and contrasted with (77):

(82a) *Jon$_i$ segir að Maria elski sjalfan sig$_i$ (Icelandic)
    John says that Mary loves self's self

(82b) *Jan$_i$ liet mij voor zichzelf$_i$ werken   (Dutch)
    John let me for himself work

(82c) Zhangsan$_i$ renwei [Lisi$_j$ hai-le ta-ziji$_{*i/j}$]   (Chinese)
    Zhangsan (m.) think Lisi (f.) hurt {*him/her}self

The ungrammatical variants of these examples are in fact just like the English
translations, which were given in (78). What they clearly show is, first, that
LD-anaphora is a property which is restricted to morphologically simple
reflexives. Second, these examples back up the conclusion we drew from the
absence of LD-reciprocals: that the definition of BD in (21') is valid in these
languages. And, third, as we already mentioned above, the ungrammaticality
of English examples like (78) isn't really due to a funny property of English,
but English lacks LD reflexives because it doesn't have a morphologically
simple reflexive *self*.

This property of LD reflexives has been exploited by many authors, beginning with Pica (1987), in developing movement analyses of LD anaphora. The basic idea is that LD reflexives undergo head-movement to AgrS (not DP-movement, as Chomsky (1986a) proposed). The Structure Preservation Constraint, which, remember, also applies to head-movement (see 2.6.3 (91)), will then prevent any non-head element from undergoing this movement. If we then make the simple and natural assumption that morphologically simple reflexives ('self' in the various languages) are heads, while morphologically complex reflexives are DPs, then we can see why only morphologically simple reflexives can be LD reflexives. We could also add that reciprocals can never be LD because they are usually morphologically complex. Pica's generalization thus supports the idea that at least some reflexives undergo movement. More precisely, it seems that LD-reflexives undergo a kind of head-movement.

Fifth property: outside of the binding domain there is no complementarity with pronouns. We saw in Section 3.1 that there is a basic complementarity between reflexives and pronouns. Principles A and B capture this, by opposing the requirement of being free (pronouns) to that of being bound (anaphors) in the same domain, the binding domain. If some reflexives in some languages are not subject to (the straightforward version of) Principle A, then it makes sense to ask about the complementarity with pronouns.

To show that this is how things work, we need both to show that pronouns are in complementary distribution with non-LD reflexives and that they are not in complementary distribution with LD reflexives. Since we know that LD reflexives are possible in contexts like (77) and that non-LD reflexives are not possible in this context, we simply need to show that pronouns are possible here (which is what we'd expect, given that Principle B is satisfied here: see English examples like *Anna$_i$ believes you to have betrayed her$_i$*). The examples in (83) show this:

(83a) Jon$_i$ segir að Maria elski hann$_i$ (Icelandic)
      John says that Mary loves him

(83b) Jan$_i$ liet [mij voor hem$_i$ werken] (Dutch)
      John let me for him work
      'John$_i$ let me work for him$_i$.'

Again, this situation confirms that in fact the standard notions of binding domain in (21') and the standard versions of Principles A and B in (20') apply in these languages. It also shows that LD reflexives are, as it were, outside the purview of Principles A and B.

In conclusion, we see that we are able to maintain a fairly conservative position with regard to binding theory. In fact, we can leave it unchanged, although we add that certain elements – morphologically simple reflexives that adjoin to AgrS – can take an antecedent under Specifier-head agreement, as suggested by Chomsky (1986a). These reflexives are exceptional in many languages in having the LD property. A plausible account for this is that they are able to undergo head-movement out of their clause, although the conditions that force and permit this movement are far from clear. In any case, we've seen that the existence of this extremely interesting (and widespread) phenomenon does not substantially disturb the core of binding theory. In Section 3.5, we'll see a theory that takes into account a much wider range of data (some of it from English) and develops an alternative to the 'standard' binding theory that we've been looking at up to now in this chapter.

3.5 Reflexivity

In this last section on binding theory I want to present a rather different kind of approach, as adopted in recent work by Tanya Reinhart and Eric Reuland (separately and together, although the most important articles are probably Reinhart and Reuland (1991, 1993)). The approach both builds on the 'standard' binding theory that we presented in 3.2 and 3.3 and incorporates many of the facts about LD reflexives that we saw in the previous section. Reciprocals are not really treated, however. It also provides interesting solutions to several long-standing problems for standard binding theory. The basic idea is that the features [± anaphor, ± pronoun] should be replaced by features of reflexivization and referentiality. In what follows I'll try to summarize the principal points of this theory.

3.5.1 Types of Anaphors and Types of Anaphora

We saw in the previous section that there are two types of reflexives: LD reflexives, those which are morphologically simple, and morphologically complex reflexives which are never LD. Reinhart and Reuland call the first type SE anaphors and the second type SELF anaphors. Let's look at what they say about each of these in turn.

Reinhart and Reuland propose that SE anaphors are Determiners, like pronouns (it is widely assumed that pronouns are Ds, an idea that was originally proposed in Postal (1969)). SE anaphors differ from pronouns in that they lack features of person, number, and gender. Because of this, these elements can't pick out a referent. In order to pick out a referent (which we might take to be a general condition on D), an SE anaphor has to combine with a head which at least has person and number features. This is why these elements undergo head-movement (either overtly or covertly, depending on the language), usually to AgrS. In this way, several of the basic properties of LD SE anaphors that we looked at in the previous section are accounted for. You can see that Pica's generalization is also accounted for; indeed much of this proposal was anticipated in the work of Pica and others.

SELF, on the other hand, is a Noun, which combines with a pronominal element (it can also combine with SE, since SE is a pronoun: we can see the combination in forms like Dutch *zichzelf*). Very importantly, SELF has the semantic function of *imposing identity on two arguments of a predicate*. So, when a DP containing SELF appears as an argument of a predicate (a verb, in the simplest case), SELF will require that two of the arguments of that verb refer to the same thing. In other words, SELF is a **reflexivizer**. On the other hand, SELF has no referential properties.

We can think of the internal structures of the different types of anaphors as in (84) (I should point out that Reinhart and Reuland do not adopt the DP hypothesis, but (84) is a reasonable adaptation of their proposals):

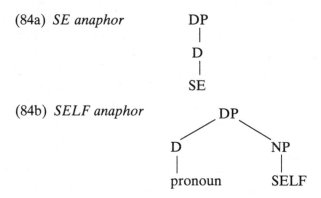

(84a) *SE anaphor*

(84b) *SELF anaphor*

More importantly, we have now isolated two properties of anaphors: the fact that they are not referential, and the fact that SELF is a reflexivizer and SE isn't. Ordinary pronouns (like *he, she,* and *it*) are referential, but are not reflexivizers. So we have the following situation:

Table 3.5 Anaphors and pronouns according to [± reflexivizer, ± R]

	SELF	*SE*	*Pronoun*
reflexivizer	+	–	–
R(eferential)	–	–	+

I'll use 'R' as shorthand for 'referential' in the sense described above: something is R if it has the features that enable it to pick out a referent. So, as I said above, if a given occurrence of D is not R then something has to happen so that it can be licensed. The two types of anaphor have the common property of being [–R], unlike pronouns (and, of course, R-expressions). So we expect both kinds of anaphor to be subject to some special condition. As we'll see, this condition is related to movement.

On the other hand, Table 3.5 groups SE anaphors and pronouns together as not being reflexivizers; being a reflexivizer is the special property of SELF anaphors.

3.5.2 Reflexivizing

The concept of 'reflexivizer' is relevant in relation to the following conditions on reflexivity, which are the central proposals for controlling the distribution of anaphors and pronouns (and, to an extent, R-expressions):

(85a) All and only REFLEXIVE PREDICATES must be REFLEXIVE-MARKED

(85b) A predicate P is REFLEXIVE iff two of its arguments are coindexed

(85c) P is REFLEXIVE-MARKED iff P has a SELF argument

So we have a basic condition, (85a), which looks very simple and natural; (85b) defines what it means for a predicate to be reflexive – again, pretty straightforward if you're familiar with the concepts of binding theory (which you should be by now!). And (85c) defines reflexive-marking (this definition will be slightly extended below).

Now we need to look at a few simple cases, to see how the definitions in (85) work. Consider the simplest instances of the operation of Principles A, B, and C (we've seen these examples before):

(86a) Brian$_i$ hates himself$_i$ (= (3a))

(86b) *Brian$_i$ hates him$_i$ (= (16))

(86c) *Brian$_i$/he$_i$ hates Brian$_i$ (= (36a))

In all these examples, the predicate is reflexive because two of its arguments are coindexed: see (85b). Example (86a) satisfies the condition in (85a), because *himself*, a SELF argument, marks the predicate as reflexive. Examples (86b and c) both fail this condition because the predicate isn't marked as reflexive.

If we contraindex the arguments to the predicate in (86), we get:

(87a) *Brian$_i$ hates himself$_j$

(87b) Brian$_i$ hates him$_j$

(87c) Brian$_i$/he$_i$ hates Brian$_j$

(In (87c), the indexing tells us that there are two different Brians, and the example is grammatical with that interpretation.) The predicate is not reflexive here. So (87a) is ruled out because a non-reflexive predicate is reflexive-marked. Examples (87b and c) are allowed, on the other hand; these are non-reflexive predicates with no reflexive marking.

A crucial part of the definition of binding domain in (20') makes reference to subjects. Now, predicates usually have subjects – in fact, let's assume that predicates *have* to have subjects. And so you might think that defining binding conditions in terms of domains involving subjects and defining them in terms of predicates amounts to much the same thing. There are some important differences, however, as we'll see later. First, though, let's linger over the similarities, so that we can see to what extent (85) can do the work of the standard binding theory. Example (85) can handle the standard Tensed-S Condition and Specified Subject Condition cases that we saw in 3.2.1, like:

(9b)   *Phil$_i$ said [that himself$_i$ was a genius]

(11b)   *Phil$_i$ believes [Loretta to admire himself$_i$]

In each of these cases, we have a reflexive-marked predicate (that is, a predicate one of whose arguments is a SELF anaphor) which is not reflexive, in the sense defined in (85b). So (85) can handle cases of this sort.

And it can also handle examples that standard binding theory has difficulty with; and this is where we see the difference between defining the domain of binding in terms of predicates and defining it in terms of subjects. One kind of example features adjunct PPs:

(88)   Don$_i$ saw a trout near him$_i$

If you apply the definition of BD in (20'), you'll see that *him* comes out as being in the same BD as *Don*. So (88) ought to violate Principle B, but it seems OK. On the other hand, since *near him* is an adjunct PP it's not an argument of the predicate. The predicate here thus isn't reflexive, according to the definition in (85b), and so there's no problem with the pronoun here. Another kind of example is:

(89)   Mick$_i$ appreciates [songs about him$_i$]

Again, (20') will tell us that *Mick* and *him* are in the same BD here, and so wrongly predicts a violation of Principle B. On the other hand, since *him* is not an argument of *appreciate*, the predicate does qualify as reflexive by (85b). And so there's no problem from the point of view of (85).

So we can see the basic approach and how it can handle some standard cases. We can also see that the notions of 'R' and of 'reflexivizer' play a central role. So far, however, you might have noticed that there's no c-command condition. In other words, unlike the standard binding theory, what we've seen of Reinhart and Reuland's theory up to now can't distinguish (87a) from (90):

(90)   *Himself$_i$ hates Brian$_i$

Here we have a reflexive-marked predicate which is reflexive, and so (85a) is satisfied, just as in (87a). Obviously we want to be able to rule out examples like (90), so more needs to be said. We'll get to a solution to this problem in a roundabout way.

3.5.3 Referentiality and Chains

According to Table 3.5, SE anaphors are [–R] and –reflexivizer. Let's look first at what it means to say that SE anaphors are not reflexivizers.

The first point is that this classification actually groups SE-anaphors with pronouns. This is arguably a good result; in many languages SE anaphors cannot have local antecedents (except under circumstances that I'll get to directly). The following Dutch example illustrates this:

(91) *Max$_i$ haat zich$_i$
     Max   hates self

The SE anaphor here is *zich*. Since this anaphor is not a reflexivizer, (91) falls foul of (85a). The predicate here is reflexive, since two of its arguments are coindexed, but there is no reflexive-marking (see (85c)). The point is that *zich* cannot function as a reflexivizer, unlike a SELF anaphor.

On the other hand, SE anaphors can appear in positions where coindexation does not create a reflexive predicate by the definition in (85b) – adjunct PPs, for example (see (88)):

(92) Max$_i$ legt het boek achter zich$_i$
     Max puts the book behind self
     'Max$_i$ puts the book behind him(self)$_i$'

You should be able to see why this example is allowed. In both (91) and (92) *zich* is functioning like a pronoun rather than like a reflexive.

Dutch is, however, fairly typical of languages which have SE anaphors, in that it allows SE anaphors to appear with predicates which are inherently reflexive, that is, predicates (usually verbs) which simply require the presence of a reflexive DP as a structural argument without that argument having any real semantic force. Here is an example:

(93) Max$_i$ schaamt zich$_i$
     Max shames self
     'Max is ashamed'

There is no possibility of having anything other than *zich* in the object position. Here *zich* just seems to fill a syntactic slot. In order to account for this kind of behaviour of inherent reflexives, we need to slightly modify the definition of reflexive-marking that I gave in (85c):

(85c') P is REFLEXIVE-MARKED iff:
     EITHER P is lexically reflexive;
     OR P has a SELF argument.

Given (85c'), we can account for the contrast between (93) and (91). Both are reflexive predicates, by (85b). The predicate in (93) is lexically defined as reflexive, and so counts as reflexive-marked in terms of (85c'). And so (93) satisfies (85a). The predicate in (91) is not a lexical reflexive, on the other hand, and so it is ruled out in the way described above.

With the exception just discussed, the system being described here groups SE anaphors with pronouns as far as the basic locality condition in (85a) is concerned. Further evidence for this comes from the following examples:

(94a) Willem$_i$ bewondert zichzelf$_i$/*zich$_i$/*hem$_i$
      Willem$_i$ admires   himself$_i$/self$_i$/him$_i$

(94b) Klaas$_i$ duwde de kar voor zich$_i$/hem$_i$/*zichzelf$_i$ uit
      Klaas$_i$ pushed the cart before self$_i$/him$_i$/himself$_i$ out

Example (94a) is simple, rather like (91). The contrast between *zichzelf* and *hem* here is a standard case of the complementary distribution of (SELF) anaphors and pronouns – we saw in connection with (86) and (87) how this is handled here. It is clear that *zich* patterns with the pronoun and not with the SELF anaphor. In (94b), we have an adjunct PP again. Here the SELF anaphor is excluded because it's not part of a reflexive predicate: see (87a). Both *zich* and *hem* are possible, again patterning alike.

One important difference between *zich* and *hem* emerges in ECM infinitives. Here *zich* is allowed, but *hem* isn't:

(95) Jan$_i$ hoorde [zich$_i$/*hem$_i$ zingen]
      John heard self/him sing
      'John heard himself sing'

Clearly, this contrast is not accounted for by grouping SE anaphors like *zich* with pronouns like *hem*. This is where the [–R] feature of SE anaphors comes into play.

At this point we need to look at the notion of **chain**. When a category is moved, it must c-command and be coindexed with its trace (as we saw in 3.3.2.2). Now, we could define chains more generally, and say that we have a chain whenever one category α c-commands and is coindexed with another category β. Also, just as in the case of binding, we can distinguish **A-chains** (chains whose **head** – the position that c-commands all the others – is in an L-related position) from **A'-chains** (chains whose head is in a non-L-related position). To handle the contrast in (95), Reinhart and Reuland propose the following general constraint on A-chains:

The Chain Condition:
(96) In a maximal A-chain the head of the chain, and only the head, must be both [+R] and Case-marked.

Being [+R] means having enough features to be able to refer to something, and, according to Table 3.5, both SE and SELF anaphors are [–R]. Pronouns, on the other hand, are [+R]. Now we can see what the contrast in (95) is due to. *Jan* can form a chain with *zich* that meets the criterion in (96), since that chain has just one Case-marked, [+R] position, the one occupied by *Jan*, and this position c-commands the other position in the chain, that occupied by *zich*. On the other hand, since *hem* is [+R] (and Case-marked), it and *Jan* cannot form a chain that satisfies (96). The chain condition (96) requires that each must head its own chain: that they have different indices.

A theoretical point can be made here: the concept of chain is usually held to be relevant for movement, but here we've used it to account for anaphora facts where nothing appears to move. If we adopt the idea that anaphors move, then we can retain the idea that chains are defined in terms of movement.

3.5.4 More on SELF Anaphors

As Table 3.5 shows, SELF anaphors differ from SE anaphors in being [+ reflexive] and are like SE anaphors in being [– R]. We looked at the main consequences of treating SELF anaphors as [+ reflexive] in Section 3.5.2. Since they are [– R], the Chain Condition in (96) prevents SELF anaphors from heading chains. This rules out examples like the following (and (90) as well):

(97a) *Myself$_i$ saw me$_i$/John$_i$

(97b) *Himself$_i$ criticized himself$_i$

(97c) *Zichzelf$_i$/hemzelf$_i$ critiseerde zich$_i$
    self-self/himself criticized self

In fact, the c-command condition that is built into the definition of chains does the work of the c-command part of the definition of binding that we gave in (7) at the beginning of this chapter. Reinhart and Reuland therefore propose that c-command does not enter into the definition of binding as such: its effects are due to (97) in combination with the fact that c-command plays a role in defining chains.

The principal condition on SELF anaphors is (85), in as much as where a predicate has a SELF argument it will count as reflexive-marked, and hence must be reflexive, having two coindexed arguments. We saw the principal effects of this approach in examples (86) and (87) above. However, you may have noticed that (85) says nothing about what happens if we have a SELF anaphor which is not an argument of a predicate (not functioning as a reflexivizer). You might think that SELF anaphors would be unavailable in this role, since they are intrinsically reflexivizers. However, what (85) really says is that SELF anaphors *that are arguments of predicates* are reflexivizers – it doesn't say anything about SELF anaphors that aren't arguments. In fact, non-argument SELF anaphors do seem to be possible. Reinhart and Reuland (1993) give the following examples:

(98a) There were five tourists in the room apart from myself

(98b) Physicists like yourself are a godsend

(98c) Max$_i$ boasted that the queen invited Lucie and himself$_i$ for a drink

In (98a and b), the anaphors have no antecedents in the sentences at all, and so they violate Principle A of the standard binding theory. Although the anaphor in (98c) has an antecedent, it is nevertheless clearly in violation of Principle A of the binding theory since the antecedent is well outside the anaphor's binding domain (which would be the lower clause).

However, the anaphors here do have antecedents in an extended sense, that goes beyond syntax: in (98a) the antecedent of *myself* is obviously the speaker/narrator; in (98b) the antecedent is the addressee and in (98c) the antecedent is the subject of the higher clause (which contains a verb of speaking). A further point to note is that the anaphors in (98) are not in complementary distribution with the corresponding pronouns:

(99a) There were five tourists in the room apart from me

(99b) Physicists like you are a godsend

(99c) Max$_i$ boasted that the queen invited Lucie and him$_i$ for a drink

It is rather hard to pin down intuitively the difference between (98) and (99). Usually, it is thought that the kinds of anaphor in examples like (98) express something about the 'point of view' of the speaker or narrator: we noted that they do in fact have antecedents in the speech situation. Because of this connection to the speaker, such a use of anaphors is called the 'logophoric' use. I can't go into a precise description of the logophoric uses of anaphors here, mainly because it is not well-understood. In any case, this wouldn't really be appropriate because, as the examples suggest, logophoricity is really an aspect of language use rather than of syntax. The one point which is relevant for syntax is that *only non-argument anaphors can be logophoric*. Where an anaphor is an argument, it must reflexivize a predicate. We can see this if we make the anaphors in (98) into arguments:

(100a) *Five tourists talked to myself in the room

(100b) *A famous physicist has just looked for yourself

(100c) *Max$_i$ boasted that the queen invited himself$_i$ for a drink

All of these examples violate (85), since they are reflexive-marked but not reflexive. This seems to be an area where Reinhart and Reuland's approach can tackle a range of facts that created difficulties for the standard binding theory.

Some languages have special forms for logophors as opposed to anaphors. This is true in the West African language Ewe, for example. Clements (1975) showed that the 'logophor' *ye* is interpreted as having the individual whose speech is being reported as its antecedent, and not the c-commanding subject. This is illustrated in (101):

(101) kɔmi$_k$ xɔ   agbalẽ tso kofi$_i$ gbɔ be wò- a- va   me kpe
      Kwami receive letter from Kofi side that Pro-T- come cast block
      nayè$_{i/*k}$
      for   LOG
      'Kwami got a letter from Kofi$_i$ saying that he should cast some blocks
      for him$_i$.'

In these languages, SELF anaphors are purely reflexive markers; the other function of SELF anaphors is taken over by the special logophoric pronouns.

3.5.5 Pronouns and the Definition of Predicate
As you can see from the discussion so far, the idea of a reflexive predicate

plays a central role in Reinhart and Reuland's system. Reflexive predicates are defined in (85b). This definition depends on a prior notion of predicate, and I haven't really given any definition of this concept up to now. In the simple cases that we've looked at it hasn't been crucial to do so. But now it's time to look a bit more closely at this notion. In the process, we'll see an interesting proposal about how to distinguish some aspects of the distribution of pronouns from SELF anaphors.

The concept of 'predicate' can have either a syntactic or a semantic definition. The syntactic definition that is relevant here is:

> *Syntactic Predicate:*
> (102) All the grammatical functions associated with a given lexical head, plus the nearest subject position.

This definition allows a subject that isn't semantically an argument of a given predicate to count as syntactically part of the predicate, something that we need in order to account for the binding facts that we find in raising predicates. The relevant kind of example is illustrated in (103):

> (103) Mick$_i$ seems to himself$_i$ [t$_i$ to be desirable]

Here *seem* forms a syntactic predicate which contains the *to*-phrase, a semantic argument of *seem*, and the nearest subject, the position which is the target of raising, occupied by *Mick*. Semantically, *Mick* is not an argument of *seem* (see Section 2.3.3 on raising). The syntactic predicate counts as reflexive by (85b), because two of its arguments are coindexed, and it is correctly reflexive-marked since a SELF anaphor is present.

Another kind of example involves an expletive subject, which semantically, of course, has no function at all. For example:

> (104) *Frank$_i$ thinks that it would bother himself$_i$ if Don made another record

By the definition in (97), *bother* forms a syntactic predicate here, since the expletive is a syntactic subject. Semantically, the nearest subject would presumably be *Frank*. However, if the predicate included *Frank*, then it would be well-formed by (85). On the other hand, if *bother* forms a complete predicate, we see that it is reflexive-marked without being reflexive (since it does not contain two coindexed arguments).

Exceptional Case-marking (ECM) clauses seem to pose some problems for this approach. As we have seen, the subject of an ECM infinitive is in the same binding domain as the arguments of the higher verb. This is illustrated by examples like (105):

> (105) Phil$_i$ expected [himself$_i$ to do better]

The subject of an ECM clause is not a *semantic* argument of the higher predicate. But examples like (105) show that, in Reinhart and Reuland's terms, it must be a part of the syntactic predicate of the main clause. Since we con-

nected Case relations to grammatical functions in 2.1, and since our definition of syntactic predicate in (102) makes reference to grammatical functions,
we might think that we can take care of (105). Let's make (102) a bit more
precise, nevertheless:

Syntactic Predicate (Revised):

(102a') The syntactic predicate formed of (a head) P is P, all its syntactic
arguments, and the external argument of P (subject)

(102b') The syntactic arguments of P are the projections assigned θ-role
or Case by P

Rule (102b') is the part that's important for ECM clauses. The subject of an ECM
clause counts as a syntactic argument of the main clause because it is Case-
marked by the verb of the main clause (or, according to checking theory, by the
AgrO of the main clause: see Section 2.6.1). Because of this, a SELF anaphor in
that position reflexivizes the main predicate, in line with (85).

However, there is a problem here: what stops *himself* reflexivizing the lower
predicate in (105)? Since *himself* receives a θ-role from the lower predicate,
it should reflexivize that predicate. In that case, we'd expect (105) to be
ungrammatical, since the predicate in the lower clause isn't reflexive. To solve
this problem, Reinhart and Reuland propose that the infinitive of ECM complements raises to the higher clause, forming a complex predicate which is
reflexive. In English, this V-raising is covert, although in many other languages
– including Dutch – it is overt. The LF for (105) is (105'), according to this
proposal:

(105') Phil$_i$ do-expected [himself$_i$ to t better]

Pronouns, on the other hand, appear to be sensitive to a *semantic* notion
of predicate. So what seems to be important here is whether two *semantic*
arguments of a predicate (elements which receive a θ-role from that predicate – see Section 2.1) refer to the same entity. We can see this from contrasts like the following:

(106a) Mick$_i$ and Keith talked about him$_i$

(106b) *Both Mick$_i$ and Keith talked about him$_i$

If the coordinate antecedent has a 'distributed' reading, in which the action
described is associated individually with each person named in the conjoined
DP, the sentence is bad. If the antecedent has a non-distributive reading,
where the action is taken to be collectively carried out by both members of
the conjunct, the pronoun is allowed. Sentence (106b) is bad because the distributive reading is forced by the presence of *both*. We can approximate the
semantic differences between the distributive and the non-distributive reading as in (107):

(107a) Mick and Keith (λx (x talked about him))   non-distributive
reading (OK)

(107b) Mick (λx (x talked about x)) and Keith (λx (x talked about him))
distributive reading (not OK)

(If you're unfamiliar with the 'lambda-notation', it's explained in the Appendix to this chapter. Read it as 'Mick and Keith are the ones who . . .' (107a), and 'Mick is the one who . . .' (107b).) What goes wrong in (107b) is that there is a semantically reflexive predicate: *x talked about x*. But this predicate isn't reflexive-marked. This is why the distributive reading of (106) is not possible.

Another contrast which shows the same thing is:

(108a) *Max rolled the carpet$_i$ over it$_i$

(108b) Max praised the carpet$_i$ underneath it$_i$

Sentence (108b) is rather absurd, but it's certainly grammatically possible with the interpretation indicated. Sentence (109a), on the other hand, is quite impossible. We've already seen (see (88)) that pronouns should be allowed in adjunct PPs, so what's the problem in (108a)? The answer emerges if we consider the semantics of the prepositions here more closely. Both *over* and *underneath* have two arguments – they express a spatial relation between two entities. In (108a), *over* expresses a spatial relation between the carpet and itself, which we could write as *over (x, x)*. Now we can see the problem: this is a semantic predicate with two arguments the same – hence it should be reflexive-marked and isn't. Sentence (108b) is acceptable because *underneath* expresses a non-reflexive relation between *Max* and *the carpet*, and so doesn't need to be reflexive-marked.

So you can see that the precise notion of predicate that's at work here is quite important. The general conclusion is that pronouns are sensitive to semantic predicates, while anaphors are sensitive to syntactic predicates (as defined in (102')).

Although there is much more to say about Reinhart and Reuland's approach, we'll have to leave it there. We've seen the essential points, which are the constraint and definitions in (85), the division among SELF anaphors, SE anaphors, and pronouns shown in Table 3.5, the constraint on chains in (96), and the two kinds of predicate just discussed. You should be able to see how this approach at once builds on and reconceptualizes the standard binding theory to which the rest of this chapter was devoted.

3.6 Conclusion

We've covered a great deal of ground in this chapter. The centrality of the material discussed here for syntactic theory should be obvious – we're dealing with a very fundamental kind of dependency and a related notion of locality. The most important points that have been covered are:

- the locality condition on (morphologically complex) anaphors (in argument positions): see 3.1.1
- the local disjoint reference condition on pronouns: see 3.1.2
- the (near-) complementary distribution of pronouns and anaphors: see 3.1
- how Principles A and B of the binding theory can account for the three points above: see 3.2.1
- the disjointness condition on R-expressions: Principle C: see 3.3.1
- PRO, the PRO theorem, and what it may (or may not) follow from: see 3.2.2.1
- control theory: see 3.2.2.2
- traces and Principles A and C: see 3.3.2
- *pro* and the null-subject parameter: see 3.3.3
- LD anaphora, notably Pica's generalization: see 3.4
- Reinhart and Reuland's theory of reflexivity: see 3.5.

Parameters Discussed in this Chapter

Here we've seen two major parameters: the null-subject parameter (3.3.3) and the possibility of long-distance anaphora (3.4).

We saw in 3.3.3 that the null-subject parameter relates the possibility of phonologically empty definite pronominal subjects of finite clauses to the possibility of free inversion. Languages that have these properties include Italian (and its many dialects, including some that at first sight appear to require subject pronouns), Spanish, (European) Portuguese, Rumanian, Greek, and many others. Languages lacking them include French and all the Germanic languages. In 4.3.2, we'll see that there's another property connected to *wh*-movement which patterns with these two properties. This parameter is arguably connected to a morphological trigger, in that it appears that AgrS must carry a sufficiently rich inflectional marking to permit recovery of the subject's person, number, and gender features.

LD anaphora is a crosslinguistically common feature, although it is not found in English. The principal observation here is Pica's generalization that LD anaphors are typically monomorphemic. This makes possible an analysis of these elements as undergoing covert head-movement to AgrS (although we noted in 3.4 that there are some technical problems with this analysis). Languages having LD anaphora include nearly all the other Germanic languages, aside from English, Italian, Chinese, Japanese, Korean, Polish, Latin, and others. Here, too, the triggering property may be morphological: being monomorphemic is clearly a morphological property of the reflexives in question.

Further Reading

The Tensed-S Condition and Specified Subject Condition were put forward in Chomsky (1973). This very difficult article is certainly worth looking at for this, and for the first statement of subjacency, which we'll discuss in Chapter 4 (see 4.2). The Disjoint Reference Condition was proposed by Lasnik (1976), another classic article that is well worth the read.

The Binding Theory of 3.2 is essentially that of Chomsky (1981, ch. 3), although many of the technical details are different principally because I've adopted different definitions of both government and c-command here. The PRO theorem is also discussed here. A collection of Lasnik's work on binding over a period of more than 20 years is Lasnik (1989); this book contains a very useful chapter entitled 'A Selective History of the Binding Theory'. A different mechanism for handling anaphoric relations is developed in Higginbotham (1980, 1981, 1983). A very important work on the syntax and semantics of reciprocals is Heim, Lasnik and May (1990).

The PRO theorem is discussed in Chomsky (1981, ch. 3). Bouchard (1984) is an early dissenter from the PRO theorem. Some discussion of how the 'null-Case' idea might derive the distribution of PRO is found in Chomsky and Lasnik (1993). Williams (1980) and Manzini (1983) present rather different theories of control; what was presented in 3.2.2.2 is loosely based on Manzini's discussion. Koster (1984) and Borer (1989) pursue the question of the relation between binding and control in different ways.

Crossover phenomena are first discussed in Postal (1971); this is another classic, if you can get hold of a copy. Wasow (1972, 1979) elaborates this theory, distinguishing 'strong' crossover (the phenomenon discussed in 3.3.2.3) from 'weak crossover', on which see the Appendix to this Chapter. L-relatedness is introduced by Chomsky and Lasnik (1993).

The principal references on null subjects are Jaeggli (1982), Rizzi (1982, ch. 4; 1986a,b), Chomsky (1981, Ch 4; 1982). All of these discuss the locality facts that we'll get to in 4.3.2, and not all of them assume that null subjects are *pro*. The best general discussion on the crosslinguistic occurrence of *pro* is Rizzi (1986a); this article focuses on object *pro*, a topic we have left aside. Another important reference on object *pro*, and on 'Chinese-style' null arguments generally, is Huang (1984). An excellent collection, reflecting the variety and importance of work on the null subject parameter, is Jaeggli and Safir (1989).

The movement account of anaphora was first proposed by Lebeaux (1983). As mentioned in the text, it is developed by Chomsky (1986a). Pica's generalization is in Pica (1987). Other important work on long-distance reflexives includes Giorgi (1984), Koster (1985, 1987), Everaert (1986) and Wexler and Manzini (1987). An important and representative collection is Koster and Reuland (1991).

Exercises

Exercise 1
In 3.3.2.2 we saw examples of super-raising, such as the following:

1. *Many students$_i$ seem that there were beaten up t$_i$ (by the police)

2. *A train$_i$ seems that there arrived t$_i$

We said that these examples are bad because DP-traces are subject to Principle A. Here Principle A is violated since the DP-trace has no antecedent in its BD. This analysis implies that (1) and (2) are parallel to (3):

3. ??They$_i$ said it would be nice for each other$_i$ to do that

Here, too, the reciprocal lacks an antecedent in its BD. And yet the ungrammaticality of (3) seems much milder than that of (1) and (2). Of the various differences between these examples, which do you think is most likely to be the crucial one in distinguishing them? You may need to compare a number of other similar examples.

Exercise 2
Principles A and B together predict the complementary distribution of pronouns and anaphors. However, what about the following pair:

1. Mick and Keith$_i$ think [that [$_{DP}$ songs about them$_i$] would sell well]
2. Mick and Keith$_i$ think [that [$_{DP}$ songs about each other$_i$] would sell well]

It has been claimed that there is a difference of interpretation here: (1) favours the meaning that the songs in question are in some sense other people's songs, while (2) favours the interpretation where the songs are Mick and Keith's own. Can we make anything of this observation (if you agree it's true) in accounting for the breakdown in complementary distribution of pronouns and anaphors here?

Exercise 3
In French, ECM clauses comparable to the familiar English ones are not found:

1. I believe George to be the best
   *Je crois Georges être le meilleur

On the other hand, (subject) control is possible with *croire* here, unlike English *believe*:

2. *I believe PRO to be the best
   Je crois PRO être le meilleur

Using the government-based Case theory described in 2.2 and the PRO theorem of 3.2.2.1, give an account of the structural difference between English and French that underlies the data in (1) and (2).

If French *de* is a prepositional complementizer similar to English *for*, then we see a further difference between English and French in (3) and (4):

3. It would be a pity for something to happen to him
   *Ce serait dommage de quelque chose lui arriver

4. *It would be a pity for PRO to leave now
   Ce serait dommage de PRO partir maintenant

Can we account for this distinction in the same way as that between (1) and (2)? What differences do we have to postulate between French Prepositions and English Prepositions? See Kayne (1984).

Appendix: Logical Binding and Syntactic Binding

The purpose of this Appendix is to introduce the concept of variable-binding in logic (for those unfamiliar with it) and to clarify its relation to syntactic anaphora of the kind that has been the subject of this entire chapter.

In predicate logic, quantifiers are said to bind variables. So, an English sentence like *Everyone likes chocolate* can be given as:

(A1) $\forall x$ (Person (x) → Like $(x, \text{chocolate})$)

This can be read as 'For all x, if x is a person, then x likes chocolate'. This 'translation' may seem cumbersome at first sight, but any logic textbook can explain why things are done this way (see Allwood, Andersson, and Dahl (1977, ch. 3)). What we're interested in is the relation between the quantifier $\forall$ and the variables x that it binds. A quantifier is said to bind a variable in its scope. The scope of the quantifier is defined as the contents of the parenthesis immediately to its right, so in (A1) the scope of the quantifier is the rest of the formula. Quantifiers are marked with late letters of the alphabet, corresponding to the variables that they bind. They can be interpreted in one of two ways in standard predicate logic, but a discussion of these matters would take us too far afield here. The essential point, however, is that the variables are interpreted as ranging over a set of constants, and each occurrence of a given variable in the scope of a quantifier must stand for the same constant on a given interpretation. So one way to interpret (A1) is by substituting constants for x and finding out if the formula in the scope of the quantifier is true. So we evaluate the truth of (A1) by evaluating the truth of (A2) for all values of x (we don't need to go into how those might be determined):

(A2) Person (a) → Like $(a, \text{chocolate})$
      Person (b) → Like $(b, \text{chocolate})$
      Person (c) → Like $(c, \text{chocolate})$
      .
      .
      .

Since it contains the universal quantifier, (A1) will be true iff (A2) is true for all values of x.

Logic textbooks often point out that logical variables are a bit like natural-language pronouns. In fact, we've seen that pronouns can be bound, as long as Principle B is satisfied, in examples like:

(A3) Phil$_i$ thinks [$_{CP}$ that he$_i$ is a genius]

Coindexing here corresponds to the pronoun designating the same logical constant (say p) as its antecedent in a predicate-logic translation. But there is another sense in which pronouns can be bound, which we see when we introduce a quantifier as the antecedent:

(A4) Everyone$_i$ thinks [$_{CP}$ that he$_i$ is a genius]

Example (A4) means 'Every person x thinks that x is a genius'. In predicate logic, it would have a translation something like (A1), but a bit more complicated, and might be interpreted along the lines described for (A2). So here *everyone* binds *he* both in the syntactic sense (coindexation and c-command respecting the binding principles) and in the logical sense that the pronoun is interpreted as a variable in its scope. The same is true where the antecedent for a reflexive is a quantifier:

(A5) Everyone$_i$ doubts himself$_i$

(A6) $\forall x$ (Doubt (x, x))

So in examples like these, the two types of binding overlap.

Nevertheless, they are distinct. We can see this by comparing (A5, A6) with (A7, A8):

(A7) Syd$_i$ doubts himself$_i$

(A8) Doubt (s, s))

Where there is no quantifier, the reflexive corresponds in value to the constant that is its syntactic antecedent. There is a clear similarity between the formulae in (A6) and (A8), in that, in both, the reflexive corresponds to a further occurrence of the preceding constant or variable.

We can elaborate this further, and get a further clue about the syntactic representation of quantified expressions, if we consider the next pair:

(A9)   Who$_i$ t$_i$ doubts himself$_i$?

(A10) *whx* (Doubt (x, x))

(A10), although a rather loose logical translation, brings out the fact that (A9) means something like 'Tell me who is the x such that x doubts x'. Again, the reflexive corresponds in semantic value to the constant/variable that is its syntactic antecedent. However, here the syntactic antecedent of the variable is the trace that A-binds it in its BD: t_i in (A9). We can think that the trace corresponds to the variable bound by the *wh*-quantifier. This is supported by cases like:

(A11) Who$_i$ saw John?

(A12) *whx* (Saw (x, John))

Here there is no anaphor in the sense of this chapter, but there is a variable *x* bound by the *wh*-quantifier.

The reflexive in (A9) acts like a logical variable because it is syntactically bound by a *wh*-trace, which has the logical property of being a variable bound by a *wh*-quantifier. The variable-binding relation between the *wh*-quantifier and its trace corresponds to A'-binding in syntax; the usual binding relation between a *wh*-element and its trace. Exactly the same holds with pronouns, except that the binding principles tell us that pronouns have to be further from their antecedents than reflexives, as in (A13):

(A13) Who$_i$ t$_i$ thinks he$_i$'s a genius ?

So we see that logical binding, at least involving *wh*-quantifiers, corresponds to syntactic A'-binding, while anaphora of the kind discussed in this chapter involves A-binding relations. A simple (probably excessively simple) way to interpret A-binding relations at LF is to assume that they correspond to the presence of identical logical constants/variables, depending on the nature of the antecedent.

The last step in this is to extend the *wh* case to all quantifiers. We know that *wh*-elements can, under certain conditions, not undergo overt movement. Nevertheless, they receive a variable binding interpretation. We can see this in examples like (A14):

(A14) Who$_i$ t$_i$ convinced who$_j$ that he$_j$ is a genius ?

With the indexing given, this example has the interpretation 'Tell me which person *x* convinced which person *y* that *y* is a genius'. So who$_j$ in (A14), although it has not undergone overt movement, is interpreted as binding a variable in exactly the way a moved *wh* does. If the variable corresponding to a moved *wh* is a trace, then the obvious thing to assume here is that the unmoved *wh* in fact does move in the derivation to LF, thereby creating a trace which can be interpreted as logically bound by the *wh* quantifier.

Now, if we allow covert movement to create LF variable-binding relations in (A14), then we can allow it in examples like (A4) and (A5). So let's assume that quantified DPs can move to an A'-position in LF; thanks to this process the trace acts like a bound variable. The LF for (A4) looks something like (A15):

(A15) Everyone$_i$ [t$_i$ thinks [$_{CP}$ that he$_i$ is a genius]]

The A'-bound trace corresponds to the 'true variable' in the interpretation, and *he* is interpreted as a variable because it is interpreted as identical to the category that A-binds it – the trace. The LF rule that creates representations like (A15) is known as Quantifier Raising, or QR. We'll say more about it in the Appendix to Chapter 4. For more on LF operations, see May (1985), Hornstein (1985, 1995).

In all the examples of pronouns or reflexives being interpreted as bound variables that we've seen up to now, the pronoun or reflexive has been c-commanded by the variable (you can check this in (A4, A5, A9, A13, and A15)). However, pronouns do not have to be c-commanded by their antecedent, as we saw in 3.1.2. So, in principle, we might get a configuration where a pronoun is not c-commanded by a variable that it is coindexed with. This arises in such configurations of 'weak crossover' (which is distinct from the 'strong crossover' discussed in 3.3.2.3), as:

(A16) *Who$_i$ does [his$_i$ mother] love t$_i$?

This example is ungrammatical on the interpretation indicated by the coin-dexing relations. It should mean 'For which x, x a person, does x's mother love x?' Here, unlike all the other examples we've looked at, the pronoun isn't c-commanded by the trace. Accordingly, we can conclude that *for a pro-noun to be interpreted as a bound variable, it must be c-commanded by an A'-bound trace.* In (A15), this requirement isn't fulfilled and the pronoun fails to have an interpretation with the indexing given. Different approaches to weak crossover have been proposed by Wasow (1972), Chomsky (1976) and Koopman and Sportiche (1982). A further argument for the existence of QR is the presence of weak-crossover effects with quantifiers, as in:

(A17) *[His$_i$ mother] loves everyone$_i$

After QR, this example has the LF representation in (A17), which is clearly parallel to (A15) and violates the condition on pronoun-interpretation in the same way:

(A18) Everyone$_i$ [[his$_i$ mother] loves t$_i$]

In conclusion, logical binding corresponds to A'-binding of variables, where the relation may be set up either by covert or overt movement to an A'-posi-tion. Anaphoric binding of the sort discussed in this chapter is A-binding. Binding in both cases is c-command combined with coindexation.

One final note: the picture presented above assumes a primitive distinction between quantificational and non-quantificational expressions, as do many kinds of logic. However, we can introduce an operator which makes anything into an expression capable of binding a variable; this is the λ-operator. It has been argued that all DPs should be interpreted this way. So *John left* might have the interpretation:

(A19) John   (λx (Left (x)))

This is read as 'John is x such that x left'. As we saw, this notation is exploited in Reinhart and Reuland's account of pronominal anaphora (see 3.5.5).

4

Locality

4.0 Introduction

This is the last chapter that deals with the technical parts of syntactic theory. As in the previous chapter, our theme is the kinds of relations that can hold among syntactic constituents. However, unlike binding relations, here we are dealing exclusively with movement dependencies, and so the theoretical construct that I'll focus on here is Move-α. What we're interested in here is 'how far' movement can go: when Move-α applies to a category α, how far away from α's original position can α be taken? It's clear that, in order to answer this question properly, we'll need a workable measure of 'distance' that can be defined over syntactic structures – figuring out what distance is in syntactic terms, and how much of it Move-α can cover, have been central currents of research in generative grammar. Here I'll give an overview of what's known.

We can set the scene for the discussion by looking at what we've already said about Move-α in earlier chapters. In Section 2.4 of Chapter 2 we looked at the properties of the different kinds of Move-α: head-movement, DP-movement, and *wh*-movement. Let's look at those again:

Head-movement:
(1a) moves a head

(1b) leaves a trace in the starting position

(1c) moves to a position c-commanding the trace

(1d) moves to the closest possible position to the trace

(1e) obeys the Structure Preservation Constraint

DP-movement:
(2a) moves a DP

(2b) leaves a trace in the starting position

(2c) moves to a position c-commanding the trace

(2d) moves to the closest possible position to the trace

(2e) obeys the Structure Preservation Constraint

(2f) only ever moves to Specifiers of functional heads

wh-*movement:*
(3a) moves a *wh*-XP

(3b) leaves a trace in the starting position

(3c) moves to a position c-commanding the trace

(3d) does NOT move to the closest possible position to its trace (or so it appears)

(3e) obeys the Structure Preservation Constraint

(3f) only ever moves to Specifiers of CP

We commented on the similarities between the different kinds of movement in 2.3. Let's see what the common factors of them are:

Move-α:
(4a) moves α = either X or XP

(4b) leaves a trace in the starting position

(4c) moves α to a position c-commanding the trace

(4d) moves α to the closest possible position to the trace (except *wh*-movement)

(4e) obeys the Structure Preservation Constraint

(4f) XP-movement only ever moves to Specifiers of functional heads; *wh*-movement is restricted to movement to SpecCP

Properties (4a, b, c, and e) are straightforward. Property (4a) just states that movement only affects some X'-entities (in fact, you might wonder why X'-level projections are inert for Move-α; one possibility, as we saw in 2.6.4, is that this is because such projections don't exist – we'll leave this aside here, however). Properties (4b, c, and e) all impose substantive constraints on Move-α and, in fact, amount to a little theory of Move-α. In fact, they fall together under the idea that we put forward in Section 3.3.2.2 of Chapter 3 that *a moved element α must bind a trace*. In terms of this idea, we can also make sense of (4f) by saying that *wh*-movement moves α to a non-L-related position, and so involves A'-binding of the trace, while DP-movement moves α to an L-related position and so involves A-binding of the trace, as we saw in 3.3.2.3.

So we have the following theory of movement, to restate what we've already seen in a synoptic form:

Move-α:

(5a) leaves a trace in the starting position

(5b) creates a binding relation between the moved category, α, and its trace (A-binding if α is in an L-related position; A'-binding if α is in a non-L-related position)

In fact, property (5a) of Move-α is a consequence of the Projection Principle (see 2.1). So the really central property that is specific to Move-α is (5b): the creation of a binding relation. So far so good (except that you might wonder about the binding relation between a moved head and its trace – let's just suppose that there can be binding, in the sense of coindexation combined with c-command, between X° elements too).

However, the locality condition in (4d) seems to be radically different for the different kinds of movement. We've seen locality conditions on both head-movement (the Head Movement Constraint, (67) in Chapter 1) and DP-Movement (Principle A of the Binding Theory). Besides Principle A, we also suggested that DP-movement may be required to move to the nearest available position: these two conditions aren't quite the same, as we'll see later. But, as we mentioned in Chapter 2, *wh*-movement doesn't seem to be constrained in the same way. *wh*-dependencies appear to be **unbounded dependencies**, able to hold across an arbitrarily large amount of syntactic material. The examples that we used to illustrate this in Chapter 2 (which were taken from classic work by Ross (1967)) were these:

(6a) What$_i$ did Bill buy t$_i$?

(6b) What$_i$ did you force Bill to buy t$_i$?

(6c) What$_i$ did Harry say you had forced Bill to buy t$_i$?

(6d) What$_i$ was it obvious that Harry said you had forced Bill to buy t$_i$?

And it seems intuitively clear that one could, circumstances permitting, interpose an arbitrary amount of material between *what* and its trace in this kind of example. One of the main goals of this chapter is to show that the unbounded nature of *wh*-dependencies is only apparent. We'll see that there is in fact a locality constraint on *wh*-movement, one comparable to the constraints on other kinds of movement. In this way, we'll eventually arrive at a unified theory of Move-α that includes (5) and a general locality condition.

As I said, the principal goal of this chapter is to show how movement theory can be unified by showing how *wh*-movement is, despite initial appearances, subject to a constraint like those which apply to head-movement and DP-movement. In Section 4.1, I'll present the evidence that *wh*-movement is not entirely unbounded – evidence which takes the form of 'island constraints', originally discussed in Ross (1967). In Sections 4.2 and 4.3, I'll present the two central locality principles that have been proposed to account for the locality of *wh*-movement: the Subjacency Principle and the Empty

Category Principle (ECP). Section 4.4 is about the concept of **barriers** (which we introduced in Chapter 2, Section 2.2.2), a first attempt to unify these two principles and integrate them with the rest of the theory. Section 4.5 deals with another kind of unification, namely the development of a theory of locality that applies to DP-movement and head-movement as well as *wh*-movement: Relativized Minimality. Finally, in Section 4.6 I'll present the most recent version of the theory of movement, Manzini's (1992) theory of locality.

4.1 Islands

Here I want to introduce the principal evidence that *wh*-dependencies are subject to constraints. The evidence, which was first systematically discussed and illustrated in Ross (1967) (although it was adumbrated in Chomsky (1964); in any case I'm going to take a number of historical liberties in my presentation), takes the form of a class of phenomena known as **islands** or **island constraints**. The terminology is metaphorical: an island is something that it's difficult to move from – at the very least you need some special means of transportation and, in fact, you can get completely stuck on one. Hence syntactic islands are those structures out of which *wh*-elements can be moved only with difficulty, if at all. It's important to see that, while island phenomena clearly show that *wh*-movement cannot apply just anywhere, they do not show us that *wh*-movement is *never* unbounded. What they show is that *wh*-movement is at least *sometimes* bounded.

As I said above, Ross discovered and illustrated many island phenomena. In the rest of this section I'll discuss the principal island phenomena that were originally identified by Ross, although a number of other constraints have been discovered in more recent work that I'll introduce as we go along. Ross instituted a terminological practice that has been largely followed ever since, that of calling each island 'The X Constraint' or 'The X Condition', where 'X' usually designates the particular structural configuration involved. Since it has at least mnemonic value, I'll follow this practice too.

The island constraints that Ross discussed are as follows:

The Complex NP Constraint (CNPC):
Ross (1986: 76) formulates this constraint as follows:

(7) No element contained in a sentence dominated by a noun phrase ... may be moved out of that noun phrase.

Putting (7) in terms of the assumptions about functional categories that we've made in earlier chapters, the CNPC prevents extraction (this term is often used for 'moving out', and I'll adopt this usage from now on) of α from a configuration like (8):

(8) $[_{DP} \cdots \quad [_{IP} \cdots \alpha \cdots]]$

The CNPC accounts for two main classes of fact: the impossibility of extraction from relative clauses, and the impossibility of extraction from the sentential complements of Nouns like *claim, fact,* and *story.* These facts are illustrated in (9). Here I've indicated the island in small capitals, with a trace in the position of α:

(9a) *Which band$_i$ did you write $[_{DP}$ A SONG WHICH $[_{IP}$ WAS ABOUT T$_i$ $]]$?

(9b) *Which band$_i$ did you believe $[_{DP}$ THE CLAIM THAT $[_{IP}$ WE HAD SEEN t$_i$ $]]$?

In (9a), the DP-island is a relative clause; in (9b) it's a DP containing a Noun and its sentential complement. In some respects, the two instances of the CNPC are distinct; for example, many speakers find sentences like (9a) worse than (9b).

Sentence (9a) should also be compared with (10):

(10) Which band$_i$ did you write $[_{DP}$ A SONG ABOUT t$_i$ $]]$?

Most people find (10) perfectly acceptable. If there is no 'reduced clause' in the complement of *song,* this fact is quite consistent with the CNPC as stated in (7) and (8). However, it is worth pointing out that the definiteness of the DP in (10) is important. The sentence deteriorates if the DP is definite, and is quite bad if there is a possessor DP in its Spec:

(11a) ??Which band$_i$ did you write $[_{DP}$ THAT SONG ABOUT t$_i$ $]]$?

(11b) *Which band$_i$ did you sing $[_{DP}$ MICK'S SONG ABOUT t$_i$ $]]$?

This fact was observed by Fiengo and Higginbotham (1981). Manzini (1992) calls this kind of case a **definiteness** island, since, as you can see, the blockage to extraction seems to be created by a definite D (remember that possessive DPs like *Mick's song* are always definite).

The Subject Condition:

Ross noticed that extraction from sentential subjects, as in (12a), was not allowed. Chomsky (1973) extended this to all cases of complex subjects. The generalization is that extraction from inside a subject is bad:

(12a) *Which rock star$_i$ was $[_{CP}$ THAT THE POLICE WOULD ARREST t$_i$ $]$ expected ?

(12b) ??Which rock star$_i$ were $[_{DP}$ ADMIRERS OF t$_i$ $]$ arrested ?

It's important to see that the Subject Condition bans extraction from within a subject, not extraction of a whole subject.

The Coordinate Structure Constraint (CSC):
(13) In a coordinate structure, no conjunct may be moved, nor may any element contained in a conjunct be moved out of that conjunct.

(Ross (1986: 99))

This means that no α can be extracted in structures like (14) (where '&' represents any kind of coordination):

(14) $[_\alpha \ldots \alpha \ldots]$ & $[_\alpha \ldots \alpha \ldots]$

This rules out examples like the following (again, the island configuration is given in small capitals):

(15a) *What$_i$ did Bill buy POTATOES AND t$_i$?

(15b) *What$_i$ did Bill buy t$_i$ AND POTATOES ?

(15c) *Which guitar$_i$ does KEITH [PLAY t$_i$] AND [SING MADRIGALS] ?

(15d) *Which madrigals$_i$ does KEITH [PLAY THE GUITAR] AND [SING t$_i$] ?

An important proviso to the CSC is that *wh*-movement can apply in coordinate structures as long as it applies **across the board**, in that identical elements are affected in each conjunct. We can see this if we compare the following examples of relative-clause formation (another instance of *wh*-movement):

(16a) Students$_i$ [WHO$_i$ t$_i$ FAIL THE FINAL EXAM] OR [WHO$_i$ t$_i$ DO NOT DO THE READING] will be executed   (Ross (1986: 109))

(16b) *This is the student$_i$ [WHO$_i$ t$_i$ FAILED THE FINAL EXAM] AND [JOHN DID THE READING]

The CSC has to a large extent resisted satisfactory theoretical treatment in the principles-and-parameters framework.

The Left Branch Condition (LBC):
This condition prevents extraction of α in the following configuration, where X is any non-null material:

(17) $[_{DP} \alpha \, X]$

Possessor DPs typically appear in the configuration in (18), and so the LBC tells us that *wh*-constituents that are possessors cannot be extracted from the DP that dominates them, as in:

(18) *Whose$_i$ did you play $[_{DP} $ t$_i$ GUITAR] ?

Possessor DPs can be left-recursive, as in (19):

(19) Mick's friend's favourite guitar

In (19), *Mick's* is on the left branch of the DP *Mick's friend*, which is in turn on the left branch of the whole DP.

(20)

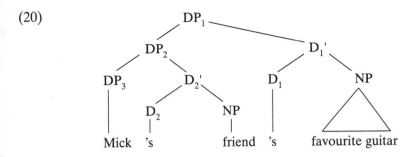

The LBC prevents extraction of the *wh*-element corresponding either to DP$_1$ or to DP$_2$:

(21a) *Whose$_i$ did you play [$_{DP}$ t$_i$ FRIEND'S FAVOURITE GUITAR] ?

(21b) *Whose friend's$_i$ did you play [$_{DP}$ t$_i$ FAVOURITE GUITAR] ?

(You might have noticed that we've treated the *'s* as a D in (20), in line with what we suggested in 1.3.2; if *whose* is really *who* + *'s*, then there might be a very simple explanation for the ungrammaticality of examples like (18) and (21): here a non-constituent made up of SpecDP and D is trying to move.) Instead of extraction from the left branch, when a possessor DP is a *wh*-element, it causes the entire DP containing the possessor to move. In other words, the grammatical version of (18) is (22):

(22) Whose guitar$_i$ did you play t$_i$?

This phenomenon, where a category moves which is not itself +*wh* but which contains a +*wh*-element, is known as **pied-piping** (the idea being that the other, non-*wh*, parts of the constituent containing the *wh*-element have to follow the *wh*-element wherever it goes, just as the rats of Hamelin followed the Pied Piper).

Up to now, I've been implicitly assuming that the island constraints are universal. This is in fact largely true; later in this chapter we'll see some examples of the kind of variation that exists across languages regarding islands, but it is mostly rather slight. However, the LBC appears to be violable in some languages. Ross gives the following examples from Russian and Latin:

(23a) Č'ju$_i$ ty   čitaješ   [$_{DP}$ t$_i$ KNIGU] ?   (Russian)
      whose you are-reading book
      'Whose book are you reading?'

(23b) Cuius$_i$ legis [$_{DP}$ t$_i$ LIBRUM] ?   (Latin)
      whose you-are-reading book
      'Whose book are you reading?'

We can add French *combien* ('how much/many') to this list:

(24) Combien$_i$ as-tu lu [$_{DP}$ t$_i$ DE LIVRES] ?
     how-many have you read of books
     'How many books have you read?'

It seems clear that the LBC is subject to parametric variation, unlike the other island constraints that we've looked at up to now. Beyond simply stating that some languages respect the LBC and others don't, at this point it's rather difficult to know what the parametric variation really consists of. It may be that it is connected to the nature of the D-position: Latin and Russian both lack overt D-elements, for example (although this doesn't explain the French fact in (24)). The precise status of the LBC is an open question at present.

The wh-*island Constraint:*
This was really the first kind of island phenomenon to be discussed, as it was first mentioned by Chomsky (1964).

The basic observation here is that a *wh*-element cannot be extracted out of clauses introduced by another *wh*-element. Now, there are two main types of clause that are introduced by *wh*-elements: questions and relatives. Relatives come under the CNPC, as we have seen. Interrogatives are thus the relevant case here:

(25a) ??Whose car were you wondering [HOW$_j$ TO FIX t$_i$ t$_j$] ?

(25b) ?*Whose car$_i$ were you wondering [HOW$_j$ YOU SHOULD FIX t$_i$ t$_j$] ?

(Since there are two instances of *wh*-movement in these examples, one to the lower SpecCP and one to the higher, there are two traces: the order of the traces is t$_{whose\ car}$ t$_{how}$ in each case, as the order of the non-*wh*-elements shows: *I fixed Bill's car with a cocktail shaker.*)

Most speakers don't find either of the examples in (25) very good, but would probably agree that there's a contrast between (25a) and (25b). Tensed *wh*-complements seem to give rise to 'stronger' ungrammaticality than infinitival ones.

The above are the main islands discussed by Ross. So we see that *wh*-movement is subject to at least the CNPC, the Subject Condition, the CSC, the *wh*-island Constraint, and (in some languages) the LBC. However, as I said above, this only shows that *wh*-movement is bounded *sometimes*. It still appears to be fundamentally different from the other instantiations of Move-α in that a *wh*-category can move over an unlimited amount of material, provided that that material contains no islands.

Ross discussed another constraint indicating that *wh*-movement may be consistently bounded, one which later became known as the 'Right Roof Constraint'. Standard *wh*-movement in questions and relatives of the kind that we've been looking at always moves the *wh*-element to the left; in fact, movement is always to SpecCP. However, there are movement rules which appear to move constituents to adjoined positions on the right of the starting point. It's rather unclear what the landing-site of rules like extraposition might be, although it seems to be a position right-adjoined to a VP or to a clausal functional category (right-adjunction structures are ruled out by Kayne's LCA, discussed in Chapter 1, but we'll gloss over that matter here).

In any case, it seems pretty clear that the landing-site of extraposition and similar operations is not an L-related position, and so the operation is a kind of *wh*-movement, in that the moved constituent A'-binds its trace. One operation of this kind is extraposition, which relates pairs like (26):

(26a) The claim [$_{CP}$ that the world was round] was made by the Greeks

(26b) The claim t$_i$ was made by the Greeks [$_{CPi}$ that the world was round]

Here the CP *that the world was round* is apparently moved to the right of the main clause. Ross observed that this operation cannot go further; that is, it is impossible to extrapose 'two clauses up'. The ungrammaticality of this kind of 'long' extraposition is shown in (27):

(27) *The proof that the claim t$_i$ was made by the Greeks was given in 1492 [$_{CPi}$ that the world was round]

Compare (27) with (28), where extraposition goes just 'one clause up':

(28) The proof that the claim t$_i$ was made [$_{CPi}$ that the world was round] by the Greeks was given in 1492

Ross showed that all operations that move material to the right are bounded in this way. So we see that only leftward *wh*-movement from non-islands is unbounded: the other cases of *wh*-movement are bounded either by islands or by the Right Roof Constraint. The obvious question to ask now is: what's special about leftward *wh*-movement from non-islands? In Section 4.2, we'll see how Chomsky (1973) dealt with this.

In this section, I've introduced a whole range of facts, all of which clearly indicate that *wh*-movement is subject to constraints of various kinds. Exactly what the theoretical interpretation of these facts should be remains to be seen; this is largely what we'll be looking at for the rest of this chapter. What we've seen is the following:

(29a) Rightward movement to A'-positions is always bounded

(29b) Leftward movement of *wh*-XPs is subject to island constraints

To recapitulate, here's a list of the island constraints we've seen:

CNPC:
(30a) *Which band$_i$ did you write [$_{DP}$ A SONG WHICH [$_{IP}$ WAS ABOUT t$_i$]] ?
*Which band$_i$ did you believe [$_{DP}$ THE CLAIM THAT [$_{IP}$ WE HAD SEEN t$_i$]] ? (see (9))

Subject Condition:
(30b) *Which rock star$_i$ was [$_{CP}$ THAT THE POLICE WOULD ARREST t$_i$] expected ?
??Which rock star$_i$ were [$_{DP}$ ADMIRERS OF t$_i$] arrested ? (see (12))

CSC:

(30c) *What$_i$ did Bill buy POTATOES AND t$_i$?

*What$_i$ did Bill buy t$_i$ AND POTATOES ?

*Which guitar$_i$ does KEITH [PLAY t$_i$] AND [SING MADRIGALS] ?

*Which madrigals$_i$ does KEITH [PLAY THE GUITAR] AND [SING t$_i$] ?

(see (16))

Left branch condition:

(30d) *Whose$_i$ did you play [$_{DP}$ t$_i$ guitar] ?

wh-*islands:*

(30e) ??Whose car were you wondering [HOW$_j$ TO FIX t$_i$ t$_j$] ?

?*Whose car$_i$ were you wondering [HOW$_j$ YOU SHOULD FIX t$_i$ t$_j$] ?

Every now and then in this book I've mentioned what a bore lists are. The reason for this is that lists don't really explain things, and what we're after when we're in the business of theory-construction is explanations. What we've seen in this section, I hope you'll agree, is a range of fascinating and complex facts (incidentally, facts that were totally unknown before the development of generative grammar, and mostly before Ross's 1967 Ph.D. dissertation). But we've just got a long list of island constraints. What we need now is some kind of unifying principle, which can tell us *why* the islands are the way they are. And, ultimately, of course, we want to link all these facts about *wh*-movement to what we've seen in connection with DP-movement and head-movement. The next sections all develop these points, beginning with the first real principle of locality: subjacency.

4.2 Subjacency

4.2.1 Successive Cyclicity

The basic idea behind subjacency was a fundamental conceptual move: we drop the assumption that *wh*-movement, at least in leftward-movement from non-islands, is unbounded. So: wh-*movement, despite appearances, is bounded.* This very important idea can only work if we assume that *wh*-movement can, like DP-movement, operate in successive cycles, or **successive-cyclically**. This idea makes it possible to, as it were, 'measure the distance' between the landing-site of a *wh*-category and its starting position.

In Section 2.3 of Chapter 2 we saw that DP-movement can give the impression of moving a DP a long way, but that each instance of apparently non-local movement can be broken down into a series of successive local hops, each of which actually moves the DP to the nearest available position. Here are the examples we saw then:

(31a) The train$_i$ seems [t'$_i$ to be likely [t$_i$ to be late]]   (2.3 (48b))

(31b) The money$_i$ seems [t'$_i$ to have been stolen t$_i$]

(31c) The train$_i$ is expected [t'$_i$ to arrive t$_i$ an hour late]

(31d) The weeds$_i$ appear [t'$_i$ to have grown t$_i$ while we were on holiday]

(31e) The patient$_i$ seems [t"$_i$ to be expected [t'$_i$ to die t$_i$]] (2.3 (49a–d))

These examples show us that raising can take place 'cyclically'. All these movements are caused by the Case Filter (or feature-checking requirements, in terms of checking theory as introduced in Section 2.6). The cyclic movement shows that a DP which is looking for Case moves to the nearest available potential Case position, looks for Case, and, if it can't find it, moves to the *next* nearest position, and so on. In Chapter 1, we also saw some examples of successive-cyclic head-movement in our discussion of verb second in 1.4.2.4 (V-to-I-to-C movement).

If the other two types of movement (which seem to be phenomenologically simpler than *wh*-movement: of course, that doesn't mean that they really are simpler) can be successive-cyclic, it's entirely reasonable to think that *wh*-movement can be too. Specifically, the proposal is that wh-*elements move successively through SpecCP*. So, the structure for a case of apparently unbounded *wh*-movement like (6c) looks like (6c'):

(6c') [$_{CP1}$ What$_i$ [$_{C'1}$ did [$_{IP1}$ Harry say [$_{CP2}$ t"$_i$ [$_{C'2}$ [$_{IP2}$ you had forced Bill [$_{CP3}$ t'$_i$ [$_{C'3}$ [$_{IP3}$ to buy t$_i$]]]] ?

Here *what* moves from its base position, occupied by t_i, first to the most embedded SpecCP (SpecCP$_3$), then to the intermediate SpecCP$_2$, and then to the matrix SpecCP$_1$. These positions are marked by the appropriately-named 'intermediate traces' *t'$_i$* and *t"$_i$*. The seemingly unbounded movement thus in fact involves a series of relatively local hops from SpecCP to SpecCP.

If we want to make sure that *wh*-movement is genuinely local in the way indicated in (6c'), then we need to make sure that it moves from SpecCP to the next SpecCP that c-commands it. The c-command condition is built into the definition of Move-α (see (5b)), so what we need to do here is make sure that *wh* always moves to the closest SpecCP. There are two parts to this: (i) we have to make sure that *wh*-movement doesn't put a *wh* category in some position other than SpecCP, and (ii) we have to make sure that *wh*-movement always goes to the closest SpecCP position.

Let's just deal with point (i) for now by saying that *wh*-movement only takes place in order to check a *wh*-feature (as proposed in 2.6.3), and SpecCP is the only position where these features can be checked. Therefore +*wh* categories will never move to any other position.

Point (ii) is where subjacency comes in. To start with, I'll give a simplified version of the original formulation in Chomsky (1973:81)):

> *Subjacency:*
> (32) In the following structure, α and β cannot be related by movement:
> ... α ... [$_{BC}$ ... [$_{BC}$ ... β ....] ..]
> where α and β are separated by more than one blocking category BC

Let's follow Chomsky's (1973) proposal in taking the blocking categories

(BCs) to be DP and IP. Now we can see how subjacency will have to go to the next SpecCP up. Consider what happens in (6c') if *wh*-movement 'skips' a SpecCP:

(6c") $[_{CP1}$ What$_i$ $[_{C'1}$ did $[_{IP1}$ Harry say $[_{CP2}$ $[_{C'2}$ $[_{IP2}$ you had forced Bill $[_{CP3}$ t'$_i$ $[_{C'3}$ $[_{IP3}$ to buy t$_i$]]]] ?

Here, *what* has moved from SpecCP3 (the position of *t'$_i$*) directly to SpecCP$_1$, skipping SpecCP$_2$. In so doing the movement crosses both IP$_2$ and IP$_1$. We've defined IP as a BC, and so this derivation, in crossing two BCs, violates subjacency. Movement through SpecCP$_2$ is necessary in order to avoid this violation. Since SpecCP$_2$ is available for *what* to transit through, (6c) is grammatical – but only with the derivation given in (6c').

4.2.2 Explaining Island Constraints

Subjacency gives us a kind of measure of syntactic distance in terms of BCs. As such, it can explain many of the island effects we saw in the previous section. Let's look at how this is done. Here are the typical CNPC violations that we saw in the previous section:

(33a)   *Which band$_i$ did you write $[_{DP}$ A SONG WHICH $[_{IP}$ WAS ABOUT t$_i$]] ?

(33b)   *Which band$_i$ did you believe $[_{DP}$ THE CLAIM THAT $[_{IP}$ WE HAD SEEN t$_i$]] ? (see (9))

Assuming successive-cyclic movement through SpecCP, (33b) has the following representation:

(33b')   *$[_{CP1}$ Which band$_i$ did $[_{IP1}$ you believe $[_{DP}$ the claim $[_{CP2}$ t'$_i$ that $[_{IP2}$ we had seen t$_i$]] ?

I've marked the BCs here in bold. The first step of movement, from the base position to SpecCP$_2$, crosses just one BC, IP$_2$. The second, on the other hand, crosses DP and IP$_1$. As such, it violates subjacency. So subjacency accounts for the complement case of the CNPC.

Now look at the relative-clause case:

(33a')   *$[_{CP1}$ Which band$_i$ did $[_{IP1}$ you write $[_{DP}$ a song $[_{CP2}$ which$_j$ $[_{IP2}$ t$_j$ was about t$_i$]] ?

Here there are two movements: one of *which* from the subject position of IP$_2$ to SpecCP$_2$, and of *which band* to SpecCP$_1$. If *which* moves first, then *which band* has to move in a single step all the way to SpecCP$_1$. This movement crosses three BCs, and so violates subjacency. If *which band* moves first, then it can presumably move cyclically through SpecCP$_2$. Movement from this position will nevertheless violate subjacency, as it crosses the two BCs DP and IP$_1$. I mentioned in 4.1 that relative-clause CNPC violations are worse than complement cases; a natural way to capture this would be by forcing the relative-clause to involve the crossing of three BCs as opposed to two in the complement case. To do this, we need to ensure that *which* moves first in (33a'). The following principle does this:

The Strict Cycle Condition:
(34) Nothing can move from a position c-commanded by an intermediate trace.

If we move *which band* to SpecCP$_2$ and on to SpecCP$_1$ in (33a') before moving *which* to SpecCP$_2$, then we'd have the following representation after the second movement of *which band* but before any movement of *which*:

(33a'') *[$_{CP1}$ Which band$_i$ did [$_{IP1}$ you write [$_{DP}$ a song [$_{CP2}$ t'$_i$ [$_{IP2}$ which was about t$_i$]] ?

Here *which* is c-commanded by the intermediate trace *t'$_i$*, and so the Strict Cycle Condition is violated. So we force the derivation where *which* moves first to SpecCP$_2$ and so *which band* crosses three BCs en route to SpecCP$_1$. This gives rise to a stronger violation of subjacency than the complement CNPC example.

Next, let's look at the Subject Condition. Here are the examples from the last section with the successive-cyclic *wh*-movements indicated:

(35a) *[$_{CP1}$ Which rock star$_i$ was [$_{IP1}$ [$_{CP2}$ t'$_i$ that [$_{IP2}$ the police would arrest t$_i$]] expected]]?

(35b) ??[$_{CP1}$ Which rock star$_i$ were [$_{IP}$ [$_{DP}$ admirers of t$_i$] arrested] ?
(see (12))

You can see straight away that the movement of *which rock star* in (35b) crosses two BCs, DP and IP. On the other hand, (35a) is allowed, since the movement can pass cyclically through SpecCP$_2$. However, it has often been suggested that subjects, meaning categories that occupy SpecIP, are always DPs. If that's true, then the correct representation of (35a) would be:

(35a') *[$_{CP1}$ Which rock star$_i$ was [$_{IP1}$ [$_{DP}$ [$_{CP2}$ t'$_i$ that [$_{IP2}$ the police would arrest t$_i$]]] expected ?

Here we can see that *which rock star* crosses two BCs on its way to SpecCP$_1$. So subjacency can account for the Subject Condition.

Subjacency can also account for *wh*-islands. Let's look at the examples we gave in the previous section (see (25)), highlighting the BCs:

(36a) ?[$_{CP1}$ Whose car were [$_{IP1}$ you wondering [$_{CP2}$ how$_j$ [$_{IP2}$ to fix t$_i$ t$_j$] ?

(36b) ?*[$_{CP1}$ Whose car$_i$ were [$_{IP1}$ you wondering [$_{CP2}$ how$_j$ [$_{IP2}$ you should fix t$_i$ t$_j$] ?

Subjacency treats both of these examples alike. Remember that the Strict Cycle Condition (see (34)) makes the movement to SpecCP$_2$ take place first every time, so the category which undergoes 'long' movement to SpecCP$_1$ crosses both IP$_2$ and IP$_1$ in both of these examples, and subjacency rules them both out. Obviously, this is basically a good result, but we'd like to know why tensed *wh*-islands are worse than infinitival *wh*-islands. So, although subjacency tells us that these examples are bad, it doesn't make any distinctions as to *degree* of ungrammaticality which is what we'd ideally like.

Next, let's see how subjacency can handle the Left Branch Condition. Here, again, is the typical example with the BCs highlighted:

(37) *Whose$_i$ did [$_{IP}$ you play [$_{DP}$ t$_i$ guitar]] ?

This example is straightforward; movement crosses IP and DP and subjacency is violated. In fact, subjacency works too well here, seemingly, since we saw that in a number of languages the LBC doesn't seem to hold (see examples (23 and 24)).

So far we've seen that subjacency does a pretty impressive job of unifying the island constraints we saw in the previous section. The CSC, however, is not so readily captured by subjacency as formulated in (32). Here are the relevant examples again:

(38a) *What$_i$ did [$_{IP}$ Bill buy [$_{DP}$ potatoes and t$_i$]] ?

(38b) *What$_i$ did [$_{IP}$ Bill buy [$_{DP}$ t$_i$ and potatoes]] ?

(38c) *Which guitar$_i$ does [$_{IP}$ Keith [$_{VP}$ [$_{VP}$ play t$_i$] and [$_{VP}$ sing madrigals]]] ?

(38d) *Which madrigals$_i$ does [$_{IP}$ Keith [$_{VP}$ [$_{VP}$ play the guitar] and [$_{VP}$ sing t$_i$]]] ?

I'm following the standard assumption that conjoined categories form a bigger category of the same kind: you 'ight note in passing that this means that coordinate structures don't fit the X'-schema that we gave in Chapter 1 – see Kayne (1994) for a recent proposal to reconcile coordination with X'-theory). Extraction out of a conjoined DP as in (38a and b) therefore violates subjacency, as you can see. However, extraction from a coordinated VP, as in (38c and d), doesn't. Here only one BC, IP, is crossed. To reconcile the CSC with subjacency, we'd need either to show that all coordinated categories were IPs or DPs or to say that the category dominating conjoined categories – whatever it is – is a BC. The former approach just won't wash empirically, and the latter amounts to restating the CSC. So the CSC poses a problem. And remember that 'across-the-board' extraction is allowed: see (16) above.

So far, we've seen that subjacency can give a unified analysis of the CNPC, the Subject Condition, some cases of the CSC, the LBC, and *wh*-islands. There are two basic kinds of problem. One is that subjacency can't handle a number of cases of the CSC; the other is that subjacency is a blanket condition that just bans certain kinds of movement, and because of this it can't distinguish extraction out of an infinitival *wh*-island from extraction out of a tensed *wh*-island. Nevertheless, it's clear that subjacency goes a good way towards giving a unified explanation for strong islands.

4.2.3 Parametric Variation

Before going on to the Empty Category Principle, I want to look at one interesting piece of apparent parametric variation in how subjacency works. Rizzi (1982) observed that, at first sight, Italian seems to allow subjacency to be violated in *wh*-islands:

(39) Tuo fratello, [a cui$_i$ mi domando [che storie$_j$ abbiano
     Your brother, to whom I   wonder   which stories they-have
     raccontato t$_i$ t$_j$], era molto preoccupato
     told   was very worried

These are tensed *wh*-islands, cases where subjacency gets it just about right for English by ruling extraction out altogether (Rizzi didn't discuss adjunct extraction, so we'll just leave that aside here). Why are they allowed in Italian?

One solution would be to say that subjacency just doesn't hold in Italian, but Rizzi shows that this isn't right. The CNPC is respected in Italian:

(40) *Tuo fratello, a cui$_i$ temo la possibilità che abbiano
     Your brother, to whom I-fear the possibility that they-have
     raccontato tutto t$_i$, ...
     told   everything, ...

Even more interestingly, Rizzi shows that the *wh*-islands of a more complicated sort do exist in Italian. Extraction from a *wh*-island inside another *wh*-island is impossible. Example (41a) gives the basic structure with one *wh*-island contained within another. This structure, like its English counterpart, is fine, since both the *wh*-movements that form the respective *wh*-islands are local, as the coindexed traces indicate. However, if we try to extract from the lowest island, ungrammaticality results in both English and Italian, as (41b) shows (in this example, I've only indicated the coindexed trace of the illicitly moved relative element):

(41a) Mi sto domandando [a chi$_i$ potrei chiedere t$_i$ [quando$_j$
      I   am wondering   to whom I-may ask   when
      dovrò   parlare di   questo argomento t$_j$]
      I'll have-to   speak about this   topic
      'I'm wondering who I can ask when I'll have to speak about this
      topic'

(41b) *Questo argomento, [di cui$_k$ mi sto domandando [a chi
      This   topic   of which I   am wondering   to whom
      potrei chiedere [quando dovrò   parlare t$_k$]]], mi
      I-may ask   when   I'll-have-to speak   to-me
      sembra sempre più   complicato
      seems ever   more complicated
      'This topic, which I am wondering who I can ask when I'll have to
      talk about, seems more and more complicated to me'

Rizzi concludes that the only reasonable solution is that subjacency holds in Italian but that *Italian has different blocking categories from English.* Specifically, the blocking categories in Italian are CP and DP, rather than IP and DP. In this way, the above data are accounted for, as we can see in (42), where the Italian BCs are highlighted:

(42a) Tuo   fratello, [a cui$_i$ mi domando [$_{CP}$ che   storie$_j$
     Your brother,   to whom I   wonder   which   stories
     abbiano   raccontato t$_i$ t$_j$], era   molto   preoccupato
     they-have told   was   very   worried

                                   ((39). One Italian BC crossed)

(42b) *Tuo fratello, a   cui$_i$ temo [$_{DP}$ la possibilità [$_{CP}$ che
     Your brother, to whom I-fear   the possibility   that
     abbiano   raccontato tutto t$_i$, ...
     they-have told   everything, ...

                                   ((40). Two Italian BCs crossed)

(42c) *Questo argomento, [di cui$_k$ mi sto domandando [$_{CP}$a chi
     This   topic   of which I   am wondering   to whom
     potrei chiedere [$_{CP}$ quando dovrò   parlare t$_k$]]], mi
     I-may ask   when   I'll-have-to speak   to-me
     sembra sempre più   complicato
     seems ever   more complicated

                                   ((41b). Two Italian BCs crossed)

And compare (39) (= (42a)) with its English counterpart: here the different BCs in the different languages are highlighted:

(43a) Tuo fratello, [a cui$_i$ mi domando [$_{CP}$ che storie$_j$ abbiano raccontato
     t$_i$ t$_j$ era molto preoccupato   (One Italian BC crossed)

(43b) *Your brother, who$_i$ [$_{IP}$ I wonder which stories [$_{IP}$ they've been
     telling t$_i$, was very worried   (Two English BCs crossed)

And so Rizzi showed that languages can differ according to which BCs they select. His analysis of the difference between English and Italian, although convincing in itself, raises another question: what is the range of choice among the BCs that UG makes available? Could we expect to find a language in which VP and AP were barriers? If not, why not? What we need is a more principled way of deciding what the possible BCs are, both in UG and at the level of the parametric choices made by different languages. This is going to be the principal topic of Section 4.4.

4.2.4 Conclusion

In this section we've seen the following points:

• the proposal that *wh*-movement is successive cyclic, and bounded by

subjacency (see (32))
- the Strict Cycle Condition (see (34))
- how subjacency accounts for (most) island constraints
- Rizzi's proposal that Italian chooses different BCs from English.

In Section 4.4, we'll come back to the question of giving a more principled account of what the class of BCs is. Before doing that, however, I want to introduce some more data regarding *wh*-movement, and the other main locality principle: the Empty Category Principle.

4.3 The Empty Category Principle

In this section, I want to introduce the Empty Category Principle (ECP). This principle constrains Move-α by imposing an LF licensing requirement on traces. Although the ECP is intended to apply to all traces, including *wh*-traces, DP-traces and head-traces, in this section I'll restrict the discussion to *wh*-traces (we'll look at how it extends to other kinds of traces in 4.5). Since it's a condition on traces rather than on movement, the ECP can be made to distinguish different kinds of traces. In this way, as we'll see in 4.3.1, it can account for the phenomenon of **argument-adjunct asymmetries**. It can also handle the constraints on *wh*-movement in languages which appear to lack an overt version of this movement, as we'll see. In 4.3.2 I'll introduce another locality phenomenon, the **complementizer-trace effect**; we'll see that the ECP can handle this, and can give a very interesting analysis of the parametric variation associated with it. Finally, 4.3.3 looks at some extensions of the ECP proposed by Kayne; in this section, I'll also introduce the intriguing phenomenon of **parasitic gaps**.

4.3.1 Argument-Adjunct Asymmetries
4.3.1.1 Lexical Government and Antecedent Government
Up to now, I've presented the constraints on *wh*-movement, whether appearing as islands or unified under subjacency, as blanket constraints on any kind of movement. But in fact there are important differences between arguments of certain types and adjunct elements with regard to extraction. These differences emerge if we compare the extraction of a direct-object *wh*-element from a *wh*-island – seen in (44) (which is the repetition of (36)) – with extraction of an adverbial element from the same island, seen in (45):

(44a) ?$[_{CP1}$ Whose car$_i$ were $[_{IP1}$ you wondering $[_{CP2}$ how$_j$ $[_{IP2}$ to fix t_i t_j $]$?

(44b) ?*$[_{CP1}$ Whose car$_i$ were $[_{IP1}$ you wondering $[_{CP2}$ how$_j$ $[_{IP2}$ you should fix t_i t_j $]$?

(45a) *How$_j$ were you wondering $[$ WHOSE CAR$_i$ TO FIX t_i t_j $]$?

(45b) *How$_j$ were you wondering $[$ WHOSE CAR$_i$ YOU SHOULD FIX t_i t_j $]$?

The difference between (44) and (45) seems to be as follows: while the argument-extraction examples in (44) are very awkward, they are intelligible; in examples like (45), on the other hand, it is all but impossible to see the interpretation that is being looked for (with *how* interpreted as modifying the lower clause, looking for an answer like 'with a spanner' in each case). This suggests that the badness of adjunct-extraction has to do with an LF condition which prevents certain kinds of interpretations. This is where the ECP, which we can think of as an LF-condition on traces, comes in. As a first formulation, let's take the following:

> *ECP:*
> (46) Traces must be properly governed

'Proper government' here means a subspecies of government. Or, more precisely, it refers to two subspecies of government:

> *Proper Government:*
> (47) either: government by a lexical head (lexical government)
>   or: government by the moved category (antecedent government)

To see how the ECP accounts for these asymmetries, we need to look again at the definition of government that I gave in 2.2.2, (16):

> *Government:*
> α, a head, governs β if and only if

(48a) α c-commands β

(48b) no barrier dominates β but not α

> *Barrier:*
> (49)   Any XP except IP

Here's the structure of a simple clause (glossing over the 'split-Infl' structure once more):

(50)

I'm assuming that adjuncts are adjoined to VP. In that case, adjuncts are not governed by anything, given the definitions in (48) and (49). Complements, on the other hand, are always governed by the lexical head that selects them. So complements are always lexically governed and adjuncts never are. This means that traces in complement position always satisfy the ECP, while adjunct traces can only satisfy the ECP by being antecedent-governed. So now we need to look more closely at antecedent-government.

We'll elaborate our conception of antecedent-government steadily over Sections 4.4 and 4.5 – in fact, we'll see that it comes close to giving us the key unifying concept for the theory of locality in 4.5. For the moment, it's enough simply to state that antecedent-government is defined in terms of blocking categories just like subjacency:

> *Antecedent Government:*
> α, a moved category, antecedent-governs β if and only if

(51a) α c-commands β

(51b) no more than one blocking category dominates β but not α

For now, we retain from the previous section the idea that IP and DP are blocking categories. You might notice that the definition of antecedent-government in (51) isn't really much like the definition of government in (48). Unifying these definitions is one of the tasks of Section 4.4.

So, given the definition of antecedent-government in (51), the ECP basically requires that an adjunct trace be subjacent to its antecedent, otherwise it will not be licensed at LF. If the trace fails to be licensed at LF, then the interpretation of the antecedent-trace relation will not be available, and the effect of uninterpretability that we noticed in (45) will arise. So, an ECP violation and a subjacency violation give different kinds of ungrammaticality: subjacency violations give rise to syntactic awkwardness, while ECP violations are usually uninterpretable on the intended reading. Sometimes, as in the case of infinitival *wh*-islands, the subjacency violation appears to be rather mild, as we've seen.

The argument-adjunct distinction can be found in the other islands that we've seen. We can see this in the following examples:

(52a) CNPC:
       *How$_i$ do you believe [the stories that [John fixed your car t$_i$]] ?

(52b) Subject Island:
       *How$_i$ would [to fix your car t$_i$] be best ?

In each of these cases, in addition to the syntactic awkwardness created by the violation of subjacency, the intended interpretation (where *how* modifies the predicate inside the island, indicated by the position of the trace inside the brackets) is all but impossible to perceive. This is because the traces fail the ECP, since they are neither lexically governed nor antecedent-governed. They are not lexically governed because they are adjuncts, and they are not antecedent-governed because their antecedent is separated from them by more than one BC (see the discussion of these island effects in the previous section).

In fact, calling these effects argument-adjunct asymmetries is slightly misleading. If you look again at the definition of lexical government, and at the clause structure in (50), you'll see that subjects are not lexically governed either. In (50), the subject position – Spec,IP – is governed by C, but C isn't lexical. So subjects ought to pattern with adjuncts as far as the asymmetries in (44) and (45) go. In fact this is basically true, as we can see from examples like (53):

(53) *Which band$_i$ were you wondering whether t$_i$ will play that song ?

If we assume that *whether* is in SpecCP here, the dependency between *which band* and its trace crosses two IPs, that is the subject trace fails to be antecedent-governed. Since the subject is not lexically governed, the sentence is very bad. On the other hand, subjects that are in positions governed by a lexical head, typically a verb, are lexically governed and so we don't find the kind of violation seen in (53):

(54) Which band$_i$ did you consider t$_i$ to be the best ?

Remember that complements to ECM Verbs like *consider* are AgrSPs: see 2.2.3. Leaving aside ECM subjects, we should really talk about 'complement/non-complement asymmetries' instead of talking about 'argument-adjunct asymmetries'. In fact, for now I'll use both terms synonymously. We'll come back to this and related points in the next subsection.

4.3.1.2 The ECP at LF: Comparative Evidence

There's very interesting and important comparative evidence that the ECP holds of LF, while subjacency holds of overt movement. This comes primarily from Huang's (1982) study of *wh*-movement and related phenomena in Chinese. As we saw in 2.6.3, *wh*-elements don't undergo overt movement in Chinese:

(55a) Zhangsan yiwei Lisi mai-le shenme?
Zhangsan think Lisi bought what
'What does Zhangsan think Lisi bought?'

(55b) Zhangsan xiang-zhidao Lisi mai-le shenme
Zhangsan wonders   Lisi bought what
'Zhangsan wonders what Lisi bought'

As we mentioned in 2.6.3, it's natural to think that Chinese behaves this way because it has a weak *wh* feature (although we also mentioned that Watanabe (1992) proposes a different view).

What we're interested in here, though, is the fact that Huang shows that *covert wh-movement in Chinese is subject to the ECP.* In other words, we don't find the island constraints that affect movement of complements that we looked at using English data in 4.1:

(56a) CNPC (relative clause):
    ni   zui   xihuan [SHEI MAI DE SHU] ?
    you most like   who buy Prt book
    'Who is the x such that you like the books x bought?'

(56b) Subject Condition:
    [WO MAI   SHENME] zui   hao ?
      I   buy   what   most good
    'What is it best that I buy?'

(56c) Argument *wh*-Island:
    ni   xiang-zhidao [WO WEISHENME MAI SHENME] ?
    you   wonder   I   why   buy what
    'What is the x such that you wonder why I bought x ?'

But we do find that adjunct *wh*-elements inside *wh*-islands cannot be interpreted. Hence (56c) cannot have the interpretation 'What is the reason x such that you wonder what I bought for x ?' Huang interprets this fact as showing that adjuncts cannot move out of *wh*-islands at LF. In other words, adjunct-traces are subject to the ECP. Huang proposes that the ECP applies to the traces of covert movement, that is, that the ECP is an LF-condition on traces while subjacency only constrains overt movement. LF-movement of complement *wh*-elements as in (55) and (56) is fine, therefore, whether these elements are in islands or not. The traces of these movements are uniformly lexically governed. On the other hand, adjunct traces fail to be antecedent-governed where their antecedent is moved out of an island (see the definition of antecedent-government in (51)); the adjunct traces fail the ECP in examples like (57a), and the interpretation is unavailable. In a similar way, we account for the ungrammaticality of sentences with a *wh*-element inside other kinds of islands – these examples contrast with those in (56a and b) (the English translations indicate the interpretation of 'why' which is relevant here; these translations are of course also ungrammatical in English with the coindexation given):

(57a) CNPC (relative clause):
    *ni   zui   xihuan [WEISHENME MAI SHU DE REN] ?
    you most like   why   buy book Prt person
    'Why$_i$ do you like [the man who bought the books t_{ij}]?'

(57b) Subject Condition:
    *[WO   WEISHENME MAI   SHU] zui   hao ?
      I   why   buy   book most like
    'Why$_i$ is [that I buy the books t_i] best ?'

Huang's work gave a very nice cross-linguistic confirmation of the existence of covert movement and of the distinction between subjacency and the ECP. However, there are clearly connections between subjacency and the ECP, in particular in that antecedent-government, as we defined it in (51), seems to be very close to subjacency. We also have to look more closely at the notions of blocking category, relevant for subjacency and antecedent-government, and barrier, relevant for government and lexical government. These are the central issues addressed by the *Barriers* system (Chomsky (1986b)); we'll look at them in detail in 4.4.

4.3.2 Complementizer-trace Effects and the Null Subject Parameter Revisited

4.3.2.1 Complementizer-trace Effects

The original motivation for the ECP didn't in fact come from the asymmetries that we've been looking at, but from Complementizer-trace effects (henceforth C-t effects). The observation here is that extraction of a subject across a complementizer is not good:

(58) *Who$_i$ did you say that t$_i$ wrote this song?

For a while in the 1970s it was thought that examples like (58) were evidence that *wh*-traces were subject to Principle A of the binding theory. In this way, (58) is assimilated to examples like:

(59) *Mick$_i$ thinks that himself$_i$ is the greatest

However, *wh*-traces are fine in object position in this kind of example, unlike anaphors:

(60a) Who$_i$ did you say that Phil admires t$_i$?

(60b) *Mick$_i$ thinks that Marianne admires himself$_i$

Comparing (58) and (60a), we see another example of a complement/non-complement asymmetry (a subject-object asymmetry in this case), and so the ECP is the relevant principle. In (58a), the subject trace is not lexically governed, unlike the object trace in (60a). If the subject trace also fails to be antecedent-governed in (58), then we can rule it out by the ECP.

According to the definition of antecedent-government in (51), however, the subject trace in (58) would be acceptable. We can see this if we look more closely at the structure of (58), taking into account successive-cyclic movement and highlighting the BCs:

(58') *[$_{CP1}$ Who$_i$ did [$_{IP1}$ you say [$_{CP2}$ t'$_i$ that [$_{IP2}$ t$_i$ wrote this song]]]] ?

Who moves from the lower subject position (SpecIP$_2$) to SpecCP$_2$, crossing just the one BC, IP$_2$. The second step of movement takes it to SpecCP$_1$, crossing just IP$_1$. So there is no step of movement that crosses two BCs here. In fact, the movement appears to be exactly the same as that which the object *wh*-element undergoes in (60a), as you should be able to see.

An important clue to what's going on in (58) comes from the grammaticality of examples like (61), where *that* has been dropped (an option which is generally available in finite complements to verbs in English):

(61) Who$_i$ did you say t$_i$ wrote this song?

Example (61) presumably looks like (62') if we take successive cyclicity into account:

(62') [$_{CP1}$ Who$_i$ did [$_{IP1}$ you say [$_{CP2}$ t'$_i$ [$_{IP2}$ t$_i$ wrote this song]]]] ?

The contrasts between (58) and (60a) and between (58) and (61) show that subject-extraction is sensitive to the presence of a complementizer: the Complementizer-trace effect.

We can account for the C-t effect in terms of the ECP if we say that the presence of the complementizer in (58) blocks antecedent government of the subject trace. Since the subject isn't lexically governed, the presence of the complementizer leads to ungrammaticality. Complements, on the other hand, are quite indifferent to the presence of the complementizer, as (60a) and (63) show:

(63) Who$_i$ did you say Phil admires t$_i$?

However, we just pointed out that the definition of antecedent government in (51) allows the subject trace to be antecedent-governed in (58). More generally, the definition in (51) won't distinguish between the presence and the absence of a complementizer.

We can handle complementizer-trace effects by adding a notion of 'minimality' to the definition of antecedent government, as follows:

> *Antecedent Government (Revised):*
> α, a moved category, antecedent-governs β if and only if

(51a') α c-commands β

(51b') no more than one blocking category dominates β but not α

(51c') there is no filled C-position that minimally c-commands β and does not c-command α

The definition of minimal c-command was given in 1.4.2 (68), as follows (and see the Appendix to Chapter 2):

> *Minimal C-command:*
> (64) α minimally c-commands β iff α c-commands β and there is no γ, such that γ both c-commands β and does not c-command α

Let's look at the relevant parts of (58) to see how (51') handles C-t effects:

(65)

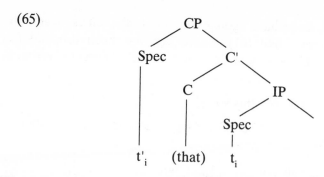

We can see that C minimally c-commands the subject: it c-commands the subject and there is nothing else that c-commands the subject without also c-commanding C. By (51c'), then, when C is overt it will block antecedent-government between the trace in SpecCP and the trace in SpecIP. Since the trace in SpecIP is not lexically governed, it will violate the ECP when C is overt. This accounts for C-t effects. On the other hand, if the Complementizer is not overt, in other words if *that* is not present, (51c') allows the subject trace to be antecedent-governed by the trace in SpecCP *(t'$_i$)*.

Rule (51c') doesn't make reference to complementizers as such, just to the presence of a filled C-position. We saw in 1.4.2.2 that in main clauses C can be filled by a moved auxiliary (I). Usually, in main-clause *wh*-questions in English, C must be filled by a moved auxiliary – in other words I-to-C movement is obligatory. However, when the subject is questioned, I-to-C movement is impossible. The following contrast shows this:

(66a) Which girl$_i$ did$_j$ he t$_j$ kiss t$_i$?

(66b) *Which girl$_i$ did$_j$ t$_i$ t$_j$ kiss him?

(66c) Which girl$_i$ t$_i$ kissed him?

(51c') tells us why I-to-C movement (which in these examples is instantiated by movement of *do*) is impossible. Where I, containing the overt element *do*, raises to C, we have a structure like (67):

(67)

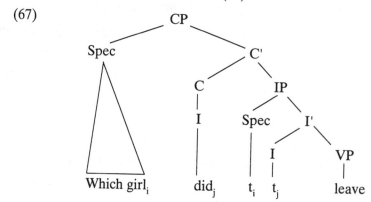

Here *did* acts like *that* in (58), and blocks the antecedent-government relation between *which girl* and its trace. Object traces are unaffected, because they are lexically governed (and here I-to-C is obligatory for reasons connected to the *wh*-criterion: see 2.6.3).

Adjuncts are not sensitive to C-t effects, as (68) shows:

(68) How$_i$ did you say [$_{CP}$ t'$_i$ (that) [$_{IP}$ he fixed your car t$_i$]] ?

The presence or absence of *that* has no effect on the grammaticality of (68). Now, adjunct traces are like subjects in not being lexically governed, so we have to see why the presence of *that* does not affect the ability of the adjunct trace t$_i$ in (68) to be antecedent-governed.

Sticking to the idea that adjuncts are adjoined to VP, t$_i$ in (68) appears in the following configuration:

(69)

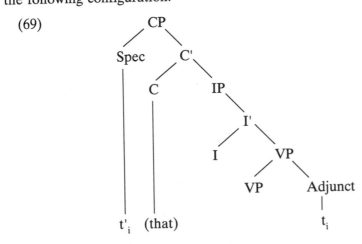

The category which minimally c-commands the adjunct in (69) is I (the VP that the adjunct adjoins to doesn't c-command it – see the discussion of adjunction in 2.6.4). The other two clauses of (51) allow t'$_i$ to antecedent-govern t$_i$; t'$_i$ c-commands t$_i$ and only one BC – IP – intervenes. We see then that it is clause (51'c) of the definition of antecedent-government that is central in accounting for C-t effects.

4.3.2.2 The Null-subject Parameter Again

C-t effects have been of great interest for comparative syntax. The basic observation was originally made by Perlmutter (1971), and has become known as **Perlmutter's generalization**. This generalization states that *null-subject languages do not show C-t phenomena* (on null-subject languages, see 3.3.3). This is illustrated by Italian sentences like (70):

(70) Chi hai   detto che ha   scritto questo libro?
     Who have-you said   that has written this   book?
     'Who did you say wrote this book?'

As you can see from the gloss and from the English translation (which, in order to be grammatical, does not contain a translation of *che* = 'that'), the extracted category *chi* is the subject of the embedded clause. The complementizer is also present (this is obligatory in this context in Italian), and the sentence is fine.

One way to handle (70) is to say that (51'c) is switched off in some languages. However, this is rather an uninteresting 'solution' to the problem, and does not offer any direct way to capture the correlation with the availability of null subjects (the ability to license *pro* in subject position, as we saw in 3.3.3). A much more interesting approach was suggested by Rizzi (1982). He connected Perlmutter's generalization to the availability of 'free inversion' in null-subject languages. In 3.3.3.3, we saw that the subjects in examples like (71) are in a postverbal position (distinct from the direct-object position – see 2.3.2), while *pro* occupies the subject position:

(71a) Hanno   telefonato molti studenti
       Have-3Pl phoned   many students (Pl)
       'Many students have phoned'

(71b) Vinceremo   noi
       Will-win-1Pl we (1Pl)
       'We will win'

Let's suppose that the postverbal subjects are in a position adjoined to VP. We can now account for Perlmutter's generalization by saying that C-t effects can be *apparently* violated in null-subject languages, since *subjects can be extracted from the adjunct-like postverbal position*. The definition of antecedent-government in (51') allows a trace in VP-adjoined position to be antecedent-governed by a trace in SpecCP whether or not C is overt. Extraction of the postverbal subject is rather like extraction of an adjunct in English, and as such is not subject to Complementizer-trace effects.

Rizzi's analysis implies that the representation of (70) is (70'a) rather than (70'b):

(70'a) $[_{CP1}$ Chi$_i$ $[_{IP1}$ *pro* hai detto $[_{CP2}$ t'$_i$ che $[_{IP2}$ *pro* ha $[_{VP}$ scritto questo libro $]$ t$_i$ $]]]]$?

(70'b) $[_{CP1}$ Chi$_i$ $[_{IP1}$ *pro* hai detto $[_{CP2}$ t'$_i$ che $[_{IP2}$ t$_i$ ha $[_{VP}$ scritto questo libro $]]]]]$?

In (70'a), *pro* in the main clause is an argumental pronoun – the silent version of *tu* ('you') – while *pro* in the embedded clause is an expletive. The expletive *pro* in the embedded clause is formally licensed by AgrS, as we saw in 3.3.3. This possibility is only open to null-subject languages, hence Perlmutter's generalization.

Rizzi's idea that the subject is extracted from postverbal position in finite clauses in null-subject languages receives direct support in certain Northern Italian dialects. In these dialects, a subject clitic appears in many persons of finite clauses as a kind of 'extra' marker of agreement; in fact, it is probably an overt AgrS. The following examples from the Florentine dialect (from Brandi and Cordin (1989)) illustrate:

(72a) Mario E   parla
      Mario SCL speaks
      'Mario speaks'

(72b) E   parla
      SCL speaks
      'He speaks'

(72c) *Parla
      speaks

(Brandi and Cordin (1989) and Rizzi (1986b) show that this element is not, despite appearances, a subject pronoun; for a detailed discussion of these clitics in many dialects of the region, see Poletto (1993).)

In 'free-inversion' sentences like (71), an expletive subject clitic appears in preverbal position in Florentine:

(73)   Gl   'ha telefonato delle ragazze
       SCL (MSG) has telephoned some girls (FPL)
       'Some girls telephoned'

As you can see, the preverbal subject clitic that appears when there is free inversion does not agree with the postverbal subject. Instead, it and the verb are in a default, third-person-masculine singular form. We can think of this subject clitic as the one that licenses an expletive *pro*. In most languages, including English, expletives are third-person-masculine singular.

Now, the really interesting and nice fact is this: *when the subject is extracted from a finite clause with an overt complementizer, the default subject clitic appears.* This is shown in (74):

(74a) Quante   ragazze tu credi che gli   abbia   parlato?
      How-many girls   you think that SCL(MSG) has (3SG) spoken
      'How many girls do you think have spoken?'

(74b) *Quante   ragazze tu credi che le   abbiano   parlato?
      How-many girls   you think that SCL(FPL) have (3PL) spoken

Example (74a) shows the clitic-agreement pattern typical of a free-inversion sentence like (73); so we conclude that the subject is extracted from the postverbal position. Example (74b) shows the preverbal clitic-agreement pattern (in other words, the subject clitic agrees with the verb). We can attribute the ungrammaticality of this sentence to the C-t effect, since the clitic-agreement pattern shows the subject is extracted from preverbal position. This sentence is then ruled out in exactly the same way as (58): the subject trace fails to be antecedent-governed due to (51'c). So this kind of example shows us that the C-t effect is operative in Italian dialects, the only way for extraction of the subject of a finite clause to be grammatical is by extracting from the postverbal position. More generally, these facts directly support the connection that Rizzi made between free inversion and Perlmutter's generalization.

Putting the discussion here together with that in 3.3.3, we see that four properties characterize null-subject languages, as opposed to non-null-subject languages:

(75a) Possibility of phonologically empty referential subject pronouns

(75b) Impossibility of overt expletive pronouns

(75c) Possibility of free inversion

(75d) Apparent absence of complementizer-trace effects

If a language allows referential *pro* in subject position, it will have the other properties in (75) (all other things being equal); if it does not, it will not have those properties. The way in which the null-subject parameter ties together a number of apparently unconnected possibilities is very elegant, and is also important for the theory of parameters, as we'll see in Chapter 5.

4.3.2.3 Conclusion
In this section, I've introduced C-t effects, and shown how an addition to the definition of antecedent-government – (51'c) – can handle these. You'll have noticed that (51'c) is hardly an elegant definition. In fact, it is rather transparently designed precisely to handle C-t effects. In that sense, although it does the job, it is clearly unsatisfactory. We also saw how Perlmutter's generalization can be handled in a way that extends the empirical coverage of the null-subject parameter and allows us to maintain that, despite initial appearances, null-subject languages do have C-t effects. In other words, antecedent government works the same way in those languages as in non-null-subject languages. In the next section, we'll continue to develop the notion of antecedent-government.

4.3.3 Connectedness, Preposition-Stranding, and Parasitic Gaps
In this section I'll briefly describe some of the proposals made by Kayne in a series of papers dating from the early to mid-1980s (collected in Kayne (1984); see particularly chapters 3 and 8). These proposals primarily concern the nature of antecedent-government. To a certain extent, they also anticipate the *Barriers* framework which is the subject of the next section. In addition to their theoretical importance, Kayne's proposals are of considerable empirical interest.

4.3.3.1 Connectedness
Let's begin by formulating the definition of antecedent government in terms of 'g-projections', as follows:

Antecedent Government (Second Revision);
α, a moved category, antecedent-governs β if and only if

(76a) α binds β

(76b) α is connected to a g-projection of γ, where γ canonically governs β

'Connected' here means 'forms a subtree of the whole tree'. G-projections (the name is intended to suggest 'government-projections') are defined in two steps. Consider first the configuration in (77):

(77)

$$\gamma \quad\nearrow^{\alpha}\searrow \quad \delta$$

By the definition in (48), γ governs δ. Moreover, γ is on the left of δ. We can call this combination of government and linear order the **canonical government relation** (for VO languages; Kayne suggests that OV languages may have a different canonical government configuration, but we'll leave that aside). In (77) α is either a g-projection of δ, or of some category β of which δ itself is a g-projection. The latter is true just where δ contains a canonical government configuration, as follows:

(78)

$$\varepsilon \quad\nearrow^{\delta}\searrow \quad \beta$$

A further condition is that the lowest head in the sequence of g-projections must be a structural Case-assigner (in terms of the government-based Case theory which Kayne was assuming – see 2.2). Finally, the usual X' projections of X (that is, X' and XP) are also g-projections of X, and of whatever X is a g-projection of.

So g-projections 'start', as it were, from a structural Case-assigner and 'go up the tree', first following the X'-projection, and then, following the canonical government configuration in (77), going to the projection of 'the next governor up'. The fact that in (77) α can be the g-projection of something which δ is the g-projection of shows that g-projections can 'percolate up' a tree. In this way, the g-projection of a deeply embedded category can go all the way to the root of a tree.

As usual, this kind of abstract notion is much easier to understand in practice. So let's take a simple example of extraction of an object (ignoring for the moment the fact that object traces are always lexically governed):

(79)   Who$_i$ did you see t$_i$?

Example (79) has the structure in (80):

(80)

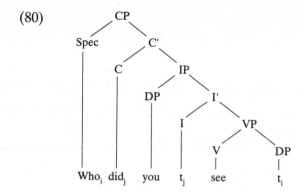

The verb *see* is a structural Case-assigner. VP (and V', not indicated here) is a g-projection of V, since it is an X'-projection of V. I' is a g-projection of V, since I and VP are in a canonical government configuration. IP is also a g-projection of V, since it is a projection of I'. C' is a g-projection of V, since C and IP are in a canonical government configuration. And because C' is a g-projection of V, so is CP. So the g-projections of V go all the way to the root of the tree, CP. V canonically governs the trace, and the moved category *who* is connected to (forms a subtree with) a g-projection of V, namely CP. Hence, by the definition of antecedent-government given in (76), *who* antecedent-governs its trace.

We'll look at two main empirical domains that this system accounts for: cross-linguistic differences in Preposition-stranding, and the interaction of the Subject Condition with parasitic gaps.

4.3.3.2 Preposition-stranding
Preposition-stranding is of interest because of the cross-linguistic differences that are found. Compare the English and French sentences in (81):

(81a) Who$_i$ did you vote for t$_i$?

(81b) *Qui$_i$ as-tu voté pour t$_i$?   (= (81a))

These sentences both have the structure in (82):

(82)

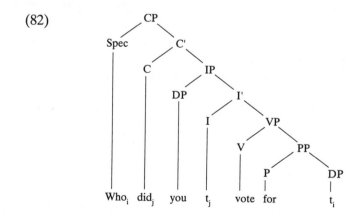

There is no independent reason to propose a structural difference between these two sentences, and yet the French one is bad while its English counterpart is good.

Let's begin by supposing that Prepositions are not lexical governors; this is not implausible, since Prepositions are in many ways like functional categories. So the trace in (82) has to be antecedent-governed in order to satisfy the ECP. In terms of the approach described above, we can see why the English sentence is good: P is a structural Case-assigner, PP is a projection and therefore a g-projection of P, and VP is a g-projection of P since V and PP are in a canonical government configuration. The rest is as described above for (79/80).

What about the French example? Here, Kayne's idea (which we mentioned briefly in Section 2.5.3) that English Prepositions are structural Case-assigners becomes crucial – or rather its inverse, namely that *French Prepositions are not structural Case-assigners*. Categories which are not structural Case-assigners are not able to project g-projections. Hence the trace of the stranded Preposition in (81b) cannot be antecedent-governed. If Prepositions are not lexical governors, then this trace fails the ECP altogether. So we are able to link the fact that English allows Preposition-stranding to our discussion of inherent Case in Section 2.5.3. This is an interesting comparative result.

4.3.3.3 Parasitic Gaps

Let's begin our discussion by looking at the Subject Condition. To see how Kayne's approach works here we have to put aside lexical government altogether. So let's just formulate the ECP as follows:

(83) Traces must be antecedent-governed

In later sections we'll return to the question of the status of lexical government. For the moment, we are entertaining the definition of antecedent-government given in (76) (this definition actually makes reference to the head that governs the trace, and so in a way subsumes lexical government). Now we can look at a typical Subject Condition violation:

(84a) * Which rock star$_i$ was that the police would arrest t$_i$ expected?

(84b) ??Which rock star$_i$ were admirers of t$_i$ arrested?

Looking first at (84a), you should be able to see that the subject CP *that the police would arrest t$_i$* is a g-projection of *arrest* – here the reasoning parallels what we saw for (79/80). But what about the rest of the structure? The relevant parts of the structure are as in (85):

(85)

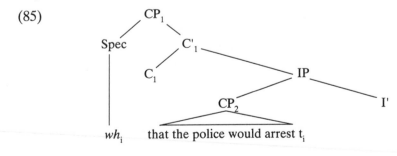

Remember that there are basically two ways of forming a g-projection: either by normal X'-projection or by a canonical government configuration of the kind in (78). IP is clearly not an X'-projection of CP_2 in (85). And neither are CP_2 and I' in a canonical government configuration (because CP_2 is to the left of I'). Therefore the g-projection of *arrest* stops at CP_2. The moved *wh*-category isn't connected to CP_2, and so the trace fails to be antecedent-governed. Successive cyclic movement won't make any difference, as the intermediate trace of such movement in $SpecCP_2$ (see (35a)) is not antecedent-governed by the moved *wh*-element for the reason just given (although the intermediate trace antecedent-governs the trace in the complement position of *arrest*).

Example (84b) is treated in just the same way as (84a). The DP *admirers of t_i* is a g-projection of *of*, but the g-projection stops there. There is therefore no way for the moved *wh*-category to be connected to the governor of its trace, and so the trace fails to be antecedent-governed.

Now the really interesting aspect of Kayne's account concerns **parasitic gaps**. Parasitic gaps can be illustrated with the following kind of contrast:

(86a) ??Which book$_i$ did you write an essay before reading t_i ?

(86b) Which book did you buy t_i before reading t_i ?

Example (86a) is rather bad (in fact, it's an example of an Adjunct Island, a kind of island that we'll look at in more detail in the next section). But (86b) is much better. In it there are two gaps for a single *wh*-element: the object of *buy* and the object of *reading*. Each of these gaps is interpreted as a variable bound by *which book*, as the interpretation of (86b) clearly shows. The gap in object position of *buy* is usually referred to as the 'real gap', and the one in the object position of *reading* is known as the 'parasitic gap'. We'll write the gap – the one which is the trace of the actual movement – as *t*, and the parasitic gap as *e*.

Without going into an analysis of the Adjunct Condition, we can see from (86) that a parasitic gap is better than a real gap in an adjunct. Kayne shows that a parasitic gap in a subject inside an adjunct is not good:

(87a) ?How many books$_i$ have you read t_i [because you knew the authors of e_i] ?

(87b) *How many books$_i$ have you read t_i [because [$_{IP}$ the authors of e_i were famous]] ?

Let's suppose that the trace inside the adjunct can be antecedent-governed by *how many books* in (87a). The trace in (87b) fails to be antecedent-governed for the same reason as that in (84): IP is not a g-projection of the subject or of anything inside the subject. We can thus account for the ungrammaticality of (87b). Since the parasitic gap is not actually related to *how many books* by movement here, we should understand antecedent-government as a condition on the *representation* formed by movement, and not as a condition on movement, since we want both traces in (87) to be antecedent-governed by the moved *wh*-element, but only one of them is the actual trace of *wh*-movement.

Kayne also discusses parasitic gaps inside subjects. These typically 'save' Subject Condition violations, as the following examples show:

(88a) ?Which rock star$_i$ do [$_{DP}$ journalists who talk to e$_i$] usually end up disgusted with t$_i$?

(88b) *Which rock star$_i$ do [$_{DP}$ journalists who talk to e$_i$] usually have blackmail in mind ?

Example (88b) is a straightforward Subject Condition violation, and we have seen how Kayne handles this kind of case. Why is (88a) better? To see this, let's look a (simplified) tree for (88a):

(89)

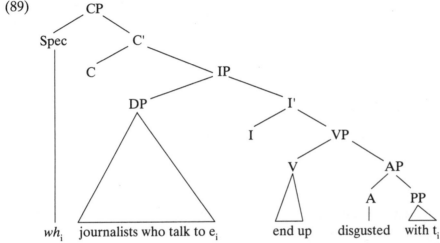

wh$_i$ journalists who talk to e$_i$ end up   disgusted   with t$_i$

One g-projection starts from *with*, and includes PP (by X'-theory), AP (canonical government), VP (canonical government), I' (canonical government), IP (X'-theory), C' (canonical government), and CP (X'-theory). So the *wh*-category is connected to *with*, the canonical governor of t$_i$. As for the parasitic gap, as long as we assume that the head of a relative canonically governs the relative clause, then the whole subject DP is a g-projection of *to*. Now, as usual, the g-projections of the category inside the subject stop here. However, there is already a subtree formed by the g-projections of *with* that the subject is connected to (forms a subtree with). And the g-projections of *with* are connected to the *wh* which binds the trace inside the subject. So, at one remove, the trace inside the subject is indeed connected to the *wh*-category. In a sense, then, the parasitic gap is truly parasitic, in that it depends on the real one in order to be antecedent-governed.

Finally, Subject Condition effects can be found with subject parasitic gaps:

(90a) ?Which rock star$_i$ do [teenagers that read articles about e$_i$] always try to imitate t$_i$?

(90b) *Which rock star$_i$ do [teenagers to whom [stories about e$_i$] are told] always imitate t$_i$?

The contrast here is clear. Example (90a) is another instance where the gap inside the subject is saved by the real gap, in the way described above. In (90b) the parasitic gap is beyond redemption, since its g-projections stop at the subject of the relative clause. As such they cannot be connected to the g-projections of the real gap, and so e$_i$ fails to be antecedent-governed. The contrast in (90) (and between (90) and standard Subject Condition cases) is strong support for an approach like Kayne's.

4.3.4 Conclusion

In this section, we've introduced and elaborated the other major principle of locality, the ECP. The ECP requires that traces be properly governed, where proper government means either government by a lexical head other than P (lexical government) or government by the moved category (antecedent-government). Our definition of government is as follows:

> *Government:*
> α, a head, governs β iff:

(48a) α c-commands β

(48b) no barrier dominates β but not α

> *Barrier:*
(49) any XP except IP

We've actually entertained two notions of antecedent-government, (51') and (76), which we repeat here:

> *Antecedent Government (Revised):*
> α, a moved category, antecedent-governs β iff:

(51a') α c-commands β

(51b') no more than one blocking category dominates β but not α

(51c') there is no filled C-position that minimally c-commands β and does not c-command α

> *Antecedent Government (Second Revision):*
> α, a moved category, **antecedent**-governs β iff:

(76a) α binds β

(76b) α is connected to a g-projection of γ, where γ canonically governs β

The distinction between lexical government and antecedent government is needed to account for argument-adjunct asymmetries of the kind we saw in

4.3.1. Condition (51b') is the same as subjacency (see 4.2). Condition (51c') is needed just for Complementizer-trace effects, as we saw in 4.3.2. Condition (76b) effectively imposes a requirement of government 'all the way along the path' from a moved element to its antecedent. Since the definition of government given in (48) refers to barriers, this implies that the notion of barrier may be relevant to the theory of locality.

Although the notions of lexical government and antecedent government do a lot of empirical work and have some theoretical depth, we clearly need to sort all this out. There are three principal issues that we need to address:

(91a) What is the correct definition of antecedent-government?

(91b) What is the relation between antecedent-government and subjacency?

(91c) What is the relation between antecedent-government and lexical government?

The next three sections are devoted to providing answers to these questions.

4.4 Barriers

This section summarizes the principal proposals in Chomsky's (1986b) monograph, *Barriers*. This was the first serious attempt to unify the theory of locality and so to provide answers to the questions raised at the end of Section 4.3.4. As the title suggests, the central notion is that of 'barrier'. We'll deal first with the proposed approach to subjacency, second with the ECP, and finally look at how the model captures the locality of head-movement and DP-movement.

4.4.1 Barriers and Subjacency

4.4.1.1 Adjunct Islands and the Condition on Extraction Domains

The central question in this section concerns the definition of the blocking categories for subjacency. Up to now, we've been assuming that these are IP and DP. But why should that be? In fact, we saw in 4.2.3 that in Italian the blocking categories are CP and DP. What is the total range of permitted variation in blocking categories and why are some categories BCs but not others? These are the questions we address here.

Our starting point is the Adjunct Condition. This is another island constraint, first noticed by Huang (1982). The observation is that extraction from inside an adjunct phrase is not allowed:

(92a) ?*Which bottle of wine$_i$ was Mick annoyed [BECAUSE KEITH DRANK t$_i$] ?

(92b) ?*Which dignitary$_i$ did the band leave the stage [WITHOUT BOWING TO t$_i$] ?

Many speakers find Adjunct Condition violations slightly less bad than

Subject Condition violations (or other island violations), which I've indicated here by '?*', as opposed to '*'. Here's (92a) with the BCs highlighted:

(92a') ?*[$_{CP1}$ Which bottle of wine$_i$ was [$_{IP1}$ Mick annoyed [$_{XP}$ because [$_{IP2}$ Keith drank t$_i$] ?

How subjacency applies depends on the precise analysis of the adjunct clause: what is XP in (92a') and what does it dominate? All the examples of embedded finite IPs that we've seen so far have been dominated by CPs, and so we probably want to say that there's a CP dominating IP$_2$ here (see 1.4.1.1). One possibility is that *because* is a complementizer. In that case, XP in (92a') is a CP and its Spec is available for successive-cyclic movement. And then there is no violation of subjacency here, as each step of movement just crosses one IP. We could block this by saying that *because* is in SpecCP, but there's really no reason to say this (except to give the right result for subjacency here); all the SpecCP elements we've seen up to now have been *wh*-elements, except for the special case of fronted XPs in verb-second languages (see 1.4.2.4). It seems more likely that *because* is a Preposition that selects a CP. In that case, there is a SpecCP position available for successive-cyclic movement and subjacency (formulated as in 4.2) cannot account for the violation here.

The fact that both subjects and adjuncts are islands is significant, since we saw in 4.3.1 that subjects and adjuncts are not lexically governed categories. Huang (1982), in fact, unified the Subject Condition and the Adjunct Condition under the following constraint, which he called the Condition on Extraction Domains (or CED):

Condition on Extraction Domains:
(93) No category can be extracted from a category which is not lexically governed

As we saw in 4.3.1, subjects and adjuncts are not lexically governed, while complements always are.

The CED is important both in theoretical and in empirical terms. From a theoretical point of view, it brings out the relationship between classical island effects of the type generally handled by subjacency and lexical government, and therefore the ECP. This suggests that a theory of subjacency of the type presented in 4.2 is missing something, since government plays no role in it. From an empirical point of view, the CED is important because it does not make reference to specific *categories* as BCs, but rather to specific *configurations*. It implies that any adjunct, whatever its category, will be an island (the implication has no real consequences for subjects, as they may well be always DPs in any case). This seems to be correct, as contrasts like the following show:

(94a) *Who$_i$ did you meet John [$_{AP}$ angry at t$_i$] ?

(94b) Who$_i$ did you make John [$_{AP}$ angry at t$_i$] ?

The category which linearly follows *John* in both examples in (94) is arguably an AP. In (94a), it is an adjunct (a secondary predicate); in (94b) it is selected by *make*. As you can see, extraction from an adjunct AP is much worse than extraction from an argument AP. It seems, then, that the function or the configuration of a category is more important for determining its islandhood than its actual category.

4.4.1.2 Defining Barriers

In many ways, the CED provided the cue for the development of the *Barriers* system. In this system, a chain of definitions is set up which begins with θ-**government**. We can think of θ-government as government by an element which assigns a θ-role to its governee. We can then define the following notions:

> *L-marking:*
> (95) α L-marks β if and only if α θ-governs β

L-marking plays a role comparable to lexical government, in that it distinguishes complements (L-marked) from subjects and adjuncts (not L-marked). Notice also that, if we stick to the basic idea that functional categories don't assign θ-roles, then the structural complements of functional categories are not L-marked.

> *Blocking category:*
> (96) α, an XP, is a BC for β if and only if α is not L-marked and α dominates β

This definition replaces the characterization of BCs as IP and DP that we gave in 4.2.1. We can now define barrier:

> *Barrier:*
> α is a barrier for β if and only if
> either:
> (97a) α is the first maximal category that dominates γ, a BC for β
> or:
> (97b) α is a BC for β, and α is not IP

Again, this definition supersedes the one we've been working with up to now. Definition (97) says that there are two ways in which something can be a barrier: either by inheritance from a BC it dominates (97a), or by simply being a blocking category, (97b). As in the simpler definition we've been using up to now, IP is excluded from the class of intrinsic barriers (remember that 'IP' means all V-related functional categories). The definition in (97) says that barrier is a relational notion rather than an absolute one – α is a barrier for β if the conditions given obtain.

Finally, we redefine subjacency in terms of barriers:

(98) In the following structure, α and β cannot be related by movement:

... α ... $[_B$ ... $[_B$ ... β .... $]$ .. $]$

where α and β are separated by more than one barrier B

So now we should go through the class of island constraints, including the Adjunct Condition, in order to see how this particular approach works.

Before looking at any bad examples of extraction, though, we have to make sure that we don't rule out any good cases. So let's take a very simple example, where nobody would doubt that extraction is possible:

(99) Who$_i$ does Phil think $[_{CP}$ t'$_i$ Loretta likes t$_i$] ?

Does the first step of movement, from t_i to t'_i, cross any barriers? In fact, yes. In (99), the direct object is extracted out of VP. Nothing θ-marks VP, and so, according to the definitions we've given, VP is not L-marked. Therefore VP is a BC for the object trace and, by (97b), a barrier for the object trace. IP, which is the first XP dominating VP, is a barrier by inheritance; see (97a). So two barriers intervene between t_i and t'_i, and subjacency should be violated. Exactly the same is true of the matrix clause; here too, VP is not L-marked and so is a BC and a barrier, making IP into a barrier and creating a subjacency violation. So we have a problem; the definitions proposed give the wrong result in some very simple, well-formed examples. The same problem arises if we assume a split-Infl clause structure, as you should be able to see.

It's clear that the problem here has to do with VP. Chomsky proposes two solutions to this. One is to assume that there is an abstract sense in which I (or some element of the I-system) θ-marks, and so θ-governs, VP. In that case, the problem is solved as VP is L-marked. The difficulty with this solution is that it extends the notion of θ-assignment rather far; it is not easy to relate whatever semantic relation may hold between I and VP to notions such as Cause and Patient (see the discussion of θ-roles in 2.1).

The other solution extends the notion of successive cyclicity one step further. Chomsky proposes the following two ideas:

(100a) Any category which doesn't receive a θ-role can be adjoined to

(100b) Only categories, not segments of categories, can be barriers

I briefly introduced the distinction between categories and segments earlier in 2.6.4. Let's recapitulate. In an adjunction structure like (101), the category adjoined to, XP, is divided into two 'segments'. Neither of these segments is the category itself, and therefore (100b) says that neither of them can be a barrier for YP:

(101)

If it's possible for YP to adjoin to XP, then, XP cannot count as a barrier for YP.

As we have seen, VP most probably is not θ-marked. Hence the object can adjoin to VP in (99). In that case, VP does not count as a barrier because neither of its segments can be a barrier. So, the true representation of (99) should be (99'):

(99') Who$_i$ does Phil [$_{VP}$ t'''$_i$ [$_{VP}$ think [$_{CP}$ t''$_i$ Loretta [$_{VP}$ t'$_i$ [$_{VP}$ likes t$_i$]]]]] ?

Here, each step of successive-cyclic movement is well-formed, as no barriers are crossed. Neither of the VPs are barriers because they can be adjoined to.

4.4.1.3 Barriers and the Island Constraints

Now we can look at the various islands. Let's begin with the CED. The CED bans extraction from categories that are not lexically governed: subjects and adjuncts. If we equate lexical government and θ-government, then we see that subjects and adjuncts are not L-marked, by (95). Since they are not L-marked, such categories are BCs, by (96). And hence, if they are not IP, they are barriers by (97b). More concretely, let's look again at the typical Subject Condition violation:

(102a) *Which rock star$_i$ was that the police would arrest t$_i$ expected ?

(102b) ??Which rock star$_i$ were admirers of t$_i$ arrested ?

Here, in each case the subject is not L-marked, and is therefore a BC (by (96)) and a barrier (by (97b)) – subjects are never IPs). Because the subject is a barrier, the IP that immediately dominates it is a barrier by inheritance (97a). Therefore movement from within the subject to the matrix SpecCP crosses two barriers, and subjacency is violated. The option of adjunction to VP plays no role here, but we have to make sure that IP is not adjoined to. Since IP is not θ-marked, it could in principle be adjoined to, given what we said in (100a). To get around this, let's just assume that IP is never available as an adjunction site. In that case, there is no derivation of (102) that does not violate subjacency.

Next consider the Adjunct Condition. I repeat the example from (92a') here:

(92a') ?*[$_{CP1}$ Which bottle of wine$_i$ was [$_{IP1}$ Mick annoyed [$_{XP}$ because [$_{IP2}$ Keith drank t$_i$] ?

Here XP, whatever its category, is not L-marked, and hence is a BC and a barrier. We've been assuming that adjuncts are adjoined to VP. In that case, IP is a barrier by inheritance. So extraction from an adjunct violates subjacency. However, there remains the possibility of adjunction to XP. Since XP is not assigned a θ-role, this is possible, in which case XP will not be a barrier and IP will not be a barrier by inheritance. This is a problem for the approach Chomsky gives in *Barriers*.

Consider next *wh*-islands. Here we're only concerned with extraction of arguments; we'll look at extraction of adjuncts in the next section. The relevant examples were given in (36):

(36a) ?$[_{CP1}$ Whose car$_i$ were $[_{IP1}$ you wondering $[_{CP2}$ how$_j$ $[_{IP2}$ to fix t_i t_j] ?

(36b) ?*$[_{CP1}$ Whose car$_i$ were $[_{IP1}$ you wondering $[_{CP2}$ how$_j$ $[_{IP2}$ you should fix t_i t_j] ?

For the version of subjacency that defines IP and DP as barriers, the crucial problem with these examples is that *whose car* has to cross two IPs on its way to SpecCP$_1$, since *how* occupies SpecCP$_2$. On the other hand, the *Barriers* system, as I've presented it so far, is unable to rule out these examples. IP can only be a barrier by inheritance, and so, given the option of VP-adjunction as described above, neither IP is a barrier in (36). The full representation of (36a), taking VP-adjunction of *whose car* into account, is (36a'):

(36a') ?$[_{CP1}$ Whose car$_i$ were $[_{IP1}$ you $[_{VP1}$ t''$_i$ $[_{VP1}$ wondering $[_{CP2}$ how$_j$ $[_{IP2}$ to $[_{VP2}$ t'$_i$ $[_{VP2}$ fix t_i t_j]]]]]]]] ?

Let's see what the barriers here are: the segments of VP$_2$ are not barriers by (100b); IP$_2$ is not a barrier because IP can only be a barrier by inheritance; CP$_2$ is not an intrinsic barrier because it's L-marked by *wonder*, but it is a barrier by inheritance from the non-L-marked IP$_2$. Finally, neither segment of VP$_1$ can be a barrier.

Chomsky concludes that this is not necessarily a bad result, given that the subjacency effect here is quite weak. Crossing one barrier gives a certain awkwardness, but not real ungrammaticality. To account for the contrast with (36b), Chomsky suggests that the most deeply embedded tensed IP can be an inherent barrier. Thus, if IP$_2$ is a barrier in (36b), and CP$_2$ is a barrier by inheritance, movement from the lower clause to the higher clause violates subjacency. It may be possible to account for Rizzi's evidence that Italian chooses different barriers (see 4.2.3) with the idea that tensed IP is never a barrier in Italian. In that case, *wh*-island configurations can be readily extracted from.

Next, the CNPC. Here, once more, are the typical examples:

(33a) *Which band$_i$ did you write $[_{DP}$ A SONG WHICH $[_{IP}$ WAS ABOUT t_i]] ?

(33b) *Which band$_i$ did you believe $[_{DP}$ THE CLAIM THAT $[_{IP}$ WE HAD SEEN t_i]] ?   (see (9))

The relative-clause example in (33a) is straightforwardly handled by the *Barriers* system. The head of a relative clause, *a song* in this example, does not θ-govern the CP that modifies it. Therefore, this CP is not L-marked, and so is both a BC and a barrier. This CP is dominated either by NP or by DP (which one depends on exactly what analysis we give to relative clauses, and that's a question I don't want to go into here), which is thus a barrier by inheritance. And so movement out of a relative clause always violates subjacency.

In (33b) no barriers are crossed by movement out of the complement to *claim*. The CP *that we had seen t$_i$* is the complement of *claim*, and so is L-marked and therefore neither a BC nor a barrier. The entire complex DP is the complement of the main verb *believe*, and so is L-marked. The NP headed by *claim* can presumably be adjoined to, since it is not θ-marked. So, as with *wh*-islands, no subjacency violation is predicted here. Unlike *wh*-islands, however, the possibility of designating tensed IP as a barrier makes no difference, since the SpecCP of the complement is available for successive-cyclic movement.

The Left Branch Condition in its simplest form cannot be handled by the *Barriers* system. That is, there is no account for the ungrammaticality of examples like the following:

(18) *Whose$_i$ did you play [$_{DP}$ t$_i$ guitar] ?

DP is L-marked here, and so is neither a BC nor a barrier. We suggested in 4.1 that the ungrammaticality of examples like (18) may be due to a condition on pied-piping that is peculiar to English, and so this is not really a problem – in fact, we want our theory of locality to allow the examples that we looked at from other languages, like (23) and (24).

On the other hand, extraction of the left branch of a left branch, as in (21a), is ruled out:

(21a) *Whose$_i$ did you play [$_{DP1}$ [$_{DP2}$ t$_i$ friend] 's favourite guitar]] ?

Here DP$_2$ is not L-marked, and so is a BC and barrier, and DP$_1$ is a barrier by inheritance. So movement of *whose* violates subjacency here. (Again, adjunction to DP$_2$ might be a possibility, with the result that neither DP$_2$ nor DP$_1$ would be a barrier. However, it may be that possessor DPs are θ-marked – perhaps by 's – but not θ-governed by anything in DP$_1$ since they occupy Spec,DP; in that case, adjunction to possessors would be impossible.)

Finally, the Coordinate Structure Constraint can't really be handled by the *Barriers* system. Let's look again at the examples we saw earlier:

(15a) *What$_i$ did Bill buy POTATOES AND t$_i$?

(15b) *What$_i$ did Bill buy t$_i$ AND POTATOES ?

(15c) *Which guitar$_i$ does KEITH [PLAY t$_i$] AND [SING MADRIGALS] ?

(15d) *Which madrigals$_i$ does KEITH [PLAY THE GUITAR] AND [SING t$_i$] ?

We could in fact handle (15a) if we assume that *and* t$_i$ is a non-L-marked XP (variants of this idea have been proposed by Munn (1993), Thiersch (1993), and Kayne (1994)). This XP would be a BC and a barrier, making the whole conjunct a barrier; and so subjacency would be violated here. Example (15b) cannot be accounted for along these lines, however. In (15c and d) it is natural to assume that the conjoined categories are not L-marked, and so are BCs and barriers. However, if they are not arguments, they can be adjoined to, and so the fact that they are barriers does not create a subjacency violation.

4.4.1.4 Conclusion

To summarize, in this section I've outlined the *Barriers* system, which consists of the definitions in (95–97), the formulation of subjacency in (98), and the further assumptions in (100). This system provides a deeper characterization of blocking categories than the earlier version of subjacency described in 4.2, and successfully accounts for the CED, the relative-clause case of the CNPC, and, with one further assumption, *wh*-islands. The possibility of adjoining to a potential barrier and moving on raises problems for the analysis of the Adjunct Condition and the relative-clause case of the CNPC. However, we have an alternative possibility for preventing VP from being a barrier in simple cases like (99): that of assuming that VP is θ-governed by I. If we assume this, we may be able to simply drop the idea that successive-cyclic adjunction can neutralize potential barriers, as examples like (99) are the main cases for which this idea is needed. For the moment, let's leave this issue open. We'll come back to it below.

4.4.2 Barriers and the ECP

In the previous subsection we saw the approach to subjacency and the characterization of blocking categories in the *Barriers* system. In this subsection, we turn to the ECP. Remember that what we're interested in is seeing how we can arrive at a unified characterization of subjacency and the ECP.

The version of the ECP that Chomsky adopts in *Barriers* is what we saw in 4.3.1.1. The ECP requires that traces be properly governed, where proper government is defined as either θ-government or antecedent-government. If we take θ-government to be broadly the same as lexical government, this corresponds to the definition of proper government that I gave in (47) of 4.3.1.1:

> *Proper Government:*
> (103) either: government by a lexical head (lexical government)
>   or: government by the moved category (antecedent-government)

Government is defined in terms of barriers, as follows:

> *Government (Revised):*
> (104) β governs α if and only if there is no barrier for α that dominates β but not α

You'll notice that this is slightly different from the definition of government we've been working with up to now. It follows from (104), combined with the definition of antecedent-government in (47) that antecedent-government is blocked by a single barrier. We see, then, that subjacency and antecedent-government are closely related: subjacency is blocked by more than one barrier; antecedent-government by a single barrier. So the approach to antecedent-government adopted in *Barriers* is like the one we assumed in (51) of 4.3.

Given these assumptions, the account of argument-adjunct asymmetries that emerges is very similar to the one described in 4.3.1.1. Let's look again at the typical contrast:

(105a) ?*[$_{CP1}$ Whose car were [$_{IP1}$ you wondering [$_{CP2}$ how$_j$ [$_{IP2}$ you should fix t$_i$ t$_j$] ?

(105b) *How$_j$ were you wondering [$_{CP}$ whose car$_i$ you should fix t$_i$ t$_j$] ?

As we saw in 4.3.1.1, the contrast here is between the awkwardness of (105a) and the uninterpretability of (105b). Although both sentences are bad, the clear difference in their status suggests that different principles are at work in each case. In (105a), subjacency is violated by the extraction of *whose car* from the *wh*-island (allowing that the finite embedded IP$_2$ is a barrier – see subsection 4.4.1.3). The trace of *whose car* satisfies the ECP, however, since it is θ-governed by *fix*. In (105b), subjacency is violated in exactly the same way as in (105a); however, here the ECP is violated since the adjunct is not θ-governed, and fails to be antecedent-governed because two barriers intervene between *how* and its trace: CP$_2$ (a barrier by inheritance from IP$_2$) and IP$_2$ (an inherent barrier if tensed).

What about the non-finite counterpart of (105b)?

(106) *How$_j$ were you wondering [$_{CP2}$ whose car$_i$ [$_{IP2}$ to fix t$_i$ t$_j$]] ?

Here IP$_2$ is non-finite, and so it is not an inherent barrier. Nevertheless, it is not L-marked and so is a BC for material it dominates. It is not a barrier, for the simple reason that we have made an exception for IP – IP can only be a barrier by inheritance. However, the fact that IP is a BC means that CP, the first XP dominating it, is also a barrier by inheritance. So CP$_2$ is a barrier, which means that *how* cannot antecedent-govern its trace here. This accounts for the ungrammaticality of (106).

Subjects are like adjuncts in typically not being θ-governed. And so an example like (53), repeated here, is ruled out because two barriers – tensed IP and CP – intervene between the trace and *which band*:

(53) *Which band$_i$ were you wondering whether t$_i$ will play that song ?

As we saw in 4.3.2.1, there is a further complication with subjects: C-t effects, as in (58):

(58) *Who$_i$ did you say that t$_i$ wrote this song?

We accounted for (58), and the contrast with the corresponding sentence without *that*, with clause (51'c) of the definition of antecedent-government:

α, a moved category, antecedent-governs β iff
(51c') there is no filled C-position that minimally c-commands β and does not c-command α

As I remarked in 4.3.2.1, although this does the job of accounting for C-t effects, it rather muddies the waters of the definition of antecedent-government.

The approach adopted in *Barriers* consists of defining a further kind of barrier, a 'minimality barrier':

Minimality Barrier:
(107) β is a minimality barrier for α if and only if:
β is an X' (other than I')
β dominates α
the head of β is lexical

Let's look more closely at (58):

(58') *Who$_i$ did you say [$_{CP}$ t'$_i$ [C' that t$_i$ wrote this song]] ?

C' fulfills the requirements for being a minimality barrier for t_i here: it is an X' (but not I'), it dominates t_i, and its head C is lexical. And so t'_i in SpecCP fails to antecedent-govern t_i, owing to the intervening minimality barrier C'. Since subjects are not θ-governed, t_i violates the ECP. Of course, if *that* is not present, then C' does not fulfil clause (c) of the definition of minimality barrier in (107) and t'_i can then antecedent-govern t_i. Minimality barriers are only relevant for government, not movement; hence the notion of 'barrier' that is relevant for subjacency does not include minimality barriers, while the one that applies to antecedent-government does, as we have just seen.

Remember that adjunct traces are not subject to C-t effects, as (68), repeated here, shows:

(68) How$_i$ did you say [$_{CP}$ t'$_i$ (that) [$_{IP}$ he fixed your car t$_i$]] ?

In *Barriers*, Chomsky takes over from Lasnik and Saito (1984) the assumption that the antecedent-government requirement applies to adjunct traces only at LF. Since *that* can delete at LF (as it has no semantic content) its overt presence makes no difference to the status of an adjunct trace. Example (68) is allowed with or without an overt *that* because *that* is in any case missing at LF. This account also extends to the absence of C-t effects in null-subject languages. If we follow Rizzi's proposal that in examples like (70) the subject is extracted from postverbal position, and assume that this position is an adjunct position, then (70) has the same status as (68):

(70) Chi   hai   detto che ha scritto questo libro?
     Who have-you said   that has written this   book?
     'Who did you say wrote this book?'

In conclusion, the *Barriers* version of the ECP covers the principal phenomena that we looked at in 4.3.1 and 4.3.2 (it doesn't handle the 'connectedness' phenomena discussed in 4.3.3, however). There is a partial unification with subjacency: antecedent-government is partly a stricter version of subjacency, since it bans the crossing of even one barrier. The ECP also makes reference to θ-government, which is indirectly implicated in the definition of BCs and barriers. However, the ECP is also sensitive to minimality barriers, while subjacency just is not; and this is the principal conceptual flaw in the attempted unification. I'll present a different version of minimality condition in 4.5, and return to the question of unifying it with subjacency in 4.6.

Before going on to those matters, however, let's reconsider the relations between *wh*-movement and the other kinds of movement, a topic that we have left to one side over the last few sections.

4.4.3 Barriers, DP-Movement, and Head-Movement

Here I want to take a brief look at how the *Barriers* system can account for the properties of DP-movement and head-movement.

4.4.3.1 DP-movement

Here we want to allow straightforward examples like those in (108) and rule out cases of 'super-raising' and 'super-passive' like (109):

(108a) John$_i$ seems t$_i$ to speak Chinese

(108b) The students$_i$ were beaten up t$_i$ (by the police)

(109a) *The train$_i$ seems that it is likely t$_i$ to be late

(109b) *The students$_i$ seem that it was told t$_i$ that there would be extra reading

In (108a), movement of *John* crosses the lower IP and the VP headed by *seems*. Here IP is L-marked by *seems*, since raising verbs select IP (see 2.3.3). VP, however, is a BC and a barrier since it is not L-marked. The subject of a complement infinitive is not θ-governed by the higher verb – we saw in 2.3.3 that raising verbs do not assign θ-roles to the subject of their infinitival complement. If t$_i$ isn't θ-governed here, it must be antecedent-governed. But the VP barrier intervenes between the trace and its antecedent.

At this point, it's useful to compare (108a) with an example of extraction of the subject of an ECM infinitive, like (54):

(54) Which band$_i$ did you consider t$_i$ to be the best ?

In 4.3.1.1, we said that the trace here is lexically governed by *consider*. However, this is a case where the switch from lexical government to θ-government has consequences: we clearly don't want to say that *consider* θ-governs the trace here. So the trace in (54) must satisfy the ECP by being antecedent-governed. Example (54) is well-formed, which means that there are no barriers at all between *which band* and its trace here. The lower IP is not a barrier, since it is non-finite. The VP headed by *consider* is a barrier, but it can be adjoined to and neutralized in that way (see 4.4.1). The matrix IP is not a barrier. So we correctly allow (54) without assuming that the trace is θ-governed. (Here and elsewhere we have to ignore the possibility that V' is a minimality barrier. Chomsky's assumption was that V' was simply not present; since this work predated the VP-internal subject hypothesis (see 2.3.4), this was tenable. I'm just going to leave this question to one side.)

Now look again at (108a). The structure of the example is broadly comparable to (54), and we want to see here too how the trace is antecedent-governed. Again, the lower IP poses no problem. But what about VP? The option of VP-adjunction is not available for DP-movement. Remember that VP-adjoined positions are A' (or non-L-related) positions (see 3.3.2.3). Movement from an A-position to an A'-position and back to an A-position is not allowed – this is referred to as 'improper movement'. We can rule out improper movement with Principle C of the binding theory if we suppose that traces in A'-positions are subject to this Principle. If we adjoin to VP and move on, a trace is left in the adjoined position. But since DP-movement moves to a Case position such as the matrix SpecIP, and since Case positions are A-positions, then the VP-adjoined trace will be A-bound. In that case, it will violate Principle C. In other words, movement from A-positions to either A- or A'-positions is allowed, and movement from A'-positions to other A'-positions is allowed, but movement from A'-positions to A-positions is NOT allowed.

If DP-movement in (108a) cannot adjoin to VP, then VP should be a barrier. The fact that the example is well-formed tells us that this can't be right. To solve this problem, Chomsky makes two proposals, both of which we have already seen in slightly different guises. First, there is a relation between V and I which we can think of as either overt or covert movement (see 1.4 and 2.6.5). Second, there is a relation between I and SpecIP: Spec-head agreement which facilitates feature-checking and/or Case-assignment (see Chapter 2, especially 2.6). We can indicate each of these relations by coindexing, and this gives the following representation for (108a):

(108a') John$_i$ I$_i$ seems$_i$ t$_i$ to speak Chinese

The coindexed elements here form a chain (see 3.5: each element c-commands and is coindexed with the next). Moreover, by the definition of government given in (104), *John* governs I and *seems* governs t$_i$. Allowing that there is a 'special relationship' between I and V which facilitates government (this seems legitimate, since we know that V-to-I movement is possible in many languages: see 1.4.1.1), then we have a chain where each element governs the next. We can in fact think of this as antecedent-government, although this is an extension of the strictly movement-based definition that we gave in (47). If we see this chain-relation as a species of antecedent government, then it follows that the trace is antecedent-governed in (108a). The crucial step in all of this involves the V–I relation. As I've already mentioned, at the price of an implausible extension of the intuitive content of θ-theory, we can simplify this picture by saying that I θ-marks VP, and therefore that VP is not a BC or a barrier.

We have no problems allowing simple passive sentences like (108b). The trace in the direct-object position is θ-governed by the verb, and so satisfies the ECP. Passives of ECM verbs like (110) are just like raising structures:

(110) George$_i$ is widely believed t$_i$ to be best

Here the considerations just raised in connection with (108) come in.

What about (109)? In (109a), we want to prevent the formation of a chain of antecedent-governors comparable to the one that allows (108a). This can be done if we take it that the coindexing that indicates Spec-head agreement and the head–head relation between I and V can only arise when those relations hold: that there is no such thing as 'accidental coindexation'. In that case, there is no way for a chain to be formed which connects the train in the matrix SpecIP with its trace in the lowest SpecIP. More concretely, we have the following relations in (109a):

(109a') *The train$_i$ I$_i$ seems$_i$ that it$_j$ is$_j$ likely$_{(j)}$ t$_i$ to be late

The train is coindexed under Spec-head agreement with I. I is coindexed with V, by their special relationship, and of course the trace of *the train* bears the same index. However, the trace is too far from *seems* to be governed by it. Hence it fails to be antecedent-governed, and, since it is not θ-governed, violates the ECP. There is another chain formed by the elements bearing the j-index here, but, even if *likely* shares that index with *is* (which is perhaps doubtful), it is of no help to the trace, since the trace hears a distinct index and there is no way of establishing any kind of equivalence between them.

Exactly the same considerations apply in (109b), as you should be able to see. So the trace of *the students* is not antecedent-governed here. However, this trace should be θ-governed since it is a direct object, and so there should be no problem. The ungrammaticality of (109b) implies that θ-government may not always be enough for well-formedness: the antecedent-government requirement seems to hold anyway. We'll come back to this point in the next section.

4.4.3.2 *Head-movement*

Turning now to head-movement, what we'd ideally like to do is to derive the Head Movement Constraint (HMC: see 1.4.2.3(67)):

The Head Movement Constraint
(111) A head X can only move to the most local c-commanding head-position

As we saw in 1.4.2.3, the HMC prevents V from moving over I to C in one step, and so it rules out examples like:

(112) *Have$_i$ he could t$_i$ done it ?

Here I'm assuming that *have* heads its own VP, and takes another VP headed by *done* as its complement. This is where it becomes crucial not to assume that I L-marks VP. If it does, then neither VP nor IP are barriers, and so (112) should be allowed. If I doesn't L-mark VP, on the other hand, VP is a BC and a barrier. IP is then a barrier by inheritance, and (112) violates both antecedent-government and subjacency (and it's safe to assume that V is not θ-marked by I). The account of (112) also appears to rule out the possibility of V-to-I movement, which is amply attested crosslinguistically (see 1.4.1.1). In the discussion of DP-movement above, I appealed to a 'special relationship' between V and I. Chomsky's proposal is that I θ-marks and therefore θ-governs VP (but not V), but that I does not L-mark VP because only lexical elements can L-mark. So we change the definition of L-marking as follows:

L-marking:
(95') α L-marks β if and only if α is a lexical category that θ-governs β

This prevents I from L-marking VP, and so VP is a BC and a barrier, as usual. However, the operation of raising V to I creates a lexical I, and such an I can then L-mark VP. Hence, V-to-I movement licenses itself, as it were. This does not affect our conclusions above regarding (112), assuming that a modal like *could* is unable to L-mark VP.

In general, I-to-C movement of the kind that creates inversion and verb-second structures (see 1.4) is allowed, since IP is not an inherent barrier. Movement from I to a position higher than C is ruled out, since CP will inherit barrierhood from IP. (Remember that throughout all of this I'm using 'I', 'IP', and so on as shorthand for the full functional structure that makes up the clause. All these categories – AgrSP, TP, AgrOP, and the others – are presumably 'defective' as barriers in the way IP is, and are similarly unable to L-mark their complement unless V moves into them. Adopting a split-Infl structure doesn't really alter anything of substance in what's gone before, but it does mean that the reality is (even) more complex than what we have seen.)

In a very important work, Baker (1988) showed that incorporation structures of the kind found in many (usually non-Indo-European) languages involve head-movement. Mohawk Noun-incorporation is an example:

(113a) Yao -wir   -a?a ye-   -nuhwe? -s   ne ka -NUHS -a?
       PRE -baby- SUF 3SgF/3N -like   -ASP the PRE -house -SUF
       'The baby likes the house'

(113b) Yao -wir   -a?a ye-   -NUHS -nuhwe? -s?
       PRE-baby -SUF 3SgF/3N -house -like   -ASP
       'The baby likes the house.'

If incorporation is head-movement, it must be subject to the conditions on movement, in particular the ECP. We can therefore predict that incorporation from subjects and from adjuncts is impossible, since such incorporation would involve crossing a barrier, with the result that the trace would not be antecedent-governed and the ECP would consequently be violated (it seems reasonable to think that heads are never θ-marked and so never θ-governed). In a survey of a wide array of languages Baker showed that there are no cases of noun-incorporation of subjects or adjuncts. In other words, we don't find examples of incorporation that would look like the following:

(114) *Ye   -WIR -nuhwe? -s ne ka   -nuhs -a? (Mohawk; see (113))
     3Sgf/3N -baby -like   the PRE-house -SUF
     'The baby likes the house'

(115) *Nofo ana a   ia (he)   (Niuean)
      live cave ABS he (in)
      'He cave-lives (in)'

Baker extends his theory of abstract incorporation to many other construction-types that are found in the world's languages. In each case, what he shows is that the head-to-head dependency can only hold between a head and its immediate complement. For example, Baker argues that one kind of causative construction involves V-to-V incorporation. This kind of causative is found in Romance, so we have:

(116) J'ai fait laver la voiture à Jean   (French)
      I've made wash the car   to John
      'I made John wash the car'

According to Baker, there is a complex verb *faire-laver* here. This complex verb is rather like verbs such as 'give' in having a direct object (*la voiture*) and an indirect object (*à Jean*). Most importantly, *faire* can only form a complex verb with a verb in its immediate complement. Again, the ECP explains this pattern: head-movement from out of a subject or an adjunct crosses a barrier and so leads to a violation of the ECP. Baker's results have made possible the development of a theory of incorporation, causatives, and many other phenomena which is fully integrated into linguistic theory. Most of the predictions that this theory makes come from the ECP.

In this section we've seen that, once certain points are clarified, the *Barriers* system can capture the basic locality constraints on DP-movement and head-movement. For DP-movement, we need to extend the notion of antecedent-government so that it relates to chains of various kinds, not just movement chains. We also saw that θ-government may not be enough for DP-traces. For head-movement, we see that the ECP subsumes the HMC, but we need a special account of why ordinary V-to-I raising is possible.

4.4.4 Conclusion

The *Barriers* framework was the first attempt to unify fully the theory of locality. We have looked at the system in some detail, and we can see what its strong and weak points are. The principal strength of the system is the central role played by the notion of 'barrier': this notion is crucial for defining government, the ECP, and subjacency. Empirically, most of the coverage of the earlier formulation of subjacency is retained (except for *wh*-islands and the complement case of the CNPC); similarly, leaving aside the 'connectedness' effects discussed in 4.3.3, *Barriers* successfully handles most of what the ECP did. As we've just seen, the approach also extends to DP-movement and head-movement. In the case of DP-movement, there are some difficulties. In the case of head-movement, the approach makes Baker's important crosslinguistic results possible.

Conceptually, however, a number of questions remain:

- What is the precise nature of the minimality condition, and why is it restricted to government and not movement relations?
- Why is θ-government seemingly 'not enough' for DP-traces?
- Why is the 'I-system' defective, in only being a barrier by inheritance rather than inherently?
- Why are adjunct traces only subject to the ECP at LF, exempting them from the full effects of the minimality condition?

Over the next two sections, answers to most of these questions will emerge. The next section focuses almost exclusively on the ECP, in that it reviews an influential alternative version of the minimality condition: Rizzi's Relativized Minimality.

4.5 Relativized Minimality

In this section I'll summarize the main points of Rizzi's (1990) theory of relativized minimality. As its name implies, the central idea is that the minimality condition shouldn't be seen as an absolute condition, but rather that each kind of movement relation – *wh*-movement, DP-movement, and head-movement – is associated with its own kind of minimality condition and is blind to the others. The relativized minimality condition is the central facet of the theory of antecedent-government. In addition to this, Rizzi proposes that θ-government can be altogether dispensed with and replaced with a simpler head-government condition. We'll look first at the proposal for antecedent-government (4.5.1) and then at the proposal for head-government (4.5.2).

4.5.1 Relativized Minimality and Antecedent-Government

4.5.1.1 A'-specifiers block A'-movement

Let's begin by looking, yet again, at the argument-adjunct asymmetries that are found in *wh*-islands:

(105a) ?*$[_{CP1}$ Whose car$_i$ were $[_{IP1}$ you wondering $[_{CP2}$ how$_j$ $[_{IP2}$ you should fix t$_i$ t$_j$] ?

(105b) *How$_j$ were you wondering [whose car$_i$ you should fix t$_i$ t$_j$] ?

Only subjacency is violated in (105a), while the ECP is also violated in (105b) since the adjunct trace must be antecedent-governed and fails to be so. Rizzi retains the account of argument extraction: complement traces are θ-governed and therefore pass the ECP – the relatively mild ill-formedness of (105a) is due to subjacency. Rizzi's observation is that in (105b) a distinct *wh*-element, *whose car*, intervenes between the moved adjunct *wh*-element and its trace. In an obvious sense, like is interfering with like here.

As we have seen, alternative accounts have been proposed for these argument-adjunct asymmetries. However, there are other cases where like appears to block like which are much harder to account for in terms of what we have seen up to now. One such case is the phenomenon of pseudo-opacity found in French. French allows certain kinds of quantifiers that are found some distance to the left of a direct object to be interpreted as quantifying that direct object, as in the following pair:

(117a) Jean a   consulté beaucoup de livres
　　　 John has consulted much   books.
　　　 'John has consulted many books'

(117b) Jean a   beaucoup consulté de livres
　　　 John has much   consulted books.
　　　 'John has consulted many books'

As we saw in 4.1, French also has one quantifier that can optionally violate the Left Branch Condition, *combien* ('how many'). This element allows either left-branch extraction or pied-piping of the quantified DP:

(118a) Combien$_i$ a-t-il   consulté t$_i$ de livres?
　　　 How-many has-he consulted of books?
　　　 'How many books has he consulted?'

(118b) Combien   de livres$_i$ a-t-il   consultés t$_i$?
　　　 How-many of books has-he consulted?
　　　 'How many books has he consulted?'

In (118b), *combien de livres* is the direct object, and so is extractable like any argument. It's reasonable to think that *combien* alone is an adjunct, since it's not θ-marked by anything. Now, if we combine the 'leftward' *beaucoup* of (117b) with extraction of *combien*, we see that only the pied-piping variant is allowed:

(119a) Combien   de livres$_i$ a-t-il   beaucoup consultés t$_i$?
　　　 How-many of books has-he much   consulted?
　　　 'How many books has he consulted a lot?'

(119b) *Combien$_i$ a-t-il   beaucoup consulté t$_i$ de livres?
　　　 How-many has-he much   consulted of books?

If we take it that *beaucoup* occupies an A'-position, presumably adjoined to VP, in these examples, then we see that, as in the case of *wh*-islands, the presence of an A'-element blocks extraction of an adjunct to an A'-position.

The third case is a further kind of island phenomenon that was originally discussed by Ross, but which we haven't introduced yet: negative islands. The basic observation is that clausal negation blocks extraction of adjuncts:

(120a)   Which car$_i$ didn't he fix t$_i$?   (Answer: The blue GTi)

(120b)   *?How$_i$ didn't HE FIX YOUR CAR t$_i$?   (*Answer: With a spanner)

The argument-adjunct asymmetry is very clear here. Rizzi also gives examples which show that the adjunct must be in the scope of negation in order for the island effect to apply. First we need to look briefly at some scope ambiguities involving negation (the concepts of 'scope' and 'scope ambiguity' and their relevance for syntactic theory are explained in the Appendix to this chapter). For example, think about the following sentence:

(121)   They don't exploit their fans [because they love them]

Example (121) is ambiguous in at least two ways (in fact, there are more possible interpretations, but they are less obvious and rather harder to see, so I'll just leave them aside). It can either mean 'Because they love them, they don't exploit their fans': only the main clause is negated, not the adjunct clause. Call this the 'main-clause negation' reading. This is probably the most natural one for (121), given the lexical items and ordinary pragmatic considerations. However, (121) also has the interpretation which we can paraphrase as 'It's not because they love them that they exploit their fans (but for some other reason)'. Here the main predicate isn't negated, just the adjunct. So call this the 'adjunct-negation' reading. So we see that, at least with *because*-type adjuncts, clausal negation allows at least two different scopes.

Now let's look at what happens if we extract a *because*-adjunct (using *why*, which naturally invites an answer with *because*):

(122)   Why$_i$ don't they exploit their fans t$_i$?

Example (122) only allows the main-clause negation interpretation. In other words, it can be answered only with something like 'Because they love them'. To put it another way, the trace of *why* can't be interpreted as being in the scope of negation. This is due to the negative island: negation blocks clausal extraction. The usual assumption about scope is that it is determined by c-command (see the Appendix to this chapter), so what the scope restriction on the interpretation of (122) tells us is that negation blocks the extraction of adjuncts within its c-command domain.

When I introduced the split-Infl hypothesis in 1.4.3, I briefly mentioned NegP. Suppose that negative clauses feature a NegP projection that is situated above TP and below AgrSP (there is some evidence that the position varies across languages, but I'll gloss over this):

(123)

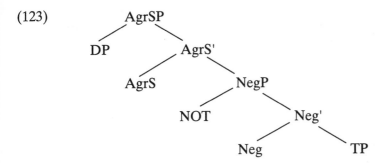

(Here, NOT refers to whatever element carries clausal negation: *not, pas, nicht*, and so forth.) It is natural to think that the position that NOT occupies isn't a GF-position. In other words, it is a non-L-related or A'-position. In that case, the negative-island effect that we saw in (120b) and (122) is a third instance of an A'-element blocking the extraction of a *wh*-adjunct.

The generalization that unifies these three cases – *wh*-islands, pseudo-opacity in French, and negative islands – is:

(124) A filled A'-position specifier α blocks antecedent government between an A'-position β that c-commands α and an adjunct trace that α c-commands.

To put it schematically, α prevents β from antecedent-governing *t* in (125), where *t* is an adjunct trace and each element c-commands the next:

(125) [... β ... [α [.... t ...]]]

In a *wh*-island case like (105b), α is a *wh*-element; in pseudo-opacity examples like (119b), α is an adverb like *beaucoup*, and in negative islands α is NOT.

4.5.1.2 A-specifiers block A-movement

Now let's look at the basic DP-movement configuration that violates the ECP – super-raising and super-passive:

(109a) *The train$_i$ seems that it is likely t_i to be late

(109b) *The students$_i$ seem that it was told t_i that there would be extra rations

Since this is DP-movement, these examples involve movement to an L-related A-position; in fact, in both of those examples the landing-site is a subject position. Now, in between the moved DP and its trace, there is another subject position occupied by *it*. Movement to this position will give well-formed results:

(126a) It seems that the train$_i$ is likely t_i to be late

(126b) It seems that the students$_i$ were told t_i that there would be extra rations

What goes wrong in (109), then, can be thought of as an element in an A-position blocking movement of another element to a higher A-position. In other words:

> (127) A filled A-position specifier α blocks antecedent government between an A-position β that c-commands α and a DP-trace that α c-commands

The similarity between (127) and (124) should be clear. Before attempting to unify them into a single principle, however, let's look at head-movement.

4.5.1.3 Heads Block Head Movement

The typical Head Movement Constraint violation looks like (112) from the previous section:

> (112) *Have$_i$ he could t$_i$ done it ?

We can rephrase the Head Movement Constraint as follows:

> (128) A head α blocks antecedent government between a head β that c-commands α and a head-trace that α c-commands

Statement (128) is little more than a restatement of the HMC as given in (67) of Chapter 1 and in (111) above. Again, there is an obvious formal similarity with the generalizations in (124) and (127).

4.5.1.4 Relativized Minimality

Relativized minimality unifies (124), (127), and (128), as follows:

> *Relativized Minimality:*
> X antecedent-governs Y only if there is no Z such that:

> (129a) Z is a typical potential antecedent governor for Y

> (129b) Z c-commands Y and does not c-command X

Now we need to know what a typical potential antecedent governor is:

> *Typical Potential Antecedent Governor:*
> (130a) Z is a typical potential antecedent governor for Y, Y in an A-chain = Z is an A-specifier c-commanding Y

> (130b) Z is a typical potential antecedent governor for Y, Y in an A'-chain = Z is an A'-specifier c-commanding Y

> (130c) Z is a typical potential antecedent governor for Y, Y in a head-chain = Z is a head c-commanding Y

Given the notion of typical potential antecedent governor as defined here, relativized minimality says that antecedent-government will be blocked in the following configuration:

(131)　[.... X_i .... 　[.... Z .... 　[... Y_i ....]]]

　　　　　　　　　　　　　　　　　　　　　　　$C = (X_i, Y_i)$

Where C is an chain of the same type (A, A', head) as the position occupied by Z, Z will block antecedent-government. If Y is an adjunct *wh*-trace, a DP-trace, or a head-trace, the result will be a violation of the ECP, since these elements all require antecedent-government. If Y is an argument *wh*-trace (as in (105a)), the structure will be well formed unless subjacency is also violated.

Relativized minimality is intended to replace the 'absolute minimality' condition of the *Barriers* system that we saw in (107). More precisely, the definition of antecedent government that is adopted is the following:

> *Antecedent Government (Third Revision):*
> X antecedent-governs Y iff:

(132a)　X and Y are coindexed

(132b)　X c-commands Y

(132c)　no barrier intervenes

(132d)　relativized minimality is respected

Principles (132a–c) are essentially as in *Barriers*, except that here 'barrier' means only 'barrier for movement' (defined in (97)). Principle (133d) replaces the 'absolute' minimality condition that I gave in (107).

According to relativized minimality, each type of chain is 'on its own track'. What is an intervener for one kind of chain has no effect on the others. So, DP-movement can cross intervening elements that block antecedent-government of *wh*-traces, such as negation:

(133) The students$_i$ weren't arrested t_i

And, of course, it can cross intervening heads – in fact, all cases of DP-movement must do this, since it is movement to a Specifier position. Conversely, head-movement can cross intervening Specifiers of both kinds – and, indeed, it must do so in order to reach higher head-positions.

Similarly, *wh*-movement is unaffected by the presence of an intervening subject position (remember that DP-movement is blocked by an intervening subject position):

(134) How$_i$ did he fix your car t_i ?

Moreover, according to relativized minimality, *wh*-movement is not affected by intervening heads. This can also be seen in (134), where adjunct movement crosses the intervening heads I and C (at least). Here we see a major difference with the 'absolute' minimality condition of (107): remember that

(107) is intended to account for C-t effects by blocking antecedent-government across a filled C-position. However, (107) doesn't really work very well: we have to prevent both I' and V' from being minimality barriers. The fact that I' isn't a minimality barrier seems to be an instance of the general 'defectivity' of the I-system in *Barriers*, but of course this is in any case a problem. And we had no real suggestion to make about V'. Conceptually, relativized minimality seems preferable to absolute minimality in that it avoids these problems. We simply drop (107) and replace it with the definition of relativized minimality in (129). At the same time, we have a unified notion of 'barrier', relevant for both subjacency and the ECP: that in (97). And relativized minimality accounts for pseudo-opacity and negative islands – two phenomena that aren't handled in the *Barriers* system.

So relativized minimality seems like a conceptual and empirical improvement on the *Barriers* approach. Except for one thing: so far there is no account of C-t effects. Without this, there is an empirical case for retaining something like the absolute minimality condition, whatever its other flaws. The next section deals with Rizzi's account of C-t effects.

4.5.2 Head Government and θ-Government

4.5.2.1 A Conjunctive ECP

As we saw at the end of the last subsection, adopting relativized rather than absolute minimality means that we need an alternative account of C-t effects. To see what needs to be done, let's look again at a typical example:

(58')   *Who$_i$ did you say [$_{CP}$ t'$_i$ [$_{C'}$ that t$_i$ wrote this song]] ?

According to relativized minimality, t'_i antecedent-governs t_i. No barrier intervenes (since we are now disregarding minimality barriers in the sense defined in (107)), and relativized minimality is respected, as no typical potential antecedent governor in an A'-specifier intervenes (see (129) and (130)). The subject trace is not θ-governed, as usual, but this is of no importance since it is antecedent-governed. So what's wrong with (58')?

Up to now, we've been working with a 'disjunctive' ECP: one that imposes an 'either–or' requirement of antecedent government or θ/lexical government. Rizzi proposes that what's needed is a 'conjunctive' ECP, as follows:
Traces must be both:

(135a)   properly head-governed, and

(135b)   either antecedent-governed or θ-governed

You can see that the disjunction of the previous formulation of the ECP is retained in (134b). Antecedent government is defined as in (132), and θ-government still distinguishes complements from non-complements. The new thing here is 'proper head-government'. We can define this notion in a way which parallels our definition of antecedent government, as follows:

Proper Head Government
X properly head-governs Y iff:

(136a) X is a lexical head, Agr or T

(136b) X c-commands Y

(136c) no barrier intervenes

(136d) relativized minimality is respected

In (58'), C doesn't properly head-govern t_i because C is not included in the class of proper head-governors. Since all traces must be properly head-governed according to Rizzi's conjunctive ECP, (58') is ruled out.

Rizzi gives a number of arguments for the conjunctive ECP. One is that objects, but not subjects, can undergo 'Heavy DP Shift', an operation that apparently places 'heavy' DPs to the right of a clause:

(137a) I would like to introduce t_i to Mannie [$_i$ all the teenagers who can play the drums]

(137b) *t_i are talented [$_i$ all the teenagers who can play the drums]

The contrast here has nothing to do with the presence of complementizers, and yet can be reduced to proper head-government. In (137a) the trace is properly head-governed by V, while in (137b) there is no proper head-governor for the subject trace present at all. It is important to see that here, as in (58'), I (AgrS) doesn't properly head-govern the trace because it doesn't c-command it. Also, if we take it that Heavy DP-Shift, rather like extraposition (see 4.2), adjoins the DP to the right of the clause, the moved DP antecedent-governs the subject trace as no barriers or A'-specifiers intervene (here it's important to bear in mind that 'intervening' is a hierarchical notion defined in terms of c-command, not a linear notion). Since antecedent-government is satisfied, the ECP must impose a further requirement – proper head-government does the job both here and in the case of Complementizer-trace effects.

The conjunctive ECP in (135), combined with the definition of proper head-government in (136), gives us the desired alternative account of C-t effects. However, we also have to account for the fact that dropping the complementizer makes examples like (58) good again. In other words, why is (62) good?

(62) [$_{CP1}$ Who$_i$ did [$_{IP1}$ you say [$_{CP2}$ t'$_i$ [$_{IP2}$ t$_i$ wrote this song]]]] ?

Rizzi proposes that the null complementizer is a kind of Agr in English. Because of this, the subject trace is properly head-governed, as Agr is defined as belonging to the class of proper head-governors in (136). The true representation for (62) thus looks more like this:

(62') [$_{CP1}$ Who$_i$ did [$_{IP1}$ you say [$_{CP2}$ t'$_i$ Agr [$_{IP2}$ t$_i$ wrote this song]]]] ?

Just looking at English, this might seem like a rather arbitrary thing to say. However, there is quite a bit of crosslinguistic evidence that agreeing complementizers exist and that they facilitate extraction of the subject.

4.5.2.2 Cross-Linguistic Evidence for Agr in C

One piece of evidence comes from French. French shows C-t effects that are very similar to those we've seen in English:

(138) *Qui_i as -tu dit qu' t_i a écrit ce livre ?
      Who have you said that has written this book ?

However, the option of deleting the complementizer (or having a null complementizer) doesn't exist in French. Instead, sentences like (138) can be 'saved' by changing *que* (which in (138) undergoes a regular phonological reduction to *qu'*) to *qui*:

(139) Qui_i as -tu dit qui t_i a écrit ce livre ?
      Who did you say QUI has written this book ?
      'Who did you say wrote this book?'

The morphological change from *que* to *qui* can be thought of as a reflex of the presence of Agr in C. In other words, *qui* is *que* + Agr, and so able to act as a proper head-governor for the subject trace. (If you try to apply the *Barriers* account of C-t phenomena that I described 4.4.2. to the French examples in (138) and (139) you'll see that both examples come out as ungrammatical.)

West Flemish has a similar alternation between *da* and *die*:

(140a) Den vent$_i$ da Pol peinst [$_{CP}$ t'$_i$ DA [Marie t$_i$ getrokken heet]]
       The man that Pol thinks   that Marie photographed has

       'The man that Pol thinks that Marie has photographed'

(140b) Den vent$_i$ da Pol peinst [$_{CP}$ t'$_i$ DIE [t$_i$ gekommen ist]]
       The man that Pol thinks   DIE come   is
       'The man that Pol thinks has come'

As with French *qui*, we can think of West Flemish *die* as *da* + Agr; hence it is able to properly head-govern the subject trace.

Some languages have very elaborate systems of agreement in Comp independently of subject extraction. One example, again given by Rizzi, is that of the Bantu language Kinande. Kinande is typical of Bantu languages in having a rich system of noun classes, which trigger various kinds of agreement processes. Among these processes is one whereby a fronted *wh*-element agrees in class with its complementizer (the Roman numerals indicate the noun classes):

(141a) IyondI yO kambale alangIra
       who-I that-I Kambale saw

(141b) aBahI   Bo   kambale   alangIra
       who-II   that-II Kambale   saw

(141c) EkIhI   kyO   kambale   alangIra
       what-VII   that-VII   Kambale saw

(141d) EBIhI   ByO   kambale   alangIra
       what-VIII that-VIII Kambale saw
       'What/who did Kambale see?'

So there is good reason to think both that C can bear agreement features and that the presence of these features can facilitate subject extraction by making C into a proper head-governor.

In our discussion of Complementizer-trace phenomena in 4.3.2.1 we also mentioned the fact that I-to-C movement is not allowed when the subject is extracted:

(66a)   Which girl$_i$ did$_j$ he t$_j$ kiss t$_i$?

(66b)   *Which girl$_i$ did t$_i$ t$_j$ kiss him?

(66c)   Which girl$_i$ t$_i$ kissed him?

In (66b) we appear to have Agr in C, since the auxiliary is dominated by AgrS and is raised to C. Why, then, is this ruled out? This suggests a further restriction on the definition of proper head government. What we want to say, in order to capture the difference between (66b) and (68), is that it is not really C that c-commands the subject trace in (66b), but AgrS. Let's look again at our definition of c-command:

    C-command:
(142) α c-commands β iff every category dominating α also dominates β

The relevant parts of (66b) look like this:

(143)

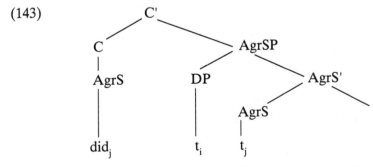

Did is an AgrS element, and the first node dominating AgrS is C, and C does not dominate the subject trace. On the other hand, in well-formed examples like (66c) and (68), we have a structure like (144):

(144)

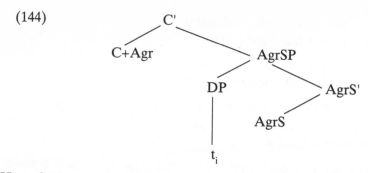

Here C+Agr c-commands the subject trace, since the first dominating node it (C') dominates the subject trace.

In 1.4.2.4 I introduced the verb-second (V2) phenomenon of the Germanic languages. We saw that one XP moves to SpecCP and the verb (plus the I-material) moves to C. In subject-initial clauses, then, we actually have subject extraction:

(145) $[_{CP}$ Ich$_i$ $[_{C'}$ las $[_{IP}$ t$_i$ schon   letztes Jahr diesen Roman $]]]$
      I   read   already last   year this   book
      'I read this book last year already'

(This analysis of subject-initial V2 clauses has been called into question by Travis (1984) and Zwart (1993).) Similarly, extraction of the subject from embedded V2 clauses is possible:

(146) Wer$_i$ hat sie gesagt $[_{CP}$ t'$_i$ ist $[_{IP}$ t$_i$ gekommen $]]$?
      Who   has she said   is   come?
      'Who did she say came?'

This implies that C in a V2 clause automatically has an Agr associated with it, and so is able to act as a proper head-governor for the subject trace. It is possible that the presence of this Agr is also connected to verb-movement to C in these constructions (this has been suggested by a number of researchers).

So we see that Rizzi offers an account of Complementizer-trace phenomena which relies on the notion of proper head-government given in (136). This approach has various crosslinguistic implications, some of which we have looked at here.

4.5.2.3 Against θ-Government

Rizzi's approach to Complementizer-trace phenomena seems to do well empirically, as we have seen. It certainly seems to do better than the notion of absolute minimality given in (107). However, the ECP now looks quite complicated, since it contains a conjunction, one of whose clauses is itself a disjunction. As a last topic under the heading of relativized minimality, let's see how this can be simplified.

The first step is to see that the complement/non-complement asymmetries that θ-government is meant to account for aren't really complement/non-complement asymmetries, but instead involve the idea of 'referentiality'. We can see this if we look at adverbial and idiomatic complements. These elements are clearly complements, and yet they behave like adjuncts for extraction (I've dropped the indices here, for reasons that will be explained below):

(147a) ??What project are you wondering [how [to make headway on t t]] ?

(147b) *What headway are you wondering [how [to make t on this project]] ?

A noun like *headway* in an idiom like *make headway on* has no reference: there's no particular thing called 'headway' that's being made; instead, the whole idiom means something like 'advance'. According to any of the various versions of the ECP that we've seen up to now, the trace of *headway* is θ-governed in (147b). But the extraction is very bad, rather like adjunct-extraction. So Rizzi suggests that what underlies complement/non-complement distinctions is the property of being referential, rather than the property of being a complement. Since, with the exception of pieces of idioms like *headway* and some adverbial or adjectival complements, complements are typically referential, most of the time the distinction can't be seen.

Instead of θ-government, then, Rizzi proposes that what underlies the complement/non-complement asymmetries the ECP deals with is the ability of referential categories to bear an index and thus be bound by their antecedent. Non-referential categories have no index and so can't be bound (see the definition of binding given in (7) of Chapter 3); this is why they're subject to a more rigorous locality condition. In Rizzi's view, aside from subjacency, there is no well-formedness condition on the relation between argument traces and their antecedents beyond what, right at the beginning of this chapter, we called the central property of Move-α: the formation of a binding relation between the moved category α and its trace. So the second clause of the ECP can be dropped for argument traces, leaving just the proper head-government requirement.

Subjects are usually referential (except for expletives, which can't be extracted). So the suggestion just made implies that subjects should pattern with objects as far as asymmetries are concerned. In fact, the only clear examples of subjects patterning with adjuncts can come under the rubric of complementizer-trace effects. This is true of (53), for example:

(53) *Which band$_i$ were you wondering whether t$_i$ will play that song ?

And conversely, it's quite clear that subjects pattern with objects rather than with adjuncts in negative islands. Compare (148) with the discussion of (122) above:

(148a) Who$_i$ don't you think we can help t$_i$?

(148b) ?Who$_i$ don't you think t$_i$ can help us ?

When they are more deeply embedded in *wh*-islands, subjects pattern with objects and against adjuncts:

(149a) ??Who$_i$ do you wonder whether we believe t$_i$ can help us ?

(149b) ?Who$_i$ do you wonder whether we believe we can help t$_i$?

(149c) *How do you wonder whether we believe [we can help Bill t] ?

(Remember that we're only interested in the lowest construal of *how* in (149c); I'm not coindexing the trace as adjuncts lack referential indices according to the theory being put forward here.) The data in (148) and (149) confirm that subjects and objects – as typically referential categories – pattern together, distinct from adjuncts.

Getting rid of θ-government is a good move as regards our treatment of DP-traces. Remember that in 4.4.3.1 we saw that DP-traces appear to require antecedent-government as well as θ-government. This question of why θ-government isn't enough partly disappears if we get rid of this notion. However, the question now becomes: why do DP-traces act like adjuncts as regards movement? DP-traces presumably bear indices, and so why isn't forming a binding relation with the antecedent enough? Rizzi's answer to this is that DP-movement always forms a θ-chain: the head of the chain must be in a Case-position and the foot of it in a θ-position. Rizzi proposes that *the locality condition on chain links is antecedent-government*, defined in terms of relativized minimality as in (132). DP-traces must be in a well-formed θ-chain, and so must be antecedent-governed by their antecedent.

All of this just leaves adjuncts, or more precisely non-referential categories. Why are such categories required to be antecedent-governed? We've just seen that antecedent-government can be viewed as a condition on chain links. Moreover, non-referential categories lack indices. So the only way they can be connected to their antecedents is by antecedent-government. In the last analysis, then, it is the non-referential nature of certain traces – typically, but not always, adjuncts – which makes them subject to a stricter locality requirement than referential traces. Chain-formation by antecedent government is a kind of last-resort strategy for connecting these traces to their antecedents. If this idea is to work, we cannot define antecedent-government itself in terms of coindexation, as we did above. So let's make a minor reformulation, as follows:

Antecedent Government (Fourth Revision):
X antecedent-governs Y iff:

(132a') X and Y are non-distinct

(132b') X c-commands Y

(132c') no barrier intervenes

(132d') relativized minimality is respected

Statement (132') differs from (132) only in that 'coindexed' has been replaced by 'non-distinct'. This allows us to maintain that non-referential traces lack indices.

Rizzi's conclusion is that (132') is *not* part of the ECP, but part of the definition of chain-formation. It is relevant for non-referential traces by default, since, being non-referential, such traces can't be bound. This is presumably why it's also relevant for heads. And it's relevant for DP-traces since such traces must be in θ-chains. It is not relevant for referential traces, since they can be bound by their antecedents, and are subject only to the proper head-government requirement of the ECP (like all traces).

4.5.3 Conclusion

Relativized minimality really leads to two main conclusions. First, antecedent-government, defined as (132'), is relevant for chain-formation. Second, the ECP consists only of a rather simple proper head-government requirement as in (136). You might have noticed that proper head-government is a slightly stipulative requirement in that it simply lists those heads that head-govern. No reason emerges for why some functional heads and not others are head-governors. Also, although Rizzi presents a very interesting theory of the ECP, the *Barriers* account of subjacency remains, along with the notion of barrier as defined in (97). In a sense, this is another result: what emerges with particular clarity from Rizzi's work is that head-movement, DP-movement, and movement of non-referential/adjunct *wh*-elements have important properties in common: all three movements are highly local, and, allowing for successive cyclicity, we can say that they always move to the nearest appropriate c-commanding position. In fact, this was part of our informal characterization of head-movement and DP-movement at the beginning of this chapter. Movement of referential/argumental *wh*-elements is much freer, on the other hand, and appears to be subject only to subjacency and the proper head-government requirement. So there are two broad types of movement, with *wh*-movement taken as a whole straddling the distinction.

We're now basically in the position of having sorted out the role of antecedent-government: as defined in (132'), antecedent-government is the condition on chain-formation. We have a residual ECP (proper head-government as in (136)) and we have subjacency, defined as in *Barriers* (see 98)). The question that remains is: can subjacency and the ECP be unified under a single locality condition? This is the question that Manzini (1992) addresses and to which we should now turn.

4.6 Locality

Manzini's system is, at the time of writing, the most comprehensive and up-to-date set of proposals on the nature of Move-α and the theory of locality. In this section, we'll come back to the questions set out at the beginning of this chapter: what we're really after is a unified, conceptually simple theory of movement relations. It should be clear from the previous section we're almost there, but not quite.

4.6.1 Some Definitions

A fundamental component of Manzini's theory is her use of two types of index. A distinction is made between 'categorial indices' and 'addresses'. Categorial indices are basically the indices we've been using all along to indicate anaphoric relations, including, of course, relations holding between traces and their antecedents. Addresses, on the other hand (the term and to some extent the idea are taken from Vergnaud (1985)) differ from categorial indices in being relational. That is, a category is addressed by being in a certain kind of relation with another category. The usual (but not the only) way that categories get addressed is by Case-assignment: a Case-assigner gives an address to the category it Case-marks (of course, it is possible to think of this in terms of Case-checking, as discussed in 2.6).

All movement dependencies involve sharing categorial indices between the moved category and its trace – again, there is nothing new here; this is precisely what we've been assuming all through this chapter (except for 4.5.2.3). The differences arise in connection with addressing. Let's look at each kind of movement in turn, distinguishing adjunct *wh*-movement from argument *wh*-movement (I'll revert to referring to the two kinds of *wh*-movement in this way, even though Rizzi argues that this is not really correct, as we have seen).

First, head-movement, as in (150) (I'm ignoring the split-Infl structure again):

(150) Jean $[_I$ embrasse$_i$] souvent $[_{VP}$ t$_i$ Marie]
      Jean   kisses   often   Marie
      'Jean often kisses Marie'

Here neither the trace nor the antecedent is in an addressed position, and so the dependency must be categorial rather than address-based. In general, since heads aren't Case-marked, head-movement cannot be an address-based dependency.

Similarly, adjunct *wh*-movement moves from a Caseless position (an adjunct) to a Caseless position (SpecCP):

(151) How$_i$ did you fix the car t$_i$?

Third, we've defined DP-movement as being movement in search of Case (see 2.3). Therefore, this cannot be an address-based dependency since only the antecedent has an address.

So we see that the inherently more local kinds of movement – head-movement, DP-movement, and adjunct *wh*-movement – do not form address-based dependencies. With these types of movement the dependency is based purely on a shared categorial index.

On the other hand, argument *wh*-traces occupy Case-marked positions.

We saw in 2.4 that this is in fact required, as the ungrammaticality of examples like (152) shows (see 2.4 (70a and b)):

(152a) *Who$_i$ does it seem [t$_i$ to speak Chinese] ?

(152b) *Who$_i$ was it believed [t$_i$ to speak Chinese] ?

In general, properties of traces are transmitted to their antecedents. So, since the trace has an address, we can regard the argument *wh*-movement dependency as an address-based dependency. The difference in the ability to form address-based dependencies corresponds to the notion of referentiality in Rizzi's work (see 4.5.2.3): this is how we distinguish the more local dependencies (adjunct *wh*-movement, DP-movement, and head-movement) from the less local argument *wh*-movement.

One more notion is needed before we can give the general locality constraint. This is the notion of a 'sequence', a neutral term intended to cover both categorial and address-based dependencies:

Sequence:
(153) (α_1 .... α_n) is a sequence iff every element in the sequence α_i is co-indexed with and c-commands the next

In other words, both types of dependencies require that each link between the antecedent and the trace c-commands the next. Now for the locality principle:

Locality:
(154) α is a dependent element iff there is an antecedent β for α and a sequence (β .... α) where no link of the sequence crosses a barrier

Definition (154) is very close to Chomsky's definition of antecedent-government in *Barriers* (see (104)), and to part of Rizzi's definition: see (132').

4.6.2 Weak Islands

Given the definitions in (153) and (154), weak islands (islands from which adjuncts can't be extracted but arguments can) can accounted for. Let's consider (for the last time) argument-adjunct asymmetries in infinitival *wh*-islands.

(155a) ?[$_{CP1}$ Whose car$_{i/K}$ were [$_{IP1}$ you wondering [$_{CP2}$ how$_j$ [$_{IP2}$ to fix t$_{i/K}$ t$_j$] ?

(155b) *How$_j$ were you wondering [whose car$_{i/K}$ to fix t$_{i/K}$ t$_j$] ?

Here the argument trace has both the index *i* and the address *K*, while the adjunct trace just has the categorial index *j*. For the purposes of this illustration, we'll just assume that CP is a barrier – we'll come to back to how barriers are determined in 4.6.4. In (155b), then, there is no sequence with index *j* where each link governs the next: CP intervenes and breaks the sequence, and so locality isn't satisfied. Again, this account should seem quite familiar since it is broadly similar to both Chomsky's and Rizzi's. However, the treatment of (155a) is quite different. Here, the categorial dependency is blocked in the same way as for the adjunct. However, the argument has the capacity to form an address-based dependency, which involves assigning the address K to all the heads intervening between $wh_{i,K}$ and the trace $t_{i,K}$. So the sequence (wh_i, C, I, V, C, I, V, t_i), all bearing the address K, is formed and the locality condition is satisfied. In this way, argument-adjunct asymmetries can be handled in terms of the single notion of locality given in (154).

There are other syntactic contexts which act like weak islands in the sense described above. One such context that we haven't mentioned up to now is the complement to factive verbs. These were discussed by Cinque (1991). 'Factive' predicates are predicates which presuppose the truth of their complement. Even if you negate the main clause, the complement clause is still taken to be true (this is one of the classic diagnostics for presupposition). Compare *regret* with *believe* in the following examples:

(156a) I don't believe that Sheena is a punk rocker

(156b) I don't regret that Sheena is a punk rocker

In (156a), there is no commitment to the truth or falsity of the proposition expressed by the complement clause: Sheena may or may not in fact be a punk rocker. In (156b), on the other hand, the fact that Sheena is a punk rocker is presupposed, taken for granted as true. Verbs that are like *regret* in this respect are known as factive verbs, while *believe* and similar verbs are non-factive.

The relevant phenomenon in the present connection is that the complements of factive verbs are weak islands, as the following sentences show:

(157a) What$_i$ do you regret [$_{CP}$ THAT YOU FIXED t$_i$] ?
(157b) *How$_i$ do you regret [$_{CP}$ THAT I FIXED YOUR CAR t$_i$] ?

As usual, *how* in (157b) should be interpreted as related to an adjunct of the *embedded* clause, not the main clause; the position of the trace inside the brackets marking the lower clause indicates this in (157b). This interpretation is completely unavailable. Manzini proposes that there is an empty *wh*-like operator in SpecCP of factive clauses, and that this is the element that makes them factive. This operator makes factive clauses structurally equivalent to *wh*-islands, and so we find the selective blocking of extraction that we find in *wh*-islands.

This kind of approach extends to both pseudo-opacity and negative islands:

(119b) *Combien$_i$ a-t-il   beaucoup consulté t$_i$ de livres?
         How-many has-he   much   consulted of books?

(120b) *?How$_i$ didn't he fix your car t$_i$?

If we assume that only one Specifier position is available for a given category, and that *beaucoup* occupies a (non-L-related) Specifier structurally close to VP – we'll discuss the precise nature of this position in 4.6.4 – while *not* occupies SpecNegP (although in (120b) it has attached to the auxiliary and raised with it while presumably, its trace still occupies SpecNegP), then each of these examples creates an analogous configuration to *wh*-islands, and the account given for (155) carries over. Here, too, it should be clear that Manzini's theory is very similar to Rizzi's.

4.6.3 Strong Islands

An important advantage of the idea of address-based dependencies and their link to Case-assignment is that it can capture the fact that certain types of NPs (or DPs) block extraction, while VPs never do. We saw in 4.4.1.3 that the *Barriers* approach can't handle the complement case of the CNPC:

(33b) *Which band$_i$ did you believe [$_{DP}$ the claim that [$_{IP}$ we had seen t$_i$]] ?   (see (9))

Complex DPs are strong islands, in the sense that they block extraction of both argument and adjunct *wh*-elements. Extraction of adjuncts is blocked by the fact that DP is a barrier (again, I'm just stating this for the moment – we'll come back to it in 4.6.4) and, unlike CP, its Specifier isn't a position that can be moved through successive-cyclically. Extraction of arguments is blocked by the fact that N has an address of its own, and so formation of an address-based sequence that passes through N is impossible. This is why complex NPs (or DPs) are islands.

Another interesting aspect of the address-based dependencies is that they can handle the fact that *wh*-islands are sensitive to tense. As I commented in 4.1, non-finite *wh*-islands more or less allow argument extraction, while tensed *wh*-islands do not. In other words, non-finite *wh*-islands are weak islands, while finite *wh*-islands are strong. Here, again, are the relevant examples:

(36a) ?[$_{CP1}$ Whose car$_i$ were [$_{IP1}$ you wondering [$_{CP2}$ how$_j$ [$_{IP2}$ to fix t$_i$ t$_j$] ?

(36b) ?*[$_{CP1}$ Whose car$_i$ were [$_{IP1}$ you wondering [$_{CP2}$ how$_j$ [$_{IP2}$ you should fix t$_i$ t$_j$] ?

Manzini suggests that this contrast can be captured by saying that finite Tense (remember that 'IP' is a cover term for TP and the other functional categories associated with V) has its own address. In that case, the address-based dependency that is required to link an argument *wh*-trace to its antecedent across a *wh*-island cannot be formed.

Similar reasoning holds for another kind of island that we briefly alluded to in 4.1. Definite DPs seem to form strong islands:

(158a) ??Which band$_i$ did [$_{IP}$ you write [$_{DP}$ that song about t$_i$]] ?

(158b) *Which band$_i$ did [$_{IP}$ you sing [$_{DP}$ Mick's song about t$_i$]] ?

(158c) Which band$_i$ did [$_{IP}$ you write [$_{DP}$ a song about t$_i$]] ?

Manzini rules out (158a) and (158b) by saying that a definite D has its own address while an indefinite one does not. Because of this, address-based dependencies cannot be formed in (158a) and (158b), while they can in (158c). (Again, we have to assume that DP is a barrier here.) So the system makes the right distinctions, to a fair degree of approximation, among these examples.

As I said above, Manzini's approach captures argument-adjunct asymmetries in terms of the idea that only argument traces can form address-based dependencies. This effectively factors out the role played by θ-government in the *Barriers* version of the ECP. The definition of locality in (154) looks very like antecedent-government – in fact, for non-addressed traces (traces of adjuncts, DP-movement, and head-movement) (154) functions almost exactly like antecedent government in both *Barriers* and relativized minimality. The major difference between Manzini's system and the *Barriers* system is the proposal that (154) also accounts for subjacency. Now let's look at how this is done.

4.6.4 Subjacency Again

The locality principle requires that the sequence linking the antecedent to the trace be such that each link governs the next. For argument traces, as we have seen, this requirement relates to an address-based dependency. So when subjacency is violated, one link of an address-based dependency must be separated from the next by a barrier (as you can see, Manzini assumes a one-barrier definition of subjacency rather than the usual two-barrier one). In order to see in detail how this works, we need to see how barriers are defined. Barriers are defined in terms of 'g-marking', as follows:

> *Barrier:*
> β is a barrier for α iff

(159a) β is a maximal projection

(159b) β dominates α

(159c) if α is g-marked, β dominates the g-marker of α

So a barrier for α is a maximal projection dominating both α and its g-marker. G-marking is a concept similar to L-marking, although it makes reference to sisterhood rather than θ-government (and is not restricted to lexical heads, as L-marking is in (95')):

> *G-Marking:*
> β g-marks α iff β is a head and:

(160a) β is a sister to α, or

(160b) β is a sister to a category that agrees with α

Subjects, adjuncts, and the CP that modifies the head of a relative clause are not sisters to a head, and therefore not g-marked. The configurations are as follows:

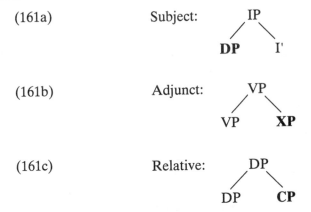

(161a)   Subject: IP
                                 / \
                               DP   I'

(161b)   Adjunct: VP
                                 / \
                                VP   **XP**

(161c)   Relative: DP
                                   / \
                                 DP   **CP**

(Again, if we follow Kayne's proposals about how phrase structure should be organized (see 1.3.4), we'll have to come up with different proposals for the positions of adjuncts and relatives; I'll leave this matter to one side here.) Since these domains are not g-marked, only clauses (159a and b) of the definition of barrier apply, and so the first maximal projection dominating the domains is a barrier. This means that no sequence of any kind can be formed between an element inside one of these domains and an element outside it. So extraction of anything, including an argument *wh*-element, from inside one of these domains will violate the locality principle.

The other principal strong islands that are discussed are the complement CNPC, tensed *wh*-islands, and definite DP-islands. We discussed these cases in the previous subsection, assuming without explanation that DP and CP are barriers. Now let's look at why these categories are barriers. In fact, the concept of barrier defined in (159) is extremely general: any maximal projection dominating a trace and its g-marker can be a barrier. This means that the assumption made above, that CP and DP are barriers, is unproblematic. The proposal is very strong, though. It means, for example, that where a direct object is extracted, VP becomes a barrier, as it dominates both the trace and the g-marker of the trace, V. However, where an argument is extracted, there are two options: either an address-based dependency can be formed, as we have seen, or extraction can pass through the A'-specifier position. Manzini assumes that all non-argument categories have an A'-specifier (for lexical categories, this would entail a complication of the notion of L-relatedness in terms of which we defined A- and A'-positions in 3.3.2.3; however, I'll leave this question to one side). This position is able to form an 'escape hatch' for extraction thanks to the second clause of the definition of g-marking given in (160). Consider the configuration where a category is successive-cyclically moved through the A'-Specifier of VP:

(162)

```
        I'
      /    \
     I      VP
          /    \
        t_i    . . . .
```

Assuming that a specifier always agrees with its head (see the discussion of this relation in 2.6), we see that I g-marks the trace here, since I is the sister of VP, a category that agrees with the trace. Since VP does not dominate I, it cannot be a barrier for the trace, because it doesn't dominate both the trace and its g-marker. However, VP is a barrier for any extraction which does not pass through its A'-specifier. This is why VP-adverbs can form weak islands, as in the case of pseudo-opacity (see (119b) above). As we saw above, argument *wh*-elements can form an address-based dependency in this case. More generally, if the Specifier position is filled in (162) (or a similar configuration in another non-argumental XP), then the only option for extraction is the formation of an address-based dependency. This is how the weak-island configurations that we looked at in 4.6.2 are created: factive islands, negative islands, and *wh*-islands.

CP, like other maximal projections, is a barrier for material it contains. Hence the only way out of CP is by formation of an address-based dependency (this option being available for argument *wh*-traces only) or by passing through the A'-specifier, SpecCP. In *wh*-islands, the A'-specifier is filled, and so all *wh*-islands block adjunct extraction. Argument extraction via an address-based dependency is possible unless some independent factor such as Tense (see 4.6.3) intervenes.

DPs are also barriers for the material they contain. Moreover, DPs are typically arguments. Developing Chomsky's proposal in *Barriers* that adjunction to arguments is impossible (see 100a), Manzini proposes that argument XPs cannot have A'-specifier positions. So the configuration in (164) never obtains with DP. For this reason DPs are always weak islands, and can become strong islands either through an intrinsic property of D (definiteness, as we saw above) or by containing a Case-marked N, as in the case of the complement CNPC. In both cases, the address-based dependency is blocked.

So we see that subjacency too can be derived from the locality principle in (154), combined with the definitions of barrier and g-marking in (159) and (160). As we saw at the end of the previous section, the other principal element of the theory of locality is proper head-government. Here the main facts to account for are C-t effects. So now let's see how Manzini's theory can deal with these, and, in particular, whether they can be unified with (154).

4.6.5 C-t Effects Again

The configuration for the Complementizer-trace effects is (163), as we have seen:

(163)

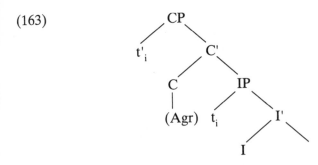

As we saw in 4.5.2.1, Rizzi argues that C must contain an abstract Agr in order for t_i to be properly head-governed. Manzini follows this basic idea, but reduces the requirement to the general locality principle of (154). In other words, the proper head-government requirement is derived, not primitive.

The basic idea is that the presence of an agreement relation is necessary in order for the subject trace to have an address. The agreement relation is optional in itself. If it does not hold, then the subject must form a categorial dependency. Since CP is a barrier for the subject trace (you can see this if you try the definitions of barrier and g-marking in (159) and (160)), SpecCP must function as an escape hatch. So, if SpecCP is filled by another *wh*-element, the sentence is bad. This is what we see in examples like (53):

(53) *Which band$_i$ were you wondering whether t$_i$ will play that song ?

This example violates locality because the trace and the antecedent are separated by the barrier CP.

So, where the agreement-in-C option is not taken, the subject must move through SpecCP. Now, SpecCP agrees with C by Specifier-head agreement, and SpecIP agrees with I by Specifier-head agreement. By transitivity of agreement, C and I also agree. So, we have agreement in C. This is manifested in English by the null alternant of *that* and in French by the presence of *qui*, as we saw in 4.5.2.1.

If, on the other hand, the agreement-in-C option is taken, then the subject trace can form an address-based dependency. Here we automatically get the null form of *that* and *qui* instead of *que*. When the subject forms an address-based dependency, it can escape from *wh*-islands and negative islands, as in (148b) and (149a):

(148b) ?Who$_i$ don't you think t$_i$ can help us ?

(149a) ??Who$_i$ do you wonder whether we believe t$_i$ can help us ?

As long as we assume that agreement in C is related to the formation of address-based dependencies, we can reduce the proper head-government requirement to the general locality principle.

4.6.6 The Nature of Move-α

So we see that Manzini is able to unify subjacency, antecedent-government, and proper head-government under a single principle. Remember that this principle also applies to DP-movement and head-movement. So the theory of Move-α reduces to (5b) – the statement that movement creates binding relations – and the locality principle in (154). In fact, since binding involves the formation of one kind of sequence (one based on categorial indices) we can collapse (5b) and (154) as follows:

> *Move-α (Final Version):*
> (164) a dependency such that there is an antecedent β for α and a sequence (β .... α) where no link of the sequence crosses a barrier

You might notice that this definition doesn't really say much about movement or about the creation of syntactic derivations. Following Rizzi's proposal for antecedent-government, it is natural to think of (164) as a condition on the formation of chains:

> *Chain:*
> (164') a dependency such that there is an antecedent β for α and a sequence (β .... α) where no link of the sequence crosses a barrier

We've seen that there are various kinds of chains: θ-chains formed by DP-movement and A-chains formed by anaphors of certain kinds (see 3.5.3); (164') can be taken as defining the class of chains which is then subdivided in various ways.

So it may turn out that we don't need Move-α at all, but simply the notion of chain given in (164'). This is an important issue, because if we don't need Move-α but can make do just with chains, then we don't really have derivations, but instead we can posit a single level of syntactic representation which contains all relevant semantic, phonological, and lexical information. The issue of whether syntax is really derivational or is instead 'representational' has been debated for over 10 years now, and is still not resolved. After all we have seen in this chapter, it should be reasonably clear that it is at best extremely hard to tell whether Move-α has an existence independently of chains.

4.7 Conclusion

This chapter has dealt with one of the most important areas of research in generative grammar. It is also worth pointing out that the phenomena discussed here, unlike those discussed in the other chapters, were completely unknown 40 years ago and have received no interesting treatment in non-generative theories. I've presented a general theory of locality, following Manzini's work, but after all the technicalities it's perhaps useful to take stock of what is in fact known about locality. I'll try to list these points below:

- despite appearances, *wh*-movement is not unbounded but local, cyclic and sensitive to islands (4.1, 4.2.1, 4.2.2)

- adjunct *wh*-movement and argument *wh*-movement show differing behaviour, with adjunct *wh*-movement being much more constrained than argument *wh*-movement (weak *vs* strong islands) (4.3.1)
- adjunct *wh*-movement patterns with DP-movement and head-movement in being blocked by a potential landing-site (relativized minimality; 4.5.1)
- argument *wh*-movement obeys the CED, the CNPC, and is sensitive to Tense and definiteness inside otherwise weak islands (4.6.3, 4.6.4)
- all movement is subject to a proper head-government requirement (4.3.2; 4.5.2; 4.6.5).

Manzini's approach captures all these observations under a single locality principle, as we saw in 4.6. This locality principle is formulated in terms of barriers, which are, in turn, defined in terms of g-marking, as we saw. The notions of barrier and g-marking are configurational notions, in that they define certain types of structures in a purely geometric way.

In recent work that sketches out the minimalist programme (see 2.6), Chomsky has suggested a seemingly rather different approach. According to this view, the essence of locality should be that any operation of movement is as 'short' as possible, in that movement should always target the closest available landing-site. In fact, relativized minimality effectively states this, since it says that a category β of the same type (A, A', head) as α – a potential landing site for α – prevents α being moved past β. So one can readily think of a 'shortest move' constraint as applying to adjunct *wh*-movement, DP-movement, and head-movement. It is not clear how this idea should extend to argument *wh*-movement, though. Here we presumably need to refer to actual rather than potential landing-sites, with the class of actual landing sites defined by subjacency in some way. At the time of writing, no proposal has been made for dealing with the locality constraints on argument *wh*-movement that fits with the minimalist conception of shortest move.

This chapter has not had much to say about comparative syntax, on the face of things at least. I've mentioned Rizzi's work on *wh*-islands in Italian, Huang's work on adjunct *wh*-elements in Chinese, and Kayne's work on Preposition-stranding. However, I hope you can see that the kinds of phenomena that are being dealt with here are fundamental to linguistic theory. The tacit assumption throughout this chapter has been that the principles that are being put forward are UG principles, subject to a small degree of parametrization. Now that you have a reasonably good idea what a number of those principles and some of the associated parameters are, it's time to take a wider view and look at the theory of parameters.

Parameters Discussed in this Chapter

As just mentioned, parametric variation has not been a central focus of this chapter. None the less, a number of parameters have been discussed to varying levels of detail. I'll now summarize and elaborate on what we've seen.

1. Some languages, like Russian and Latin, appear systematically able to violate the Left Branch Condition, while languages like English cannot (see 4.1). We suggested that this might be connected to the absence of overt D-elements in these languages. French can apparently violate the LBC in the sole instance of *combien*, a quite mysterious fact.

2. In 4.3.1.2 we saw that there is variation as to the level at which *wh*-movement can take place. In Chinese, *wh*-movement is always covert (but see Watanabe (1992), Aoun and Li (1994)). Many languages pattern like Chinese: Japanese, Korean, Armenian, and others. In French, main-clause *wh*-movement is optionally overt or covert, depending on register, while *wh*-movement in embedded [+*wh*] clauses is always obligatory:

> (165a) Quelle fille a-t-il embrassée?   (Standard/literary French)
>   Which girl has he kissed?

> (165b) Il a embrassé quelle fille?   (Colloquial French)
>   He has kissed which girl?
>   Which girl did he kiss?'

> (165c) Je me demande quelle fille il a embrassée (Both registers)
>   'I wonder which girl he has kissed'

> (165d) *Je me demande il a embrassé quelle fille
>   I wonder he kissed which girl

In English, a single *wh*-element moves to the Specifier of a [+*wh*] CP; where there is more than one *wh*-element in a clause, the others do not move overtly:

(166)   Who$_i$ t$_i$ said what ?

As mentioned in the Appendix to Chapter 3, however, the interpretation of the *wh*-element *in situ* (*what* in (168)) as a quantifier binding a variable implies that we should assume that it moves covertly to Spec,CP. If so, the LF of (166) might look like (166'):

(166')   Who$_i$ what$_j$ t$_i$ said t$_j$?

Some languages, including most of the Slavic languages, overtly form multiple questions that look like (166'). This is shown in the Russian example in (167):

(167)   Kto čto kogda skazal?
        who what when said?
        'Who said what when?'

There are interesting differences among these languages as regards the multiple *wh* structures: see Rudin (1988) for discussion.

3. In 4.2.3 we saw Rizzi's evidence that Italian has slightly different BCs from English. Sportiche (1981) showed that French patterns like Italian. You might have noticed that we didn't see a way to integrate this variation into Manzini's version of subjacency in 4.6.4.

4. In (75), we saw the full effects of the null subject parameter, as described by Rizzi (1982). We recapitulate these here:

(75a) Possibility of phonologically empty referential subject pronouns

(75b) Impossibility of overt expletive pronouns

(75c) Possibility of free inversion

(75d) Apparent absence of Complementizer-trace effects

In 3.3.3, we suggested that the trigger for the null-subject parameter was the presence of verbal inflection that permits the identification of the referential properties of subject *pro*; we also discussed some problems for this idea. A number of researchers, notably Safir (1985), have denied that the properties listed in (75) correlate. Certainly, a superficial survey of languages will show that they do not. However, (75) is not a statement of an implicational relation of the Greenbergian kind that we discussed in Chapter 1 (see 1.3.3), but a statement of properties that follow from the availability of referential *pro* in a system of a given kind. If we look across all the languages of the world, we are likely to bring a number of extra unknown variables into play that may well disturb these correlations; but this would not affect their theoretical validity.

5. English allows Preposition-stranding; French doesn't. Most of the Scandinavian languages pattern like English (although Icelandic is a special case: see Kayne (1984)). In Dutch and German, the complement of a Preposition can only be extracted if the *wh*-element takes on a particular form into which the Preposition appears to be incorporated (see van Riemsdijk (1978)); archaic English shows the same phenomenon, as in *the person **whereof** I spoke*. In Welsh, the Preposition must agree with the *wh*-trace, giving something like *the person I spoke of+3sg* (see Hendrick (1988) – although Hendrick does not treat these cases as extraction). We saw in 4.3.3.2 that the difference between English and French can be related to the differing status of Prepositions as Case-assigners in these languages: see 2.5.3.

Further Reading

In this chapter more than the others, I've mentioned the central readings in the text; so here there'll be rather more repetition than in the other Further Reading sections.

wh-islands are discussed briefly and rather inconclusively in Chomsky (1964). Otherwise, the reference for island phenomena is Ross (1967), published in almost unaltered form as Ross (1986). This is a classic text of generative grammar, and contains a wealth of insight and information. It remains a very influential piece of work. A good up-to-date discussion of island phenomena, including the division into weak and strong islands, is Cinque (1991). The first chapter of Manzini (1992) is an excellent overview, and is perhaps the best thing to read after this chapter.

Subjacency was first formulated in Chomsky (1973), an article which, as I said in the Further Reading to Chapter 3, is difficult but worth looking at. Successive cyclicity and the Strict Cycle Condition are also introduced here. The other major works on subjacency are Chomsky (1977), Rizzi (1982, ch. 2) (on the parametric variation between English and Italian; in this article, originally circulated in 1977, the idea of parametric variation appears for the first time), Huang (1982) (showing that it doesn't apply to covert *wh*-movement; argument–adjunct asymmetries and the Condition on Extraction Domains are first discussed here), Lasnik and Saito (1984, 1992), Chomsky (1986b) (*Barriers*), Cinque (1991), and Manzini (1992).

The Empty Category Principle was first proposed in Chomsky (1981). Several of the chapters of Kayne (1984) develop the idea in various ways; here the account of Preposition-stranding and the theory of connectedness are proposed. An approach comparable to connectedness is put forward by Pesetsky (1982). In addition to the references given under subjacency in the previous paragraph, all of which also deal with the ECP, important work on the ECP is found in Aoun (1985, 1986), Aoun, Hornstein, Lightfoot and Weinberg (1987) – Aoun's theory of 'generalized binding' largely anticipates relativized minimality.

Parasitic gaps were first discussed by Taraldsen (1979). Chomsky (1982, 1986b) discusses them in detail, and proposes quite different theories. Other important works on this phenomenon, in addition to Kayne (1984), are Engdahl (1983, 1985), Bennis and Hoekstra (1984), Longobardi (1985), and Frampton (1989).

The remaining topics of the chapter – barriers, relativized minimality, and locality – are discussed in the eponymous monographs by Chomsky (1986b), Rizzi (1990), and Manzini (1992) respectively. After reading this chapter, you should be able to tackle that material: indeed, I hope much of it will seem familiar. The important recent works on the theory of movement that I haven't gone into detail about here are Cinque (1991) and Lasnik and Saito (1992).

The question of whether Move-α has an existence independently of chain-formation was first raised in Chomsky (1981, ch. 6). The idea that Move-α should be reduced to chain-formation is argued for notably by Sportiche (1983), Brody (1985, 1995), and Rizzi (1986c). Moreover, both Rizzi (1990) and Manzini (1992) present theories that are broadly compatible with this view, as we have seen. The opposite view, namely that Move-α exists independently of properties of chains, is espoused by Lasnik and Saito (1984, 1992) and Chomsky (1986b). The minimalist organization of the grammar (see 2.6.2) appears to be 'derivationalist', but see Brody (1995) for a 'representationalist' version of minimalism.

Exercises

Exercise 1
We haven't said much in this chapter about extraction of APs, although we mentioned in 2.4 that *wh*-APs exist and can be moved. However, there are some surprising constraints on AP-extraction. Here is a range of different kinds of APs:

1. John considers Bill [$_{AP}$ intelligent]   (epistemic)
2. John made Mary [$_{AP}$ angry]   (causative)
3. We hammered the metal [$_{AP}$ flat]   (resultative)
4. Keith took the stage [$_{AP}$ drunk]   (circumstantial)
5. Kazuo ate the fish [$_{AP}$ raw]   (depictive)

Try extracting these APs (with *how*) in this environment and in weak-island contexts. Try also to see whether the different kinds of APs are selected (by seeing whether the verbs are grammatical, or have the same meaning, without them). What generalizations can you arrive at here?

Exercise 2
Chomsky (1977) showed that a range of constructions, including *easy-to-please* constructions as in (1) and comparatives as in (2), involve movement of a null *wh*-phrase (a null operator: see 3.2.2.2):

1. John is easy to please
2. Ruth is stranger than Richard is

Chomsky used three main diagnostics for *wh*-movement:

3. It leaves a gap
4. It is apparently unbounded
5. It obeys subjacency

Show that these diagnostics apply to the operations in (1) and (2). This will entail showing the positions both of the gap and of the empty operator. (Hint regarding (2): many dialects of English express (2) as *Ruth is stranger than what Richard is.*)
   Why can't we analyse *easy-to-please* constructions as involving the following movement dependency (possibly mediated by cyclicity)?

6. John$_i$ is easy to please t$_i$

Finally, following on from our brief discussion of control in 3.2.2.2, what does the interpretation of the PRO subject of *to please* tell us here?

Exercise 3
Consider the following parasitic-gap data:
   This is the book that I filed t . . .

1. . . . without reading *e*

2. *. . . before hearing the rumour that the author had plagiarized *e*

3. *. . . after wondering whether I should throw away *e*

4. *. . . after the author of *e* had come to dinner

5. *. . . after going on holiday without reading *e*

What does this tell you about parasitic gaps? How best might they be analysed, especially in the light of Exercise 2?

Exercise 4

Look again at the contrast between (27) and (28), which illustrates the Right Roof Constraint:

(27) *The proof that the claim t_i was made by the Greeks was given in 1492 $[_{CP_i}$ that the world was round]

(28) The proof that the claim t_i was made $[_{CP_i}$ that the world was round] by the Greeks was given in 1492

There's a simple explanation for the rightward-boundedness of movement in terms of subjacency and successive cyclicity. Or is there? Think about it.

Exercise 5

In Modern Greek, factive islands are strong islands. That is, they block extraction of both arguments and adjuncts (this was discovered by Roussou (1993)):

1. *Pjon$_i$ thimase   pu   sinandises t_i?
   Who   you-remember that you-met?
   'Who do you remember that you met?'

2. *Pote$_i$ thimase   pu   sinandises ti   Maria t_i?
   When you-remember that you-met   the Maria?
   'When do you remember that you met Maria?'

How might we integrate this fact in a theory like Manzini's? These factive complements have a special complementizer (*pu*); might this fact be significant?

Exercise 6

We saw in 4.4.3.2 that noun-incorporation cannot move the head of a subject DP into the verb. In that case, what do you make of the following Onandaga example?

1. Ka- hi- hw-   i   ne? o-   HSAHE? T-a?
   3n- spill- CAUSE- ASP the PRE- bean-SUF
   'The beans spilled'

2. Ka-   HSAHE? T- ahi- hw-   i
   3n-   bean-   spill- CAUSE- ASP
   'The beans spilled'

The solution to this problem should become apparent if you re-read Section 2.3.2.

Exercise 7
Anaphors can occur inside DPs, as we have seen. These DPs can, under the right circumstances, undergo *wh*-movement, giving sentences like (1):

1. [$_{DPj}$ Which songs about himself$_i$] does Mick$_i$ particularly like t$_j$?

To bring (1) into line with the binding theory, we have to propose that there is an LF operation of reconstruction which 'puts the *wh*-DP back' in the position of the trace. Once in the position of the trace, the reflexive can be bound in conformity with Principle A, as you should be able to see.

Barss (1986) discussed more complicated cases of reconstruction, such as the following:

2. [$_{DPj}$ Which songs about himself$_i$] did Mick$_{(i)}$ say that Keith$_{(i)}$ likes t$_j$?

As the indexing indicates, either Mick or Keith can be the antecedent of himself in (2). How can we account for this using successive cyclicity?

A further complication arises where a VP is fronted. Here only the lowest interpretation is available. We can see this if we disambiguate the possible antecedents as in (3):

3. *[$_{VPj}$ Talk about himself$_i$], Mick$_i$ said that Sheena never did t$_j$

4. [$_{VPj}$ Talk about himself$_i$], Sheena said that Mick$_i$ never did t$_j$

Can you think of a way to exploit the VP-internal subject hypothesis (2.3.4) and the binding theory in order to account for (3) and (4) as well as the contrast with (2)? See Huang (1993).

Appendix: Syntactic Scope and Logical Scope

In the Appendix to the last chapter, I introduced the operation of Quantifier Raising (QR) and the idea that there is covert *wh*-movement in the mapping to LF. I also introduced the idea of logical scope. Here I want to follow up that discussion and introduce some ideas about the relation between syntactic scope and logical scope.

We saw in the last Appendix that in predicate logic the scope of a quantifier is the contents of the parenthesis to its right in the formula. We also saw that logical variable-binding corresponds to an A'-binding relation (in the sense of c-command and coindexation) between a quantifier and its trace (the trace is technically a *wh*-trace in all instances, subject to Principle C of the binding theory). A natural extension of this is to say that *the scope of a quantifier is its c-command domain at LF.*

Now, clauses can contain two quantifiers which can show relative scope ambiguities. Here is an example:

(A1) Someone loves everyone

The two interpretations of (A1) are: (i) that there is a single maximally philanthropic individual, i.e. one lover for the whole world, and (ii) that everyone has a lover. The difference is this: in reading (i) everyone has the same lover, while in reading (ii) everyone may have a different lover. (You might notice that reading (i) entails reading (ii), that is, reading (ii) will be true whenever reading (i) is true; but reading (ii) does not entail reading (i), as reading (ii) can be true where people have different lovers, but reading (i) is false on this interpretation.)

In predicate logic, we can represent the different readings as follows (translating 'someone' and 'everyone' slightly inaccurately as 'pure' quantifiers):

(A2) (i) $\exists x \ (\forall y \ (\ \text{Love} \ (x, \ y)))$
(ii) $\forall y \ (\ \exists x \ (\ \text{Love} \ (x, \ y)))$

The relative scope of the quantifiers is clearly indicated by their order in the formulae. The rules of interpretation will guarantee that the entailment relations come out correctly, something that we don't need to go into here (see Allwood, Andersson and Dahl (1977), for example).

If, in our LF-representations, scope is determined by c-command, then relative scope should be determined by relative c-command. The ambiguity of (A1) implies that there must be two distinct LF representations, one in which *someone* c-commands *everyone*, and one in which the relations are the other way around. The earliest theory of LF was May (1977), and he proposed that these c-command asymmetries arose as the result of different orders of adjunction to IP. So, on this view, the two readings of (A1) correspond to the LFs in (A3):

(A3) (i) $[_{IP}$ someone$_i$ $[_{IP}$ everyone$_j$ $[_{IP}$ t$_i$ loves t$_j$ $]]]$
(ii) $[_{IP}$ everyone$_j$ $[_{IP}$ someone$_i$ $[_{IP}$ t$_i$ loves t$_j$ $]]]$

It's clear that where one quantifier Q_i has wider relative scope than another quantifier Q_j, Q_i c-commands Q_j – and conversely. C-command relations thus feed into the semantic interpretation rules at the LF interface, so as to determine the different entailment relations.

More recently, Hornstein (1995) has developed a variant theory which exploits the same basic idea – that scope relations are determined by c-command relations – in a minimalist framework. Hornstein adopts the analysis of transitive clauses that we sketched in 2.6; subjects are base-generated in Spec,VP and objects in the complement of V. By LF, the subject raises to Spec,AgrSP and the object to Spec,AgrOP. Hornstein adopts one further minimalist assumption that I haven't mentioned up to now: that traces are really copies of moved categories (this is an idea with potentially far-reaching implications, as you can probably see). In both PF and LF, one copy of a moved element must be deleted. In PF, this is the one we've been calling a trace – the one you don't hear. *But you don't have to delete the same one in LF.* To see how this can be made into an account of relative scope, let's look at the representation of a sentence containing two quantifiers prior to copy-deletion:

(A4) $[_{SpecAgrSP}$ someone ... $[_{SpecAgrOP}$ everyone $[_{VP}$ someone loves everyone]]]

Now you must delete one copy of each quantifier, and at LF you're free to decide which. If you delete the upper copy of *someone* but the lower copy of *everyone*, then you get an interface representation like (A5):

(A5) $[_{SpecAgrSP}$ ... $[_{SpecAgrOP}$ everyone $[_{VP}$ someone loves]]]

This gives us reading (ii). If you delete the lower copy of *someone*, you get reading (i) whatever you do with *everyone*, and the same result ensues if you delete the upper occurrence of *everyone*. The crucial point, however, is that the copy + deletion approach gives us the possibility of two different LFs corresponding to the different relative scopes. And we retain the idea that relative scope is determined by c-command relations. Hornstein's approach does not appeal to a special rule like QR; the DPs are raised for checking reasons (this implies that they are in A-positions; combined with the fact they don't have traces in the sense we've seen up to now, this entails that a different approach to variable-binding has to be adopted: see Hornstein (1995) for details).

wh-elements can interact scopally with other quantifiers, as in (A6):

(A6) What did everyone buy for Bill?

Here *what* can be either inside or outside the scope of *everyone*. That is, the sentence can be either asking for a single answer ('everyone got together and bought him a gold watch') or a 'pair-list' answer ('Mick bought him a yacht; Keith bought him a spoon; Charlie bought him a record token', etc.). On the first interpretation, *what* is outside the scope of *everyone* – so we have one answer for everyone. On the second interpretation, the scope relations are reversed, and so everyone has a (potentially) different answer. There has been quite a bit of work on these interactions, starting with May (1985).

When two *wh*-quantifiers appear together in a single clause, they typically require a pair-list reading:

(A7) To whom did Johnny dedicate which song?

The natural answer to this question consists of pairs of people and songs. Higginbotham and May (1981) proposed that what happens here is that a complex *wh*-quantifier is created at LF by the absorption of the two *wh*-elements in Spec,CP at LF:

(A8) $[_{CP}$ {To whom$_i$, which song$_j$} [did Johnny dedicate t_j t_i]] ?

(I'm avoiding the technical details of absorption here.)

Finally, *wh*-movement at LF appears to show C-t effects. This is shown by the phenomenon of superiority, illustrated by the following contrast:

(A9)   Who$_i$ t$_i$ drank what$_j$?

(A10) *What$_j$ did who$_i$ drink t$_j$?

If *who* has to raise at LF, we can attribute the ungrammaticality of (A10) to the general impossibility of extracting a subject following a filled complementizer: the C-t effect discussed at length in this chapter. Note that we must then assume that there is a null *wh* complementizer in embedded clauses in order to account for superiority effects in embedded clauses (see 1.4.2.2):

(A11) *I can't remember what$_j$ who$_i$ drank t$_j$

If we adopt the Rizzi-Manzini account of C-t effects discussed in 4.5.2 and 4.6.5, one that relies on Spec-head agreement in CP, then this requirement must extend to LF.

The proposal that relative scope is determined by c-command is not restricted to quantifiers, but extends to negation, for example. We see this if we look again at an example of ambiguous scope of negation, as in (121), repeated from 4.5.1:

(121) They don't exploit their fans [because they love them]

As we noticed in 4.5.1, negation here can have main-clause scope (giving the interpretation that they love their fans, and therefore don't exploit them), or adjunct scope (giving the interpretation that they exploit their fans for some reason other than love). Now, we've assumed throughout our discussion of adjuncts in this chapter that they are adjoined to VP. We've also assumed that negation is situated outside VP (see 1.4.1 in particular), perhaps in NegP. Since NegP c-commands VP and VP-adjuncts, the scope ambiguity of (121), and in particular the fact that extraction of the adjunct can only give an interpretation where the adjunct is outside the scope of negation (as we saw in (122)), indicate that the adjunct can appear higher up than VP. It seems that we must allow different levels of attachment of adjuncts, in order to capture the scope ambiguities with negation that we observe. A natural possibility would be to allow adjunction to AgrSP (this would be a problem for the *Barriers* account of the CED (see 4.4.1.3), but not for Manzini's – you should be able to see this if you look again at 4.6.4). Something further needs to be said so as to allow negation to apply *only* to the adjunct when it has adjunct scope. I'll leave this as an open question.

As you might imagine, I haven't covered all there is to say about LF here. My excuse for this is that LF is an invariant level, and the focus of this book is on comparative syntax – hence things that vary across languages. The most up-to-date book on LF is Hornstein (1995).

5

Principles, Parameters, and Language Acquisition

5.0 Introduction

In this chapter, I don't intend to present any more of the mechanics of syntactic theory. Instead, I want to look at how the things we've seen in the earlier chapters relate to language acquisition and language learnability. In 5.1, I'll go through the argument for the existence of an innate language faculty that comes from the poverty of the stimulus to language acquisition. In 5.2 we'll look at how the 'principles-and-parameters' approach to language universals and language acquisition can give us a handle on this problem. Here we'll briefly outline the implications of the principles-and-parameters approach for language acquisition. Finally, in 5.3, I'll say something about the implications of the principles-and-parameters approach for the study of historical change in language.

5.1 The Argument from the Poverty of the Stimulus

5.1.1 The Nature of the Final State

In this section I review the well-known argument for the innateness of the language faculty that stems from the observed poverty of the stimulus to language acquisition. The idea is that the stimulus to language acquisition is deficient in two ways, which we will refer to as the *noisiness* and the *incompleteness* of the input to language acquisition.

Before considering the argument in detail, it is perhaps worthwhile to recall the nature of adult competence, or the kind of knowledge that makes up the adult I-language. Of course, the entire book up to now has been about this. The detailed, intricate complexity of the language faculty should be very apparent to you by now. It's only when one is aware of this complexity that one can fully appreciate the force of the argument from the poverty of the stimulus.

So let's look at some of the things an adult native speaker of English knows. Speakers of English can distinguish sentences with the grammatical SVO order from those with other imaginable orders, as illustrated by the following sentences:

(1a) John read the book   (SVO)

(1b) *John the book read   (SOV)

(1c) *Read John the book   (VSO)

This knowledge is never explicitly taught, and yet all English speakers have fully mastered it. What we are witnessing, even with examples as simple as this, is a complex interaction of universal principles and different parameter settings as we saw in Chapters 1 and 2.

The above example might seem to verge on the banal. However, it is easy to give more complex instances. In one type of interrogative sentence in English, the *wh*-word appears initially and an auxiliary verb must invert over the subject. Hence an interrogative corresponding to (1a) might be (2):

(2) How many books has John read?

Here, owing to the *wh*-criterion (see 2.6.3), placing the auxiliary verb in front of the subject is obligatory. However, this operation cannot take place in embedded questions, or in exclamations. Compare (3):

(3a) *How many books John has read?

(3b) I can't remember how many books John has/*has John read

(3c) What a lot of books John has/*has John read!

The above examples give an indication of the complexity of the facts of word order even in very simple sentences. They also show the interplay of principles and parameters. Adult speakers command the mechanisms that produce these patterns effortlessly.

We've also seen facts involving the interpretation of sentences, specifically pronouns. In general, a pronoun can have as an antecedent a DP that is outside its binding domain, or it can simply indicate an individual present in the non-linguistic context, as in:

(4) John said that he would fail

Here, *he* can take *John* as its antecedent (this is perhaps the most natural interpretation out of context), or it could refer to some other male individual. As we saw in the Appendix to Chapter 3, pronouns can also function as logical variables where the NP they 'stand for' is quantified, as in:

(5) Every student thinks he will fail

Example (5) has the natural interpretation '$\forall x$, x a student, x thinks x will fail'. It can also have the interpretation where *he* designates some contextually given individual. *wh*-expressions also act like quantified expressions:

(6) Which student thinks he will fail?

Example (6) has the interpretation 'For which x, x a student, x thinks x will fail?'. Again, the interpretation where *he* simply designates some unspecified individual is also possible.

However, under certain conditions, the bound-variable interpretation is unavailable for pronouns. Compare (7) with (6):

(7) Which student does he think will fail?

Example (7) simply cannot be interpreted to mean 'For which x, x a student, x thinks x will fail?', unlike (6). The only interpretation available for the pronoun here is that it refers to some contextually given male individual. This fact is implicitly known by speakers of English, and yet it is implausible to the point of absurdity to suppose that it has somehow been learnt or taught. We saw in Chapter 3 that this fact can be ascribed to Principle C of the binding theory – the same principle that rules out sentences like *He$_i$/John$_i$ saw John$_i$*.

Finally, consider *wh*-movement. We have seen numerous instances of argument-adjunct asymmetries in the foregoing, such as:

(8a) Who didn't John dance with ?

(8b) *How didn't John dance?

These seemingly simple sentences are subject to complex and rigorous constraints that native speakers effortlessly command and yet have never been given any explicit instruction in. Or take the contrasts in superiority that we discussed in the Appendix to Chapter 4:

(9a) I can't remember who drank what

(9b) *I can't remember what who drank

Given the great simplicity of these sentences, it is hardly likely that processing constraints play any role in ruling out the bad ones. Nor do any proposed communicative principles get us very far: it's obvious that (9b) is trying to mean the same as (9a) – the syntax just won't let it. Once again, the facts are clear; any speaker of English has a quite amazing unconscious knowledge of his or her native language. It need hardly be pointed out that this kind of knowledge is not explicitly taught or learnt in any sense; indeed most speakers of English are blissfully unaware that they possess such knowledge. And, of course, there's nothing special about English: the same observations can be made, *mutatis mutandis*, for any natural language and its speakers.

The above paragraphs are intended simply as a reminder of what we have seen in looking at the theory of adult competence. What we see is a cognitive system of immense richness and complexity. So, the question we really need to ask now is: where does this knowledge come from? How do adults acquire their competence? To put it another way, having seen something of the nature of the final state, let us now ask what the initial state must be like in order to produce such a final state. It is here that the question of the poverty of the stimulus plays a crucial role. Essentially, the argument is that the circumstances of language acquisition are such that we must suppose that the lion's share of the intricate knowledge that makes up the final state must be present at the initial state, in other words, that this knowledge is innate.

5.1.2 The Nature of the Stimulus

If we claimed that the initial state was impoverished, or perhaps even non-existent, then we would have to attribute much (or all) of the richness of the final state to the stimulus. The stimulus to language acquisition would have to be such that the kind of competence that we have ample evidence for could be gleaned from it, perhaps aided by general learning strategies of some kind.

Let's make the relevant concepts more specific (the following discussion is based on Atkinson (1992: 11–31)). We take learning to involve four things: (a) a learner; (b) data available to the learner; (c) a procedure by means of which the learner selects hypotheses; and (d) a criterion for learning. Here we are most interested in the nature of (b) in relation to the final state of language acquisition. We take (a) as given, and defer discussion of (c) and (d).

In the earliest work on learnability theory (the study of what kinds of formal properties languages must have, given that they are learnable), Gold (1967) makes a useful distinction between 'text presentation' and 'informant presentation'. Text presentation involves presenting only positive instances of the target language to the learner, so that the learner has only well-formed sentences of the target language. Informant presentation involves presenting both well-formed and ill-formed sentences to the learner, with the relevant information as to the status of each sentence. Note that there are two differences between the modes of presentation: (i) text presentation does not feature ill-formed sentences while informant presentation does; and (ii) text presentation does not feature information about well-formedness while informant presentation does. It is intuitively clear that informant presentation would facilitate the learner's task (and it is easy to demonstrate this with certain classes of formal languages).

Which of the two modes of presentation most closely approximates to the circumstances of language acquisition? The question falls into two parts, since there are two differences between text presentation and informant presentation: (i) do children have information as to the well-formedness of the linguistic data they are exposed to? (ii) are children exposed to ill-formed sentences? The answer to the first of these questions appears to be 'no', while the answer to the second is 'yes'. Let us look at them in turn.

Concerning (i), there is no doubt that adults simply do not present children with systematic instances of ill-formed sentences. Direct information regarding grammaticality of the kind summarized by the linguist's use of an asterisk in ungrammatical sentences is clearly not available to the child. However, the possibility that some kind of implicit information may be available to children has been discussed in the literature on child language. The best-known study is Brown and Hanlon (1970), which shows that factors such as correction, negative reinforcement, or the child failing to get what she wants are not sensitive to grammatical well-formedness. It is also well known that children appear to pay little heed to correction. A famous example of this is reported in McNeill (1966):

(10) CHILD: Nobody don't like me.
    MOTHER: No, say 'Nobody likes me'.
    CHILD: Nobody don't like me.
    (dialogue repeated eight times)
    MOTHER: Now listen carefully, say 'Nobody likes me'.
    CHILD: Oh! Nobody don't likes me!

It seems that the child's experience is closer to that of text presentation than that of informant presentation in this first sense, then. Children have no information as to the well-formedness of the strings they are exposed to (or, if they have it, they appear to ignore or misinterpret it).

On the other hand, children are exposed to ill-formed sentences. Actual language use, performance in the sense of Chomsky (1965), involves incomplete sentences, slips of the tongue, speech errors, and so on. While the proportion of such 'mistakes' in the primary linguistic data for language acquisition may be debatable (see Newport, Gleitman and Gleitman (1977)), their existence is not in doubt. It is intuitively clear that even a small proportion of ill-formed utterances, not flagged as such, make the child's task significantly harder. Chomsky (1980) points out that the child's situation is comparable to attempting to induce the rules of chess by observing players who occasionally break those rules without giving any indication that they are doing so.

We see that the input to language acquisition is noisy text in the sense that it contains an indeterminate quantity of covertly ill-formed sentences. This was what Chomsky (1965) meant by his discussion of the degenerate nature of the stimulus. The intuition that the 'noise' introduced by performance errors makes the child's task harder is confirmed by Osherson, Stob, and Weinstein (1982, 1984, 1986), who show that there are classes of languages which are learnable by a computable learning function on the basis of standard text but not on the basis of noisy text.

It is very difficult to reconcile this conclusion with the idea that the kinds of knowledge adults have can be induced from the input text alone with no specification of the initial state. The noisiness of the input to language acquisition leads us to exclude some imaginable grammars *a priori* by specifying aspects of the initial state. The richer the final state, the more we are led to attribute to the initial state. The great richness of the final state tempts us to attribute a great deal of linguistic competence to the initial state. In this way, the degenerate nature of the stimulus can be overcome and we understand better how language acquisition may take place.

5.1.3 The Incompleteness of the Input

In work on learnability theory, it is often assumed that a complete text, that is, all the well-formed sentences of the language, must be presented to the learner (this is certainly the case for the influential 'identification in the limit' paradigm of Gold (1967) and much subsequent work). This assumption is obviously invalid for language acquisition. Thus, the input to language acquisition is incomplete. This is the other major aspect of the poverty of the stimulus, and a further reason to identify much of the final state of competence as being present in the initial state.

Of course, it would be impossible to present all the well-formed sentences of any natural language to a learner. This is because the syntax of natural languages contains recursive structures which can, in principle, be indefinitely iterated so as to produce sentences of unlimited length. It is clear, then, that the final state is a system with infinite capacity. Since humans are finite beings, this infinite capacity must be grounded in some finite cognitive capacity. This was the original reason for supposing that a recursive system of PS-rules must form part of the language faculty. As we saw in Chapter 1, the PS-rules have been replaced by the phrase-structure templates of X'-theory.

Another consequence of the infinite nature of natural language is that acquirers can only be exposed to a tiny portion of a given language as the input to language acquisition. It is therefore likely that some children may not be exposed to certain kinds of input. The result of this ought to be adults with widely differing kinds of competence within a single language community, a situation which (while acknowledging the problematic and extrinsic nature of the notion 'language community' – see the Introduction) we do not find.

A further consideration arises from the richness and detail of adult competence. As we mentioned in 5.1.1, it is preposterous to suppose that evidence that gives rise to the kind of adult knowledge that we have seen is available in the input to language acquisition. It is also entirely plausible that some acquirers simply never come across sentences of the relevant kind. This point is developed in much greater detail and with further exemplification in Hornstein and Lightfoot (1981, Introduction) and in Chomsky (1986a).

It is clear, then, that the input to language acquisition may contain significant gaps. As with noisy input, Osherson, Stob, and Weinstein (op. cit.) have shown that there are classes of languages which are learnable from complete texts, but which are not learnable from incomplete texts.

The incompleteness of the input to language acquisition supports the postulation of a rich initial state for language acquisition in a straightforward way. Language acquisition must result from the interaction of conditions within the learner, (the initial state), and conditions outside the learner, (the input). The less of the final state there is in the input, the more of it must be attributed to the initial state. The richness of the final state, combined with poverty of the stimulus, lead us to conclude that much of the final state must already be present in the initial state. In other words, a very significant part of our linguistic competence must be innate.

In fact, the best way of dealing with the argument from the poverty of the stimulus would be to assume that *all* adult linguistic knowledge stems directly from the initial state. The states in between the initial state and the final state – the observed stages of language acquisition (see 5.2) – could be treated as purely the reflection of cognitive maturation. The obvious reason for not doing this is the existence of variant final states manifested in the socio-cultural entities we call languages. This is where principles and parameters theory comes in.

As we have seen, what principles and parameters theory says is that most of our linguistic competence – the principles of UG – are innate. What is open to variation are the parametric values that the principles can take on. It's clear, then, that what we need to do is to establish the division of labour between principles and parameters in such a way as to make the experience that fixes parameters available in the impoverished stimulus. We also want, as far as possible, to approximate the ideal situation in which all of the final state is present in the initial state. For both of these reasons, we want our parameters to be very simple – I'll come back to this point below.

This concludes our discussion of the poverty of the stimulus argument. We are now in a position to see the attractiveness of the idea that large parts of our linguistic ability are innately based. This idea seems to be the only one which can explain the facts of language competence and language acquisition – facts which, in a real sense, have been the subject matter of this book. It is now time to look at the similarities and differences between languages that we've seen in the preceding chapters in the light of this conclusion.

5.2 Language Acquisition and Parameter Setting

Principles and parameters theory evolved as a means of resolving the tension between the need to posit a very rich UG as a consequence of the poverty of the stimulus argument and the variation which can be seen among the world's languages. More precisely, the following three statements seem to hold (we actually introduced these in the Introduction in a slightly different way):

- there exists a rich, innate language faculty which is a species characteristic
- there are no racial or cultural biases towards given languages or language types
- there is clear evidence that a sentence (or syntactic structure) which is well-formed in one natural language L may be ill-formed in some other natural language L'.

The main argument for the first of these points comes from the poverty of the stimulus, as we saw in the previous section. We take the second point as given, since, in the context of an innate language faculty, to deny it would amount to positing genetically given cognitive differences between races or cultures. Moreover, there is ample evidence for its correctness in immigrant communities the world over: a child of any ethnic background will learn the language of his/her surroundings as a native speaker, while immigrant parents often struggle for many years with the language of their adopted country. The third point should also be quite obvious by now – in the preceding chapters we've seen numerous cases where a structure that is well formed in one language is ill formed in another.

So the above three statements seem to hold. However, taken together, they come close to deriving a contradiction. How can an innate language faculty which is uniform across the species give rise to such superficially different adult I-languages?

As we have seen, the principles and parameters conception of UG allows for crosslinguistic variation by associating with the principles of UG a small number of parameters of variation. The idea is that a given principle may be able to instantiate itself in slightly different ways, along minimally differing parameters. Thus principles can be associated with different parametric values. A given association of principles with parametric values will give rise to a particular grammatical system; an I-language. We have seen numerous examples of this sort in the preceding chapters.

More precisely, constructing a theory of principles and parameters means simultaneously doing three things:

(11a) claiming what is invariant and what is variant in UG

(11b) predicting the dimensions along which language typologies might be constructed

(11c) predicting what features might develop in the course of language acquisition (although here maturational factors might also intervene)

Correspondingly, the hallmarks of parameters will be:

(12a) simplicity: the evidence which triggers parameter values must be readily available in the impoverished stimulus

(12b) 'typologizability': parameters should give rise to coherent language typologies, and explain those typological generalizations that are observed

(12c) instability in acquisition: we might expect to individuate stages of parameter-fixation in language acquisition; also, if UG 'matures' during the course of language acquisition, we might think that parameters – or perhaps parameter values – come 'on line' at different times

The fact that very simple aspects of experience may set quite abstract parameters which have far-reaching consequences for the resulting system makes language acquisition 'chaotic' in the sense of complexity theory.

In (13), I list the parameters that we've seen in this book. The list is a 'cleaned-up' version of the lists that have appeared at the end of each chapter, and some parameters been left out either because they are not compatible with other proposals that we've seen (as in the case of the X'-linearization parameters of Chapter 1 (21), which are incompatible with Kayne's LCA of 1.3.4), or because they don't connect interestingly to any other property (as in the case of the ability of Portuguese AgrS to assign Nominative in infinitives: see 2.2.2). I've also tried to state the parameters in a uniform way, following a format which allows them to be thought of as binary options (see below).

> *Some Parameters:*

(13a) i. Is D morphologically realized? Yes: English (*the*), Swedish (*-et*). No: Latin. See 1.2.3. Languages lacking overt D may be able to violate the Left Branch Condition, as in Russian and Latin (see 4.1)

    ii. If (i) is Yes, is D an affix? Yes: Swedish. No: English

(13b) i. Does the I-system have strong V-features? Yes: French. No: English (see 1.4.1.1)

    ii. If (i) is Yes, does the highest V-related functional category have strong N-features? Yes: French-type SVO languages. No: VSO languages (such as Celtic languages, see 2.7.1)

    iii. If (i) is No, does AgrO have a strong N-feature? Yes: SOV systems (see 2.7.2)

(13c) Does root C have features attracting V and an XP to its checking domain? Yes: V2 (Germanic languages, apart from English). No: non-V2. See 1.4.2.4

(13d) i. Is abstract Case morphologically marked? Yes: Latin, German, English. No: Thai, Chinese

    ii. If (i) is Yes, is abstract Case marked on all DPs? Yes: Latin, German. (In German, D bears Case-marking; in Latin, Nouns (and nominal modifiers) do so – Latin D can't show morphological case owing to the value of (a) above.) No: English, French. (We can assume that the default value here is 'pronouns only'.) (2.0)

    iii. If (i) is Yes, is *inherent* abstract Case morphologically marked? Yes: Latin, German, French. No: English. (Because of this, English Prepositions only assign Accusative – 2.5.3. This in turn may explain why English allows Preposition-stranding (see 4.3.3.2))

> (The values of (ii) and (iii) imply that French marks abstract inherent Case in the pronominal system – see Kayne (1984))

(13e) Does AgrS have enough inflectional content to recover the features of *pro* in Spec,AgrSP? Yes: a null-subject language with the properties of (76) of Chapter 4, as described by Rizzi (1982)

(13f) Is there a monomorphemic reflexive? Yes: LD anaphora possible (all non-English Germanic, Italian, Chinese, Japanese, Korean, Polish, Latin, and so on). No: no LD anaphora (3.4)

(13g) i. Is *wh*-movement overt? Yes: English, French, Slavic, and so on. No: Chinese, Japanese, Korean, Armenian, and so on (2.6.3)
       ii. If (i) is Yes: can more than one *wh*-element move overtly to the Specifier of a [+WH] CP? No: English, French. Yes: Slavic (parameters discussed in Chapter 4)

(13h) Is the lowest finite IP a barrier? Yes: English. No: Italian, French (see 4.2.3)

(You may find that working through these statements and understanding how they are integrated with the material presented in the earlier chapters is a good revision exercise.)

Are the parameters listed in (13) simple in the sense of (12a)? That is, can their values be gleaned from the impoverished stimulus by the language acquirer? Parameters (13a, d, and e) depend on simple morphological properties: the presence or absence of Determiners, case and a particular kind of agreement inflection in the trigger experience. Parameter (13f) depends on the presence of a different kind of morphological entity, a monomorphemic reflexive, while (13b) may depend on morphological properties too; it has been suggested that verb-movement is correlated with a particular kind of inflectional marking (different from that required by the null-subject parameter). Parameters (13c) (verb second) and (13g) (overt *vs* covert *wh*-movement) may be directly triggered by word order: in both cases it's the contents of root Spec,CP and C that are crucial. It is clear that the trigger experience for (13h) must be less simple. So, we can perhaps conclude that simple morphological properties and root word-order properties can give the required trigger experience for setting our parameters – with the glaring exception of (13h). (Lightfoot (1991) in fact proposed that trigger experience must be restricted to root clauses.)

Regarding (12b), we've discussed some of the typological correlations that we find (see 1.3.3, 2.7, and 3.3.3.3 in particular). Here matters are never simple, as each new language puts us in the position of a language acquirer: we have to start our analysis from scratch with no idea of what the system may be like – we only have imperfect guesses based on data from past experience. In fact, we are worse off than language acquirers, as they 'know' what can vary in UG and we're trying to find out: they have a theory; we only have data.

Here I want to leave (12b) aside, since we've already discussed it a little, and concentrate on (12c). What is the evidence regarding parameter-setting in language acquisition? Let's make a couple of simplifying assumptions. We can take it that all parameters are binary (or can be formulated in a binary way, as in (13)). Because of this, we can consider parameters as the truth values of contingent statements about grammars (in this sense, the principles of

UG would be the necessary truths about grammars). This is implicit in formulating the parameters as Yes/No questions in (13). Really, we should reformulate (13a, i), for example, as follows:

(14) D is morphologically realized (true/false)

In line with common practice in semantics, we can state the truth values as members of the set $\{1,0\}$. Then we are in a position, given an ordering of the set of parameters, to give the set of parameter values of a given language as a binary number n. (Some of the parameters in (13) contain implicational statements, like (13a, ii); this simply amounts to saying that certain combinations of '01' or '10' will never be allowed, which, of course, may simplify the task of acquisition and also suggests that there are 'networks' of parameters.) In these terms, the task of acquisition consists of assigning truth values to each parameter, and, ultimately, of finding the correct string of 1s and 0s – the binary number – which characterizes the target grammar. You can think of this as the grammar's bar-code if you like. For example, if we take the parameters in (13), we have the following values for English:

(15) (13a) i. 1
           ii. 0
     (13b) i. 0
           ii. 0
           iii. 0
     (13c)   0
     (13d) i. 1
           ii. 0
           iii. 0
     (13e)   0
     (13f)   0
     (13g) i. 1
           ii. 0
     (13h)   1

English is characterized as 10000010000101. In a fully developed theory of parameters, this statement alone could be used to derive all the features of English listed in (13). However, the day when we'll be able to do that is still quite distant.

Within this general framework, various questions arise. The most important concern the nature of the initial state and the way in which successive grammars are triggered before the adult grammar is attained. On a purely theoretical level, it is possible to idealize the acquisition process as being instantaneous. However, studies of child language have shown that children pass through a number of stages before attaining adult-like competence. These intermediate stages can be thought of as interim grammars, which approximate but do not adequately match the target grammar.

There are basically three ways in which we can conceptualize the process of parameter-setting, and these are not necessarily mutually contradictory or exclusive. Parameter settings may be initially open and filled in by experience; they may initially correspond to a random setting with the correct setting eventually arrived at by exposure to data; they may be preset to a default (or unmarked) value, with the deviations from the maximally unmarked system being reached through acquisition. If we indicate an open setting (neither 1 nor 0) by '*' and default values for parameters as 0, we can schematize these respective conceptions as follows:

(16a) [... ******* ...] (open settings)

(16b) [... 101010 ...]   (random settings)

(16c) [... 000000 ...]   (default settings)

I can't go in detail into the merits and demerits of each of these possibilities here. Two issues, both of them somewhat controversial, bear on the choice among them. The first is the question of whether maturation plays any role in acquisition. It has been suggested (most influentially by Borer and Wexler (1987)) that certain principles of UG may not be available at early stages of acquisition. Rather, they develop as the child grows, as part of the general process of maturation. In that case, we could think of certain positions in the bit string as being without a parameter value at earlier stages. The basic problem with this view is that it represents a less restrictive option than the idea that all child grammars are subject to the same constraints as adult grammars, in that it implicitly allows child grammars that would violate 'adult UG' (although they wouldn't violate 'general UG', of course). For this reason, it is a hypothesis that requires very strong empirical support.

The second issue concerns the theory of markedness: what are the default settings of parameters, and is there a corresponding default grammar (of which (16c) might be a representation)? The idea that parameters have a preset default value is an attractive one, and it has been evoked in many studies, beginning with the pioneering work of Hyams (1986). Bickerton (1984) suggested that creoles represent the maximally unmarked grammar; his idea was that since they are constructed on the basis of pidgins, which are essentially codes which use natural-language words but lack a natural-language grammar, creoles must manifest a 'pure', untainted instantiation of UG. This essentially means the default system (it cannot mean a system with all parameters open, as by hypothesis such a system could not 'run'; it could not produce or interpret data). Bickerton's idea is attractive, but the question is whether there is really a good reason to grant such a special status to creoles. This is an area of considerable controversy in creole studies. In general, the absence of any clear theory of markedness makes it difficult for proposals of this kind to be properly evaluated (although see also the contributions to deGraff and Pierce (1996)).

One proposal that has been made is known as the Subset Condition (see Berwick (1985)). Berwick observed that the set of well-formed sentences in some languages is a subset of that of other languages. Given the lack of 'negative evidence' for language acquisition, that is the fact that children have access only to raw data with no commentary as to the grammaticality of that data (see 5.1.1), children must avoid falling into 'superset traps', or positing a grammar which generates a superset of the target language, since there will never be evidence to force the child to 'retreat' to the target grammar. Accordingly, it may be that subset grammars – or parameter-values giving rise to subset grammars – are unmarked.

What do the observed facts of child-language acquisition tell us about the options in (16)? Clearly, the relationship between the recorded utterances of children (which represent a kind of E-language, in the sense of the Introduction) and the questions about the acquisition of I-language that we are asking is very indirect and must be mediated by linguistic theory. Nevertheless, certain tendencies in acquisition seem clear. All of these revolve, in one way or another, around the way in which children acquire the morphological system of their native language and the implications which that may have for syntax.

One observation originates in Hyams (1986). She points out that children acquiring English seem to allow sentences in which pronominal subjects are not phonetically realized; they seem to allow null subjects, at a certain stage of acquisition. Thus such children utter sentences like (17), which are of course ungrammatical as declaratives in adult English:

(17) Eat apples

Hyams suggests that children initially set the null-subject parameter to the Italian value, and only indirectly learn the English value on exposure to particular sentence types later (the details of how this happens need not concern us unduly here).

Aldridge (1988) and Radford (1986, 1990) developed Hyams's work into a more general proposal. They noticed that children at the 'two-word stage' of acquisition (a few months either side of the second birthday) lacked many of the grammatical formatives of adult language. They suggested that this was due to a lack of functional categories at this stage, and that the functional categories emerge with maturation.

Of our parameters, (13a) and (13e) are quite clearly triggered by the presence of morphological material in the functional system (and some of the others may be). If we assign '0' to the absence of morphology, then we see that the Aldridge-Radford approach implies a starting-point to acquisitions like (16c).

However, Wexler (1994), Pierce and Deprez (1993), and Pierce (1992) have recently shown that the two-word stage does not lack all grammatical information, but only some crucial elements. In particular, it seems that the grammatical category of finiteness (as opposed to the semantic concept of tense) is missing. As we saw in Chapter 2, finiteness is such a pervasive part of the verbal system of most languages that the resulting child grammars appear to be very different from adult ones.

A theoretical development which coalesces with the line of research just outlined is Chomsky's recent (1993) proposal that all parameters should concern the morphological realization of functional categories (see 2.6). If this very strong hypothesis can be maintained (which would entail a rethinking of some of the parameters discussed above, especially (13h)), then we may be able to move towards a conception of acquisition which takes something like (16c) as its starting point, given the research results just mentioned.

Research in these areas is still ongoing. A very welcome recent development has been a proliferation of research into the acquisition of a number of languages in addition to English; see in particular Pierce (1992), Pierce and Deprez (1993), Wexler (1994), Rizzi (1996), and the collection in Hoekstra and Schwartz (1994) and the references given there. In this way, our overall knowledge of the phenomena connected to language acquisition is certainly increasing. Although many questions still remain open, the principles-and-parameters theory has provided an essential framework for research.

Finally, a brief word about second-language (L2) acquisition. It should be clear that from the perspective adopted here that this is potentially a very different animal. The most salient difference compared to first-language (L1) acquisition lies in the nature of the final state: L2 acquirers often fail to reach the target of acquisition, remaining in some 'interlanguage' state of 'imperfect' acquisition. The question of whether interlanguage grammars are I-languages in good standing has been controversial. The current consensus is that they are, in that they reflect UG properties (see the Introduction to Hoekstra and Schwartz (1994)). Interlanguages are a reflection of I-languages that simply fail to produce the (partly normative, partly teleological) goal of native-speaker-like L2 behaviour. The alternative view is that interlanguages are non-UG constructs based on general learning strategies, but with a grammatical structure that is either parasitic on that of the L1 or not a UG system at all.

In any case, the initial state of L2 acquisition seems to be like that in (16b), in that I-languages differ randomly within the space defined by UG. This may be different from the situation with L1 acquisition, as we have just seen. It is presumably this fact that underlies the phenomenon of 'L1 interference', much discussed in work on L2 acquisition. Maturation may also play a role in that, past puberty, the capability of forming a new grammar may simply be lost (see Lenneberg (1967)). All of these questions are interconnected in various ways and are quite controversial. Again, principles and parameters theory forms the essential framework for research.

5.3 Historical Change in Language

In this final section I'd like to raise an issue which is traditionally connected to comparative linguistics: language change. That languages change historically can't be doubted. It's enough for an English speaker to attempt to decipher a page of *Beowulf* to be convinced. Moreover, the results of 19th-century linguistics tell us that many of today's separate languages have common ancestors. This very strongly suggests that historical change in language is more than just a matter of changing conventions – something deeper and more interesting for linguistic theory is at work. In fact, a moment's thought reveals that language change must involve change in parameter values: we know that English and German descend from Proto West Germanic, a language probably spoken in southern Denmark around the time of Christ. No records remain of this language, but much of its phonology and morphology, and a sizeable part of the lexicon, can be reconstructed using the techniques developed by historical linguists. We also know that Modern English and Modern German have some differing parameter values: for example, German is OV in embedded clauses and V2 in main clauses while English has neither property. It follows that either English or German (or possibly both) has changed these parameter values at some point in the last 2,000 years.

We can illustrate the same point very simply and directly with V-to-I movement. We saw in 1.4.1.1 that French finite main verbs move to I while English ones don't. This can be seen from the fact that finite main verbs precede the negative element *pas* in French, while they follow this element in English:

(18a) Jean (ne) MANGE PAS du chocolat
       *Jean (ne) PAS MANGE du chocolat

(18b) *John LIKES NOT chocolate
       John does NOT LIKE chocolate

In terms of the checking theory introduced in 2.6, we can say that French I (or AgrS) has a strong V-feature, triggering verb-movement, while English AgrS has a weak feature (see 2.6.3 for details). This is a parametric difference between Modern English and Modern French (it is in fact, parameter (13b, i) above). Now, earlier English, up until approximately 1600 (or slightly before), shows the French order in negative sentences. The following example has a vaguely 'Shakespearean' ring to it for many English speakers, and all English speakers recognize that it is not grammatical Modern English:

(19) Wepyng and teres CONFORTETH NOT dissolute laghers

This example is typical of English up to the 16th century. So we see that a parameter has changed its value in the recorded history of English. In fact, statistical studies of 16th-century texts reveal the change actually happening (see Kroch (1989) on this). Other examples, still from the history of English, include the fact that Old English was like Modern German in being OV and V2; Modern English, of course, lacks both of these properties. Also, I mentioned in passing in 3.3.3.2 that Old French was a null-subject language; Modern French, however, is not (as we also saw in that section).

So there can be no doubt that parameters can change their values in historical time. Historical work in the principles and parameters framework faces a challenge which synchronic work does not. If we isolate a parametric difference between, say, English and Italian, then we can simply describe the parameter and its consequences, and ideally say something about the typology it implies and the trigger experience that sets it (of course, these are by no means trivial tasks). Then our job is done and we can go to the beach (see Anderson (1982)). If, however, we isolate a parametric difference between one historical stage of English and another, then we need to explain not just what the parameter is and what its effects are, but *how, at some point in the generation-to-generation transmission of language, the new value was favoured over the older one.*

Now, textbooks in historical linguistics will tell you that all sorts of factors can cause language change: war, invasion, migration, contact with other civilizations, and so on. It is also often said that change can be internally driven: a linguistic system can become unstable and spontaneously change its properties. From the perspective of principles and parameters theory, the natural way to look at parametric change is as parameter resetting (there are, of course, other kinds of change, like borrowing words, but these are of less theoretical interest). That is, the older grammar has at least one parameter set differently from the new grammar: in the example from 16th-century English given above, in the older grammar AgrS has a strong V-feature and in the new grammar it has a weak V-feature. If we regard the innovations as arising through language acquisition (again, this is an old idea in historical linguistics), then the new system will gradually displace the old one as the older generation dies out. The speakers of the innovating grammar will transmit their system to their children, and the language will have changed.

The really intriguing (and difficult) aspect of such a scenario for parameter change comes up if we compare this with what I said about parameter-setting in the previous section. Language acquisition proceeds through setting values of open parameters on the basis of experience. In my discussion in the previous section, I tacitly assumed, along with almost all work on language acquisition, that the trigger experience accurately reflects the older generation's grammar, so that acquisition replicates the adult system. However, language change arguably tells us that this is not always so. The conditions of language change are such that the *trigger experience may set parameter-values which are different from those which produced it.* If this is true, then a close investigation of the conditions of language change may tell us something very important about the nature of the trigger experience.

Language change is important in another way. It is well known that a change spreads through a speech community in certain well-defined ways (see Labov (1972)). This is a fact about E-language (see the Introduction), which need not concern us unduly. However, if a change spreads only part-way through the community before that community is divided by some historical vicissitude (again a matter of no concern to linguistic theory), then we have two communities, one with one parameter value and one with another. Often, although again this depends on non-linguistic factors like politics and culture, these communities will refer to themselves as having different languages. This is how older languages can divide into new ones; something like this must have happened with the Fall of the Roman Empire in western Europe, ultimately giving rise to the Romance languages. To a very large extent, then, the existence of different languages (in the everyday socio-political sense of that term) is a result of the internal dynamic of parameter change combined with the external accidents of history. We cannot make a theory of history, and in that sense we will never understand why there are different E-languages. But we can, using the notions of principles and parameters theory, make a theory of how I-languages differ, how they can be acquired, and how they can change.

Glossary

A-chain A chain whose **head** in sense (ii) (q.v.) is in an A-position (also known as an L-related position: see 3.3.2.3).

A'-chain A chain whose **head** in sense (ii) (q.v.) is in an A'-position (also known as a non-L-related position: see 3.3.2.3).

abstract Case A feature assigned to DPs which identifies them as taking on a particular grammatical function.

across the board Extraction (q.v.) from a coordinate structure that affects parallel positions in each conjunct.

adjunction The operation of a **movement rule** (q.v.) so as to create a new position attached to the target of movement. The attachment site is structurally located between two segments of the target category. Opposed to substitution, which is movement to an already existing position.

anaphor In **binding theory** (q.v.), a nominal subject to Principle A.

antecedent (of an anaphoric nominal). The nominal to which the anaphoric nominal is semantically related.

argument-adjunct asymmetries Refers to the differential **extraction** (q.v.) possibilities of adjuncts (e.g. adverbials of various kinds) and arguments (in particular **complements** (q.v.) in various kinds of **islands** (q.v.).)

barrier A node which potentially blocks the operation of **movement rule** (q.v.), the formation of a **chain** (q.v.) and/or the relation of government. Barriers play a central role in constraining **unbounded dependencies** (q.v.): see 4.4.

binding theory The theory of the anaphoric relations among nominals, the principal topic of Chapter 3.

canonical government relation A notion used by Kayne (1984) in the definition of g-projections. A combination of government and linear order, such that in VO languages canonical government is from left to right, and in OV languages from right to left.

category variable A node label that is intended to range over some class of syntactic category labels, e.g. the 'X' of X'-theory, whose value can be any **lexical category** (q.v.) or **functional category** (q.v.).

c-command A structural relation among the positions in a syntactic representation (a **labelled bracketing** (q.v.) or a **phrase marker** (q.v.). C-command can be defined in various ways, as discussed in the Appendix to

Chapter 2. The relation plays a fundamental role in many aspects of syntax, including notably **binding theory** (q.v.) and **chains** (q.v.).

chain Non-trivial chains are formed by **movement rules** (q.v.). In a well-formed chain, the **head** in sense (ii) (q.v.) **c-commands** (q.v.) all other positions. More generally, each link of the chain c-commands and is coindexed with, i.e. binds, the next. Any category can be regarded as a chain; categories which do not undergo movement form trivial chains, consisting of just one position.

checking domain The structural domain within which abstract features of categories are 'checked' (and therefore eliminated from the derivation) in **checking theory** (q.v.).

checking theory The minimalist extension of the theory of **abstract Case** (q.v.): see 2.7.

competence The tacit knowledge an adult has of the grammar of his/her language. The syntactic part of competence consists, in the view advocated in this book, of **principles** (q.v.) of **universal grammar** (q.v.) with the associated **parameters** (q.v.) fixed. Competence is usually contrasted with performance, which refers to the actualization of competence in behaviour.

complement A category whose presence is required by a **head** in sense (i) (q.v.), usually a consequence of a lexical property of a head. For example, transitive verbs require a direct object as their complement. In X'-theory, the complement of X is the sister of X and the daughter of the **intermediate projection** (q.v.) X'.

complementizer-trace effect The fact that in languages with a negative setting for the **null-subject parameter** (q.v.) subjects cannot undergo **extraction** (q.v.) from a position immediately following a complementizer.

constituency tests Operations of various kinds that can be applied to a sentence (or other syntactic structure) in order to show the constituency relations in that structure. These tests are not dealt with in detail here; see Ouhalla (1994: 17ff.) for more discussion.

crossover phenomena The impossibility for a pronoun to take as its antecedent a category which has 'moved over' it. The effect is handled by Principle C of the **binding theory** (q.v.) in the theory described here.

definiteness A semantic property of nominals (DPs or NPs). A definite nominal refers to something which is taken to exist and to be known to both speaker and hearer in the context of utterance. The use of the definite article in a language like English also implies exhaustive reference to the members of the set of entities denoted by the Noun. Indefinite nominals imply none of the above, and so may be used with no commitment to the existence, the familiarity or the exhaustive reference to the set denoted by the Noun.

derived structures Structures derived by **movement** (q.v.) from other structures. Derived structures always contain at least one non-trivial **chain** (q.v.).

empty categories terminals (q.v.) that are filled by material lacking a phonological realization.

endocentric   An endocentric category has a **head** in sense (i) (q.v.). X'-theory implies that all categories are endocentric.

exocentric   An exocentric category lacks a **head** in sense (i) (q.v.). Until the development of the theory of **functional categories** (q.v.), described in 1.4, clauses were often thought to be exocentric. X'-theory implies that exocentric categories do not exist.

extraction   Refers to a **movement rule** (q.v.), often in relation to the possibility of movement of a category from a position inside an **island** (q.v.) to one outside an island.

free inversion   Refers to the possibility in languages with a positive setting for the **null-subject parameter** (q.v.) for the subject to appear postverbally in what seems to be a VP-internal position.

functional categories   As opposed to **lexical categories** (q.v.) in sense (ii). Categories containing primarily grammatical information. Functional categories tend to be occupied by closed-class elements, and are often realized by affixes or other material smaller than words. They are often not phonetically realized at all. In much current work, including versions of the minimalist programme, functional categories are held to be the locus of **parameters** (q.v.), in the sense that cross-linguistically variant properties of grammars are thought to be exclusively properties of functional categories.

grammatical function   Refers to the traditional roles in sentence grammar such as 'subject', 'direct object', 'indirect object', etc. In the theory described here, grammatical functions are defined structurally, as configurations in which **abstract Case** (q.v.) is assigned.

head   (i) The **lexical category** in sense (i) of this term (q.v.) which is the 'principal element' of a complex syntactic category and the only element of a simple category. The head determines many properties of the category it belongs to, including the actual label of category. In X'-theory all categories must have a head. The head of the **maximal projection** (q.v.) XP is written X or X°. (ii) The position in a chain (q.v.) which **c-commands** (q.v.) all other positions in that chain.

intermediate projections   In X'-theory, the single-bar projection of a **head** in sense (i) (q.v.), e.g. N', V', A'.

islands (or **islands constraints**)   Syntactic configurations which do not permit **movement rules** (q.v.) to move categories from positions inside them to positions outside them.

labelled bracketing   A mode of representation of syntactic structure in which each constituent is given in square brackets (e.g. [constituent]), with a subscripted category label on the left bracket indicating the grammatical category of the constituent. Labelled bracketings are equivalent to tree diagrams (or **phrase markers** (q.v.)); they represent the same information in a different way.

lexical categories   (i) As opposed to **phrasal categories** (q.v.), categories which only dominate a single lexical item; in X'-theory lexical categories in this sense are always **heads** in sense (i) (q.v.). (ii) As opposed to **functional categories** (q.v.), categories whose head is a substantive lexical item, e.g. Noun, Verb, or Adjective.

lexicon The 'dictionary' of a language. At the very least, the lexicon is a list of the words of a language associated with a specification of idiosyncratic phonological, syntactic, and semantic information.

maximal projection In X'-theory, the projection of a **head** in sense (i) (q.v.) which contains the **specifier** (q.v.) and the **complement** (q.v.) of the head, and may contain adjoined categories also. A maximal projection is not immediately dominated by further projections of the same category, except possibly for further segments in **adjunction** (q.v.) structures.

morphological case A feature of the inflectional system of many languages whereby nominal material (typically Nouns, Determiners, and adnominal modifiers) is marked for **grammatical function** (q.v.) and/or **thematic role** (q.v.).

movement rule An operation that converts one **phrase marker** (q.v.) or **labelled bracketing** (q.v.) into another by taking a constituent of the initial phrase marker (or labelled bracketing) and copying it in a different position, followed (generally) by deletion of the constituent in its original position. In this way, manipulations of word order can be handled. Movement rules always give rise to **derived structures** (q.v.) containing non-trivial **chains** (q.v.).

non-terminals Nodes which dominate other nodes in a tree diagram, i.e. which have immediate constituents (see example (iv), p. 7 of the Introduction). In many theories of syntax, words cannot be non-terminal nodes and category labels must be.

null-subject parameter The **parameter** (q.v.) which determines whether a language allows the **empty category** (q.v.) *pro* to function as the definite subject of a finite clause.

parameters (of **universal grammar** (q.v.)) Associated to **principles** (q.v.) of Universal Grammar, parameters define the syntactic variation among languages. Section 5.2 discusses a number of aspects of the nature of parameters in more detail.

parasitic gaps In constructions in which there are two empty positions that appear to correspond to a single case of *wh*-movement, the parasitic gap is the position which appears to be the 'extra' one (generally inside an adjunct or a subject category).

Perlmutter's generalization The observation that languages with a positive value for the **null-subject parameter** (q.v.) do not show the **complementizer-trace effect** (q.v.).

phrasal categories Categories which are the **maximal projections** (q.v.) of a **head** in sense (i) (q.v.). Phrasal categories may consist only of a **head**, or they may contain a **recursive** (q.v.) structure, in principle of unlimited size.

phrase marker (or tree diagram) Equivalent to **labelled bracketing** (q.v.), as a way of representing syntactic structures. Constituency relations are represented by the immediate constituent(s) of a category (in the sense of example (iv), p. 7 of the Introduction) being placed under a node bearing the label of that category and joined to it by a vertical or diagonal line.

phrase structure rules Rules of the general format $X \rightarrow Y\ Z$ (read as 'rewrite X as the sequence $Y\ Z$'). These rules specify the linear order and hierarchical dominance/constituency relations of syntactic categories, such as X in this example.

pied-piping The phenomenon whereby a *wh*-element that undergoes *wh*-movement takes along other parts of a constituent to which it belongs.

POSS-*ing* gerundives An English construction containing a nominal marked as a possessor which functions as a subject, and a verb affixed with -*ing*, e.g. *John's playing his guitar all night (bothered me)*.

principles (of **universal grammar** (q.v.)) These are the fundamental state-ments that define the invariant common core of universal grammar. Principles are modulated by **parameters** (q.v.) in the grammar of an indi-vidual language.

pronoun (or **pronominal**) A nominal subject to Principle B of the **binding theory** (q.v.).

quantification The semantic property of referring to some specified portion of a set. In predicate logic, there are two quantifiers, the existential quan-tifier $\exists$ (meaning 'at least one'), and the universal quantifier $\forall$ (meaning 'all'). Natural languages have much more complex quantification systems, and can, owing to their **recursive** (q.v.) property, form an infinite number of quantifiers.

raising constructions Constructions in which the subject of an infinitival complement undergoes a **movement rule** (q.v.) placing it in the subject position of the predicate which selects the infinitival.

recursive (rule application). The ability of (a set of) rules to apply to its own output, as in for example the phrase-structure rule $X \rightarrow Y\ X$. Here the application of the rule creates the condition for its reapplication, and so on *ad infinitum*. Recursive rules make possible the generation of infinite structures from a finite set of symbols, which is a fundamental property of natural-language syntax.

Referring (R-) expressions Nominals with independent semantic content, subject to Principle C of the **binding theory** (q.v.).

reflexivizer A morpheme which, according to Reinhart and Reuland's the-ory of reflexivity (see 3.5) requires the semantic identity of two arguments of the predicate with which it is associated.

root-embedded asymmetry Describes the situation in which a syntactic operation found in root clauses is not found in embedded clauses, or vice versa. A well-known example, discussed in 1.4.2.4, is the verb-second rule of German.

specifier In X'-theory, if YP is the specifier of X YP is the sister of the **inter-mediate projection** of X, X', and the daughter of the **maximal projection** of X, XP.

successive cyclic The property of **movement rules** (q.v.) that requires them to 'transit through' intermediate positions in the formation of seemingly **unbounded dependencies** (q.v.). The idea of successive cyclicity implies that the existence of unbounded dependencies is illusory.

syntactic binding In **binding theory** (q.v.), the formal mechanism which captures anaphoric relations, a combination of **c-command** (q.v.) and co-indexing. Related to but distinct from logical binding: see the Appendix to Chapter 3.

syntactic derivation Usually just called a 'derivation'. A series of **phrase-markers** (q.v.) or **labelled bracketings** (q.v.) which represent a single sentence and which are related together by **movement rules** (q.v.) or other transformational operations of copying or deletion of constituents.

syntax The word comes from Greek roots meaning 'putting together', and is the study of precisely that: how smaller elements are combined into larger ones in natural language. The principal sense of the term usually (and certainly in this book) refers to the specific case of how sentences are formed from words and other constituents.

terminals Nodes which do not dominate anything, i.e. have no immediate constituents (see example (iv), p. 7 of the Introduction). The terminals are the 'leaves' of a tree diagram. In many theories, words must be terminals and syntactic category labels can't be.

thematic roles (or **θ-roles**) Lexico-semantic features of predicates, which designate the way in which their arguments participate in the eventuality they describe.

unaccusative hypothesis The idea that intransitive Verbs fall into two distinct classes: those whose single argument is the underlying subject (unergatives), and those whose single argument is the underlying object (unaccusatives).

unbounded dependency The property of **movement rules** (q.v.) whereby they appear to be able to move categories across arbitrarily large stretches of material.

universal grammar In generative grammar, the theory of the innate human language faculty. The faculty is common to all humans, hence universal in the sense being common to all languages. The principal syntactic differences among languages are handled by **parameters** (q.v.).

Bibliography

Abney, S. (1987) *The English Noun Phrase in its Sentential Aspect*. PhD dissertation, MIT.

Aldridge, M. (1988) *The Acquisition of INFL*, University College of North Wales Monographs in Linguistics, 1.

Allwood, J., Andersson, L.-G. and Dahl, Ö. (1977) *Logic in Linguistics*. Cambridge: Cambridge University Press.

Anderson, J. (1971) *The Grammar of Case: Towards a Localistic Theory*. Cambridge: Cambridge University Press.

Anderson, S. (1982) 'Where's Morphology?' *Linguistic Inquiry* 13: 571–612.

Aoun, J. (1985) *A Grammar of Anaphora*. Cambridge, Mass.: MIT Press.

Aoun, J. (1986) *Generalized Binding*. Dordrecht: Foris.

Aoun, J., Hornstein, N., Lightfoot, D. and Weinberg, A. (1987) 'Two Types of Locality', *Linguistic Inquiry* 18: 537–77.

Aoun, J. and A. Li (1994) '*Wh*-in-Situ: Syntax of LF', *Linguistic Inquiry* 24: 199–238.

Atkinson, M. (1992) *Children's Syntax*. Oxford: Blackwell.

Baker, L. (1991) 'The Syntax of English *Not*: The Limits of Core Grammar', *Linguistic Inquiry* 22: 387–430.

Baker, M. (1988) *Incorporation: A Theory of Grammatical-Function Changing*. Chicago: Chicago University Press.

Baker, M., Johnson, K. and Roberts, I. (1989) 'Passive Arguments Raised', *Linguistic Inquiry* 20: 219–251.

Barss, A. (1986) *Chains and Anaphoric Dependence*. PhD dissertation, MIT.

Barss, A. and H. Lasnik (1986) 'A Note on Anaphora and Double Objects', *Linguistic Inquiry* 17: 347–54.

Belletti, A. (1988) 'The Case of Unaccusatives', *Linguistic Inquiry* 19: 1–35.

Belletti, A. (1990) *Generalized Verb Movement*. Turin: Rosenberg and Sellier.

Belletti, A. and L. Rizzi (1988) 'Psych Verbs and θ-Theory', *Natural Language and Linguistic Theory* 6: 291–352.

Benmamoun, E. (1991) 'Negation and Verb Movement', in T. Sherer (ed.), *Proceedings of NELS* 21: 17–31.

Bennis, H. and T. Hoekstra (1984) 'Gaps and Parasitic Gaps', *The Linguistic Review* 4: 29–87.

Berwick, R. (1985) *The Acquisition of Syntactic Knowledge*. Cambridge, Mass.: MIT Press.

den Besten, H. (1983) 'On the Interaction of Root Transformations and Lexical Deletive Rules', in W. Abraham (ed.), *On the Formal Syntax of the Westgermania*. Amsterdam: John Benjamins.

Bickerton, D. (1984) 'The Language Bioprogram Hypothesis', *Behavioral and Brain Sciences* 7: 173–221.

Blake, B. (1994) *Case*. Cambridge: Cambridge University Press.

Borer, H. (1984) *Parametric Syntax*. Dordrecht: Foris.

Borer, H. (1989) 'Anaphoric Agr', in O. Jaeggli and K. Safir (eds.), *The Null Subject Parameter*. Dordrecht: Kluwer, 69–110.

Borer, H. and K. Wexler (1987) 'The Maturation of Syntax', in T. Roeper and E. Williams (eds.), *Parameter Setting*. Dordrecht: Kluwer, 123–72.

Borsley, R. D. (1991) *Syntactic Theory: A Unified Approach*. London: Edward Arnold.

Borsley, R. D. (forthcoming) *Modern Phrase Structure Grammar*. Oxford: Blackwell.

Borsley, R. D. and I. Roberts (eds.) (1996), *The Syntax of the Celtic Languages*. Cambridge: Cambridge University Press.

Bouchard, D. (1984) *On the Content of Empty Categories*. Dordrecht: Foris.

Brandi, L. and P. Cordin (1989) 'Two Italian Dialects and the Null Subject Parameter', in O. Jaeggli and K. Safir (eds.), *The Null Subject Parameter*. Dordrecht: Kluwer, 111–42.

Bresnan, J. (1972) *Theory of Complementation in English*. PhD dissertation, MIT.

Bresnan, J. (1982a) 'Control and Complementation', *Linguistic Inquiry* 13: 343–434.

Bresnan, J. (1982b) *The Mental Representation of Grammatical Relations*. Cambridge, Mass.: MIT Press.

Brody, M. (1985) 'On the Complementary Distribution of Empty Categories', *Linguistic Inquiry* 16: 505–46.

Brody, M. (1995) *Lexico-Logical Form*. Cambridge, Mass.: MIT Press.

Brown, R. and C. Hanlon (1970) 'Derivational Complexity and the Order of Acquisition in Child Speech', in J. R. Hayes (ed.), *Cognition and the Development of Language*. New York: Wiley, 155–207.

Burzio., L. (1986) *Italian Syntax: A Government-Binding Approach*. Kluwer: Dordrecht.

Chomsky, N. (1955) *The Logical Structure of Linguistic Theory*. New York: Plenum (published in 1975).

Chomsky, N. (1957) *Syntactic Structures*. The Hague: Mouton.

Chomsky, N. (1964) *Current Issues in Linguistic Theory*. The Hague: Mouton.

Chomsky, N. (1965) *Aspects of the Theory of Syntax*. Cambridge, Mass.: MIT Press.

Chomsky, N. (1970) 'Remarks on Nominalizations', in R. Jacobs and P. S. Rosenbaum (eds.), *English Transformational Grammar*. Waltham, Mass.: Ginn, 184–221.

Chomsky, N. (1973) 'Conditions on Transformations', in S. Anderson and P.

Kiparsky (eds.), *A Festschrift for Morris Halle.* New York: Holt, Rinehart and Winston, 232–86.

Chomsky, N. (1976) 'Conditions on Rules of Grammar', *Linguistic Analysis* 2(4).

Chomsky, N. (1977) 'On WH-Movement', in A. Akmajian, P. Culicover, and T. Wasow (eds.), *Formal Syntax.* New York: Academic Press.

Chomsky, N. (1980) *Rules and Representations.* New York: Columbia University Press.

Chomsky, N. (1981) *Lectures on Government and Binding.* Dordrecht: Foris.

Chomsky, N. (1982) *Some Concepts and Consequences of the Theory of Government and Binding.* Cambridge, Mass.: MIT Press.

Chomsky, N. (1986a) *Knowledge of Language: Its Nature, Origin and Use.* New York: Praeger.

Chomsky, N. (1986b) *Barriers.* Cambridge, Mass.: MIT Press.

Chomsky, N. (1991) 'Some Notes on Economy of Derivation and Representation', in R. Friedin (ed.), *Principles and Parameters in Comparative Grammar,* 417–54.

Chomsky, N. (1993) 'A Minimalist Program for Linguistic Theory', in K. Hale and S. J. Keyser (eds.), *The View from Building 20.* Cambridge, Mass.: MIT Press, 1–52.

Chomsky, N. (1995) 'Categories and Transformations', ms. MIT.

Chomsky, N. and H. Lasnik (1993) 'Principles and Parameters Theory', in J. Jacobs, A. von Stechow, W. Sternefeld, and T. Vennemann (eds.), *Syntax: An International Handbook of Contemporary Research.* Berlin: de Gruyter.

Cinque, G. (1991) *Types of A'-Dependencies.* Cambridge, Mass.: MIT Press.

Clements, N. (1975) 'The Logophoric Pronoun in Ewe: Its Role in Discourse', *Journal of West African Languages,* 10: 141–77.

Comrie, B. (1981) *Language Universals and Linguistic Typology.* Chicago: Chicago University Press.

Croft, W. (1990) *Universals and Typology.* Cambridge: Cambridge University Press.

Duffield, N. (1995) *Particles and Projections in Irish Syntax.* Dordrecht: Kluwer.

Emonds, J. (1976) *A Transformational Approach to English Syntax: Root, Structure-Preserving and Local Transformations.* New York: Academic Press.

Emonds, J. (1978) 'The Verbal Complex V-V' in French', *Linguistic Inquiry* 9:151–75.

Emonds, J. (1980) 'Word Order in Generative Grammar', *Journal of Linguistic Research* 1:33–54.

Engdahl, E. (1983) 'Parasitic Gaps', *Linguistics and Philosophy* 6: 534.

Engdahl, E. (1985) 'Parasitic Gaps, Resumptive Pronouns and Subject Extractions', *Linguistics* 23: 3–44.

Everaert, M. (1986) *The Syntax of Reflexivization.* Dordrecht: Foris.

Faltz, L. (1977) *Reflexivization: A Study in Universal Syntax.* PhD dissertation, UC Berkeley.

Fiengo, R. and J. Higginbotham (1981) 'Opacity in NP', *Linguistic Analysis* 7: 395–422.

Fillmore, C. (1968) 'The Case for Case', in E. Bach and J. Harms (eds.), *Universals in Linguistic Theory*, 1–88.

Frampton, J. (1990) 'Parasitic Gaps and the Theory of *Wh*-Chains', *Linguistic Inquiry* 21: 49–78.

Fukui, N. and P. Speas (1986) 'Specifiers and Projections', in N. Fukui, T. Rapoport, and E. Sagey (eds.), *Papers in Theoretical Linguistics: MIT Working Papers in Linguistics,* 128–172.

Gazdar, G., Klein, E., Pullum, G. and Sag, I. (1985) *Generalized Phrase Structure Grammar*. Cambridge, Mass.: Harvard University Press.

Giorgi, A. (1984) 'Towards a Theory of Long-Distance Anaphora: A GB Approach', *The Linguistic Review* 3: 307–359.

Giorgi, A. and G. Longobardi (1991) *The Syntax of Noun Phrases*. Cambridge: Cambridge University Press.

Gold, E. (1967) 'Language Identification in the Limit', *Information and Control* 16: 447–74.

deGraff, M. and A. Pierce (1996) *Creoles, Diachrony and Language Acquisition*. Cambridge, Mass.: MIT Press.

Greenberg, J. (1963) 'Some Universals of Grammar with Particular Reference to the Order of Meaningful Elements', in J. Greenberg (ed.), *Universals of Language*. Cambridge, Mass.: MIT Press.

Grimshaw, J. (1990) *Argument Structure*. Cambridge, Mass.: MIT Press.

Gruber, J. (1965) *Studies in Lexical Relations*. PhD dissertation, MIT.

Haegeman, L. (1995) *The Syntax of Negation*. Cambridge: Cambridge University Press.

Hale, K., Jeanne, L. M. and Platero, P. (1977) 'Three Cases of Overgeneration', in A. Akmajian, P. Culicover and T. Wasow (eds.), *Formal Syntax*. New York: Academic Press.

Hale, K. and S. J. Keyser (1993) 'On Argument Structure and the Lexical Expression of Syntactic Relations', in K. Hale and S.J. Keyser (eds.), *The View from Building 20*. Cambridge, Mass.: MIT Press, 53–109.

Hawkins, J. (1983) *Word Order Universals*. New York: Academic Press.

Hawkins, J. (ed) (1988) *Explaining Language Universals*. Oxford: Blackwell.

Heim, I., Lasnik, H. and May, R. (1991) 'Reciprocity and Plurality', *Linguistic Inquiry* 22: 63–101.

Hendrick, R. (1988) *Anaphora in Celtic and Universal Grammar*. Dordrecht: Kluwer.

Higginbotham, J. (1980) 'Pronouns and Bound Variables', *Linguistic Inquiry* 11: 679–708.

Higginbotham, J. (1981) 'Reciprocal Interpretation', *Journal of Linguistic Research* 1: 97–117.

Higginbotham, J. (1983) 'Logical Form, Binding and Nominals', *Linguistic Inquiry* 16: 547–93.

Higginbotham, J. (1985) 'On Semantics', *Linguistic Inquiry* 16: 547–593.

Higginbotham, J. and R. May (1981) 'Questions, Quantifiers and Crossing', *The Linguistic Review* 1: 41–79.

Hoekstra, T. and B. Schwartz (eds.), (1994) *Language Acquisition Studies in Generative Grammar*. Amsterdam: John Benjamins.

Hornstein, N. (1985) *Logic as Grammar*. Cambridge, Mass.: MIT Press.

Hornstein, N. (1995) *Logical Form*. Oxford: Blackwell.

Hornstein, N. and D. Lightfoot (1981) *Explanation in Linguistics*. London: Longman.

Huang, C.T.J. (1982) *Logical Relations in Chinese and the Theory of Grammar*. PhD dissertation, MIT.

Huang, C.T.J. (1984) 'On the Distribution and Reference of Empty Pronouns', *Linguistic Inquiry* 15: 531–74.

Huang, C.T.J. (1993) 'Reconstruction and the Structure of VP: Some Theoretical Consequences', *Linguistic Inquiry* 24.

Hurford, J. (1994) *Grammar: A Student's Guide*. Cambridge: Cambridge University Press.

Hyams, N. (1986) *Language Acquisition and the Theory of Parameters*. Dordrecht: Kluwer.

Iatridou, S. (1990) 'About AGR(P)', *Linguistic Inquiry* 21:551–77.

Jackendoff, R. (1972) *Semantic Interpretation in Generative Grammar*. Cambridge, Mass.: MIT Press.

Jackendoff, R. (1977) *X'-Theory*. Cambridge, Mass.: MIT Press.

Jaeggli, O. (1982) *Topics in Romance Syntax*. Dordrecht: Foris.

Jaeggli, O. (1986) 'Passive' *Linguistic Inquiry* 17: 587–633.

Jaeggli, O. and K. Safir (eds.), (1989) *The Null Subject Parameter*. Dordrecht: Kluwer.

Jones, R. and A. Thomas (1977) *The Welsh Language: Studies in its Syntax and Semantics*. Cardiff: University of Wales Press.

Kayne, R. (1975) *French Syntax*. Cambridge, Mass.: MIT Press.

Kayne, R. (1984) *Connectedness and Binary Branching*. Dordrecht: Foris.

Kayne, R. (1989a) 'Notes on English Agreement', *CIEFL Bulletin*, Hyderabad, India.

Kayne, R. (1989b) 'Facets of Romance Past Participle Agreement,' in P. Benincà (ed.), *Dialect Variation on the Theory of Grammar*. Dordrecht: Foris, 85–104.

Kayne, R. (1991) 'Romance Clitics, Verb Movement and PRO', *Linguistic Inquiry* 22: 647–86.

Kayne, R. (1993) 'The Antisymmetry of Syntax', ms. CUNY.

Kayne, R. (1994) *The Antisymmetry of Syntax*. Cambridge, Mass.: MIT Press.

Keenan, E. (1988) *Universal Grammar: 15 Essays*. London: Croom Helm.

Keyser, S. J. and T. Roeper (1984) 'On the Middle and Ergative Constructions in English', *Linguistic Inquiry* 15: 381–416.

Kitagawa, Y. (1986) *Subjects in Japanese and English*. PhD dissertation, University of Massachusetts, Amherst.

Koopman, H. (1984) *Verb Movement and Universal Grammar*. Dordrecht: Foris.

Koopman, H. and D. Sportiche (1982) 'Variables and the Bijection Principle', *The Linguistic Review* 2: 139–60.

Koopmann, H. and D. Sportiche (1991) 'The Position of Subjects', *Lingua* 85:

211–58.

Koster, J. (1984) 'On Binding and Control', *Linguistic Inquiry* 15: 417–59.

Koster, J. (1985) 'Reflexives in Dutch', in J. Guéron, H. G. Obenauer and J.-Y. Pollock (eds.), *Grammatical Representation*. Dordrecht: Foris.

Koster, J. (1987) *Domains and Dynasties: The Radical Autonomy of Syntax*. Dordrecht: Foris.

Koster, J. and E. Reuland (eds.) (1991) *Long Distance Anaphora*. Cambridge: Cambridge University Press.

Kroch, A. (1989) 'Reflexes of Grammar in Patterns of Language Change', *Journal of Language Variation and Change* 1: 199–244.

Kuroda, Y. (1988) 'Whether We Agree or Not: A Comparative Syntax of English and Japanese,' in W. Poser (ed.), *Papers from the Second International Workshop on Japanese Syntax*. Center for the Study of Language and Information, Stanford University.

Labov, W. (1972) *Language in the Inner City*. Philadelphia: University of Pennsylvania Press.

Lasnik, H. (1976) 'Remarks on Coreference', *Linguistic Analysis* 2: 122.

Lasnik, H. (1989) *Essays on Anaphora*. Dordrecht: Kluwer.

Lasnik, H. and M. Saito (1984) 'On the Nature of Proper Government', *Linguistic Inquiry* 14: 235–89.

Lasnik, H. and M. Saito (1991) 'On the Subject of Infinitives', *Proceedings of the Chicago Linguistics Society*, 27: 324–43.

Lasnik, H. and M. Saito (1992) *Move-α*. Cambridge, Mass.: MIT Press.

Lebeaux, D. (1983) 'A Distributional Difference between Reciprocals and Reflexives', *Linguistic Inquiry* 14: 723–30.

Lenneberg, E. (1967) *Biological Foundations of Language*. New York: Wiley.

Levin, B. and M. Rappaport (1986) 'The Formation of Adjectival Passives', *Linguistic Inquiry* 17: 623–62.

Levin, B. and M. Rappaport-Hotav (1995) *Unaccusativity*. Cambridge, Mass.: MIT Press.

Lightfoot, D. (1991) *How to Set Parameters*. Cambridge, Mass.: MIT Press.

Lightfoot, D. and N. Hornstein (1994) *Verb Movement*. Cambridge: Cambridge University Press.

Longobardi, G. (1985) 'Connectedness, Scope and C-command', *Linguistic Inquiry* 16: 163–92.

McCloskey, J. (1983) 'A VP in a VSO language', in G. Gazdar, E. Klein, and G. K. Pullum (eds.), *Order, Concord and Constituency*. Dordrecht: Foris.

McCloskey, J. (1991), 'Clause structure, ellipsis and proper government in Irish', *Lingua* 85: 259–302.

McCloskey, J. (1996), 'On the scope of verb-movement in Irish', *Natural Language and Linguistic Theory* 14: 47–104.

McLuhan, M. (1964) *Understanding Media: The Extensions of Man*. New York: McGraw-Hill.

McNeill, D. (1966) 'Developmental Psycholinguistics,' in F. Smith and G. Miller (eds.), *The Genesis of Language: A Psycholinguistic Approach*. Cambridge,

Mass.: MIT Press, 15–84.

Manzini, M.-R. (1983) 'On Control and Control Theory', *Linguistic Inquiry* 14: 421–46.

Manzini, M.-R. (1992) *Locality: A Theory and Some of its Empirical Consequences*. Cambridge, Mass.: MIT Press.

Marantz, A. (1984) *On the Nature of Grammatical Relations*. Cambridge, Mass.: MIT Press.

May, R. (1977) *The Grammar of Quantification*. PhD dissertation, MIT.

May, R. (1985) *Logical Form: Its Structure and Derivation*. Cambridge, Mass.: MIT Press.

Mohammad, M. (1988) *The Sentential Structure of Arabic*. PhD dissertation, University of Southern California.

Munn, A. (1993) *Topics in the Syntax and Semantics of Coordinate Structures*. PhD dissertation, University of Maryland.

Newport, E., Gleitman, L. and Gleitman, H. (1977) ' "Mother, I'd Rather Do It Myself": Some Effects and Non-effects of Maternal Speech Style', in C. E Snow and C.A. Ferguson (eds.), *Talking to Children, Language Input and Acquisition*. Cambridge: Cambridge University Press.

Osherson, D., Stob, M. and Weinstein, S. (1982) 'Learning Strategies', *Information and Control* 53: 32–51.

Osherson, D., Stob, M. and Weinstein, S. (1984) 'Learning Theory and Natural Language', *Cognition* 17:128.

Osherson, D., Stob, M. and Weinstein, S. (1986) *Systems That Learn*. Cambridge, Mass.: MIT Press.

Ouhalla, J. (1994) *Introducing Transformational Grammar*. London: Edward Arnold.

Perlmutter, D. (1971) *Deep and Surface Structure Constraints in Syntax*. New York: Holt, Rinehart and Winston.

Perlmutter, D. (1978) 'Impersonal Passives and the Unaccusative Hypothesis', *Proceedings of the Fourth Annual Meeting of the Berkeley Linguistics Society*, 157–89.

Perlmutter, D. (ed.) (1983) *Studies in Relational Grammar I*. Chicago: University of Chicago Press.

Perlmutter, D. and P. Postal (1984) 'The 1-Advancement Exclusiveness Law', in D. Perlmutter and C. Rosen (eds.), *Studies in Relational Grammar II*. Chicago: Chicago University Press.

D. Perlmutter and C. Rosen (eds.) (1984), *Studies in Relational Grammar II*. Chicago: Chicago University Press.

Pesetsky, D. (1982) *Paths and Categories*. PhD dissertation, MIT.

Pica, P. (1987) 'On the Nature of the Reflexivization Cycle', *Proceedings of NELS* 17 2: 483–99.

Pierce, A. (1992) *Language Acquisition and Syntactic Theory: A Comparative Analysis of French and English Child Grammars*. Dordrecht: Kluwer.

Pierce, A. and V. Deprez (1993) 'Negation and Functional Projections in Early Grammar', *Linguistic Inquiry* 24: 25–68.

Poletto, C. (1993) *La Sintassi dei Clitici Soggetto nei Dialetti Italiani Settentrionali*, Doctoral Dissertation, Universities of Venice and Padua.

Pollard, C. and I. Sag (1994) *Head Driven Phrase Structure Grammar*. Chicago: Chicago University Press.

Pollock, J.-Y. (1989) 'Verb Movement, Universal Grammar and the Structure of IP', *Linguistic Inquiry* 20: 365–424.

Postal, P. (1969) 'On the So-Called "Pronouns" in English' in D. Reibel and S. Schane (eds.), *Modern Studies in English*. Englewood Cliffs, NJ: Prentice-Hall, 201–24.

Postal, P. (1971) *Crossover Phenomena*. New York: Holt, Rinehart and Winston.

Postal, P. (1974) *On Raising*. Cambridge, Mass.: MIT Press.

Postal, P. (1986) *Studies in Passive Clauses*. Albany, N.Y.: State University of New York Press.

Radford, A. (1986) 'Small Children's Small Clauses', *Bangor Research Papers in Linguistics*, 1. Bangor: University of Wales.

Radford, A. (1990) *Syntactic Theory and the Acquisition of English*. Oxford: Blackwell.

Reinhart, T. and E. Reuland (1991) 'Anaphors and Logophors: An Argument Structure Perspective', in Koster, J. and E. Reuland (eds.) (1991), *Long Distance Anaphora*. Cambridge: Cambridge University Press, 283–321.

Reinhart, T. and E. Reuland (1993) 'Reflexivity', *Linguistic Inquiry* 24.

van Riemsdijk, H. (1978) *A Case Study in Syntactic Markedness: The Binding Nature of Prepositional Phrases*. Dordrecht: Foris.

Rizzi, L. (1982) *Issues in Italian Syntax*. Dordrecht: Foris.

Rizzi, L. (1986a) 'Null Objects in Italian and the Theory of *pro*', *Linguistic Inquiry* 17: 501–57.

Rizzi, L. (1986b) 'On the Status of Subject Clitics in Romance,' In O. Jaeggli and C. Silva-Corvalán (eds.), *Studies in Romance Syntax*. Dordrecht: Foris, 391–419.

Rizzi, L. (1986c) 'On Chain Formation', in H. Borer (ed.), *The Syntax of Pronominal Clitics: Syntax and Semantics*, 19. New York: Academic Press.

Rizzi, L. (1988) 'The Structural Uniformity of Syntactic Categories', in *Proceedings of the Conference on the Basque Language*, Eusko Jaurlaritzaren Argitalpen-Zerbitzu Nagusia/Servicio Central de Publicaciones del Gobierno Vasco, Vitoria/Gasteiz.

Rizzi, L. (1990) *Relativized Minimality*. Cambridge, Mass.: MIT Press.

Rizzi, L. (1991) 'Residual Verb Second and the WH-Criterion', *University of Geneva Technical Reports in Formal and Computational Linguistics*, 2.

Rizzi, L. (1996) 'Some Notes on Linguistic Theory and Language Development: The Case of Root Infinitives', *Language Acquisition* 6.

Rizzi, L. and I. Roberts (1989) 'Complex Inversion in French', *Probus* 1: 1–39.

Roberts, I. (1987) *The Representation of Implicit and Dethematized Subjects*. Dordrecht: Foris.

Roberts, I. and U. Shlonsky (1996) 'Pronominal Enclisis and VSO Languages', in R. D. Borsley and I. Roberts (eds.), *Comparative Celtic Syntax*. Cambridge: Cambridge University Press, 171–99.

Rosenbaum, P. (1967) *The Grammar of English Predicate Complement Constructions*. Cambridge, Mass.: MIT Press.

Ross, J. R. (1967) *Constraints on Variables in Syntax*. PhD dissertation, MIT.

Ross, J.R. (1986) *Infinite Syntax!* Norwood, NJ: Ablex.

Roussou, A. (1993) 'Factivity, Factive Islands and the *that-t* Filter', in *Proceedings of CONSOLE* 1.

Rouveret, A. and J.-R. Vergnaud (1980) 'Specifying Reference to the Subject: French Causatives and Conditions on Representations', *Linguistic Inquiry* 11: 97–202.

Rudin, J. (1988) 'On Multiple Questions and Multiple WH-Fronting', *Natural Language and Linguistic Theory* 6: 445–502.

Safir, K. (1985) *Syntactic Chains*. Cambridge: Cambridge University Press.

Shopen, T. (1985) *Language Typology and Syntactic Description*. Cambridge: Cambridge University Press.

Sportiche, D. (1981) 'Bounding Nodes in French', *The Linguistic Review* 1: 219–46.

Sportiche, D. (1983) *Structural Invariance and Asymmetry in Syntax*. PhD dissertation, MIT.

Sproat, R. (1985) 'Welsh Syntax and VSO Structure', *Natural Language and Linguistic Theory* 3: 173–216.

Stowell, T. (1981) *The Origins of Phrase Structure*. PhD dissertation, MIT.

Taraldsen, T. (1979) 'The Theoretical Interpretation of a Class of Marked Extractions', in A. Belleti, L. Brandi and L. Rizzi (eds.), *Theory of Markedness in Generative Grammar*. Pisa: Scuola Normale.

Thiersch, C. (1993) 'On the Formal Properties of Constituent Coordination', *GLOW Newsletter* 30: 70–71.

Tomaselli, A. (1989) *La sintassi del verbo finito nelle lingue germaniche*. PhD dissertation, University of Pavia.

Travis, L. (1984) *Parameters and Effects of Word Order Variation*. PhD dissertation, MIT.

Travis, L. (1991) 'Parameters of Phrase Structure and Verb-Second Phenomena', in R. Friedin (ed.), *Principles and Parameters in Comparative Grammar*. Cambridge, Mass.: MIT Press, 339–364.

Vergnaud, J.-R. (1985) *Dépendances et niveaux de représentation en syntaxe*. Amsterdam: John Benjamins.

Vikner, S. (1994) *Verb Movement and Expletive Subjects in the Germanic Languages*. Oxford/New York: Oxford University Press.

Wasow, T. (1972) *Anaphoric Relations in English*. PhD dissertation, MIT Press.

Wasow, T. (1979) *Anaphora in Generative Grammar*. Ghent: E. Story-Scientia.

Watanabe, A. (1992) '*Wh*-in-situ, Subjacency and Chain Formation', *MIT Occasional Papers in Linguistics*, 2.

Watanabe, A. (1993) *Case Absorption*. PhD dissertation, MIT.

Webelhuth, G. (ed.) (1995), *Government and Binding Theory and the Minimalist Program*. Oxford: Blackwell.

Wexler, K. (1994) 'Finiteness and Head Movement in Early Child Grammars', in D. Lightfoot and N. Hornstein (eds.), *Verb Movement*. Cambridge: Cambridge

University Press, 305–50.

Wexler, K. and M.-R. Manzini (1987) 'Parameters, Learnability and Binding Theory', *Linguistic Inquiry* 18: 413–44.

Williams, E. (1980) 'Predication', *Linguistic Inquiry* 11: 203–38.

Williams, E. (1981) 'Argument Structure and Morphology', *The Linguistic Review* 1: 81–114.

Williams, E. (1994) 'A Reinterpretation of the Evidence for Verb Movement in French', in D. Lightfoot and N. Hornstein (eds.), *Verb Movement*. Cambridge: Cambridge University Press, 189–206.

Zagona, K. (1992) *Verb Phrase Syntax*. Dordrecht: Kluwer.

Zubizarreta, M.-L. (1987) *Levels of Representation in the Lexicon and Syntax*. Dordrecht: Foris.

Zwart, J.-W. (1993) *Dutch Syntax*. PhD dissertation, University of Groningen.

Subject Index

A(rgument)
  A-binding 124–39, 148, 181–2, 184–5
  A-chain 170, 236, 254
  A-movement (*see also* passives, raising, unaccusatives) 69–80, 235,
  A-position 148, 161, 228, 235–6, 263
  A-Specifiers 235–6
A'
  A'-binding 181–2, 184–5, 261
  A'-chain 170, 236–7
  A'-movement (*see also* *wh*-movement) 181–2, 190–1, 228, 232–5
  A'-position 148, 233, 181–2, 191, 228, 235, 251
  A'-Specifiers 232–5, 236–7, 238, 239, 251–2
absorption
  Case- 71–2, 93
  wh- 263–4
address 246–7, 249, 250, 253
  address-based dependency 245–53
adjacency 108
adjectives 13, 15, 20, 22, 23, 25, 27, 56, 61, 62, 63, 71, 74, 96
  and Case theory 63, 71, 87–92
  and raising 91–2
Adjunct Condition 217–9, 220, 221, 224
Adjunct Island 201, 214
adjunction 102, 103, 123, 190, 207, 220–1, 222, 223, 224, 228, 252, 262, 264
adjuncts 168, 169, 170, 175, 207, 218, 243, 244, 264
  extraction from *see* Adjunct Island, Adjunct condition
  movement and ECP (*see also* argument-adjunct asymmetry) 197, 199, 200, 201, 208, 219, 221, 225, 230, 232–5, 237–8, 246–9, 251, 252, 255, 260
  -traces 201, 203, 226, 232–3, 235, 237–8, 250
Agent 57–8, 61, 70, 74, 75, 84, 88, 90, 220
Agreement 17, 32, 38, 41–4, 56, 65, 80, 97, 104, 109, 119, 121, 122–3, 154–5, 159, 208–9, 240–2, 253, 274
  abstract 103–4, 155, 159
  domain 103
  features 102
  past participle 43–4

Spec(ifier)-head 43, 65–6, 67, 69, 92, 96, 97–99, 102–4, 228, 229, 252, 253, 264
Agr 42
  weak *vs.* strong Agr 102
  AgrP 41–4, 47, 57
  AgrSP 43, 65–7, 67–8, 76–79, 83, 90, 96–97, 108–9, 111–13, 148, 156–7, 230, 262–3, 264, 273
  AgrOP 43–4, 47, 79, 101, 110, 148, 230, 262–3
  Agr in C 240–2, 253
anaphora 4, 165–6, 177
  Long-distance (LD) anaphora 158–65, 176, 179–82, 274
anaphors (*see also* reflexives, reciprocals)
  binding theory and 124–82
  [± anaphor] 139–42, 149
antecedent 125, 180–2, 243, 246–7, 266
  and binding 125–130
  and chains 228, 244–5, 254
antecedent government 199–202, 203–7, 208, 210–7, 224–39, 244–5, 247, 250, 253–4
anti-agreement 109
arbitrary interpretation 135–6
arc-pair grammar 116
argument (*see also* A-position) 59–61, 69, 73–4, 94, 118, 166, 167
asymmetric c-command *see* c-command asymmetry
  argument *vs.* adjunct 199–204, 216, 224–5, 232–4, 247–50, 258, 267
  complement *vs.* non-complement 202, 204, 242–4
  root *vs.* embedded 36–38, 41, 46, 155–6
auxiliary 31–32, 44, 80
  inversion 36–7, 156, 206, 241, 266
  selection of *have vs. be* 74

barrier 69, 104, 121, 123, 186, 198, 217–32, 237–8, 247, 249, 250–2, 255, 258, 274
  definition 64, 119, 200, 219, 250
  and ECP 224–7, 238
  status of IP 64, 123
  and subjacency 217–24, 238, 254
  and government 67–8, 204
binary-branching 118–19, 118

Author Index

Language Index